## Other Books By Bill Welch

The Baseball Analysis And Reporting System
American League Report

The Baseball Analysis And Reporting System
National League Report

# The Tenth Man

## —How Major League Baseball Teams—
### Can Gain a 2 to 3 Run Advantage
### Every Game

## By Bill Welch

With Jeff Moses

A Baseball Analysis And Reporting System Publication

The Tenth Man

"A BARS book."
Includes index.
ISBN 0-929633-00-8

# Contents

*"The first guy who can crack this mystery, who learns to get maximum efficiency from the computer, is going to have quite an edge."*

Tony Larussa
Manager, Oakland A's

# Introduction: The BARS System

Perhaps more than any other major sport, baseball lends itself to statistical review and analysis. Individual batting averages, runs-batted-in totals, home run totals, win-loss records (for pitchers), ERAs, strikeout totals and many other statistics are familiar to anyone with an interest in the game.

But there are more crucial statistics when considering strategy in key moments of actual play. When batters such as George Brett or Don Mattingly come to the plate with runners on second and third in the late innings of a close game, everyone knows that they are capable of driving in the runners.

Batting averages and RBI totals become superficial at such moments. Opposing managers and players need to know what specific weaknesses (and strengths) each hitter has against right- and left-handed pitchers, how these strengths and weaknesses vary when the hitter is ahead or behind in the count, and where fielders should position themselves to have the greatest chance of making the out.

Experience and intuition determine the decisions made in such key moments. A manager's notebook is based on years of observation and thought. But the key to any system is the accuracy and amount of information taken into account.

**The Baseball Analysis and Reporting System** (The BARS System) is a privately owned organization that uses a nationwide scouting system and an IBM 4331 mainframe computer to analyze some of the most fundamental aspects of the game. Managers and players can use this system as a tool to help make decisions based on much more complete and detailed information than would normally be available to them.

The powerful computer used by the BARS System may not be able to think like an experienced baseball coach or manager, but it does have the advantage of being able to record and make sense out of many more events of actual play than any one person could ever see or remember.

In its May 12, 1988 issue, the Grand National Scene Magazine wrote, "By definition a computer is no more than an electronic machine that has the capability of supplying rapid and complex calculations, as well as compiling and selecting data. Once you program it — that is, tell it what you want it to do — the computer is easily able to 'out think' the smartest human."

The BARS System uses the computer to keep track of information that is too vast and complex for a human being to work with. The BARS computer generates reports and charts that are easy to understand, so that the data gathered over many seasons can be put to practical use.

## How The BARS System Works

The BARS System scouts games on a pitch-by-pitch basis to record the results of every pitch. The strike zone is divided into a nine-location grid so that the exact location of every pitch can be recorded. This grid is the basis for much of the information generated by the BARS System. By keeping track of the type of pitch (fastball, curve, slider, etc.) that is thrown to each location, very unique and exacting statistics can be recorded.

The following chart is for a right-handed hitter. The Inside and Outside columns would be reversed for a left-handed hitter.

|  | Inside | Middle | Outside |
|---|---|---|---|
| High | High Inside | High Over The Middle | High Outside |
| Medium | Medium-High Inside | Medium Over The Middle | Medium-High Outside |
| Low | Low Inside | Low Over The Middle | Low Outside |

The BARS System calculates exact batting percentages for each location. The percentages are calculated separately for fastballs, curves, sliders and change-ups. They are further separated when a hitter is facing right-handed and left-handed pitchers, and when the batter is ahead, behind and even in the count.

Batting charts such as these give an exact display of a hitter's strengths and weaknesses. Such charts can be used by opposing pitchers when preparing to face particular hitters, or by a hitter who wants to take a close look at his own performance.

A more complete description of the BARS System batting charts will be given in the following chapters, along with examples of the batting charts for many of the game's top hitters.

## Fielding Strategy

**It has been found that, on the average, each major league team allows between two and three base hits per game which could be prevented by following the BARS System fielding strategy.**

Using the recorded results of pitches to the nine locations, the BARS System computer positions each fielder so that an exact fielding strategy can be made for each hitter on a pitch-by-pitch basis.

The BARS System has discovered that very precise long-term trends can be determined about the distance and direction a player hits a particular type and location of pitch. For example, fielders might need to be positioned one way for a high-inside fastball, while being positioned differently for a low-inside fastball.

The BARS System fielding strategy is correct 90 percent of the time. This means that by following the BARS System fielding strategy, the fielders would be positioned correctly 90 percent of the time for balls hit to their locations. BARS System analysts have found that current fielding strategy positions fielders correctly only 70 to 75 percent of the time. The difference in percentages between the BARS System strategy and current fielding strategy means that unnecessary base hits are being allowed by each team in every game.

It has been found that, on the average, each major league team allows between two and three base hits per game which could be prevented by following the BARS System fielding strategy. By following accurate fielding strategy, balls that now fall for singles, doubles and triples could be fielded and turned into outs.

The significance of this cannot be overemphasized. In 1987, Boston had the highest average number of hits per game, 9.6, and Houston had the lowest, 8.6. Considering that a team averages about nine hits per game, an average of two or three hits per game represents from 20 percent to 33 percent of all hits. Preventing this large number of hits would make a tremendous difference in a team's standing over the course of a 162-game schedule, especially since many games are decided by one or two runs.

In addition, the BARS System fielding strategy would allow fielders to cut off many hits that now go for extra bases. By being in position to reach hit balls more quickly, fielders could hold many runners to singles instead of doubles and to doubles instead of triples. Preventing such extra bases would directly reduce the number of runs allowed.

Numerous examples of games in which the BARS System fielding strategy could have prevented hits and extra-base hits (including many hits that produced game-winning RBIs) are shown in the following chapters, along with a complete description of the fielding strategy.

### BARS System Pitching, Field Chart And Batting-Order Reports

The BARS System also uses the nine-location grid and pitch-by-pitch scouting to analyze the performance of individual pitchers. These reports can be used by opposing hitters when preparing to face a particular pitcher, or by a pitcher to analyze his own performance.

Two detailed reports are generated for each pitcher. The Pitch Information Report shows the types of pitches (fastball, curve, slider, etc.) a particular pitcher tends to throw in different runners-on-base situations and different ahead- and behind-in-the-count situations. The Pitch Location Report shows where in the strike zone a pitcher tends to throw each type of pitch, based on different runners-on-base situations.

The BARS System also generates the Batting-Order Report, which shows nine offensive categories that give a complete evaluation of a hitter's offensive performance, and the Fielding Chart, which is a graphic representation of the baseball field with an exact indication of where each of an individual player's hit balls landed.

Each of these reports will be described in detail in later chapters.

### Number Of Games Scouted

---

**Whitey Herzog, Manager of the St. Louis Cardinals, said: "The BARS System has an incredible amount of information, and it is extremely useful for any manager. It is unbelievable that the BARS System has scouted over 800 games each of the last few seasons."**

---

In 1987, the BARS System scouted 838 games (482 in the American

League and 356 in the National). Many teams had well over half of their games scouted during the 1987 season. The Yankees had 88 games scouted, the Red Sox 90, the Orioles 93, the Tigers 78, the Royals 113, the Cubs 137, the Astros 66, and the Braves 88. Many teams had 40, 50 or 60 games scouted.

Eight hundred and seventy-five games were scouted in 1986 (473 in the American League and 402 in the National). In 1985, 875 games were also scouted (457 in American, 418 in National). In 1984, 740 games were scouted (352 in American, 338 in National). And in 1983, 455 games were scouted (240 American, 215 National). For a team-by-team record of the number of games scouted, please see Chapter Sixteen. Also included in Chapter Sixteen are interesting figures that show the magnitude of the data collected by the BARS System over the last five years.

The large number of games scouted over the last five years is the basis for the great accuracy of the BARS System, because the higher the number of instances a computer has to work with, the greater the degree of accuracy. At present, the fielding strategy is correct about 90 percent of the time. As additional games are scouted, the accuracy of the BARS System will increase even further.

## How Information Is Gathered In The BARS System

BARS System scouts record the details and results of every pitch on a specially prepared form called the Scouting Report.

The Scouting Report is designed so that the details of every pitch, every hit and every defensive play can easily and accurately be recorded on computer for complete analysis.

When the BARS System was first started, a scout had to attend each game and sit behind home plate as close to the field as possible to accurately judge the type of pitch (fastball, curve, slider, etc.) and the location of each pitch in the strike zone.

It has been found, however, that much greater accuracy is possible by scouting games on television. The camera allows closer observation than when attending a game. Even television and radio announcers can't see details of the type and location of each pitch as well from where they sit as a scout can on television. Camera work is done so well today that a BARS scout can record every detail needed for complete game analysis.

The BARS System uses four full-time scouts, four satellite dishes and four video cassette recorders. This allows games from all over the country to be watched day and night. Also, the use of VCRs allows the scouts to replay events that weren't seen perfectly the first time, thereby scouting each play with the greatest accuracy.

In addition to the four full-time scouts, one person works full-time checking the accuracy of the information gathered. This person also coordinates many of the statistics that are generated by the BARS System.

The BARS System records:

1. The exact location of every pitch. The BARS System designates nine locations in and around the strike zone. This information allows each hitter's batting average to be calculated within each grid location. Also, a complete record can be kept of where each pitcher throws his pitches.

2. The type of pitch: fastballs, curves, sliders, knuckleballs, screwballs, sinkerballs, split-fingered fastballs and change-ups.

3. Exact details of the results of every hit: runners advanced, runs scored, runs driven in, errors, direction and distance the ball was hit, etc.

4. Called-strikes and swing-strikes, balls, fouls, walks, bunts and bunt attempts, passed balls, balks, stolen bases, sacrifices, accuracy of throws, whether the second baseman or shortstop covered second, etc. — all events in the game are recorded on a pitch-by-pitch basis. Even the playing time of the game, temperature, wind direction, wind speed, field condition and attendance are recorded.

The Scouting Report is described in detail in Chapter Sixteen. Chapter Seventeen describes the attention to accuracy and detail that is maintained when recording the BARS information into the computer.

## The Computer In Baseball — A Powerful Tool

This book describes a system for computerized scouting and analysis that could produce a revolution in baseball.

Revolution is the correct word, because once the BARS System principles are introduced into actual major league play, many fundamental activities in baseball will have to be completely reinterpreted. Once a person understands the concepts presented in this book, he can never again look at a baseball game in quite the same way.

Until now it has been common for fielders to take positions when a batter comes to the plate and to hold those positions, with minor adjustments, through every pitch made to the batter, whether the pitches are fastballs, curves or other types of pitches, and whether they are high inside, low inside or to other locations around the strike zone.

It has been common to accept base hits that result from this inexact fielding strategy as inevitable and unpreventable. But after reading this book, a person will not be able to accept the common opinion that nothing can be done to prevent such base hits. It will be understood that for maximum fielding effectiveness, fielders must adjust their positions on a pitch-by-pitch basis, using a comprehensive fielding strategy such as the one presented in the BARS System.

Even hits that now seem totally unpreventable, such as doubles down the lines or line-drive singles that fall in front of charging outfielders, will have to be re-examined. This book will show numerous instances in which outfielders could have caught line-drive singles or cut off extra-base hits if they had been positioned according to the BARS System fielding strategy.

Winning baseball is an ongoing accumulation of small advantages. The strategic edge that can be gained by knowing on a pitch-by-pitch basis what the best pitch is, or where the fielders should be positioned, can prove immensely valuable to a team's performance.

Sports today is big business, and no business of size operates without computers. The advantages which can be gained by using computers will be so quickly apparent that when one team starts, the competition will follow just to keep up.

## Fan Enjoyment, The True Purpose Of The BARS System

Inevitably, computers will take their place in baseball strategy, as they have in football, basketball and most other sports. This and upcoming BARS System publications will perhaps encourage such use, but that is not the central goal of this book.

The BARS System is designed for baseball fans. The batting charts, the fielding strategy, the pitching charts, the batting-order report and other BARS statistics offer a richness to baseball reporting and scouting that has never before been available. Using this book and future BARS magazines and newspapers, fans can keep up to date and enjoy the BARS information as they watch games at the stadium or at home on television.

The founders of the BARS System have a deep love and appreciation of the grand game of baseball, and hopefully these feelings have been expressed on every page of this book. It was out of love for the game and for the enjoyment of the fans that this book was written.

## *Personal Comments*

Chapter One talks about the BARS System batting and fielding charts, using Don Mattingly's charts as examples. It also delves into one of the biggest debates in the game today: why so many home runs are being hit.

I think the main reason for the increasing number of home runs is that pitchers today throw more fastballs than ever before. When looking at the BARS batting charts it becomes obvious that more fastballs are thrown than all other types of pitches combined. Hitters know that if they just wait for a fastball in a certain spot, they'll eventually get it. I've read hundreds of articles about why more home runs are being hit, but I don't believe anyone has mentioned that hitters are waiting more for fastballs.

Along this line, several years ago I was playing golf at Pine Valley in New Jersey. I was the guest of John McMullen, who owns the Houston Astros, and it was one of the nicest experience I've ever had. Yogi Berra was also a guest and one evening I talked with him about hitting. "Yogi," I said, "I'll bet you're glad you played when you did. Not that pitching wasn't real good back then, but how would you like to hit against these 90-mile-per-hour fastballs?"

Yogi said that he'd love to hit against today's pitchers. "All you'd have to look for is fastballs," he said. "They don't mix 'em up with breaking balls or change-ups like they did when I played." He said he used to have to look for three or four different types of pitches. Now all he'd have to do is mainly look for one type of pitch. "I'd just dig in and wait for the fastball," Yogi said. "I think I'd be just as good or an even better hitter now."

There's no real mystery to the increasing number of home runs. Ted Williams said that no matter how hard a pitcher throws, a good hitter will be able to hit a fastball — if he's looking for it. This book shows how many more fastballs are thrown than other pitches. I think the majority of pitchers are just going on brute power. Most teams are reluctant to even sign a young pitcher unless he has a 90-mile-per-hour fastball. A lot of people may lament the change, but it's a fact of the game today.

# Chapter One

## The Best Way To Get A Batter Out

In his classic book, *The Science of Hitting*[1], Ted Williams designed a chart showing his preference of pitches in the strike zone. The heart of the plate he called his "happy zone" — where he would expect to hit about .400 over the long run. The outer edges of the plate were locations where he would expect to hit for lower percentages.

The following chart is the strike zone as the left-handed Williams would see it from his position in the batter's box looking out at the pitcher.

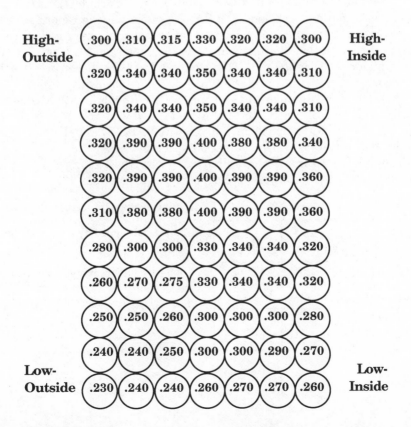

High-Outside

High-Inside

Low-Outside

Low-Inside

This chart is fascinating for baseball fans. Williams explained that the percentages in the upper part of the strike zone are higher than in the lower because he personally was a better high-ball hitter. He said that each player would have his own set of percentages in the various locations because some are better low-ball hitters, some better outside hitters, etc. Even so, the basic principle illustrated in the chart holds true for almost every hitter: pitches over the center of the plate are easier to hit, while pitches on the corners are trickier.

Williams' chart is a composite of all types of pitches he would receive — all fastballs, curves, sliders, etc. Also, it is a composite of all count situations and does not differentiate between his expected performance against left- and right-handed pitchers. He did not differentiate between these variables because his chart is an approximation of his overall experience — not an exact calculation as in the BARS System.

## BARS System Super Summary Charts

The BARS System calculates exact batting percentages using a chart somewhat like the one Williams used. The area in and around the strike zone is divided into nine locations. The BARS System batting report, which is called the Super Summary Report because it is a composite of several BARS System reports, calculates a separate batting-average grid for fastballs, curves, sliders and change-ups. These four pitches were chosen because they are the most representative of the types of pitches thrown.

Dick Howser, manager of the Kansas City Royals in 1985 when the Royals used the BARS System (the year they won the World Series), requested that change-ups be included in the BARS System batting report to show how hitters perform against off-speed pitches.

The following sample chart illustrates how the batting average and other statistics are displayed for each of the nine locations.

Batting average for the specific location.

Total at-bats ended by pitches to the location.

Total base hits resulting from pitches to the location.

| 7 / 0 | 25 / 8 | 7 / 3 |
|---|---|---|
| 0 | 320 | 428 |
| 64 / 27 | 33 / 13 | 28 / 10 |
| 421 | 393 | 357 |
| 17 / 3 | 28 / 9 | 11 / 3 |
| 176 | 321 | 272 |

Notice that a separate batting percentage is calculated for each of the nine locations of each grid. This batting percentage appears to the lower left of the fraction in each location. For greater clarity, the decimal point is not included. The number above and to the left of the slash in each location indicates the total number of at-bats that were ended by pitches to that location (strike outs plus hit balls). The number below and to the right of the slash indicates the number of base hits resulting from pitches to that location.

Overall, six separate Super Summary Reports are printed for each batter:

1. When ahead in the count against right-handed pitchers
2. When behind in the count against right-handed pitchers
3. Overall for all counts against right-handed pitchers
4. When ahead in the count against left-handed pitchers
5. When behind in the count against left-handed pitchers
6. Overall for all counts against left-handed pitchers

The breakdown into these different categories is important because, as will be seen in following chapters, a batter may hit the same type and location of pitch very differently when facing right- and left-handed pitchers and when ahead and behind in the count.

It is generally considered that when the batter is ahead in the count, he has the advantage over the pitcher. When the batter is behind in the count, the pitcher has the advantage.

The BARS System designates the batter ahead in the count when the count is 1-0 (one ball and no strikes), 3-0, 3-1, 2-0 and 2-1. The batter is behind in the count when the count is 0-1, 0-2, 1-2 and 2-2. The other ball and strike counts — 0-0, 1-1 and 3-2 — are designated as even counts.

## Don Mattingly's Batting Report

The Super Summary batting charts of Don Mattingly, first baseman for the New York Yankees, will be used as examples.

It should be noted that the BARS System batting percentage will not correspond exactly with a player's official batting percentage, because the BARS batting charts are a composite of a player's record over many seasons. Also, the BARS System does not scout every game in which a player is involved. However, the high percentage of games scouted does allow an excellent representation of a player's overall performance.

The overall average includes Mattingly's performance against all types of pitches that the BARS System records (fastballs, curves, sliders, change-ups, sinkerballs, split-fingered fastballs, knuckleballs and screwballs). The grids beneath the overall average show Mattingly's performance against individual types of pitches. For simplicity's sake, only Mattingly's performance against fastballs and curves is shown here. In many instances throughout the book, the grids for fastballs, curves, sliders and change-ups are shown.

### Don Mattingly   Left-Handed Hitter
### Against All Right-Handed Pitchers All Teams
### Overall Batting Average Is .323

**Fastball Average .366**

|      | Outside | Middle | Inside |
|------|---------|--------|--------|
| High | 37 / 432 / 16 | 32 / 343 / 11 | 14 / 571 / 8 |
| Med  | 115 / 286 / 33 | 39 / 435 / 17 | 31 / 290 / 9 |
| Low  | 35 / 457 / 16 | 70 / 400 / 28 | 23 / 304 / 7 |

**Curve Average .313**

|      | Outside | Middle | Inside |
|------|---------|--------|--------|
| High | 4 / 1000 / 4 | 2 / 0 / 0 | 1 / 0 / 0 |
| Med  | 22 / 272 / 6 | 3 / 333 / 1 | 6 / 500 / 3 |
| Low  | 8 / 375 / 3 | 12 / 250 / 3 | 9 / 111 / 1 |

### Don Mattingly   Left-Handed Hitter
### Against All Left-Handed Pitchers All Teams
### Overall Batting Average Is .320

**Fastball Average .345**

|      | Outside | Middle | Inside |
|------|---------|--------|--------|
| High | 7 / 0 / 0 | 25 / 320 / 8 | 7 / 428 / 3 |
| Med  | 64 / 421 / 27 | 33 / 393 / 13 | 28 / 357 / 10 |
| Low  | 17 / 176 / 3 | 28 / 321 / 9 | 11 / 272 / 3 |

**Curve Average .305**

|      | Outside | Middle | Inside |
|------|---------|--------|--------|
| High | 3 / 333 / 1 | 3 / 333 / 1 | 6 / 166 / 1 |
| Med  | 16 / 312 / 5 | 8 / 500 / 4 | 9 / 333 / 3 |
| Low  | 16 / 250 / 4 | 10 / 200 / 2 | 1 / 1000 / 1 |

A superficial look at Don Mattingly's Super Summary Report shows that he hits just about as well against left-handed as against right-handed pitchers.

His overall BARS Super Summary batting average against left-handers is .320. Against right-handers it is .323.

But a closer look shows many items of interest that could be useful for opposing pitchers. By focussing on locations in which Mattingly has lower percentages, pitchers can gain an advantage.

One of the first items of note when looking at the Super Summary batting chart is the extremely large number of fastballs thrown in comparison to curves. This is the case for every hitter. The number of fastballs far exceeds the total of all other types of pitches combined (curves, sliders, sinkers, change-ups, etc.).

Considering that Mattingly hits .345 against fastballs thrown by left-handers and .366 against fastballs thrown by right-handers, the question can be raised: why do pitchers continue to throw him so many fastballs?

Either they think they can get him out with fastballs (obviously they are wrong), or in general most pitchers do not have enough confidence in their other pitches.

Notice that Mattingly, who bats left-handed, has no significantly weak locations against fastballs thrown by right-handed pitchers. He hits even low-outside fastballs well (.457). Most fastballs to Mattingly are thrown outside, and he has little problem with them.

When facing left-handed pitchers, however, Mattingly has several problem locations against fastballs. Note that when thrown low-outside fastballs by left-handers, he hits only .176 and when thrown high-outside fastballs, he is 0 for 7. Left-handers should throw him high-outside or low-outside if they are going to give him fastballs. Right-handers should be wary of fastballs altogether. They would do much better by mixing in other pitches.

One weak point Mattingly has against breaking pitches thrown by right-handers is the low-inside location. His curveball average in that location is .111 on 1 for 9.

## Mattingly Ahead And Behind In The Count

Mattingly's Super Summary batting report on the following page shows that he hits better against right-handed pitchers when ahead in the count (.386) than when behind in the count (.314).

### Don Mattingly   Left-Handed Hitter
### Against All Right-Handed Pitchers When Ahead In The Count
### Batting Average Is .386

**Fastball Average .406**

|      | Outside | Middle | Inside |
|------|---------|--------|--------|
| High | 9/555/5 | 10/300/3 | 7/571/4 |
| Med  | 53/339/18 | 26/461/12 | 10/300/3 |
| Low  | 21/428/9 | 42/452/19 | 9/333/3 |

**Curve Average .666**

|      | Outside | Middle | Inside |
|------|---------|--------|--------|
| High | 1/1000/1 | 0/0/0 | 0/0/0 |
| Med  | 5/800/4 | 0/0/0 | 2/1000/2 |
| Low  | 0/0/0 | 2/0/0 | 2/500/1 |

### Don Mattingly   Left-Handed Hitter
### Against All Right-Handed Pitchers When Behind In The Count
### Batting Average Is .314

**Fastball Average .359**

|      | Outside | Middle | Inside |
|------|---------|--------|--------|
| High | 14/285/4 | 11/454/5 | 6/500/3 |
| Med  | 27/333/9 | 4/500/2 | 9/222/2 |
| Low  | 5/400/2 | 10/300/3 | 3/666/2 |

**Curve Average .320**

|      | Outside | Middle | Inside |
|------|---------|--------|--------|
| High | 3/0/0 | 1/0/0 | 0/0/0 |
| Med  | 9/222/2 | 0/0/0 | 0/0/0 |
| Low  | 3/0/0 | 8/375/3 | 1/0/0 |

Against left-handed pitchers, Mattingly hits better when he is behind in the count (.346 when behind, .308 when ahead).

### Don Mattingly   Left-Handed Hitter
### Against All Left-Handed Pitchers When Ahead In The Count
### Batting Average Is .308

Fastball Average .300

| | Outside | Middle | Inside |
|---|---|---|---|
| High | 2 / 0 / 0 | 9 / 444 / 4 | 2 / 500 / 1 |
| Med | 33 / 333 / 11 | 18 / 388 / 7 | 14 / 285 / 4 |
| Low | 7 / 0 / 0 | 14 / 214 / 3 | 4 / 250 / 1 |

Curve Average .470

| | Outside | Middle | Inside |
|---|---|---|---|
| High | 1 / 0 / 0 | 0 / 0 / 0 | 3 / 333 / 1 |
| Med | 5 / 600 / 3 | 1 / 0 / 0 | 3 / 666 / 2 |
| Low | 2 / 500 / 1 | 2 / 500 / 1 | 0 / 0 / 0 |

### Don Mattingly   Left-Handed Hitter
### Against All Left-Handed Pitchers When Behind In The Count
### Batting Average Is .346

Fastball Average .380

| | Outside | Middle | Inside |
|---|---|---|---|
| High | 4 / 0 / 0 | 5 / 0 / 0 | 1 / 0 / 0 |
| Med | 16 / 625 / 10 | 2 / 500 / 1 | 4 / 500 / 2 |
| Low | 9 / 333 / 3 | 7 / 428 / 3 | 2 / 0 / 0 |

Curve Average .230

| | Outside | Middle | Inside |
|---|---|---|---|
| High | 0 / 0 / 0 | 0 / 0 / 0 | 2 / 0 / 0 |
| Med | 2 / 0 / 0 | 2 / 500 / 1 | 1 / 0 / 0 |
| Low | 3 / 333 / 1 | 3 / 333 / 1 | 0 / 0 / 0 |

## Fielding Strategy

In each Super Summary Report there are areas of strength and weakness. By focussing on a hitter's weak batting locations, a pitcher will have a greater  chance of getting the hitter out. But there is another aspect to getting a hitter out: proper fielding.

As mentioned in the Introduction, the BARS System has found that trends develop in a hitter's performance when large numbers of instances are taken into consideration.

For example, a hitter will tend to hit low-inside fastballs a certain direction and distance, while hitting high-inside fastballs a different direction and distance. The BARS System computer uses these trends to determine the best fielding locations for the three outfielders, the shortstop and the second baseman.

Direction and distance will also vary against different pitchers, but it is rarely possible to gather enough information about how a hitter performs against a specific pitcher to get an accurate projection. Even when categorizing against right- and left-handed pitchers, 90 percent accuracy has been attained.

Each hitter has his own characteristic trends. Direction and distance of hit balls will vary with the type of pitch, location of pitch, when facing right- and left-handed pitchers and when ahead and behind in the count.

Not every ball a batter hits will follow these trends, but it has been found that the BARS System fielding strategy is correct 90 percent of the time. This allows great accuracy in the positioning of fielders and complements the pitching strategy to provide the best possible way to get a batter out.

The Super Summary shows fielding strategy for each of the nine locations for fastballs, curves, sliders and change-ups. The following chart shows the fastball fielding strategy from Mattingly's Super Summary against right-handed pitchers.

Notice that there are nine fielding categories, one for each of the nine locations in the strike zone. In each of these categories the best fielding location for each fielder is shown. These positions are calculated by computer, based on the direction and distance of the many balls that Mattingly has hit in each of the pitch locations during the past seasons.

## Don Mattingly   Left-Handed Hitter
## Against All Right-Handed Pitchers All Teams

Fastball Average .366

|  | Outside | Middle | Inside |
|---|---|---|---|
| High | 37/ 432/16 | 32/ 343/11 | 14/ 571/8 |
| Med | 115/ 286/33 | 39/ 435/17 | 31/ 290/9 |
| Low | 35/ 457/16 | 70/ 400/28 | 23/ 304/7 |

1. MEDIUM-HIGH OUTSIDE FASTBALLS

   BATTING AVERAGE .286
   *PLAY*
   LEFTFIELDER       Deep in straightaway left field
   CENTERFIELDER     Deep in straightaway center field
   RIGHTFIELDER      Deep in straightaway right field
   SHORTSTOP         Up middle (shifted toward second base)
   SECOND            Normal position

2. MEDIUM-HIGH INSIDE FASTBALLS

   BATTING AVERAGE .290
   *PLAY*
   LEFTFIELDER       Deep in straightaway left field
   CENTERFIELDER     Deep in straightaway center field
   RIGHTFIELDER      Deep in straightaway right field
   SHORTSTOP         Normal position
   SECOND            Shifted toward first base

3. LOW-INSIDE FASTBALLS

   BATTING AVERAGE .304
   *PLAY*
   LEFTFIELDER       Deep in straightaway left field
   CENTERFIELDER     Deep in straightaway center field
   RIGHTFIELDER      Deep and shifted toward center field
   SHORTSTOP         Normal position
   SECOND            Shifted toward second base

4. HIGH-OVER-MIDDLE FASTBALLS

   BATTING AVERAGE .343
   *PLAY*
   LEFTFIELDER       Medium-deep and shifted toward the left
                     field line
   CENTERFIELDER     Deep in straightaway center field
   RIGHTFIELDER      Deep in straightaway right field
   SHORTSTOP         Up middle (shifted toward second base)
   SECOND            Shifted toward first base

5.  LOW-OVER-MIDDLE FASTBALLS

    BATTING AVERAGE .400
    *PLAY*
    | | |
    |---|---|
    | LEFTFIELDER | Deep in straightaway left field |
    | CENTERFIELDER | Deep in straightaway center field |
    | RIGHTFIELDER | Deep in straightaway right field |
    | SHORTSTOP | Up middle (shifted toward second base) |
    | SECOND | Normal position |

6.  HIGH-OUTSIDE FASTBALLS

    BATTING AVERAGE .432
    *PLAY*
    | | |
    |---|---|
    | LEFTFIELDER | Deep and shifted toward the left field line |
    | CENTERFIELDER | Deep in straightaway center field |
    | RIGHTFIELDER | Deep in straightaway right field |
    | SHORTSTOP | Up middle (shifted toward second base) |
    | SECOND | Shifted toward first base |

7.  MEDIUM-OVER-MIDDLE FASTBALLS

    BATTING AVERAGE .435
    *PLAY*
    | | |
    |---|---|
    | LEFTFIELDER | Deep and shifted toward center field |
    | CENTERFIELDER | Medium-deep in straightaway center field |
    | RIGHTFIELDER | Deep and shifted toward the right field line |
    | SHORTSTOP | Normal position |
    | SECOND | Normal position |

8.  LOW-OUTSIDE FASTBALLS

    BATTING AVERAGE .457
    *PLAY*
    | | |
    |---|---|
    | LEFTFIELDER | Deep and shifted toward the left field line |
    | CENTERFIELDER | Deep and shifted toward left field |
    | RIGHTFIELDER | Deep and shifted toward center field |
    | SHORTSTOP | Normal position |
    | SECOND | Shifted toward first base |

9.   HIGH-INSIDE FASTBALLS

BATTING AVERAGE .571
    *PLAY*
LEFTFIELDER        Deep and shifted toward the left field line
CENTERFIELDER   Deep and shifted toward right field
RIGHTFIELDER      Deep and shifted toward the right field line
SHORTSTOP         Normal position
SECOND               Shifted toward first base

When each fielder plays in the suggested position, which varies for each type and location of pitch, the overall fielding strategy for the team will be correct about 90 percent of the time.

The best way to get Mattingly out with a fastball thrown by a right-handed pitcher is to throw to the location in which he has the lowest average. In this case Mattingly's lowest percentage is .286, which is in the medium-high outside location. In addition, positioning the fielders according to the suggested fielding strategy will increase the chances of getting Mattingly out.

MEDIUM-HIGH OUTSIDE FASTBALLS
(THROWN TO MATTINGLY BY RIGHT-HANDED PITCHERS)

BATTING AVERAGE .286
    *PLAY*
LEFTFIELDER        Deep in straightaway left field
CENTERFIELDER   Deep in straightaway center field
RIGHTFIELDER      Deep in straightaway right field
SHORTSTOP         Up middle (shifted toward second base)
SECOND               Normal position

The chart on the following page shows how differently the fielders would have to be positioned to achieve maximum defensive coordination when the pitch is to the low-outside location.

LOW-OUTSIDE FASTBALLS
(THROWN TO MATTINGLY BY RIGHT-HANDED PITCHERS)

BATTING AVERAGE .457
    *PLAY*
LEFTFIELDER        Deep and shifted toward the left field line
CENTERFIELDER      Deep and shifted toward left field
RIGHTFIELDER       Deep and shifted toward center field
SHORTSTOP          Normal position
SECOND             Shifted toward first base

The left fielder would have to shift toward the left field line; the center fielder would have to shift toward left field; and the right fielder would have to shift toward center field. The shortstop would have to shift more into his normal position and the second baseman would have to shift toward first.

Thus, every fielder would be required to shift in order to be correctly positioned on a low-outside fastball as compared to a medium-high outside fastball. If they did not shift, they would be completely out of position for one of the pitches, and the chances are that they would have difficulty fielding a hit ball.

Notice that in Mattingly's #1, #2 and #5 categories each of the three outfielders is required to be positioned deep and straightaway. In each of the other six categories, at least one of the outfielders needs to shift to a different position to have the best chance to get Mattingly out.

Chapter Seven will discuss implementing the BARS System fielding strategy in actual play, but even a casual glance at Mattingly's fielding categories shows how easy it would be to position fielders correctly for each pitch.

The first pitch to Mattingly could be a fastball to the medium-high outside location, which has his lowest fastball average (.286). The second pitch could be a fastball to the medium-high inside location, which has his second-lowest fastball average (.290). The third pitch could be a low-over-the-middle fastball (.400). This strategy would move the ball around in the strike zone and enable the outfielders to remain in their same positions.

Variations could be used each time Mattingly came to the plate, mixing in fastballs, curves, sliders, etc., to different locations of the strike zone. This would keep Mattingly (or any hitter) off balance and allow fielders to shift as little as possible.

Fielding strategy information is also generated by the BARS System for curves, sliders and change-ups. In addition, separate fielding charts are generated for each of these pitches when a batter is ahead in the count and behind in the count. As will be shown in later chapters, such exactness is necessary to insure that each fielder is properly positioned.

One question that can be raised about this pitch-by-pitch procedure is whether many pitchers are accurate enough to consistently hit the desired location. The strategy may call for a low-inside fastball, for example, but the pitcher may actually end up throwing a medium-high inside fastball, a high-inside fastball, or even a high-outside fastball.

These inaccuracies will occur, but since the fielders have to be positioned somewhere anyway, they should be positioned according to an overall coordinated strategy that offers the highest percentage of getting the batter out. A team will have the greatest possible edge using the BARS System fielding strategy if the pitcher can throw the ball to the planned location.

Since the fielding strategy is accurate 90 percent of the time, positioning fielders according to the suggested strategy for any particular pitch location will tend to lower a hitter's average in that location.

For instance, Mattingly may hit .457 against low-outside fastballs, but if all fielders were properly positioned for pitches to him in that location, his average in that location would decline. The same is true of all locations in the Super Summary.

Thus, it is just as important — if not more important — to position fielders correctly for particular types and locations of pitches as it is to pitch to a hitter's weaknesses. It does not matter whether a hitter has been batting .300 or even .400 in a particular location, if the fielders know where to position themselves.

Notice that the first and third basemen are not represented in the fielding strategy. The first baseman is not included because often he is forced to play out of position when holding a runner near the bag.

The third baseman is usually not under this obligation. It has been found that many hits result from the third baseman being out of position, thus the fielding strategy for third baseman is now being worked out by the BARS System.

There has been an ongoing question in baseball whether it is best to position the third baseman near the line in key situations so that he can cut off possible doubles or to keep him in his regular position.

When the BARS System positioning is completed for third basemen, strategy will be available on an exact basis for each batter, based not on theory or conjecture, but on exact statistical trends.

[1] Ted Williams and John Underwood, *The Science of Hitting*, Simon and Schuster, Inc., New York, 1986.

## Personal Comments

I first started thinking about the BARS System when I was at the University of Arizona. I started charting pitches when I was on the baseball team there. We played a lot of intersquad games from the middle of September to the middle or end of October. I kept track of the direction and distance players hit the ball, and our coach was surprised when I took unusual fielding positions against the hitters. He was alarmed at some of the strategy I used, but the ball consistently came to me.

That's when I began thinking about designing a system that would allow fielders to be in the best possible position for each pitch. It seemed it would be possible. After all, the same basic thing happens over and over when a pitcher throws to a hitter. The pitcher's mound is about 60 feet from the plate, it's always about the same height, the bat is always round and so is the ball, and there are such a large number of major league games played each year that an adequate amount of information could be gathered for each player.

The charting I did at Arizona wasn't nearly as accurate as what we do now with the BARS System, because I didn't know where each pitch was going to be thrown. I might have known that it was going to be a fastball or curveball — that was about it. The fielders never knew where the pitch was going over the plate, and I imagine that a lot of times the pitcher didn't know either.

But at the major league level, pitchers are fairly accurate. Very few pitchers in the majors try to throw the ball low inside and have it go low outside. There's a pretty good chance it's going to be on the inside part of the plate if that's where they want it to be. If they couldn't do that, they wouldn't be in the big leagues.

I used to talk about my ideas with a good friend of mine, Bob Fairchild, who is the football coach at the high school in Chillicothe, Missouri. Bob is one of the most successful coaches in the country with a record of 225 wins, 42 losses and 2 ties, and I respect his opinion very much. I talked with him so often about this that he finally got irritated and told me to stop talking about it and do it. That's what got me started in the BARS System.

I knew I would have to use a computer to retain all the information about the type and location of pitches, and to coordinate the location of each pitch with where each ball was hit. My family is in banking and, of course, we had a computer at the bank. When I got out of school, I knew that no one had ever done anything like what I was thinking of, so I decided to give it a shot.

It took about a year for me to write up the plans, and about four months to get the first basic program working, but we still didn't have any information to use in the program. That was about '69 or '70. I was interviewed by Sports Illustrated on the topic of using computers for scouting. That was in '72, I think. They were very interested in the general possibilities, but I knew that I had to get exact information if anything was going to really work.

That's about the time I went to the Kansas City Royals and met with Ewing Kaufmann, who owns the Royals. Mr. Kaufmann was impressed, so he flew me out to Los Angeles in his private jet, and I started travelling with the team. I hired a man named Ed Douglas to work with me. We'd sit right behind the catcher, if we could, and one of us would write down the type and location of pitches and the other would chart the hits. That's how the BARS System first started, just following the Royals around the league.

For three straight years Ed Douglas and another BARS scout travelled with the Royals, but nothing really came of it. The Royals decided it wasn't very useful, and the only thing I gained out of it was Ed. He did such a phenomenal job of scouting for me that I talked him into coming back and working in the bank, and now he's president.

I had collected so much information in those three years that the field charts, on which we record the location of hits, were just a big jumble. I wanted to use this information to position the fielders for each pitch, but there was so much information, so many hits crammed on the page, that I knew it would take a computer to decipher it. Chapter Fifteen in this book has an example of a field chart with various hit balls. From this example you can see that it would be almost impossible to make use of this information without a computer.

At that point, I knew my old system wasn't going to work, so I needed to design a new one. I wanted to let the computer do all the work. I thought that if I designated specific areas for each outfielder and for the shortstop and second baseman, the computer could coordinate where each ball was hit with the type, location and count of each pitch.

At that time our bank had grown and we needed a new computer, so we bought an IBM 4331, which was large enough to handle all the BARS System information in addition to the computer volume required by the bank. The baseball program I needed designed was extremely complicated and required a top-quality programmer. Fortunately, a man named Larry Birch worked for the company that sold us the computer. I asked him if he would moonlight for me, and he turned out to be a fabulous programmer. I was very fortunate to get him. He worked out the Super Summary Program the way it is now, with the nine locations on the batting grid and the fielding strategy for each location. Larry is still working for me, designing a program to forecast the scores of games. I now lease time on the computer for the BARS System, paying the bank just like other firms who use the computer for their accounting or other needs.

When satellite dishes came out, I started watching more and more games on TV. I thought about scouting games using the dish. It turns out that on TV you can see what kind of pitches are thrown and where they are in the strike zone better than when you're at the park. Steve Boros had already been using TV to see the pitches, I believe.

So I hired a full-time scout. The first year we scouted 350 games, almost all of them from TV. The next year we scouted 500 or 600 games. More games were being televised all the time, so I added three more full-time scouts. We now get about a third of all the games that are played. We've scouted over 800 games each of the last three seasons.

Now we have so much information and are covering so many games that we're getting tremendous accuracy in our statistics. Bub Baker, who works for me on the BARS System, just sits and watches games all year to make sure our information is right. He was with me when I went back to the Royals with my new Super Summary Program. He sat right between Mr. Fogelman and Mr. Kaufmann, co-owners of the Royals, during a game. We were up in Mr. Fogelman's private booth. Bub would tell them what a pitcher was going to pitch to every hitter, and the BARS System was right 75 percent of the time on the type of pitch and 66 percent of the time on the location of the pitch. And we were right 90 percent of the time on where the ball would be hit, judging from the type and location of the pitch, the count, and whether the pitcher was right- or left-handed.

They got the biggest kick out of it. Say, for instance, that the pitcher threw a fastball medium-high and outside, and that the pitch was hit to right center field for a double. We would show them on the Super Summary that for that particular type and location of pitch, on that particular count, the hitter would be expected to hit the ball to right center field. It was clear that if the center fielder or right fielder had been positioned according to the BARS System, one of them would have been positioned just right to catch the ball, instead of allowing it to fall in for a double. The computer was right 90 percent of the time.

The Royals decided to use the BARS System for a year. Dick Howser, who was the Royals' manager then, gave the deciding vote. The Royals were having a hard time with Larry Parrish of the Texas Rangers. They just couldn't get him out. I pointed out on the BARS charts that Parrish is extremely good at hitting breaking balls when he's behind in the count. He's especially good at breaking balls thrown away from him by right-handed pitchers.

That struck a chord with Dick Howser because he hadn't realized that Parrish was hitting for such a high average when behind in the count. He thought that the Royals' pitchers had been throwing Parrish the right kind of pitches, but the BARS System pointed out that outside curves were just what Parrish wanted. The following Super Summary charts show that Parrish hits .647 against medium-high outside curves when he's behind in the count.

### Larry Parrish    Right-Handed Hitter
### When Behind In The Count Against Right-Handed Pitchers

**Fastball Average .404**                    **Curve Average .450**

| | Inside | Middle | Outside | | Inside | Middle | Outside |
|---|---|---|---|---|---|---|---|
| High | 1/ 0 / 0 | 1/ 0 / 0 | 3/ 333 / 1 | | 0/ 0 / 0 | 2/ 1000 / 2 | 1/ 0 / 0 |
| Med | 6/ 166 / 1 | 5/ 600 / 3 | 10/ 400 / 4 | | 3/ 333 / 1 | 2/ 500 / 1 | 17/ 647 / 11 |
| Low | 7/ 285 / 2 | 8/ 625 / 5 | 1/ 1000 / 1 | | 2/ 0 / 0 | 3/ 333 / 1 | 10/ 200 / 2 |

### Larry Parrish    Right-Handed Hitter
### When Ahead In The Count Against Right-Handed Pitchers

**Fastball Average .433**                    **Curve Average .393**

| | Inside | Middle | Outside | | Inside | Middle | Outside |
|---|---|---|---|---|---|---|---|
| High | 2/ 500 / 3 | 4/ 500 / 2 | 2/ 1000 / 2 | | 0/ 0 / 0 | 3/ 666 / 2 | 1/ 0 / 0 |
| Med | 15/ 133 / 2 | 20/ 550 / 11 | 44/ 454 / 20 | | 2/ 500 / 1 | 5/ 800 / 4 | 12/ 333 / 4 |
| Low | 7/ 285 / 2 | 24/ 541 / 13 | 9/ 222 / 2 | | 1/ 0 / 0 | 5/ 200 / 1 | 4/ 250 / 1 |

As I said, we're getting more information all the time. We have information on every player in the major leagues. We have an extremely large amount of information on some of the players who have been around for several years and who play frequently.

In the last few years I've been thinking about getting this information out to baseball fans. I wrote this book so people could see the BARS System and understand all the details. We're planning to publish a BARS System newspaper soon with all the information so fans can take it right to the ballpark with them or follow along as they watch a game on TV. Any fan who uses the BARS newspaper will know more than the players and the managers about how to pitch a hitter and where fielders should be positioned to defense him. That's what really excites me about the program now — getting the information to baseball fans so they can enjoy it. It could be that baseball teams will ultimately start using the BARS System because the fans are so interested, but the most important thing to me is that people enjoy it. That would make all my work worthwhile.

# Chapter Two

# The Hitters

The BARS System generates batting charts for every player in the major leagues. In this chapter the Super Summary batting charts of many top hitters are examined.

Each hitter has six Super Summary batting charts.

1. When ahead in the count against right-handed pitchers
2. When behind in the count against right-handed pitchers
3. Overall for all counts against right-handed pitchers
4. When ahead in the count against left-handed pitchers
5. When behind in the count against left-handed pitchers
6. Overall for all counts against left-handed pitchers

The overall BARS System batting averages will not match exactly with a hitter's official average, because the BARS System batting charts are a composite of a player's performance over several seasons. Since 1984, over one-third of the games in the major leagues have been scouted. Therefore, the BARS System records are an excellent representation of a player's hitting record.

The batting charts in this chapter were the latest available. For this reason they may not match a player's charts in other chapters.

As noted in Chapter One, many more fastballs are thrown than other types of pitches. Often, more fastballs are thrown than all other types of pitches combined. This allows hitters to expect fastballs, to wait for them and to time their swings to them.

Ted Williams said that all great hitters can hit fastballs, no matter how fast the pitcher is. The BARS System shows that even average hitters usually hit fastballs well. Most hitters have a high overall fastball average as recorded by the BARS System. Their curve, slider and change-up averages are usually lower — in many cases much lower.

The BARS System believes that the increasing number of home runs in the majors is primarily due to the large number of fastballs thrown. Hitters today can in many cases avoid swinging at breaking and off-speed pitches altogether. They can wait for fastballs and put full weight into their swings. The result is an increasing number of home runs.

Pitchers should become aware of this and throw more breaking and off-speed pitches. But the emphasis today is to pitch with speed. Pitchers with a hard fastball are usually brought up from the minors more quickly than finesse pitchers. Most clubs are reluctant to even sign pitchers who do not have a hard fastball.

Many pitchers in the majors lack confidence in their breaking pitches in tight situations. Hitters know this, and time their swings accordingly.

As Ted Williams said in *The Science of Hitting*, "The trouble with the average pitcher is his hardheadedness. He has too inflated an opinion of what he's got. Say it's his fastball. He thinks he can throw it anytime, anyplace, anywhere. If you hit his fastball, he still gives it to you again."

This is a fact in major league pitching today. There are more fastballs and fewer breaking pitches thrown. The result is more home runs.

The following Super Summary batting charts show at a glance the large number of fastballs thrown in comparison to other types of pitches. In many cases, so few sliders and change-ups were thrown that these two grids are not included.

This chapter discusses the hitting charts of six top hitters in the game today. Chapter Eighteen discusses the charts of many other top hitters.

## Super Summary For Wade Boggs

Left-handed Wade Boggs of the Boston Red Sox hits for a consistently high average. He performs better against right-handed than against left-handed pitchers.

### Wade Boggs    Left-Handed Hitter
### Against All Right-Handed Pitchers All Teams
### Overall Batting Average Is .352

| | Fastball Average .348 | | | Curve Average .482 | | |
|---|---|---|---|---|---|---|
| | Outside | Middle | Inside | Outside | Middle | Inside |
| High | 28/178 / 5 | 33/333 / 11 | 19/526 / 10 | 4/1000/ 4 | 9/111 / 1 | 5/400 / 2 |
| Med | 173/341 /59 | 57/438 /25 | 84/404 /34 | 19/631 /12 | 10/500 / 5 | 23/695 /16 |
| Low | 20/150 / 3 | 47/340 /16 | 41/292 /12 | 5/200 / 1 | 15/400 / 6 | 24/333 / 8 |

Slider Average .307          Change-Up Average .290

| | Outside | Middle | Inside | Outside | Middle | Inside |
|---|---|---|---|---|---|---|
| High | 0 / 0 0 | 2 / 500 1 | 3 / 333 1 | 2 / 1000 2 | 2 / 500 1 | 0 / 0 0 |
| Med | 6 / 166 1 | 2 / 1000 2 | 14 / 214 3 | 6 / 166 1 | 7 / 571 4 | 4 / 250 1 |
| Low | 5 / 200 1 | 10 / 400 4 | 10 / 300 3 | 3 / 0 0 | 3 / 0 0 | 4 / 0 0 |

To remind the reader, each of the nine locations in a grid represents the results of pitches thrown to that location.

In the fastball chart shown on the opposite page, 173 instances were recorded in which Boggs ended an at-bat receiving a pitch to the medium-high outside location. This means the BARS System recorded 173 instances in which Boggs struck out or hit the ball when thrown a medium-high outside fastball.

The number beneath the slash (59) represents the number of base hits that Boggs made on pitches to that location. The 59 divided by 173 is Boggs' average for that location (.341). The overall fastball average above the fastball chart (.348) represents the average for all nine locations.

Looking at Boggs' charts, notice his strong performance in all waist-high fastball and curve locations. His only weaknesses against fastballs are in the low-outside and high-outside locations.

Boggs goes to the opposite field (left field) with inside fastballs when he hits fly balls, but he pulls to the right side of the infield when he hits grounders.


MEDIUM-HIGH INSIDE FASTBALLS

BATTING AVERAGE .404
   *PLAY*
LEFTFIELDER          Deep and shifted toward the left field line
CENTERFIELDER        Medium-deep in straightaway center field
RIGHTFIELDER         Deep and shifted toward center field
SHORTSTOP            Up middle (shifted toward second base)
SECOND               Shifted toward first base

Boggs' performance against curve balls is exceptional. His .482 overall curve average is one of the highest recorded by the BARS System. Note his strength against all waist-high curves (.631 against medium-high outside,

.500 against medium-over-the-middle, and a brilliant .695 against medium-high inside).  His only two weak curve locations are low-outside (.200) and high-over-the-middle (.111).

Boggs' overall slider average (.307) is high, but he has several weak locations.  His medium-high inside, low-outside, and medium-high outside locations are weaknesses that pitchers can focus on.

His overall change-up average (.290) is good, but notice his weakness against low change-ups.

Boggs is known as a hitter who performs well when he is behind in the count.  His BARS System Super Summary shows that he hits better when behind in the count than when ahead.  Few slider and change-up instances were recorded, so those grids are not shown.  The overall composite batting average therefore includes pitches that are not shown.

### Wade Boggs    Left-Handed Hitter
### Against Right-Handed Pitchers When Behind In The Count
### Batting Average Is .393

| | Fastball Average .343 | | | Curve Average .500 | | |
|---|---|---|---|---|---|---|
| | Outside | Middle | Inside | Outside | Middle | Inside |
| High | 10/400 / 4 | 7/142 / 1 | 8/500 / 4 | 4/1000 / 4 | 6/166 / 1 | 3/333 / 1 |
| Med | 49/367 / 18 | 10/300 / 3 | 18/500 / 9 | 6/666 / 4 | 6/666 / 4 | 10/600 / 6 |
| Low | 7/285 / 2 | 10/200 / 2 | 12/166 / 2 | 2/0 / 0 | 8/750 / 6 | 11/181 / 2 |

## Wade Boggs    Left-Handed Hitter
## Against Right-Handed Pitchers When Ahead In The Count
## Batting Average Is .363

| | Fastball Average .362 | | | Curve Average .631 | | |
| --- | --- | --- | --- | --- | --- | --- |
| | Outside | Middle | Inside | Outside | Middle | Inside |
| High | 4/ 250 / 1 | 9/ 555 / 5 | 5/ 400 / 2 | 0/ 0 / 0 | 0/ 0 / 0 | 1/ 1000 / 1 |
| Med | 64/ 375 / 24 | 23/ 260 / 6 | 34/ 323 / 11 | 6/ 833 / 5 | 2/ 0 / 0 | 5/ 800 / 4 |
| Low | 4/ 0 / 0 | 15/ 400 / 6 | 16/ 500 / 8 | 0/ 0 / 0 | 2/ 0 / 0 | 3/ 666 / 2 |

Boggs' behind-in-the-count averages present several weaknesses. His low-inside and high-over-the-middle fastball locations are below .200, and his low-over-the-middle location is an even .200. His low-inside curve location could also be a point of attack for pitchers.

When ahead in the count, Boggs' fastball and curve averages are extremely high. His .375 against medium-high outside fastballs is excellent.

It is interesting to see how differently Boggs hits medium-high inside curves when he is ahead and behind in the count. There are no recorded instances of hit balls to the shortstop or second baseman in the following charts.

MEDIUM-HIGH INSIDE CURVEBALLS
(THROWN TO BOGGS WHEN HE IS AHEAD IN THE COUNT)

BATTING AVERAGE .800
   *PLAY*
| | |
| --- | --- |
| LEFTFIELDER | Deep in straightaway left field |
| CENTERFIELDER | Deep and shifted toward left field |
| RIGHTFIELDER | Deep and shifted toward the right field line |

MEDIUM-HIGH INSIDE CURVEBALLS
(THROWN TO BOGGS WHEN HE IS BEHIND IN THE COUNT)

BATTING AVERAGE .600
   *PLAY*
| | |
| --- | --- |
| LEFTFIELDER | Medium-deep and shifted toward center field |
| CENTERFIELDER | Deep and shifted toward right field |
| RIGHTFIELDER | Deep in straightaway right field |

## Boggs Against Left-Handed Pitchers

Against left-handed pitchers, Boggs hits fastballs well but has trouble with curves.

### Wade Boggs    Left-Handed Hitter
### Against All Left-Handed Pitchers All Teams
### Overall Batting Average Is .310

**Fastball Average .356**

|      | Outside | Middle | Inside |
|------|---------|--------|--------|
| High | 5/ 400 /2 | 19/ 368 /7 | 14/ 214 /3 |
| Med  | 66/ 318 /21 | 23/ 391 /9 | 55/ 436 /24 |
| Low  | 6/ 166 /1 | 35/ 371 /13 | 18/ 333 /6 |

**Curve Average .206**

|      | Outside | Middle | Inside |
|------|---------|--------|--------|
| High | 1/ 1000 /1 | 6/ 166 /1 | 1/ 1000 /1 |
| Med  | 13/ 76 /1 | 5/ 200 /1 | 11/ 272 /3 |
| Low  | 7/ 0 /0 | 10/ 400 /4 | 4/ 0 /0 |

**Slider Average .250**

|      | Outside | Middle | Inside |
|------|---------|--------|--------|
| High | 1/ 0 /0 | 0/ 0 /0 | 0/ 0 /0 |
| Med  | 10/ 200 /2 | 0/ 0 /0 | 6/ 166 /1 |
| Low  | 4/ 500 /2 | 11/ 181 /2 | 4/ 500 /2 |

**Change-Up Average .250**

|      | Outside | Middle | Inside |
|------|---------|--------|--------|
| High | 0/ 0 /0 | 1/ 0 /0 | 1/ 1000 /1 |
| Med  | 2/ 0 /0 | 0/ 0 /0 | 0/ 0 /0 |
| Low  | 0/ 0 /0 | 0/ 0 /0 | 0/ 0 /0 |

With the exception of low-outside and high-inside fastballs, Boggs hits every fastball location well. His .436 against medium-high inside fastballs is very strong. He sends these inside pitches to the opposite field when he hits fly balls, and to the right side of the infield when he hits grounders.

MEDIUM-HIGH INSIDE FASTBALLS
(THROWN TO BOGGS BY LEFT-HANDED PITCHERS)

BATTING AVERAGE .436
*PLAY*
LEFTFIELDER        Deep and shifted toward the left field line
CENTERFIELDER      Medium-deep in straightaway center field
RIGHTFIELDER       Medium-deep and shifted toward center field
SHORTSTOP          Up middle (shifted toward second base)
SECOND             Shifted toward first base

Many of Boggs' curveball locations against left-handed pitchers are weak. His medium-high outside and low-outside averages are very low. Overall, he hits sliders only adequately against left-handers. Few change-up instances were recorded.

Boggs hits much better against left-handers when ahead in the count.

### Wade Boggs    Left-Handed Hitter
### Against Left-Handed Pitchers When Ahead In The Count
### Average Is .382

Fastball Average .419                    Curve Average .250

| | Outside | Middle | Inside | | Outside | Middle | Inside |
|------|---------|--------|--------|---|---------|--------|--------|
| High | 1/1000 / 1 | 7/428 / 3 | 6/166 / 1 | | 0/0 / 0 | 1/0 / 0 | 0/0 / 0 |
| Med  | 28/357 / 10 | 11/636 / 7 | 25/520 / 13 | | 0/0 / 0 | 2/0 / 0 | 0/0 / 0 |
| Low  | 0/0 / 0 | 19/368 / 7 | 8/250 / 2 | | 0/0 / 0 | 1/1000 / 1 | 0/0 / 0 |

### Wade Boggs    Left-Handed Hitter
### Against Left-Handed Pitchers When Behind In The Count
### Average Is .293

| | Fastball Average .313 | | | Curve Average .200 | | |
|---|---|---|---|---|---|---|
| | Outside | Middle | Inside | Outside | Middle | Inside |
| High | 3 / 333 / 1 | 1 / 0 / 0 | 4 / 250 / 1 | 1 / 1000 / 1 | 2 / 0 / 0 | 1 / 1000 / 1 |
| Med | 14 / 357 / 5 | 5 / 200 / 1 | 15 / 333 / 5 | 5 / 200 / 1 | 1 / 0 / 0 | 5 / 200 / 1 |
| Low | 2 / 500 / 1 | 3 / 333 / 1 | 4 / 250 / 1 | 3 / 0 / 0 | 4 / 250 / 1 | 3 / 0 / 0 |

Notice how strongly he hits fastballs when ahead. His .520 average against medium-high inside fastballs is excellent. His .636 against medium-over-the-middle fastballs should serve as a warning for left-handers to avoid these pitches to Boggs when he is ahead in the count.

## Super Summary For George Brett

George Brett, left-handed hitter for the Kansas City Royals, consistently hits for a high percentage. Like Wade Boggs, Brett hits better against right-handed pitchers.

### George Brett    Left-Handed Hitter
### Against All Right-Handed Pitchers All Teams
### Overall Batting Average Is .339

| | Fastball Average .370 | | | Curve Average .308 | | |
|---|---|---|---|---|---|---|
| | Outside | Middle | Inside | Outside | Middle | Inside |
| High | 24 / 166 / 4 | 62 / 274 / 17 | 14 / 428 / 6 | 4 / 250 / 1 | 4 / 500 / 2 | 2 / 0 / 0 |
| Med | 110 / 400 / 44 | 82 / 500 / 41 | 57 / 315 / 18 | 27 / 444 / 12 | 17 / 352 / 6 | 20 / 400 / 8 |
| Low | 33 / 333 / 11 | 86 / 360 / 31 | 18 / 444 / 8 | 7 / 0 / 0 | 26 / 153 / 4 | 13 / 307 / 4 |

Slider Average .362

| | Outside | Middle | Inside |
|---|---|---|---|
| High | 0/ 0 / 0 | 2/ 500 / 1 | 3/ 333 / 1 |
| Med | 3/ 666 / 2 | 9/ 777 / 7 | 21/ 285 / 6 |
| Low | 5/ 200 / 1 | 14/ 142 / 2 | 12/ 416 / 5 |

Change-Up Average .314

| | Outside | Middle | Inside |
|---|---|---|---|
| High | 2/ 0 / 0 | 14/ 428 / 6 | 1/ 1000 / 1 |
| Med | 16/ 250 / 4 | 8/ 625 / 5 | 9/ 111 / 1 |
| Low | 4/ 250 / 1 | 12/ 333 / 4 | 4/ 0 / 0 |

With the exception of the high-outside location, Brett has no weak fastball locations. His .500 average against medium-over-the-middle fastballs is exceptional, especially when considering the high number of recorded instances in that location (82 instances). His .400 average in the medium-high outside location is equally impressive because of the number of recorded instances (110).

Brett has been thrown so many pitches over the heart of the plate in his career that he knows he can wait for his pitch. He's patient. That's one of the reasons he's a great hitter.

Brett's strength with waist-high pitches continues into the curveball locations. If not for several very weak curve locations (low-outside and low-over-the-middle), Brett's overall curve average would be nearly as high as his overall fastball average.

His slider averages are also strong. Notice that he has the same two weak locations against sliders that he has against curveballs (low-outside and low-over-the-middle). He hits most change-up locations well, although several weak locations bring his overall change-up average down.

Brett hits medium-high outside fastballs almost exactly the same direction and distance that Wade Boggs does, going to the opposite field with fly balls and pulling grounders to the right side of the infield.

MEDIUM-HIGH OUTSIDE FASTBALLS

BATTING AVERAGE .400
   *PLAY*
LEFTFIELDER        Deep and shifted toward the left field line
CENTERFIELDER      Deep in straightaway center field
RIGHTFIELDER       Deep and shifted toward center field
SHORTSTOP          Up middle (shifted toward second base)
SECOND             Shifted toward first base

He hits medium-high outside curves deep to all fields.

MEDIUM-HIGH OUTSIDE CURVEBALLS

BATTING AVERAGE .444
  *PLAY*
LEFTFIELDER        Deep and shifted toward the left field line
CENTERFIELDER      Deep and shifted toward left field
RIGHTFIELDER       Deep and shifted toward the right field line
SHORTSTOP          Up middle (shifted toward second base)
SECOND             Normal position

Against right-handed pitchers, Brett hits better when ahead in the count.

## George Brett    Left-Handed Hitter
### Against Right-Handed Pitchers When Ahead In The Count
### Batting Average Is .387

Fastball Average .408

|      | Outside | Middle | Inside |
|------|---------|--------|--------|
| High | 11/ 181 / 2 | 28/ 285 / 8 | 7/ 285 / 2 |
| Med  | 61/ 442 / 27 | 51/ 647 / 33 | 41/ 341 / 14 |
| Low  | 16/ 437 / 7 | 55/ 309 / 17 | 9/ 444 / 4 |

Curve Average .447

|      | Outside | Middle | Inside |
|------|---------|--------|--------|
| High | 1/ 1000/ 1 | 1/ 1000/ 1 | 1/ 0 / 0 |
| Med  | 7/ 714 / 5 | 5/ 200 / 1 | 8/ 500 / 4 |
| Low  | 1/ 0 / 0 | 9/ 222 / 2 | 5/ 600 / 3 |

Slider Average .368

|      | Outside | Middle | Inside |
|------|---------|--------|--------|
| High | 0/ 0 / 0 | 1/ 0 / 0 | 3/ 333 / 1 |
| Med  | 1/ 0 / 0 | 7/ 857 / 6 | 11/ 363 / 4 |
| Low  | 1/ 0 / 0 | 8/ 125 / 1 | 6/ 333 / 2 |

Change-Up Average .307

|      | Outside | Middle | Inside |
|------|---------|--------|--------|
| High | 0/ 0 / 0 | 6/ 500 / 3 | 1/ 1000/ 1 |
| Med  | 8/ 125 / 1 | 2/ 500 / 1 | 6/ 166 / 1 |
| Low  | 0/ 0 / 0 | 3/ 333 / 1 | 0/ 0 / 0 |

## George Brett    Left-Handed Hitter
### Against Right-Handed Pitchers When Behind In The Count
### Batting Average Is .330

#### Fastball Average .353

|  | Outside | Middle | Inside |
|---|---|---|---|
| High | 2/ 500 / 1 | 12/ 166 / 2 | 4/ 250 / 1 |
| Med | 16/ 562 / 9 | 7/ 142 / 1 | 6/ 166 / 1 |
| Low | 1/ 0 / 0 | 15/ 466 / 7 | 2/ 500 / 1 |

#### Curve Average .258

|  | Outside | Middle | Inside |
|---|---|---|---|
| High | 2/ 0 / 0 | 1/ 1000 / 1 | 0/ 0 / 0 |
| Med | 7/ 285 / 2 | 4/ 250 / 1 | 5/ 400 / 2 |
| Low | 1/ 0 / 0 | 9/ 111 / 1 | 2/ 500 / 1 |

#### Slider Average .266

|  | Outside | Middle | Inside |
|---|---|---|---|
| High | 0/ 0 / 0 | 1/ 1000 / 1 | 0/ 0 / 0 |
| Med | 0/ 0 / 0 | 1/ 0 / 0 | 5/ 200 / 1 |
| Low | 1/ 0 / 0 | 4/ 0 / 0 | 3/ 666 / 2 |

#### Change-Up Average .428

|  | Outside | Middle | Inside |
|---|---|---|---|
| High | 1/ 0 / 0 | 3/ 666 / 2 | 0/ 0 / 0 |
| Med | 4/ 500 / 2 | 1/ 0 / 0 | 1/ 0 / 0 |
| Low | 2/ 500 / 1 | 2/ 500 / 1 | 0/ 0 / 0 |

Brett's fastball, curve and slider averages go up when he is ahead in the count. His overall fastball average of .408 is very high. In particular, notice his .442 against medium-high outside fastballs and .647 against medium-over-the-middle fastballs. The high-outside location is his only weakness against fastballs when ahead in the count.

His curve and slider averages both jump sharply when he is ahead. His change-up average falls when he is ahead, mainly due to low averages in the medium-high inside and medium-high outside locations.

## Brett Against Left-Handed Pitchers

Brett's averages fall against all types of pitches when he faces left-handed pitchers. He continues to hit fastballs well, but has difficulty with curves, sliders and change-ups.

### George Brett    Left-Handed Hitter
### Against All Left-Handed Pitchers All Teams
### Overall Batting Average Is .276

Fastball Average .314

| | Outside | Middle | Inside |
|---|---|---|---|
| High | 6/ 333 /2 | 21/ 523 /11 | 13/ 461 /6 |
| Med | 68/ 264 /18 | 31/ 354 /11 | 38/ 315 /12 |
| Low | 14/ 142 /2 | 25/ 240 /6 | 13/ 307 /4 |

Curve Average .287

| | Outside | Middle | Inside |
|---|---|---|---|
| High | 4/ 500 /2 | 14/ 285 /4 | 5/ 400 /2 |
| Med | 22/ 363 /8 | 15/ 400 /6 | 16/ 187 /3 |
| Low | 9/ 111 /1 | 15/ 200 /3 | 1/ 0 /0 |

Slider Average .186

| | Outside | Middle | Inside |
|---|---|---|---|
| High | 1/ 0 /0 | 3/ 0 /0 | 0/ 0 /0 |
| Med | 10/ 100 /1 | 3/ 666 /2 | 2/ 0 /0 |
| Low | 9/ 0 /0 | 10/ 400 /4 | 5/ 200 /1 |

Change-Up Average .166

| | Outside | Middle | Inside |
|---|---|---|---|
| High | 0/ 0 /0 | 0/ 0 /0 | 0/ 0 /0 |
| Med | 2/ 500 /1 | 3/ 0 /0 | 5/ 200 /1 |
| Low | 1/ 1000 /1 | 6/ 0 /0 | 1/ 0 /0 |

Brett's three weak fastball locations (low-outside, low-over-the-middle, and medium-high outside) bring down his overall fastball average. He hits several fastball locations against left-handers very well (.523 in high-over-the-middle and .461 in high-inside).

He has difficulty with low curves, low sliders, and low change-ups. He also has trouble with medium-high inside pitches of these three types.

Against left-handed pitchers, Brett tends to hit medium-high outside and medium-high inside fastballs straightaway to all fields. He goes more to the opposite field with medium-high outside and medium-high inside curves.

Brett hits slightly better when behind in the count against left-handers.

### George Brett   Left-Handed Hitter
### Against Left-Handed Pitchers When Ahead In The Count
### Batting Average Is .299

Fastball Average .333

| | Outside | Middle | Inside |
|---|---|---|---|
| High | 2 / 0 / 0 | 10 / 700 / 7 | 7 / 285 / 2 |
| Med | 38 / 236 / 9 | 21 / 380 / 8 | 24 / 375 / 9 |
| Low | 5 / 200 / 1 | 12 / 250 / 3 | 7 / 428 / 3 |

Curve Average .270

| | Outside | Middle | Inside |
|---|---|---|---|
| High | 1 / 0 / 0 | 6 / 333 / 2 | 3 / 333 / 1 |
| Med | 7 / 285 / 2 | 7 / 428 / 3 | 6 / 333 / 2 |
| Low | 2 / 0 / 0 | 4 / 0 / 0 | 1 / 0 / 0 |

### George Brett   Left-Handed Hitter
### Against Left-Handed Pitchers When Behind In The Count
### Batting Average Is .323

Fastball Average .343

| | Outside | Middle | Inside |
|---|---|---|---|
| High | 2 / 500 / 1 | 3 / 0 / 0 | 3 / 666 / 2 |
| Med | 10 / 300 / 3 | 4 / 500 / 2 | 4 / 250 / 1 |
| Low | 1 / 0 / 0 | 3 / 333 / 1 | 2 / 500 / 1 |

Curve Average .346

| | Outside | Middle | Inside |
|---|---|---|---|
| High | 1 / 1000 / 1 | 4 / 250 / 1 | 1 / 0 / 0 |
| Med | 6 / 333 / 2 | 5 / 400 / 2 | 3 / 0 / 0 |
| Low | 2 / 500 / 1 | 4 / 500 / 2 | 0 / 0 / 0 |

## Super Summary For Dave Winfield

Dave Winfield, right-handed hitter for the New York Yankees, hits well against both left- and right-handed pitchers.

First, against right-handers:

### Dave Winfield    Right-Handed Hitter
### Against All Right-Handed Pitchers All Teams
### Overall Batting Average Is .267

Fastball Average .299

|      | Inside | Middle | Outside |
|------|--------|--------|---------|
| High | 20/150 /3 | 35/457 /16 | 14/357 /5 |
| Med  | 46/304 /14 | 34/352 /12 | 115/313 /36 |
| Low  | 21/95 /2 | 48/291 /14 | 44/250 /11 |

Curve Average .288

|      | Inside | Middle | Outside |
|------|--------|--------|---------|
| High | 4/500 /2 | 8/500 /4 | 2/500 /1 |
| Med  | 13/384 /5 | 8/250 /2 | 33/272 /9 |
| Low  | 1/0 /0 | 12/333 /4 | 30/166 /5 |

Slider Average .233

|      | Inside | Middle | Outside |
|------|--------|--------|---------|
| High | 1/0 /0 | 13/307 /4 | 1/1000 /1 |
| Med  | 4/500 /2 | 8/500 /4 | 36/222 /8 |
| Low  | 4/0 /0 | 11/90 /1 | 29/172 /5 |

Change-Up Average .176

|      | Inside | Middle | Outside |
|------|--------|--------|---------|
| High | 0/0 /0 | 1/0 /0 | 4/250 /1 |
| Med  | 1/0 /0 | 2/0 /0 | 5/400 /2 |
| Low  | 1/0 /0 | 0/0 /0 | 3/0 /0 |

With the exceptions of high-inside and low-inside, Winfield's fastball locations are strong. His high-over-the-middle average of .457 is excellent.

Winfield pulls medium-high outside fastballs and hits them deeply to left and center fields. His .313 average against medium-high outside fastballs is very good considering the large number of instances (115) recorded in this location against right-handed pitchers.

MEDIUM-HIGH OUTSIDE FASTBALLS

BATTING AVERAGE .313
*PLAY*
LEFTFIELDER      Deep and shifted toward the left field line
CENTERFIELDER    Deep in straightaway center field
RIGHTFIELDER     Deep and shifted toward center field
SHORTSTOP        Up middle (shifted toward second base)
SECOND           Normal position

Winfield scatters hits in many fastball locations.

HIGH-OVER-THE-MIDDLE FASTBALLS

BATTING AVERAGE .457
*PLAY*
LEFTFIELDER      Medium-deep and shifted toward center field
CENTERFIELDER    Deep in straightaway center field
RIGHTFIELDER     Deep and shifted toward center field
SHORTSTOP        Shifted toward third base
SECOND           Normal position

LOW-OVER-THE-MIDDLE FASTBALLS

BATTING AVERAGE .291
*PLAY*
LEFTFIELDER      Medium-deep and shifted toward the left field line
CENTERFIELDER    Deep and shifted toward left field
RIGHTFIELDER     Deep in straightaway right field
SHORTSTOP        Normal position
SECOND           Shifted toward first base

Winfield also scatters curveballs.

MEDIUM-HIGH OUTSIDE CURVEBALLS

BATTING AVERAGE .272
*PLAY*
LEFTFIELDER      Deep and shifted toward the left field line
CENTERFIELDER    Medium-deep and shifted toward left field
RIGHTFIELDER     Deep in straightaway right field
SHORTSTOP        Shifted toward third base
SECOND           Shifted toward first base

He has trouble with low-outside curves (.166), although every other curve location is adequate.

Winfield has great difficulty with low sliders and with medium-high outside sliders. These present noticeable weaknesses for pitchers to attack.

Against right-handed pitchers, Winfield hits better when behind in the count.

### Dave Winfield   Right-Handed Hitter
### Against Right-Handed Pitchers When Ahead In The Count
### Batting Average Is .296

**Fastball Average .326**

| | Inside | Middle | Outside |
|---|---|---|---|
| High | 10 / 100 / 1 | 13 / 538 / 7 | 4 / 500 / 2 |
| Med | 22 / 318 / 7 | 16 / 250 / 4 | 43 / 325 / 14 |
| Low | 5 / 400 / 2 | 23 / 217 / 5 | 17 / 470 / 8 |

**Curve Average .458**

| | Inside | Middle | Outside |
|---|---|---|---|
| High | 1 / 1000 / 1 | 2 / 500 / 1 | 0 / 0 / 0 |
| Med | 2 / 500 / 1 | 2 / 1000 / 2 | 8 / 250 / 2 |
| Low | 0 / 0 / 0 | 3 / 333 / 1 | 6 / 500 / 3 |

**Slider Average .225**

| | Inside | Middle | Outside |
|---|---|---|---|
| High | 0 / 0 / 0 | 4 / 250 / 1 | 0 / 0 / 0 |
| Med | 3 / 333 / 1 | 3 / 333 / 1 | 10 / 200 / 2 |
| Low | 3 / 0 / 0 | 4 / 0 / 0 | 4 / 500 / 2 |

**Change-Up Average .000**

| | Inside | Middle | Outside |
|---|---|---|---|
| High | 0 / 0 / 0 | 0 / 0 / 0 | 0 / 0 / 0 |
| Med | 1 / 0 / 0 | 1 / 0 / 0 | 0 / 0 / 0 |
| Low | 0 / 0 / 0 | 0 / 0 / 0 | 0 / 0 / 0 |

### Dave Winfield  Right-Handed Hitter
### Against Right-Handed Pitchers When Behind In The Count
### Batting Average Is .333

Fastball Average .333

| | Inside | Middle | Outside |
|---|---|---|---|
| High | 2/ 500 / 1 | 8/ 250 / 2 | 3/ 333 / 1 |
| Med | 9/ 333 / 3 | 5/ 800 / 4 | 25/ 360 / 9 |
| Low | 6/ 0 / 0 | 11/ 272 / 3 | 3/ 333 / 1 |

Curve Average .322

| | Inside | Middle | Outside |
|---|---|---|---|
| High | 1/ 0 / 0 | 1/ 1000 / 1 | 1/ 0 / 0 |
| Med | 5/ 600 / 3 | 2/ 0 / 0 | 11/ 363 / 4 |
| Low | 0/ 0 / 0 | 2/ 0 / 0 | 8/ 250 / 2 |

Slider Average .333

| | Inside | Middle | Outside |
|---|---|---|---|
| High | 0/ 0 / 0 | 5/ 200 / 1 | 1/ 1000 / 1 |
| Med | 1/ 1000 / 1 | 1/ 0 / 0 | 14/ 357 / 5 |
| Low | 1/ 0 / 0 | 5/ 200 / 1 | 5/ 400 / 2 |

Change-Up Average .400

| | Inside | Middle | Outside |
|---|---|---|---|
| High | 0/ 0 / 0 | 1/ 0 / 0 | 1/ 1000 / 1 |
| Med | 0/ 0 / 0 | 0/ 0 / 0 | 2/ 500 / 1 |
| Low | 1/ 0 / 0 | 0/ 0 / 0 | 0/ 0 / 0 |

His overall fastball averages are about the same when ahead and when behind. Notice, however, his strength against low-outside fastballs when ahead in the count (.470), against high-over-the-middle when ahead (.538) and his relatively low medium-over-the-middle average when ahead (.250). His 0-for-6 record in the low-inside location when behind indicates a weakness.

Winfield hits curves well both when ahead and behind. His .458 overall average when ahead is very strong. In general, he has trouble with low curves when he is behind.

Winfield's performance against sliders when behind in the count is one of the strengths of his charts. His .357 average against medium-high outside sliders and .400 against low-outside sliders show that he can hit these two highly pitched slider locations well.

## Winfield Against Left-Handed Pitchers

Winfield's overall curve average is lower against left-handed pitchers than against right-handers, but his fastball average is higher.

### Dave Winfield   Right-Handed Hitter
### Against All Left-Handed Pitchers All Teams
### Overall Batting Average Is .260

#### Fastball Average .312

|      | Inside    | Middle    | Outside   |
|------|-----------|-----------|-----------|
| High | 6 / 333 / 2 | 13 / 384 / 5 | 20 / 400 / 8 |
| Med  | 25 / 280 / 7 | 18 / 500 / 9 | 70 / 300 / 21 |
| Low  | 15 / 266 / 4 | 28 / 321 / 9 | 26 / 153 / 4 |

#### Curve Average .225

|      | Inside    | Middle    | Outside   |
|------|-----------|-----------|-----------|
| High | 1 / 0 / 0 | 4 / 250 / 1 | 4 / 250 / 1 |
| Med  | 7 / 285 / 2 | 2 / 1000 / 2 | 22 / 318 / 7 |
| Low  | 13 / 76 / 1 | 10 / 100 / 1 | 8 / 125 / 1 |

#### Slider Average .333

|      | Inside    | Middle    | Outside   |
|------|-----------|-----------|-----------|
| High | 0 / 0 / 0 | 1 / 0 / 0 | 1 / 0 / 0 |
| Med  | 7 / 142 / 1 | 0 / 0 / 0 | 5 / 400 / 2 |
| Low  | 4 / 500 / 2 | 3 / 666 / 2 | 3 / 333 / 1 |

#### Change-Up Average .111

|      | Inside    | Middle    | Outside   |
|------|-----------|-----------|-----------|
| High | 0 / 0 / 0 | 0 / 0 / 0 | 4 / 0 / 0 |
| Med  | 1 / 0 / 0 | 0 / 0 / 0 | 7 / 142 / 1 |
| Low  | 1 / 0 / 0 | 1 / 0 / 0 | 13 / 153 / 2 |

Winfield's low-outside location is his only fastball weakness.

LOW-OUTSIDE FASTBALLS
(THROWN TO WINFIELD BY LEFT-HANDED PITCHERS)

BATTING AVERAGE .153
*PLAY*

| | |
|---|---|
| LEFTFIELDER | Deep in straightaway left field |
| CENTERFIELDER | Deep and shifted toward right field |
| RIGHTFIELDER | Medium-deep and shifted toward the right field line |
| SHORTSTOP | Shifted toward third base |
| SECOND | Normal position |

He hits medium-high outside fastballs deep and fairly straightaway.

MEDIUM-HIGH OUTSIDE FASTBALLS
(THROWN TO WINFIELD BY LEFT-HANDED PITCHERS)

BATTING AVERAGE .300
*PLAY*

| | |
|---|---|
| LEFTFIELDER | Deep in straightaway left field |
| CENTERFIELDER | Deep and shifted toward left field |
| RIGHTFIELDER | Deep in straightaway right field |
| SHORTSTOP | Normal position |
| SECOND | Shifted toward first base |

He pulls medium-high inside pitches to left field and the left side of the infield, but tends to hit high-inside pitches to the opposite field, as do many hitters.

HIGH-INSIDE FASTBALLS
(THROWN TO WINFIELD BY LEFT-HANDED PITCHERS)

BATTING AVERAGE .333
*PLAY*

| | |
|---|---|
| LEFTFIELDER | No instances recorded |
| CENTERFIELDER | Short and shifted toward left field |
| RIGHTFIELDER | Deep and shifted toward the right field line |
| SHORTSTOP | Up middle (shifted toward second base) |
| SECOND | No instances recorded |

Winfield has difficulty with low curves thrown by left-handers. Most of the time he strikes out on low curves or grounds them to the left side of the infield.

He pulls medium-high outside curves and hits them deeply to all fields.

MEDIUM-HIGH OUTSIDE CURVEBALLS
(THROWN TO WINFIELD BY LEFT-HANDED PITCHERS)

BATTING AVERAGE .318
*PLAY*
LEFTFIELDER          Deep and shifted toward the left field line
CENTERFIELDER        Deep and shifted toward left field
RIGHTFIELDER         Deep and shifted toward center field
SHORTSTOP            Shifted toward third base
SECOND               No instances recorded

With the exception of the medium-high inside location, Winfield hits well against sliders thrown by left-handers, but he has difficulty with change-ups. When Winfield is thrown a change-up, fielders must adopt the proper fielding strategy for the pitch, because he hits change-ups differently than he does other types of pitches.

LOW-OUTSIDE CHANGE-UPS
(THROWN TO WINFIELD BY LEFT-HANDED PITCHERS)

BATTING AVERAGE .153
*PLAY*
LEFTFIELDER          Medium-deep and shifted toward the left field line
CENTERFIELDER        Short in straightaway center field
RIGHTFIELDER         No instances recorded
SHORTSTOP            Shifted toward third base
SECOND               No instances recorded

As he does against right-handed pitchers, Winfield hits left-handers better when he is behind in the count.

### Dave Winfield   Right-Handed Hitter
### Against Left-Handed Pitchers When Behind In The Count
### Batting Average Is .364

Fastball Average .440

| | Inside | Middle | Outside |
|---|---|---|---|
| High | 1 / 1000 / 1 | 1 / 1000 / 1 | 5 / 600 / 3 |
| Med | 7 / 142 / 1 | 4 / 750 / 3 | 15 / 400 / 6 |
| Low | 4 / 500 / 2 | 6 / 500 / 3 | 7 / 285 / 2 |

Curve Average .181

| | Inside | Middle | Outside |
|---|---|---|---|
| High | 0 / 0 / 0 | 0 / 0 / 0 | 1 / 0 / 0 |
| Med | 1 / 0 / 0 | 1 / 1000 / 1 | 4 / 250 / 1 |
| Low | 0 / 0 / 0 | 3 / 0 / 0 | 1 / 0 / 0 |

### Dave Winfield   Right-Handed Hitter
### Against Left-Handed Pitchers When Ahead In The Count
### Batting Average Is .261

Fastball Average .282

| | Inside | Middle | Outside |
|---|---|---|---|
| High | 3 / 0 / 0 | 4 / 500 / 2 | 6 / 500 / 3 |
| Med | 7 / 285 / 2 | 8 / 375 / 3 | 36 / 333 / 12 |
| Low | 4 / 0 / 0 | 11 / 181 / 2 | 6 / 0 / 0 |

Curve Average .277

| | Inside | Middle | Outside |
|---|---|---|---|
| High | 1 / 0 / 0 | 1 / 0 / 0 | 1 / 0 / 0 |
| Med | 2 / 0 / 0 | 1 / 1000 / 1 | 8 / 375 / 3 |
| Low | 0 / 0 / 0 | 2 / 0 / 0 | 2 / 500 / 1 |

It is interesting that Winfield hits fastballs better when behind in the count and curveballs better when ahead. The opposite is true for most hitters because they look for breaking pitches when behind and for fastballs when ahead.  Winfield also hits curveballs better when ahead against right-handed pitchers.

## Super Summary For Ryne Sandberg

Ryne Sandberg, right-handed hitter for the Chicago Cubs, is an excellent fastball hitter with a better overall average against right-handed pitchers.

### Ryne Sandberg   Right-Handed Hitter
### Against All Right-Handed Pitchers All Teams
### Overall Batting Average Is .299

Fastball Average .351

|  | Inside | Middle | Outside |
|---|---|---|---|
| High | 47 / 404 / 19 | 99 / 373 / 37 | 58 / 275 / 16 |
| Med | 91 / 384 / 35 | 53 / 547 / 29 | 210 / 371 / 78 |
| Low | 33 / 272 / 9 | 189 / 354 / 67 | 140 / 235 / 33 |

Curve Average .236

|  | Inside | Middle | Outside |
|---|---|---|---|
| High | 4 / 250 / 1 | 10 / 200 / 2 | 16 / 125 / 2 |
| Med | 13 / 153 / 2 | 5 / 600 / 3 | 61 / 262 / 16 |
| Low | 8 / 250 / 2 | 25 / 320 / 8 | 82 / 207 / 17 |

Slider Average .284

|  | Inside | Middle | Outside |
|---|---|---|---|
| High | 3 / 0 / 0 | 7 / 285 / 2 | 6 / 166 / 1 |
| Med | 10 / 400 / 4 | 6 / 500 / 3 | 90 / 355 / 32 |
| Low | 4 / 0 / 0 | 17 / 294 / 5 | 82 / 207 / 17 |

Change-Up Average .104

|  | Inside | Middle | Outside |
|---|---|---|---|
| High | 0 / 0 / 0 | 0 / 0 / 0 | 0 / 0 / 0 |
| Med | 5 / 200 / 1 | 1 / 0 / 0 | 9 / 222 / 2 |
| Low | 5 / 0 / 0 | 7 / 142 / 1 | 21 / 47 / 1 |

Sandberg's fastball locations are strong throughout. His only weakness is the .235 in his low-outside fastball location. He hits low-outside fastballs to the opposite field.

LOW-OUTSIDE FASTBALLS

BATTING AVERAGE .235
> PLAY

| | |
|---|---|
| LEFTFIELDER | Deep and shifted toward center field |
| CENTERFIELDER | Deep and shifted toward right field |
| RIGHTFIELDER | Medium-deep and shifted toward the right field line |
| SHORTSTOP | Up middle (shifted toward second base) |
| SECOND | Normal position |

Considering the large number of total instances in many of his fastball locations, his high averages are exceptional. Sandberg hits medium-high outside fastballs (.371) straightaway and deep; he scatters medium-high inside fastballs (.384) to all fields.

MEDIUM-HIGH INSIDE FASTBALLS

BATTING AVERAGE .384
*PLAY*
LEFTFIELDER         Deep and shifted toward the left field line
CENTERFIELDER       Medium-deep and shifted toward left field
RIGHTFIELDER        Medium-deep and shifted toward the right field line
SHORTSTOP           Shifted toward third base
SECOND              Normal position

Sandberg hits high-inside fastballs deep and straightaway, but he tends to pull medium-over-the-middle fastballs. Sandberg's extremely high .547 average in the medium-over-the-middle location should stand as a firm warning to pitchers to stay on the corners when pitching to him.

HIGH-INSIDE FASTBALLS

BATTING AVERAGE .404
*PLAY*
LEFTFIELDER         Deep in straightaway left field
CENTERFIELDER       Deep in straightaway center field
RIGHTFIELDER        Deep in straightaway right field
SHORTSTOP           Shifted toward third base
SECOND              Normal position

Sandberg has difficulty with curveballs thrown by right-handers. He has numerous weak locations. His strongest average is .320 in the low-over-the-middle curve location. He tends to pull these pitches. He also pulls medium-high outside curves.

MEDIUM-HIGH OUTSIDE CURVEBALLS

BATTING AVERAGE .262
*PLAY*
LEFTFIELDER         Deep and shifted toward the left field line
CENTERFIELDER       Deep and shifted toward left field
RIGHTFIELDER        Deep in straightaway right field
SHORTSTOP           Shifted toward third base
SECOND              Shifted toward first base

He hits well against sliders, posting a strong .355 against medium-high outside sliders. His .207 average in the low-outside slider location and his .166 in the high-outside are weak. He hits medium-high outside sliders deep and straightaway to all fields, while tending to hit low-outside sliders medium-deep to the opposite field (right field).

Sandberg has great difficulty with change-ups. He hits low change-ups very poorly.

Against right-handers, Sandberg hits very strongly when ahead in the count.

### Ryne Sandberg   Right-Handed Hitter
### Against Right-Handed Pitchers When Ahead In The Count
### Batting Average Is .388

#### Fastball Average .422

|      | Inside | Middle | Outside |
|------|--------|--------|---------|
| High | 19/ 578 /11 | 39/ 435 /17 | 23/ 304 / 7 |
| Med  | 33/ 454 /15 | 21/ 571 /12 | 100/ 450 /45 |
| Low  | 4/ 500 / 2 | 97/ 422 /41 | 64/ 296 /19 |

#### Curve Average .230

|      | Inside | Middle | Outside |
|------|--------|--------|---------|
| High | 0/ 0 / 0 | 0/ 0 / 0 | 1/ 0 / 0 |
| Med  | 0/ 0 / 0 | 0/ 0 / 0 | 9/ 222 / 2 |
| Low  | 2/ 500 / 1 | 5/ 200 / 1 | 9/ 222 / 2 |

#### Slider Average .365

|      | Inside | Middle | Outside |
|------|--------|--------|---------|
| High | 0/ 0 / 0 | 2/ 0 / 0 | 0/ 0 / 0 |
| Med  | 0/ 0 / 0 | 2/ 1000/ 2 | 28/ 357 /10 |
| Low  | 1/ 0 / 0 | 3/ 333 / 1 | 16/ 375 / 6 |

#### Change-Up Average .250

|      | Inside | Middle | Outside |
|------|--------|--------|---------|
| High | 0/ 0 / 0 | 0/ 0 / 0 | 0/ 0 / 0 |
| Med  | 0/ 0 / 0 | 0/ 0 / 0 | 1/ 0 / 0 |
| Low  | 0/ 0 / 0 | 1/ 1000/ 1 | 2/ 0 / 0 |

**Ryne Sandberg  Right-Handed Hitter**
**Against Right-Handed Pitchers When Behind In The Count**
**Batting Average Is .311**

Fastball Average .333          Curve Average .282

|  | Inside | Middle | Outside | | Inside | Middle | Outside |
|------|--------|--------|---------|---|--------|--------|---------|
| High | 6/<br>500 / 3 | 16/<br>375 / 6 | 9/<br>444 / 4 | | 1/<br>1000 / 1 | 2/<br>500 / 1 | 6/<br>0 / 0 |
| Med | 21/<br>333 / 7 | 8/<br>500 / 4 | 32/<br>281 / 9 | | 3/<br>0 / 0 | 3/<br>333 / 1 | 31/<br>290 / 9 |
| Low | 12/<br>333 / 4 | 32/<br>312 / 10 | 20/<br>250 / 5 | | 1/<br>0 / 0 | 11/<br>454 / 5 | 27/<br>259 / 7 |

Slider Average .367          Change-Up Average .300

|  | Inside | Middle | Outside | | Inside | Middle | Outside |
|------|--------|--------|---------|---|--------|--------|---------|
| High | 1/<br>0 / 0 | 1/<br>1000 / 1 | 0/<br>0 / 0 | | 0/<br>0 / 0 | 0/<br>0 / 0 | 0/<br>0 / 0 |
| Med | 4/<br>500 / 2 | 1/<br>1000 / 1 | 19/<br>421 / 8 | | 1/<br>1000 / 1 | 0/<br>0 / 0 | 3/<br>333 / 1 |
| Low | 0/<br>0 / 0 | 1/<br>0 / 0 | 22/<br>272 / 6 | | 0/<br>0 / 0 | 1/<br>0 / 0 | 5/<br>200 / 1 |

Sandberg looks for fastballs when ahead in the count and hits them with great authority. His overall .422 average against fastballs when he is ahead in the count is one of the highest recorded by the BARS System, considering the high number of instances in many of the locations. His .450 average against medium-high outside fastballs (with 100 recorded instances) is sensational. He tends to hit these medium-high outside pitches straightaway to all fields.

His fastball averages are also solid when behind in the count. The .250 in his low-outside location is the only average that approaches being a weakness.

Sandberg hits curves better when behind in the count. He pulls low-over-the-middle curves (.454) and medium-high outside curves (.290).

MEDIUM-HIGH OUTSIDE CURVEBALLS
(THROWN TO SANDBERG WHEN HE IS BEHIND IN THE COUNT)

BATTING AVERAGE .290
   *PLAY*
LEFTFIELDER          Deep and shifted toward the left field line
CENTERFIELDER        Deep and shifted toward left field
RIGHTFIELDER         Deep in straightaway right field
SHORTSTOP            Shifted toward third base
SECOND               Shifted toward first base

## Sandberg Against Left-Handed Pitchers

Sandberg has a lower overall average against left-handed pitchers than he does against right-handed pitchers.

### Ryne Sandberg   Right-Handed Hitter
### Against All Left-Handed Pitchers All Teams
### Overall Batting Average Is .271

Fastball Average .302

| | Inside | Middle | Outside |
|---|---|---|---|
| High | 7 / 2  **285** | 17 / 3  **176** | 20 / 4  **200** |
| Med | 30 / 7  **233** | 10 / 3  **300** | 70 / 20  **285** |
| Low | 10 / 2  **200** | 51 / 23  **450** | 56 / 18  **321** |

Curve Average .250

| | Inside | Middle | Outside |
|---|---|---|---|
| High | 1 / 0  **0** | 3 / 1  **333** | 3 / 0  **0** |
| Med | 6 / 4  **666** | 1 / 0  **0** | 20 / 6  **300** |
| Low | 14 / 2  **142** | 22 / 5  **227** | 18 / 4  **222** |

Slider Average .212

| | Inside | Middle | Outside |
|---|---|---|---|
| High | 3 / 0  **0** | 0 / 0  **0** | 0 / 0  **0** |
| Med | 4 / 0  **0** | 0 / 0  **0** | 5 / 2  **400** |
| Low | 8 / 0  **0** | 8 / 3  **375** | 5 / 2  **400** |

Change-Up Average .236

| | Inside | Middle | Outside |
|---|---|---|---|
| High | 0 / 0  **0** | 1 / 0  **0** | 1 / 0  **0** |
| Med | 0 / 0  **0** | 0 / 0  **0** | 12 / 5  **416** |
| Low | 3 / 0  **0** | 5 / 1  **200** | 16 / 3  **187** |

He has several weak fastball locations and these bring his overall fastball average down. Notice that he hits low-over-the-middle (.450) and low-outside fastballs well (.321), but every other location is considerably lower than against right-handed pitchers.

He pulls both medium-high outside and medium-high inside fastballs, but hits low-outside and low-over-the-middle fastballs fairly straightaway to all fields.

Sandberg's curve averages are slightly higher against left-handers than against right-handers. He has difficulty with low curves, but hits medium-high outside and medium-high inside curves well. It is interesting to note that he pulls all low curves (for low averages), while hitting medium-high curves to the opposite field (for high averages).

MEDIUM-HIGH OUTSIDE CURVEBALLS
(THROWN TO SANDBERG BY LEFT-HANDED PITCHERS)

BATTING AVERAGE .300
    *PLAY*
LEFTFIELDER       Deep in straightaway left field
CENTERFIELDER    Deep and shifted toward right field
RIGHTFIELDER     Deep and shifted toward the right field line
SHORTSTOP        Shifted toward third base
SECOND           Normal position

LOW-OUTSIDE CURVEBALLS
(THROWN TO SANDBERG BY LEFT-HANDED PITCHERS)

BATTING AVERAGE .222
    *PLAY*
LEFTFIELDER       Deep and shifted toward the left field line
CENTERFIELDER    Medium-deep and shifted toward left field
RIGHTFIELDER     Deep and shifted toward center field
SHORTSTOP        Normal position
SECOND           Normal position

Sandberg hits sliders and change-ups poorly against left-handers, although he does have several strong locations in these two charts. Every outfielder should play Sandberg to pull the ball when medium-high outside change-ups are thrown.

MEDIUM-HIGH OUTSIDE CHANGE-UPS
(THROWN TO SANDBERG BY LEFT-HANDED PITCHERS)

BATTING AVERAGE .416
  *PLAY*
LEFTFIELDER        Medium-deep and shifted toward the left field line
CENTERFIELDER      Deep and shifted toward left field
RIGHTFIELDER       Medium-deep and shifted toward center field
SHORTSTOP          Up middle (shifted toward second base)
SECOND             Shifted toward first base

Sandberg hits better against left-handed pitchers when ahead in the count.

**Ryne Sandberg    Right-Handed Hitter**
**Against Left-Handed Pitchers When Ahead In The Count**
**Batting Average Is .310**

Fastball Average .314

|      | Inside | Middle | Outside |
|------|--------|--------|---------|
| High | 250 $^4/_1$ | 200 $^5/_1$ | 200 $^5/_1$ |
| Med  | 375 $^8/_3$ | 500 $^6/_3$ | 250 $^{40}/_{10}$ |
| Low  | 500 $^2/_1$ | 400 $^{25}/_{10}$ | 310 $^{29}/_9$ |

Curve Average .352

|      | Inside | Middle | Outside |
|------|--------|--------|---------|
| High | 0 $^0/_0$ | 0 $^1/_0$ | 0 $^0/_0$ |
| Med  | 0 $^0/_0$ | 0 $^0/_0$ | 666 $^3/_2$ |
| Low  | 500 $^2/_1$ | 428 $^7/_3$ | 0 $^4/_0$ |

**Ryne Sandberg   Right-Handed Hitter**
**Against Left-Handed Pitchers When Behind In The Count**
**Batting Average Is .260**

Fastball Average .274

|      | Inside | Middle | Outside |
|------|--------|--------|---------|
| High | 500 $^2/_1$ | 666 $^3/_2$ | 333 $^6/_2$ |
| Med  | 111 $^9/_1$ | 0 $^0/_0$ | 363 $^{11}/_4$ |
| Low  | 0 $^2/_0$ | 222 $^9/_2$ | 222 $^9/_2$ |

Curve Average .227

|      | Inside | Middle | Outside |
|------|--------|--------|---------|
| High | 0 $^0/_0$ | 500 $^2/_1$ | 0 $^1/_0$ |
| Med  | 750 $^4/_3$ | 0 $^1/_0$ | 200 $^5/_1$ |
| Low  | 0 $^1/_0$ | 0 $^6/_0$ | 0 $^2/_0$ |

**Super Summary For Steve Sax**

Steve Sax, right-handed hitter for the Los Angeles Dodgers, is a good fastball hitter. He has trouble with curves thrown by right-handed pitchers, but hits curves thrown by left-handed pitchers extremely well.

First against right-handers:

### Steve Sax    Right-Handed Hitter
### Against All Right-Handed Pitchers All Teams
### Overall Batting Average Is .306

Fastball Average .347

| | Inside | Middle | Outside |
|---|---|---|---|
| High | 24/ 291 / 7 | 53/ 283 / 15 | 16/ 187 / 3 |
| Med | 49/ 408 / 20 | 22/ 318 / 7 | 64/ 359 / 23 |
| Low | 21/ 333 / 7 | 63/ 476 / 30 | 36/ 250 / 9 |

Curve Average .216

| | Inside | Middle | Outside |
|---|---|---|---|
| High | 3/ 333 / 1 | 8/ 125 / 1 | 2/ 0 / 0 |
| Med | 6/ 166 / 1 | 10/ 300 / 3 | 20/ 400 / 8 |
| Low | 3/ 0 / 0 | 16/ 187 / 3 | 15/ 66 / 1 |

Slider Average .333

| | Inside | Middle | Outside |
|---|---|---|---|
| High | 0/ 0 / 0 | 4/ 750 / 3 | 3/ 0 / 0 |
| Med | 3/ 666 / 2 | 5/ 600 / 3 | 10/ 600 / 6 |
| Low | 1/ 0 / 0 | 7/ 285 / 2 | 27/ 148 / 4 |

Change-Up Average .375

| | Inside | Middle | Outside |
|---|---|---|---|
| High | 2/ 500 / 1 | 2/ 0 / 0 | 0/ 0 / 0 |
| Med | 1/ 1000/ 1 | 0/ 0 / 0 | 6/ 500 / 3 |
| Low | 2/ 500 / 1 | 5/ 400 / 2 | 6/ 166 / 1 |

Sax's fastball averages are strong in all locations except high-outside and low-outside. He hits his three most highly pitched locations excellently — medium-high outside (.359), medium-high inside (.408) and low-over-the-middle (.476). Each of these three locations has a high number of recorded instances.

Sax hits medium-high outside fastballs mostly to the opposite field (right field).

MEDIUM-HIGH OUTSIDE FASTBALLS

BATTING AVERAGE .359
  *PLAY*
LEFTFIELDER          Deep and shifted toward center field
CENTERFIELDER        Deep in straightaway center field
RIGHTFIELDER         Deep and shifted toward the right field line
SHORTSTOP            Up middle (shifted toward second base)
SECOND               Normal position

He hits medium-high inside fastballs mostly straightaway.

MEDIUM-HIGH INSIDE FASTBALLS

BATTING AVERAGE .408
  *PLAY*
LEFTFIELDER          Medium-deep in straightaway left field
CENTERFIELDER        Short and shifted toward left field
RIGHTFIELDER         Medium-deep in straightaway right field
SHORTSTOP            Normal position
SECOND               Normal position

Sax's medium-high inside fastball chart shows that fielders must be positioned specifically for each type and location of pitch. Who would have thought that for medium-high inside fastballs the center fielder would need to play Sax short and shifted toward left field?
Sax hits low-over-the-middle fastballs to all fields.

LOW-OVER-THE-MIDDLE FASTBALLS

BATTING AVERAGE .476
  *PLAY*
LEFTFIELDER          Deep and shifted toward the left field line
CENTERFIELDER        Deep in straightaway center field
RIGHTFIELDER         Deep and shifted toward the right field line
SHORTSTOP            Up middle (shifted toward second base)
SECOND               Normal position

Sax has trouble with low curveballs. He hits these pitches medium-deep to straightaway center and right fields. He has no recorded instances of hitting a low curve thrown by a right-handed pitcher to left field. However, he hits medium-high curves very well.

MEDIUM-HIGH OUTSIDE CURVEBALLS

BATTING AVERAGE .400
   *PLAY*
| | |
|---|---|
| LEFTFIELDER | Deep and shifted toward the left field line |
| CENTERFIELDER | Medium-deep in straightaway center field |
| RIGHTFIELDER | Medium-deep and shifted toward center field |
| SHORTSTOP | Normal position |
| SECOND | No instances recorded |

    Sax hits sliders well overall, with very high averages in the medium-high locations. The .148 average in his low-outside slider location is weak. Low-outside is his most highly pitched slider location, and presents a target for pitchers to focus on.
    Sax's change-up averages are strong throughout with the exception in the low-outside location.
    Sax hits nearly 100 points higher against right-handed pitchers when he is ahead in the count.

**Steve Sax   Right-Handed Hitter**
**Against Right-Handed Pitchers When Ahead In The Count**
**Batting Average Is .377**

Fastball Average .406         Curve Average .375

| | Inside | Middle | Outside | | Inside | Middle | Outside |
|---|---|---|---|---|---|---|---|
| High | 11/ 363 / 4 | 29/ 344 / 10 | 3/ 0 / 0 | | 0/ 0 / 0 | 3/ 333 / 1 | 0/ 0 / 0 |
| Med | 26/ 423 / 11 | 15/ 266 / 4 | 29/ 448 / 13 | | 0/ 0 / 0 | 3/ 333 / 1 | 6/ 500 / 3 |
| Low | 9/ 444 / 4 | 31/ 548 / 17 | 12/ 333 / 4 | | 0/ 0 / 0 | 3/ 333 / 1 | 1/ 0 / 0 |

### Steve Sax   Right-Handed Hitter
### Against Right-Handed Pitchers When Behind In The Count
### Batting Average Is .287

Fastball Average .281

| | Inside | Middle | Outside |
|---|---|---|---|
| High | 4 / 500 / 2 | 13 / 230 / 3 | 4 / 250 / 1 |
| Med | 8 / 375 / 3 | 1 / 0 / 0 | 18 / 222 / 4 |
| Low | 6 / 0 / 0 | 7 / 428 / 3 | 3 / 666 / 2 |

Curve Average .236

| | Inside | Middle | Outside |
|---|---|---|---|
| High | 2 / 500 / 1 | 4 / 0 / 0 | 2 / 0 / 0 |
| Med | 3 / 333 / 1 | 4 / 250 / 1 | 10 / 400 / 4 |
| Low | 2 / 0 / 0 | 7 / 285 / 2 | 4 / 0 / 0 |

All of Sax's averages go up when he is ahead in the count. His overall fastball average of .406 is excellent. His fastball averages are strong throughout. The exception is, strangely, in his medium-over-the-middle location (.266). Sax hits medium-high outside fastballs deep to center and deep down the right field line both when ahead and behind. When behind, he has no recorded instances of hitting a medium-high outside fastball to left field.

MEDIUM-HIGH OUTSIDE FASTBALLS
(THROWN WHEN SAX IS AHEAD IN THE COUNT)

BATTING AVERAGE .448
   *PLAY*

| | |
|---|---|
| LEFTFIELDER | Deep and shifted toward center field |
| CENTERFIELDER | Deep in straightaway center field |
| RIGHTFIELDER | Deep and shifted toward the right field line |
| SHORTSTOP | Up middle (shifted toward second base) |
| SECOND | Normal position |

He also hits curveballs better when ahead in the count. This is not unusual for a hitter, but the large difference in percentages when ahead and behind (nearly 150 points) indicates that Sax feels much more in command when ahead.

He hits sliders and curves well when behind. Little information is available for these pitches, however.

## Sax Against Left-Handed Pitchers

Sax hits very well against left-handed pitchers. His fastball average is good and his curve average exceptional.

### Steve Sax   Right-Handed Hitter
### Against All Left-Handed Pitchers All Teams
### Overall Batting Average Is .324

Fastball Average .322          Curve Average .538

|  | Inside | Middle | Outside | | Inside | Middle | Outside |
|---|---|---|---|---|---|---|---|
| High | 4 / 250 / 1 | 13 / 307 / 4 | 10 / 100 / 1 | | 3 / 333 / 1 | 1 / 0 / 0 | 1 / 0 / 0 |
| Med | 15 / 533 / 8 | 1 / 0 / 0 | 39 / 487 / 19 | | 0 / 0 / 0 | 2 / 1000 / 2 | 7 / 571 / 4 |
| Low | 5 / 0 / 0 | 22 / 272 / 6 | 18 / 111 / 2 | | 4 / 250 / 1 | 5 / 800 / 4 | 3 / 666 / 2 |

Sax has numerous weak fastball locations against lefties. The high-inside and all the low locations are weak.

His medium-high outside fastball average of .487 is excellent, as is his .533 average in medium-high inside. To be effective when pitches are thrown to these two locations, fielders need to be positioned differently.

MEDIUM-HIGH OUTSIDE FASTBALLS
(THROWN TO SAX BY LEFT-HANDED PITCHERS)

BATTING AVERAGE .487
    *PLAY*
LEFTFIELDER        Deep in straightaway left field
CENTERFIELDER    Medium-deep in straightaway center field
RIGHTFIELDER     Deep and shifted toward center field
SHORTSTOP        Normal position
SECOND            Normal position

MEDIUM-HIGH INSIDE FASTBALLS
(THROWN TO SAX BY LEFT-HANDED PITCHERS)

BATTING AVERAGE .533
*PLAY*

| | |
|---|---|
| LEFTFIELDER | Medium-deep and shifted toward center field |
| CENTERFIELDER | Deep in straightaway center field |
| RIGHTFIELDER | Deep and shifted toward the right field line |
| SHORTSTOP | Up middle (shifted toward second base) |
| SECOND | Normal position |

Notice that left-handers threw Sax only one recorded medium-over-the-middle fastball. Sax popped it up medium-deep into straightaway left field. This single pitch over the heart of the plate shows that lefties pitched Sax extremely carefully, keeping the ball over the corners of the plate. If they could keep their fastballs low, they would have a better chance of getting him out.

Sax hits curves thrown by left-handers very well. He does not have a weak curve location, although few curves were thrown to him in the high locations.

In the low-over-the-middle curve location, Sax got four base hits through the hole between the third baseman and shortstop. His two hits in the low-outside location were to medium-deep left field down the line. He scattered his hits in the medium-high outside curve location.

MEDIUM-HIGH OUTSIDE CURVEBALLS
(THROWN TO SAX BY LEFT-HANDED PITCHERS)

BATTING AVERAGE .571
*PLAY*

| | |
|---|---|
| LEFTFIELDER | Deep and shifted toward the left field line |
| CENTERFIELDER | Medium-deep and shifted toward left field |
| RIGHTFIELDER | Medium-deep and shifted toward center field |
| SHORTSTOP | Normal position |
| SECOND | No instances recorded |

Sax hits 100 points better against left-handed pitchers when he is ahead in the count than when he is behind.

### Steve Sax    Right-Handed Hitter
### Against Left-Handed Pitchers When Ahead In The Count
### Batting Average Is .384

Fastball Average .338

|  | Inside | Middle | Outside |
|---|---|---|---|
| High | 1 / 1000 / 1 | 9 / 444 / 4 | 3 / 0 / 0 |
| Med | 6 / 500 / 3 | 1 / 0 / 0 | 22 / 454 / 10 |
| Low | 2 / 0 / 0 | 14 / 214 / 3 | 7 / 142 / 1 |

Curve Average 1.000

|  | Inside | Middle | Outside |
|---|---|---|---|
| High | 0 / 0 / 0 | 0 / 0 / 0 | 0 / 0 / 0 |
| Med | 0 / 0 / 0 | 0 / 0 / 0 | 2 / 1000 / 2 |
| Low | 0 / 0 / 0 | 1 / 1000 / 1 | 0 / 0 / 0 |

### Steve Sax    Right-Handed Hitter
### Against Left-Handed Pitchers When Behind In The Count
### Batting Average Is .285

Fastball Average .368

|  | Inside | Middle | Outside |
|---|---|---|---|
| High | 1 / 0 / 0 | 2 / 0 / 0 | 2 / 0 / 0 |
| Med | 4 / 750 / 3 | 0 / 0 / 0 | 4 / 500 / 2 |
| Low | 0 / 0 / 0 | 3 / 333 / 1 | 3 / 333 / 1 |

Curve Average .571

|  | Inside | Middle | Outside |
|---|---|---|---|
| High | 1 / 0 / 0 | 0 / 0 / 0 | 0 / 0 / 0 |
| Med | 0 / 0 / 0 | 1 / 1000 / 1 | 3 / 333 / 1 |
| Low | 0 / 0 / 0 | 0 / 0 / 0 | 2 / 1000 / 2 |

**Super Summary For Darryl Strawberry**

Darryl Strawberry, left-handed hitter for the New York Mets, is a fastball hitter who hits for a higher BARS System average against left-handed pitchers.

First, against right-handers:

### Darryl Strawberry    Left-Handed Hitter
### Against All Right-Handed Pitchers All Teams
### Overall Batting Average Is .287

#### Fastball Average .320

|  | Outside | Middle | Inside |
|---|---|---|---|
| High | 24 / 208 / 5 | 43 / 418 / 18 | 19 / 157 / 3 |
| Med | 64 / 312 / 20 | 26 / 423 / 11 | 35 / 342 / 12 |
| Low | 31 / 193 / 6 | 44 / 386 / 17 | 17 / 294 / 5 |

#### Curve Average .242

|  | Outside | Middle | Inside |
|---|---|---|---|
| High | 2 / 0 / 0 | 6 / 500 / 3 | 0 / 0 / 0 |
| Med | 9 / 555 / 5 | 5 / 800 / 4 | 5 / 0 / 0 |
| Low | 10 / 0 / 0 | 23 / 173 / 4 | 10 / 100 / 1 |

#### Slider Average .264

|  | Outside | Middle | Inside |
|---|---|---|---|
| High | 0 / 0 / 0 | 4 / 0 / 0 | 1 / 0 / 0 |
| Med | 2 / 0 / 0 | 1 / 1000 / 1 | 6 / 500 / 3 |
| Low | 2 / 0 / 0 | 7 / 714 / 5 | 11 / 0 / 0 |

#### Change-Up Average .222

|  | Outside | Middle | Inside |
|---|---|---|---|
| High | 6 / 166 / 1 | 1 / 1000 / 1 | 1 / 0 / 0 |
| Med | 9 / 555 / 5 | 2 / 500 / 1 | 2 / 0 / 0 |
| Low | 5 / 0 / 0 | 6 / 0 / 0 | 4 / 0 / 0 |

Strawberry has weaknesses against fastballs in the high-inside, high-outside and low-outside locations. He tends to pull inside fastballs to right field and go with outside fastballs to left field.

MEDIUM-HIGH OUTSIDE FASTBALLS

BATTING AVERAGE .312
    PLAY
LEFTFIELDER          Deep and shifted toward the left field line
CENTERFIELDER        Medium-deep in straightaway center field
RIGHTFIELDER         Deep in straightaway right field
SHORTSTOP            Normal position
SECOND               Normal position

MEDIUM-HIGH INSIDE FASTBALLS

BATTING AVERAGE .342
   *PLAY*

| | |
|---|---|
| LEFTFIELDER | Deep in straightaway left field |
| CENTERFIELDER | Deep in straightaway center field |
| RIGHTFIELDER | Deep and shifted toward the right field line |
| SHORTSTOP | Normal position |
| SECOND | Normal position |

    Strawberry's strong fastball averages down the middle of the plate serve as a warning to pitchers. His fastball weaknesses are on the corners.

    Curveballs are a different story. He has significant weaknesses in each of the three low curveball locations and in the medium-high inside curveball location. This is in contrast to his high percentages in several other curveball locations.

    Strawberry's slider averages vary from excellent to poor through the locations. He hits low-over-the-middle sliders at a .714 clip, but against low-inside sliders he is 0-for-11.

    His difficulty with low pitches extends into the change-up chart. The BARS System has not yet recorded a hit for him in the low change-up locations.

    Against right-handed pitchers, Strawberry hits slightly better when behind in the count.

**Darryl Strawberry    Left-Handed Hitter**
**Against Right-Handed Pitchers When Behind In The Count**
**Batting Average Is .381**

Fastball Average .526        Curve Average .318

| | Outside | Middle | Inside | | Outside | Middle | Inside |
|---|---|---|---|---|---|---|---|
| High | 666 / 2 (3) | 333 / 3 (9) | 0 / 0 (1) | | 0 / 0 (1) | 333 / 1 (3) | 0 / 0 (0) |
| Med | 500 / 5 (10) | 1000 / 2 (2) | 1000 / 1 (1) | | 750 / 3 (4) | 1000 / 3 (3) | 0 / 0 (1) |
| Low | 333 / 1 (3) | 714 / 5 (7) | 500 / 1 (2) | | 0 / 0 (4) | 0 / 0 (4) | 0 / 0 (2) |

### Darryl Strawberry   Left-Handed Hitter
### Against Right-Handed Pitchers When Ahead In The Count
### Batting Average Is .352

Fastball Average .358                Curve Average .333

| | Outside | Middle | Inside | Outside | Middle | Inside |
|---|---|---|---|---|---|---|
| High | 5/<br>400 / 2 | 15/<br>466 / 7 | 10/<br>300 / 3 | 0/<br>0 / 0 | 1/<br>1000/ 1 | 0/<br>0 / 0 |
| Med | 30/<br>333 /10 | 14/<br>500 / 7 | 17/<br>352 / 6 | 2/<br>1000/ 2 | 1/<br>0 / 0 | 3/<br>0 / 0 |
| Low | 13/<br>153 / 2 | 21/<br>333 / 7 | 6/<br>500 / 3 | 1/<br>0 / 0 | 6/<br>166 / 1 | 1/<br>1000/ 1 |

Strawberry's fastball chart when behind in the count includes several locations with little information, but his averages in the medium-high outside and low-over-the-middle locations are excellent. When ahead in the count, his only weak fastball location is low-outside. When ahead, he hits medium-high outside fastballs straightaway to all positions and medium-high inside fastballs to the opposite field.

MEDIUM-HIGH INSIDE FASTBALLS
(THROWN TO STRAWBERRY WHEN HE IS AHEAD IN THE COUNT)

BATTING AVERAGE .352
   *PLAY*

| | |
|---|---|
| LEFTFIELDER | Deep and shifted toward the left field line |
| CENTERFIELDER | Deep in straightaway center field |
| RIGHTFIELDER | Deep and shifted toward center field |
| SHORTSTOP | Up middle (shifted toward second base) |
| SECOND | Shifted toward second base |

Notice Strawberry's weakness against low curves when he is behind in the count. This improves only slightly when he is ahead in the count.

### Strawberry Against Left-Handed Pitchers

Against left-handed pitchers, Strawberry's fastball average is near .300, but his curve average is low.

**Darryl Strawberry   Left-Handed Hitter**
**Against All Left-Handed Pitchers All Teams**
**Overall Batting Average Is .234**

Fastball Average .290                    Curve Average .209

| | Outside | Middle | Inside | | Outside | Middle | Inside |
|------|---------|--------|--------|---|---------|--------|--------|
| High | 5/ 200 / 1 | 9/ 333 / 3 | 8/ 0 / 0 | | 1/ 1000 / 1 | 2/ 0 / 0 | 1/ 0 / 0 |
| Med | 18/ 444 / 8 | 10/ 400 / 4 | 35/ 257 / 9 | | 6/ 333 / 2 | 6/ 333 / 2 | 6/ 333 / 2 |
| Low | 7/ 142 / 1 | 14/ 500 / 7 | 11/ 90 / 1 | | 14/ 71 / 1 | 4/ 250 / 1 | 3/ 0 / 0 |

Notice Strawberry's fastball weaknesses in the upper and lower corner locations. His medium-high inside location is less than adequate (.257). If left-handed pitchers would stay inside with their fastballs they would have an edge on Strawberry. The following chart shows that he hits inside fastballs to the opposite field.

MEDIUM-HIGH INSIDE FASTBALLS
(THROWN TO STRAWBERRY BY LEFT-HANDED PITCHERS)

BATTING AVERAGE .257
   *PLAY*
LEFTFIELDER       Deep and shifted toward the left field line
CENTERFIELDER     Deep and shifted toward left field
RIGHTFIELDER      Deep and shifted toward center field
SHORTSTOP         Normal position
SECOND              Normal position

He hits medium-outside fastballs thrown by left-handers fairly straightaway to the outfield and to the right side of the infield.

MEDIUM-HIGH OUTSIDE FASTBALLS
(THROWN TO STRAWBERRY BY LEFT-HANDED PITCHERS)

BATTING AVERAGE .444
*PLAY*

| | |
|---|---|
| LEFTFIELDER | Deep in straightaway left field |
| CENTERFIELDER | Medium-deep in straightaway center field |
| RIGHTFIELDER | Deep and shifted toward center field |
| SHORTSTOP | Up middle (shifted toward second base) |
| SECOND | Shifted toward first base |

Strawberry tends to pull low-over-middle fastballs thrown by left-handers, but he hits high-over-the-middle fastballs straightaway to all fields.

HIGH-OVER-THE-MIDDLE FASTBALLS
(THROWN TO STRAWBERRY BY LEFT-HANDED PITCHERS)

BATTING AVERAGE .333
*PLAY*

| | |
|---|---|
| LEFTFIELDER | Short in straightaway left field |
| CENTERFIELDER | Medium-deep in straightaway center field |
| RIGHTFIELDER | Deep in straightaway right field |
| SHORTSTOP | Shifted toward third base |
| SECOND | Normal position |

Against left-handed pitchers, Strawberry's batting percentages are about the same when ahead and when behind in the count. His ahead and behind charts are not shown.

## Super Summary For Bob Horner

Right-handed Bob Horner, former Atlanta slugger now playing with St. Louis, is a first-rate fastball hitter who has considerable difficulty with curves thrown by right-handers.

**Bob Horner Right-Handed Hitter**
**Against All Right-Handed Pitchers All Teams**
**Overall Batting Average Is .276**

Fastball Average .352

| | Inside | Middle | Outside |
|------|--------|--------|---------|
| High | 11 / 364 / 4 | 42 / 357 / 15 | 17 / 294 / 5 |
| Med | 53 / 283 / 15 | 38 / 500 / 19 | 85 / 282 / 24 |
| Low | 31 / 451 / 14 | 64 / 390 / 25 | 36 / 333 / 12 |

Curve Average .155

| | Inside | Middle | Outside |
|------|--------|--------|---------|
| High | 1 / 0 / 0 | 12 / 0 / 0 | 1 / 1000 / 0 |
| Med | 11 / 272 / 3 | 13 / 538 / 7 | 37 / 108 / 4 |
| Low | 5 / 0 / 0 | 27 / 111 / 3 | 22 / 90 / 2 |

Slider Average .155

| | Inside | Middle | Outside |
|------|--------|--------|---------|
| High | 1 / 0 / 0 | 1 / 1000 / 1 | 0 / 0 / 0 |
| Med | 2 / 500 / 1 | 3 / 666 / 2 | 22 / 318 / 7 |
| Low | 4 / 250 / 1 | 12 / 166 / 2 | 17 / 176 / 3 |

Change-Up Average .375

| | Inside | Middle | Outside |
|------|--------|--------|---------|
| High | 0 / 0 / 0 | 0 / 0 / 0 | 0 / 0 / 0 |
| Med | 2 / 500 / 1 | 2 / 1000 / 2 | 6 / 500 / 3 |
| Low | 2 / 0 / 0 | 0 / 0 / 0 | 4 / 0 / 0 |

Notice that Horner does not have a weak fastball location against right-handers. The .282 and .283 in his medium-high outside and medium-high inside locations show a consistency that is more than adequate for a hitter of Horner's power.

An analysis of several locations shows that Horner scatters the ball to all fields.

MEDIUM-HIGH OUTSIDE FASTBALLS

BATTING AVERAGE .282
   *PLAY*
| | |
|---|---|
| LEFTFIELDER | Deep and shifted toward center field |
| CENTERFIELDER | Deep in straightaway center field |
| RIGHTFIELDER | Deep and shifted toward center field |
| SHORTSTOP | Normal position |
| SECOND | Normal position |

## MEDIUM-HIGH INSIDE FASTBALLS

BATTING AVERAGE .283
*PLAY*

| | |
|---|---|
| LEFTFIELDER | Deep and shifted toward the left field line |
| CENTERFIELDER | Medium-deep in straightaway center field |
| RIGHTFIELDER | Medium-deep and shifted toward center field |
| SHORTSTOP | Shifted toward third base |
| SECOND | Normal position |

Horner hits low-outside fastballs to right field and pulls low-inside fastballs to left.

## LOW-OUTSIDE FASTBALLS

BATTING AVERAGE .333
*PLAY*

| | |
|---|---|
| LEFTFIELDER | Medium-deep and shifted toward center field |
| CENTERFIELDER | Deep and shifted toward right field |
| RIGHTFIELDER | Deep and shifted toward the right field line |
| SHORTSTOP | Normal position |
| SECOND | Shifted toward first base |

## LOW-INSIDE FASTBALLS

BATTING AVERAGE .451
*PLAY*

| | |
|---|---|
| LEFTFIELDER | Deep and shifted toward the left field line |
| CENTERFIELDER | Deep and shifted toward left field |
| RIGHTFIELDER | Medium-deep and shifted toward center field |
| SHORTSTOP | Shifted toward third base |
| SECOND | No instances recorded |

In contrast to his excellent performance against fastballs, Horner has difficulty against curves. His .155 overall curve average is nearly 200 points lower than his .352 overall fastball average.

Notice especially Horner's weaknesses in the low-outside (.090), medium-high outside (.108) and low-over-the-middle (.111) curve locations. In addition, he is 0-for-12 against high-over-the-middle curves and 0-for-5 against low-inside curves. These weaknesses give pitchers ample targets for attack.

Of course pitchers do not want to throw Horner a high-over-the-middle curve, but it does show that a pitcher can make a mistake with a curve and Horner may not hurt him.

Horner has difficulty getting low-outside curves out of the infield.

## LOW-OUTSIDE CURVES

**BATTING AVERAGE .090**
*PLAY*

| | |
|---|---|
| LEFTFIELDER | No recorded instances |
| CENTERFIELDER | Deep and shifted toward left field |
| RIGHTFIELDER | No recorded instances |
| SHORTSTOP | Normal position |
| SECOND | No recorded instances |

In general, Horner hits curves deeply to the outfield, but since his curve averages are low, it seems that he mostly hits long outs. His medium-high outside location illustrates this.

## MEDIUM-HIGH OUTSIDE CURVES

**BATTING AVERAGE .108**
*PLAY*

| | |
|---|---|
| LEFTFIELDER | Deep and shifted toward the left field line |
| CENTERFIELDER | Deep and shifted toward left field |
| RIGHTFIELDER | Deep in straightaway right field |
| SHORTSTOP | Normal position |
| SECOND | Normal position |

Horner's slider and change-up averages are higher than his curve average. He has trouble with low sliders, but he hits waist-high sliders well.

### Horner Against Left-Handed Pitchers

Horner does not hit fastballs as well overall against left-handers as he does against right-handers, but he hits curves better.

### Bob Horner Right-Handed Hitter
### Against All Left-Handed Pitchers All Teams
### Overall Batting Average Is .286

Fastball Average .318          Curve Average .316

| | Inside | Middle | Outside | | Inside | Middle | Outside |
|---|---|---|---|---|---|---|---|
| High | 5/200 / 1 | 14/357 / 5 | 14/357 / 5 | | 0/0 / 0 | 3/333 / 1 | 0/0 / 0 |
| Med | 14/500 / 7 | 9/444 / 4 | 40/275 /11 | | 5/600 / 3 | 4/750 / 3 | 15/266 / 4 |
| Low | 10/200 / 2 | 29/413 /12 | 22/136 / 3 | | 6/0 / 0 | 9/0 / 0 | 18/444 / 8 |

The fastball chart shows that Horner has several distinct fastball weaknesses. His low-outside (.136) and low-inside (.200) locations are definitely weak, and his medium-high outside location (.275) is only adequate.

Nonetheless, his strong locations buoy up his overall fastball average of .318.

Notice in the following charts how differently several fielders would have to play against Horner when defending against pitches to the low-inside and low-outside locations.

LOW-OUTSIDE FASTBALLS
(THROWN TO HORNER BY LEFT-HANDED PITCHERS)

BATTING AVERAGE .136
   *PLAY*
LEFTFIELDER          Short and shifted toward the left field line
CENTERFIELDER        Deep in straightaway center field
RIGHTFIELDER         Deep in straightaway right field
SHORTSTOP            Shifted toward third base
SECOND               Shifted toward first base

## LOW-INSIDE FASTBALLS
### (THROWN TO HORNER BY LEFT-HANDED PITCHERS)

BATTING AVERAGE .200
*PLAY*

| | |
|---|---|
| LEFTFIELDER | Deep and shifted toward center field |
| CENTERFIELDER | Deep in straightaway center field |
| RIGHTFIELDER | Deep and shifted toward center field |
| SHORTSTOP | Normal position |
| SECOND | Normal position |

Notice how radically the left fielder needs to shift to be positioned correctly. The right fielder, the shortstop and the second baseman also need to shift. Only the center fielder would be able to remain in the same position if maximum fielding effectiveness were to be achieved against these two locations of pitches.

Horner hits curves against left-handed pitchers better than against right-handed pitchers. His two main weaknesses are in the low-inside and low-over-the-middle curve locations.

Notice how differently Horner hits low-outside and medium-high outside curves.

## LOW-OUTSIDE CURVES
### (THROWN TO HORNER BY LEFT-HANDED PITCHERS)

BATTING AVERAGE .444
*PLAY*

| | |
|---|---|
| LEFTFIELDER | Medium-deep and shifted toward the left field line |
| CENTERFIELDER | Short in straightaway center field |
| RIGHTFIELDER | Medium-deep and shifted toward the right field line |
| SHORTSTOP | Shifted toward third base |
| SECOND | Shifted toward second base |

## MEDIUM-HIGH OUTSIDE CURVES
### (THROWN TO HORNER BY LEFT-HANDED PITCHERS)

BATTING AVERAGE .266
*PLAY*

| | |
|---|---|
| LEFTFIELDER | Deep and shifted toward the left field line |
| CENTERFIELDER | Deep and shifted toward left field |
| RIGHTFIELDER | Deep in straightaway right field |
| SHORTSTOP | Shifted toward third base |
| SECOND | Normal position |

Fewer instances are recorded for Horner's slider and change-up record against left-handers, but his strengths and weaknesses are evident.

## Horner's Four-Home Run Game, July 6, 1986

When Atlanta played Montreal on July 6th in the 1986 season, Horner had an extraordinary day. In five trips to the plate, he hit four home runs. This feat has been accomplished only ten other times in baseball history.

With Horner's ability to hit fastballs, it seems that pitchers would feed him a steady diet of breaking and off-speed pitches to keep him off balance. But on that day, three of the four homers Horner hit were from fastballs. This is an example of what is often found in the BARS reports: pitchers tend to pitch to their own strengths, rather than to the batter's weaknesses.

On Horner's first at-bat, in the bottom of the second inning against right-handed pitcher Andy McGaffigan, Horner fell behind in the count one ball to two strikes. There were no outs and no runners on base. The 1-2 pitch was a high-inside fastball that Horner hit over the left-field fence near the line.

Horner's second homer was in the bottom of the fourth inning, also against McGaffigan. No runners were on base, there were two outs, and the count was no balls and no strikes. The first pitch was a fastball, waist-high over the middle of the plate. Horner slammed it far over the left center field fence. McGaffigan obviously did not want to throw a fastball to Horner directly over the heart of the plate.

Horner's third homer against McGaffigan was in the bottom of the fifth. There were two outs, runners on first and second, and a full count of three balls and two strikes. The 3-2 pitch was a medium-high inside slider that Horner hit over the straightaway left-field fence.

Horner's fourth homer was in the bottom of the ninth. McGaffigan had been relieved by Tim Burke, also a right-hander. With two outs and no one on base, Horner hit Burke's first pitch, a low-inside fastball, over the fence in deep left center. It was Horner's fourth long home run of the day.

The only time Horner was out during the day was his fourth time at bat, when he foul-popped a medium-high inside fastball down the first base line.

The BARS System Scouting Report shows that Horner swung at every first pitch delivered to him in his five at-bats during the day.

| Time At Plate | First Pitch |
|---|---|
| First At-Bat | Fastball high inside, swinging strike |
| Second At-Bat | Fastball medium over middle, home run |
| Third At-Bat | Fastball medium-high inside, fouled off |
| Fourth At-Bat | Fastball medium-high inside, fouled off |
| Fifth At-Bat | Fastball low inside, home run |

It is evident that Horner swings often at the first pitch. Yet the first pitch thrown to him each time he came to the plate was a fastball — his strongest pitch. And each time it was in a location that was tailor-made for him to hit a long one.

Pitchers should be more aware of a batter's strengths. Studying the BARS System batting charts would inform them of what to look for in certain situations.

As mentioned at the beginning of this chapter, the BARS System analysts feel that the increasing number of home runs in the majors is the result of the large number of fastballs that are being thrown in comparison with other types of pitches. Hitters expect fastballs and wait for them. A look at Horner's batting charts against right- and left-handed pitchers shows how many more fastballs are thrown to him than other types of pitches, though he is one of the finest fastball hitters in the game.

That day the pitchers were lucky. Montreal won 11-8 even though Horner drove in six runs with his four homers. Even so, it didn't do much for McGaffigan's ERA.

## _Personal Comments_

Steve Boros helped me set up the Super Summary Report. He suggested that when I didn't have much information for a certain pitching location, say for a low-inside or low-outside fastball, I could use the fielding information for other inside or outside fastballs. It seemed to him that hitters would probably hit most inside fastballs similarly and most outside fastballs similarly, so he suggested that until I had enough information for a certain location, I just group all inside or outside locations together.

I did that for awhile, but when we had a lot of information, we found that in many cases there is a significant difference in how a batter hits even a low-outside fastball compared to a medium-high outside fastball. I don't say this to make Steve look bad in any way, but just to point out that until we had gathered a large amount of information and had a computer analyze it, even a tremendously experienced baseball person had no idea how differently batters hit pitches in adjoining locations over the strike zone.

The BARS System is 90 percent accurate when positioning fielders. This shows that fielders can't afford to take just one position for a batter, then hold that position through all the pitches that are thrown to him. It's not enough for fielders to play hitters to pull or to not pull the ball. If they do, fielders will be out of position for a lot of pitches, and even a pitcher's best pitches may go to waste.

# Chapter Three

## Refined Fielding Strategy

When a hitter comes to the plate, opposing fielders take positions to defend against him based on the knowledge they and their manager have about his tendencies to pull the ball, hit the ball to the opposite field, bunt the ball, etc. In general the fielders position themselves when a hitter comes to bat and maintain these positions for every pitch thrown to him.

But when the strategy between the pitcher and catcher is to have the first pitch be a high-inside fastball, the second pitch a low-outside curve, the third pitch a low-inside slider, etc., the hitter is being thrown pitches that he will tend to hit in varying directions and distances. When the fielders remain in one position through all the pitches to a hitter, they are not adjusting as they should to each pitch.

The BARS System Super Summary Report simply and clearly illustrates the best defensive fielding position for each fielder on each pitch. The BARS System's computer calculates the best possible fielding strategy for the outfielders, the shortstop and the second baseman for pitches to each of the nine locations of the strike zone. These computer calculations are based upon the direction and distance of balls that a batter has hit over the past seasons.

The BARS System fielding strategy is accurate 90 percent of the time. This accuracy would allow each team to prevent an average of two to three hits per game — hits that are now being allowed.

To show the importance of adjusting the fielding strategy on a pitch-by-pitch basis, Super Summaries of several top players will be examined. The chart on the following page shows George Brett's BARS System fastball record. As discussed in Chapter One, fielding strategy is generated by computer for each of the nine fastball locations. Fielding strategy is also generated for curveballs, sliders and change-ups.

In this instance, only Brett's fastball performance will be discussed. These suggested optimal fielding positions are calculated by computer analysis of the hundreds of balls Brett hit during the years 1983-1987.

## George Brett  Left-Handed Hitter
## Against All Right-Handed Pitchers All Teams

Fastball Average .370

|  | Outside | Middle | Inside |
|---|---|---|---|
| High | 24/ 166 / 4 | 62/ 274 / 17 | 14/ 428 / 6 |
| Med | 110/ 400 / 44 | 82/ 500 / 41 | 57/ 315 / 18 |
| Low | 33/ 333 / 11 | 86/ 360 / 31 | 18/ 444 / 8 |

An examination of the fielding strategy required for Brett's two weakest fastball locations (high-outside and high-over-the-middle) shows why it is necessary to adjust fielding positions on a pitch-by-pitch basis.

1. HIGH-OUTSIDE FASTBALLS

   BATTING AVERAGE .166
   *PLAY*
   LEFTFIELDER        Deep in straightaway left field
   CENTERFIELDER      Deep and shifted toward left field
   RIGHTFIELDER       Medium-deep and shifted toward center field
   SHORTSTOP          Normal position
   SECOND             Normal position

2. HIGH-OVER-MIDDLE FASTBALLS

   BATTING AVERAGE .274
   *PLAY*
   LEFTFIELDER        Deep and shifted toward center field
   CENTERFIELDER      Deep in straightaway center field
   RIGHTFIELDER       Deep in straightaway right field
   SHORTSTOP          Up middle (shifted toward second base)
   SECOND             Normal position

The above two categories show that even a slight difference in pitch location (from high-outside to high-over-the-middle) would require shifting all outfielders toward the right field line.

The difference is even greater in Brett's medium-high fastball categories.

6.  MEDIUM-HIGH OUTSIDE FASTBALLS

> BATTING AVERAGE .400
> > *PLAY*
>
> LEFTFIELDER        Deep and shifted toward the left field line
> CENTERFIELDER      Deep in straightaway center field
> RIGHTFIELDER       Deep and shifted toward center field
> SHORTSTOP          Up middle (shifted toward second base)
> SECOND             Shifted toward first base

9.  MEDIUM-OVER-THE-MIDDLE FASTBALLS

> BATTING AVERAGE .500
> > *PLAY*
>
> LEFTFIELDER        Deep and shifted toward center field
> CENTERFIELDER      Medium-deep in straightaway center field
> RIGHTFIELDER       Deep and shifted toward the right field line
> SHORTSTOP          Normal position
> SECOND             Shifted toward first base

Long-term computer analysis shows that even though the two pitching locations are only inches apart, the suggested optimal positions for the left fielder and right fielder are completely different in these two categories. The shortstop is also required to shift.

If Brett were at the plate for four or five pitches, presumably each pitch would be to a different location around the strike zone and be varied among fastballs, curves, sliders, etc. Thus, if the fielders maintained the same positions for all the pitches to Brett, they would be out of position for many of the pitches.

**Shifting For Inside And Outside Pitches**

Most fielders do not change positions for even the widest variances of pitches. Few fielders change positions even for an outside fastball as opposed to an inside fastball. But notice the difference inside and outside pitches make in fielding strategy when defending against Dale Murphy, right-handed slugger for the Atlanta Braves.

## Dale Murphy    Right-Handed Hitter
## Against All Right-Handed Pitchers All Teams

Fastball Average .319

|  | Inside | Middle | Outside |
|------|--------|--------|---------|
| High | 16/62 / 1 | 47/340 / 16 | 31/258 / 8 |
| Med | 76/302 / 23 | 60/366 / 22 | 118/347 / 41 |
| Low | 35/257 / 9 | 126/365 / 46 | 67/268 / 18 |

Murphy's second-worst fastball category (low-inside) requires almost completely different fielding positions than his fourth-worst category (low-outside).

2.  LOW-INSIDE FASTBALLS

BATTING AVERAGE .257
   *PLAY*
LEFTFIELDER            Deep and shifted toward the left field line
CENTERFIELDER          Medium-deep in straightaway center field
RIGHTFIELDER           Deep and shifted toward center field
SHORTSTOP              Normal position
SECOND                 Shifted toward first base

4.  LOW-OUTSIDE FASTBALLS

BATTING AVERAGE .268
   *PLAY*
LEFTFIELDER            Medium-deep and shifted toward center field
CENTERFIELDER          Deep and shifted toward right field
RIGHTFIELDER           Deep and shifted toward the right field line
SHORTSTOP              Normal position
SECOND                 Normal position

To be in the best fielding position, each outfielder is required to adjust for inside and outside pitches. The second baseman must also adjust.

If fielders took and held one position when Murphy came to the plate, they would be completely out of position for pitches to one of these two locations.

Even hitters who consistently pull the ball tend to hit certain types and locations of pitches to the opposite field.

Jack Clark, right-handed hitter for the New York Yankees, is well-known for his tendency to pull the ball. But the BARS System fielding strategy shows that Clark consistently tends to hit some types and locations of pitches to the opposite field.

Against right-handed pitchers Clark hits high-outside fastballs to the opposite field.

### Jack Clark   Right-Handed Hitter
### Against All Right-Handed Pitchers All Teams

Fastball Average .312

|  | Inside | Middle | Outside |
|---|---|---|---|
| High | 16/<br>125 / 2 | 29/<br>275 / 8 | 15/<br>333 / 5 |
| Med | 17/<br>411 / 7 | 16/<br>625 / 10 | 49/<br>367 / 18 |
| Low | 6/<br>0 / 0 | 36/<br>333 / 12 | 21/<br>95 / 2 |

HIGH-OUTSIDE FASTBALLS

BATTING AVERAGE .333
>    *PLAY*

| | |
|---|---|
| LEFTFIELDER | No recorded instances |
| CENTERFIELDER | Deep in straightaway center field |
| RIGHTFIELDER | Deep and shifted toward the right field line |
| SHORTSTOP | No recorded instances |
| SECOND | Shifted toward first base |

Fielders that are positioned for Clark to pull the ball will find themselves out of position about 90 percent of the time when Clark hits a high-outside fastball.

Many times a batter will tend to hit fly balls one direction, while hitting ground balls another. Jack Clark's performance against fastballs can again be used as an example.

MEDIUM-HIGH INSIDE FASTBALLS

BATTING AVERAGE .411
*PLAY*
LEFTFIELDER          Deep and shifted toward the left field line
CENTERFIELDER    Deep and shifted toward left field
RIGHTFIELDER      Deep in straightaway right field
SHORTSTOP           Normal position
SECOND                 Shifted toward first base

Thus if the shortstop and second baseman played Clark to pull the ball, even on inside pitches they would be out of position for most of the balls hit in their directions. The outfielders would have to play Clark to pull, but the shortstop would have to play straightaway and the second baseman shifted toward first.

**High, Medium-High And Low Pitches Require Special Adjustment**

The Super Summary fielding report for Kent Hrbek, left-handed power hitter for the Minnesota Twins, shows that even shifting for inside and outside pitches is not entirely adequate for achieving correct fielding position.

**Kent Hrbek    Left-Handed Hitter
Against All Right-Handed Pitchers All Teams**

Fastball Average .297

| | Outside | Middle | Inside |
|---|---|---|---|
| High | 19/263 / 5 | 28/392 / 11 | 3/0 / 0 |
| Med | 71/380 / 27 | 22/500 / 11 | 33/212 / 7 |
| Low | 19/210 / 4 | 36/166 / 6 | 14/142 / 2 |

To be in the best position for high-outside, medium-high outside and low-outside fastballs, the fielders need to make significant fielding adjustments.

## OUTSIDE FASTBALLS

|  | HIGH<br>(.263) | MEDIUM-HIGH<br>(.380) | LOW<br>(.210) |
|---|---|---|---|
| LEFTFIELDER | Deep center | Deep straight | Deep line |
| CENTERFIELDER | Deep right | Deep straight | Deep left |
| RIGHTFIELDER | Deep straight | Deep straight | No instances |
| SHORTSTOP | Normal | Normal | Toward third |
| SECOND | Normal | Normal | Toward first |

The left fielder is required to be in a different fielding position for each of the three pitching locations. On high-outside pitches, the left fielder should play deep toward center field, on medium-high outside pitches, he should play deep in straightaway left field, and for low-outside pitches he should play deep and shifted toward the left field line.

The center fielder is also required to play in a different fielding position for each pitch location. The right fielder is not required to shift, but the shortstop and the second baseman need to shift on low-inside fastballs.

These illustrations from the Super Summary Reports of Brett, Murphy, Clark and Hrbek are based upon the BARS System findings that hitters tend to hit certain types and locations of pitches in the same direction time after time. They will not always hit the same way, but over a large number of instances the direction and distance will tend to be the same, just as in the law of averages trends develop when larger numbers of instances are taken into account.

Fielders may find themselves in the correct position simply by chance in any given situation, but over the long term they would be able to position themselves correctly 90 percent of the time by using the statistics presented in the BARS System.

### Shifting When Ahead And Behind In The Count

It should be noted that hitters tend to hit even the same type and location of pitch differently when ahead and when behind in the count. This is not the case for all hitters, but must be considered if complete accuracy in fielding position is to be achieved.

An example can be found in the Super Summary Report for Dale Murphy, right-handed hitting outfielder for the Atlanta Braves. When ahead and when behind in the count, Murphy tends to hit even low-outside fastballs in different directions.

In the following example, the right fielder and the shortstop would be required to shift according to the count for a low-outside fastball thrown to Murphy. The other fielders are not required to shift, so their fielding positions are not indicated.

### Dale Murphy   Right-Handed Hitter
### Against All Right-Handed Pitchers All Teams

| | When Ahead .403 | | | | When Behind .339 | | |
|------|---------|---------|---------|------|---------|---------|---------|
| | Inside | Middle | Outside | | Inside | Middle | Outside |
| High | 3/ 0 / 0 | 17/ 647 /11 | 10/ 500 / 5 | | 1/ 1000/ 1 | 12/ 250 / 3 | 7/ 142 / 1 |
| Med | 33/ 424 /14 | 28/ 392 /11 | 58/ 413 /24 | | 18/ 333 / 6 | 14/ 357 / 5 | 23/ 347 / 8 |
| Low | 17/ 294 / 5 | 63/ 365 /23 | 24/ 375 / 9 | | 4/ 0 / 0 | 17/ 529 / 9 | 13/ 307 / 4 |

LOW-OUTSIDE FASTBALLS WHEN AHEAD IN THE COUNT

BATTING AVERAGE .375
   *PLAY*
LEFTFIELDER         ——
CENTERFIELDER   ——
RIGHTFIELDER      Deep and shifted toward center field
SHORTSTOP         Normal position
SECOND             ——

LOW-OUTSIDE FASTBALLS WHEN BEHIND IN THE COUNT

BATTING AVERAGE .307
   *PLAY*
LEFTFIELDER         ——
CENTERFIELDER   ——
RIGHTFIELDER      Deep and shifted toward the right field line
SHORTSTOP         Shifted toward third base
SECOND             ——

Even greater contrast is presented by Fred Lynn's performance against fastballs. Lynn, a left-handed hitter, tends to pull the ball more when ahead in the count than when behind.

## Fred Lynn   Left-Handed Hitter
### Against All Right-Handed Pitchers All Teams

| | When Ahead .367 | | | | When Behind .416 | | |
|---|---|---|---|---|---|---|---|
| | Outside | Middle | Inside | | Outside | Middle | Inside |
| High | 3/ 666 / 2 | 10/ 500 / 5 | 1/ 0 / 0 | | 0/ 0 / 0 | 6/ 666 / 4 | 2/ 0 / 0 |
| Med | 37/ 351 / 13 | 15/ 533 / 8 | 17/ 411 / 7 | | 10/ 400 / 4 | 4/ 750 / 3 | 4/ 500 / 2 |
| Low | 1/ 1000 / 1 | 13/ 230 / 3 | 9/ 0 / 0 | | 1/ 0 / 0 | 4/ 250 / 1 | 5/ 200 / 1 |

MEDIUM-HIGH OUTSIDE FASTBALLS WHEN AHEAD IN THE COUNT

BATTING AVERAGE .351
*PLAY*

| | |
|---|---|
| LEFTFIELDER | Deep and shifted toward center field |
| CENTERFIELDER | Deep in straightaway center field |
| RIGHTFIELDER | Deep in straightaway right field |
| SHORTSTOP | Up middle (shifted toward second base) |
| SECOND | Shifted toward first base |

MEDIUM-HIGH OUTSIDE FASTBALLS WHEN BEHIND

BATTING AVERAGE .400
*PLAY*

| | |
|---|---|
| LEFTFIELDER | Deep in straightaway left field |
| CENTERFIELDER | Deep and shifted toward left field |
| RIGHTFIELDER | Medium-deep and shifted toward center field |
| SHORTSTOP | Up middle (shifted toward second base) |
| SECOND | Normal position |

Notice that with the exception of the shortstop, every fielder is required to shift to the right (that is, to play for more of a pull) when the left-handed Lynn is ahead in the count.

Most players tend to pull fastballs more when they are ahead in the count. This may be because when a hitter is ahead he is looking for fastballs and can time his swing better.

On the opposite side of the coin, there is a slight tendency for hitters to pull curves more when they are behind in the count. This tendency is not as pronounced, but still must be taken into consideration.

Dale Murphy and Fred Lynn, like most good hitters, wait for their pitch when ahead in the count. When ahead in the count against right-handers, 72 percent of the balls Murphy hits are fastballs. When he is behind in the count, only 55 percent are fastballs. Almost the same percentages apply to Lynn. When he is ahead in the count, 72 percent of the balls he hits are fastballs. When behind, 59 percent are fastballs.

This indicates that these hitters are waiting for fastballs when ahead and for curves when behind. And they are adjusting their swings to the expected type of pitch.

Ryne Sandberg, right-handed hitter for the Chicago Cubs, tends to hit medium-high inside fastballs differently when ahead and when behind in the count.

### Ryne Sandberg   Right-Handed Hitter
### Against All Right-Handed Pitchers All Teams

When Ahead .422

| | Inside | Middle | Outside |
|---|---|---|---|
| High | 19/ 578 /11 | 39/ 435 /17 | 23/ 304 / 7 |
| Med | 33/ 454 /15 | 21/ 571 /12 | 100/ 450 /45 |
| Low | 4/ 500 / 2 | 97/ 422 /41 | 64/ 296 /19 |

When Behind .311

| | Inside | Middle | Outside |
|---|---|---|---|
| High | 6/ 500 / 3 | 16/ 375 / 6 | 9/ 444 / 4 |
| Med | 21/ 333 / 7 | 8/ 500 / 4 | 32/ 281 / 9 |
| Low | 12/ 333 / 4 | 32/ 312 /10 | 20/ 250 / 5 |

MEDIUM-HIGH INSIDE FASTBALLS WHEN AHEAD IN THE COUNT

BATTING AVERAGE .454

*PLAY*

| | |
|---|---|
| LEFTFIELDER | Medium-deep and shifted toward the left field line |
| CENTERFIELDER | Short in straightaway center field |
| RIGHTFIELDER | Deep and shifted toward center field |
| SHORTSTOP | Shifted toward third base |
| SECOND | Normal position |

MEDIUM-HIGH INSIDE FASTBALLS WHEN BEHIND IN THE COUNT

BATTING AVERAGE .333
   *PLAY*
LEFTFIELDER          Medium-deep in straightaway left field
CENTERFIELDER        Deep and shifted toward left field
RIGHTFIELDER         Medium-deep and shifted toward the right field line
SHORTSTOP            Shifted toward third base
SECOND               Normal position

Each outfielder would need to shift when Sandberg is ahead or behind in the count.


### Different Types of Pitches (Fastballs, Curves, Sliders, etc.)

When pitchers throw a change-up, curve or slider, they lose the advantage of making the batter hit a different type of pitch if the fielders are not properly positioned to field the resulting hit.

Examine the differences in required fielding strategy when pitching Jim Rice (RH) of the Boston Red Sox a medium-high outside fastball and a medium-high outside curve.

### Jim Rice   Right-Handed Hitter
### Against All Right-Handed Pitchers All Teams

Fastball Average .329                Curve Average .323

|      | Inside | Middle | Outside | Inside | Middle | Outside |
|------|--------|--------|---------|--------|--------|---------|
| High | 21/ 238 / 5 | 16/ 312 / 5 | 13/ 307 / 4 | 5/ 200 / 1 | 7/ 0 / 0 | 3/ 333 / 1 |
| Med  | 67/ 432 / 29 | 35/ 314 / 11 | 117/ 341 / 40 | 14/ 428 / 6 | 20/ 400 / 8 | 34/ 382 / 13 |
| Low  | 39/ 333 / 13 | 51/ 333 / 17 | 29/ 137 / 4 | 3/ 333 / 1 | 18/ 333 / 6 | 26/ 230 / 6 |

The best fielding strategy for medium-high outside curves and fastballs is shown on the following page.

## MEDIUM-HIGH OUTSIDE FASTBALLS

BATTING AVERAGE .341
  *PLAY*
LEFTFIELDER          Deep and shifted toward center field
CENTERFIELDER        Deep in straightaway center field
RIGHTFIELDER         Medium-deep in straightaway right field
SHORTSTOP            Normal position
SECOND               Normal position


## MEDIUM-HIGH OUTSIDE CURVES

BATTING AVERAGE .382
  *PLAY*
LEFTFIELDER          Medium-deep and shifted toward center field
CENTERFIELDER        Deep and shifted toward left field
RIGHTFIELDER         Deep and shifted toward center field
SHORTSTOP            Normal position
SECOND               Shifted toward first base

All fielders except the shortstop must play differently for a curve as opposed to a fastball. The same is true for most batters when considering a slider, split-fingered fastball, change-up, or any other type of pitch.


### Significance of the Fielding Strategy

An entire book could be written about players who hit differently when ahead or behind in the count, when different types and locations of pitches are thrown, and when facing left- and right-handed pitchers. The differences in depth and direction of hits are often so significant that every fielder is required to shift.

This exactness is the most valuable aspect of the BARS System fielding strategy. Use of the BARS System fielding strategy would turn average defensive teams into highly effective, coordinated units. Fielders could be positioned for maximum efficiency on a pitch-by-pitch basis, and the results would be evident in nearly every game played.

In a 162-game season, the prevention of two to three hits per game would have an immense impact. It is not difficult to imagine the difference in a team's final standing if over the course of a season it prevented 300 to 400 base hits (and the ensuing runs) that would otherwise be allowed.

The following chapters give examples of hits in actual games that could have been prevented by using the BARS fielding strategy. These examples are shown to give authenticity to what would otherwise be mere theory. The 90 percent accuracy in fielding strategy that the BARS System achieves is the result of careful, accurate scouting in thousands of games during the past seasons. As a result, the BARS System is a practical, reliable tool that can be used by any team.

## Personal Comments

A short time ago I happened to watch Johnny Bench's Saturday TV show. Each week he teaches fundamentals of baseball for young players, using humor to keep things lively for kids.

Tommy Lasorda was a guest on that particular show, and when I tuned in he was surrounded by a group of youngsters. He was emphatic about how important it is for a fielder to get a good jump on the ball. That was his lesson to them. He said that even a few inches can make all the difference.

What he said is good baseball sense, of course, but what struck me is that if a few inches make such a difference, how much difference would 10, 15 or even 20 feet make? That's how much closer a fielder would be to a hit ball in many cases if he followed the BARS System fielding strategy.

Over and over in games you'll see ground balls that just slip by the infielders, or hard-hit drives that fall just a few feet in front of the outfielders. By being in the right position before the pitch, a fielder would have more than a good jump on the ball. If he was a good fielder and quick to react, he'd be in the best possible position to start.

The BARS fielding strategy is correct 90 percent of the time. By following it, each team could prevent two or three base hits every game. By positioning fielders correctly, a team could also cut off many extra base hits. This wouldn't reduce the number of base hits but would hold runners to fewer bases and prevent runs.

I think the time will come when following this system, or one just like it, will make good baseball sense — just like the advice Tommy Lasorda was giving. A good player will still want to get a jump on the ball, but by being properly positioned when the pitch is made, he'll have an edge.

# Chapter Four

## Examples Of The BARS System Fielding Strategy

As discussed in previous chapters, the BARS System fielding strategy is based on computer calculations that find trends in the direction and distance a batter has hit certain types and locations of pitches in the past. These trends are often based on dozens and even hundreds of previous balls that a batter has hit.

The computer analyzes these trends to find the best position for each fielder on a pitch-by-pitch basis. As has been shown, pitches in different locations and even in different ball-strike count situations may require different fielding positions by one or more of the fielders.

### The Infielders

Many ground-ball base hits that find their way through the infield could be prevented by positioning the shortstop and second baseman according to the BARS System fielding strategy.

The three positions that the BARS System suggests for the shortstop are: shifted toward third base, normal position, and shifted toward second base. The three positions for the second baseman are: shifted toward second base, normal position, and shifted toward first base. Please see the diagram on the following page.

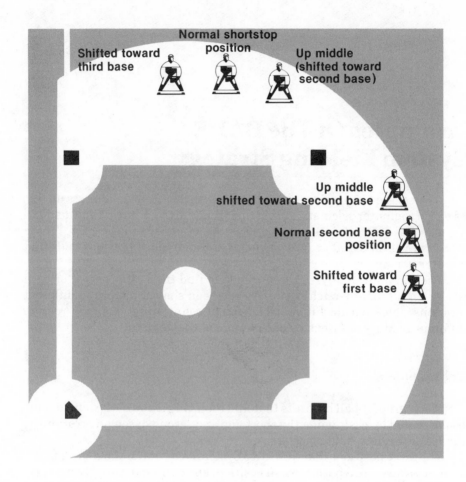

### Example Of A Preventable Base Hit

On September 30, 1986, the Toronto Blue Jays were playing New York at Yankee Stadium. In the bottom of the first inning, with no outs and a runner on first base, Don Mattingly (batting left-handed) came to the plate to face Toronto pitcher Dave Stieb (right-handed).

On the 3-1 pitch Stieb threw a medium-high inside fastball that Mattingly hit on the ground between the first and second basemen. Toronto's second baseman was playing in his normal straightaway position and couldn't quite reach the ball as it skipped through the infield into right field for a single.

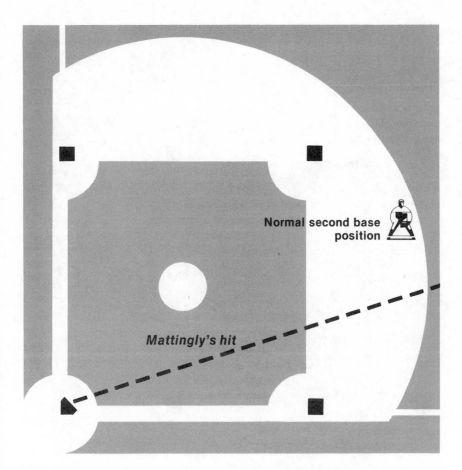

Normal second base position

Mattingly's hit

If Toronto's second baseman had been playing shifted toward first base (which would have positioned him about ten feet closer to first base), he would have been perfectly positioned to field the ball. He could have forced the runner at second and possibly started a double play.

In any case, he could have prevented the base hit by fielding the ball and throwing Mattingly out at first base. See diagram on the following page.

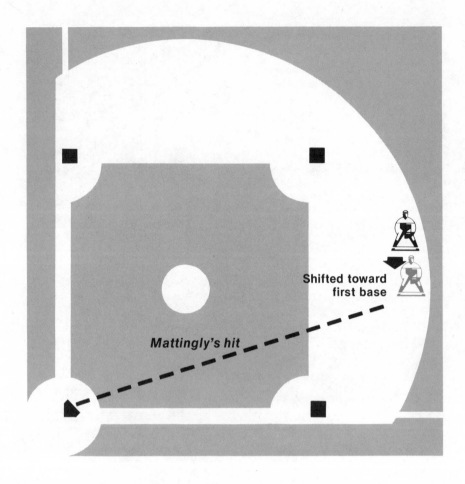

The following BARS System Super Summary chart shows where each of the fielders should have been positioned on the pitch for maximum effectiveness.

**BARS SYSTEM SUPER SUMMARY:**

MEDIUM-HIGH INSIDE FASTBALLS
(THROWN WHEN MATTINGLY IS AHEAD IN THE COUNT)

*PLAY*
LEFTFIELDER          Medium-deep in straightaway left field
CENTERFIELDER        Medium-deep and shifted toward left field
RIGHTFIELDER         Deep in straightaway right field
SHORTSTOP            Normal position
**SECOND**           **Shifted toward first base**

If the second baseman had been positioned according to the BARS System fielding strategy for this particular type and location of pitch, he would have been playing shifted toward first base and would have been able to field the ball. In the game, the second baseman was playing in his normal straightaway fielding position and barely missed getting to the ball.

It is interesting to note that if Mattingly had been behind in the count instead of ahead, the BARS fielding strategy would have called for the second baseman to play at the normal second baseman position instead of shifted toward first base.

### Don Mattingly    Left-Handed Batter
### Against All Right-Handed Pitchers All Teams

Fastball Average .366

|  | Outside | Middle | Inside |
|---|---|---|---|
| High | 37 / 432 / 16 | 32 / 343 / 11 | 14 / 571 / 8 |
| Med | 115 / 286 / 33 | 39 / 435 / 17 | 31 / 290 / 9 |
| Low | 35 / 457 / 16 | 70 / 400 / 28 | 23 / 304 / 7 |

It can be said that hitters, especially good hitters like Mattingly, will adjust to any fielding strategy and still hit balls through the infield for base hits. But the computer analysis of the BARS System has been proven correct more than 90 percent of the time. This means that when a team's fielders position themselves according to the BARS System fielding strategy, each fielder will be in the correct position for 90 percent of the balls hit to his location.

## Strategy For Outfielders

The BARS System fielding strategy has nine fielding positions for each outfielder. The fielding positions for the left fielder are:

> Deep and shifted toward the left field line
> Deep in straightaway left field
> Deep and shifted toward center field
> Medium-deep and shifted toward the left field line
> Medium-deep in straightaway left field
> Medium-deep and shifted toward center field
> Short and shifted toward the left field line
> Short in straightaway left field
> Short and shifted toward center field

The same basic fielding positions are designated for the center and right fielders.

By positioning each outfielder on a pitch-by-pitch basis, the BARS System can assure very exacting fielding strategy.

## Example Of A Preventable Hit To The Outfield

On May 13, 1987, the California Angels were playing at Detroit. With two outs in the bottom of the first inning, Detroit's Larry Herndon (RH) came up to bat against John Candelaria (LH). There were runners on first and second.

Herndon fell behind in the count 1-2, then hit a medium-high outside fastball to deep left-center field. The California center fielder, Gary Pettis, was playing medium-deep in straightaway center and couldn't get to the ball. It dropped for a base hit, driving in the runner from second with what proved to be the game-winning RBI.

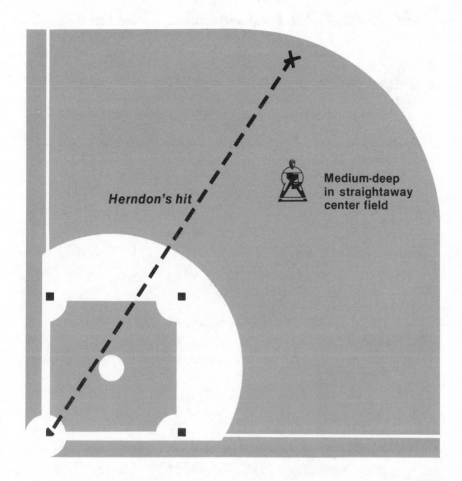

Herndon's hit

Medium-deep
in straightaway
center field

If Pettis had been playing deep and shifted toward left field instead of medium-deep and straightaway, he could have caught the ball, preventing the hit and the run and ending the inning. The BARS System fielding strategy suggests that on this particular type and location of pitch to Herndon, the center fielder play deep in center and shifted toward left field. Please see the diagram on the following page.

**BARS: CENTERFIELDER Deep and shifted toward left field**

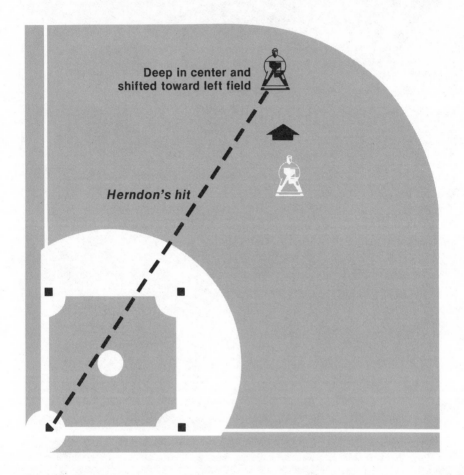

Deep in center and shifted toward left field

Herndon's hit

The California center fielder would have been perfectly positioned to catch the ball and prevent this key hit if he had followed the BARS System fielding strategy.

Herndon hit this medium-high outside fastball when he was behind in the count (1-2). It is interesting to note that if he had been ahead in the count, every fielder would have needed to be in a different position for maximum fielding effectiveness.

**Larry Herndon    Right-Handed Batter**
**Behind In The Count Against Left-Handed Pitchers**

Fastball Average .323

|        | Inside | Middle | Outside |
|--------|--------|--------|---------|
| High   | 3/ 333 / 1 | 2/ 1000/ 2 | 3/ 333 / 1 |
| Med    | 2/ 500 / 1 | 2/ 500 / 1 | 14/ 71 / 1 |
| Low    | 4/ 750 / 3 | 2/ 0 / 0 | 2/ 500 / 1 |

MEDIUM-HIGH OUTSIDE FASTBALLS
(THROWN WHEN HERNDON IS BEHIND IN THE COUNT)

BATTING AVERAGE .071
    *PLAY*
LEFTFIELDER          No instances recorded
CENTERFIELDER        Deep and shifted toward left field
RIGHTFIELDER         Medium-deep and shifted toward the right field line
SHORTSTOP            Normal position
SECOND               Normal position

**Larry Herndon    Right-Handed Batter**
**Ahead In The Count Against Left-Handed Pitchers**

Fastball Average .358

|        | Inside | Middle | Outside |
|--------|--------|--------|---------|
| High   | 0/ 0 / 0 | 3/ 666 / 2 | 5/ 400 / 2 |
| Med    | 5/ 200 / 1 | 9/ 555 / 5 | 11/ 181 / 2 |
| Low    | 5/ 0 / 0 | 11/ 454 / 5 | 4/ 500 / 2 |

MEDIUM-HIGH OUTSIDE FASTBALLS
(THROWN WHEN HERNDON IS AHEAD IN THE COUNT)

BATTING AVERAGE .181

*PLAY*

| | |
|---|---|
| LEFTFIELDER | Deep in straightaway left field |
| CENTERFIELDER | Deep in straightaway center field |
| RIGHTFIELDER | Deep in straightaway right field |
| SHORTSTOP | Up middle (shifted toward second base) |
| SECOND | Up middle |

To achieve maximum fielding effectiveness, every fielder would have needed to be shifted to a different position if Herndon had been ahead in the count instead of behind.

## Line-Drive Singles

Even some base hits that are now considered routine and completely unpreventable, such as line-drive singles that fall in front of outfielders, can be prevented by properly positioning the fielders.

On May 4, 1987, San Francisco was playing at St. Louis. With one out and runners on first and second in the top of the eighth, San Francisco's Jose Uribe (batting RH) came to the plate to face Ricky Horton (LH).

The first pitch to Uribe was a high-over-the-middle fastball that Uribe lined into left field for a single, driving in Candy Maldonado from second base with the game's winning run.

The ball was hit to medium-deep left field. The St. Louis left fielder, Vince Coleman, was playing deep in straightaway left and couldn't reach the ball.

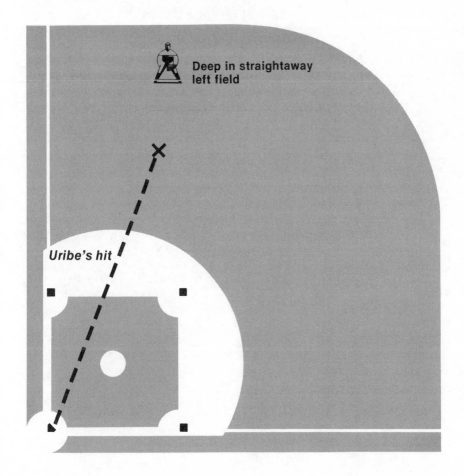

**Deep in straightaway left field**

*Uribe's hit*

If Coleman had been playing medium-deep instead of deep, he could have made the catch, preventing the hit and the run.

### BARS: LEFTFIELDER  Medium-deep in straightaway left field

Coleman could have made the catch if he had been positioned medium-deep in straightaway left field as suggested by the BARS System fielding strategy.  See diagram on the following page.

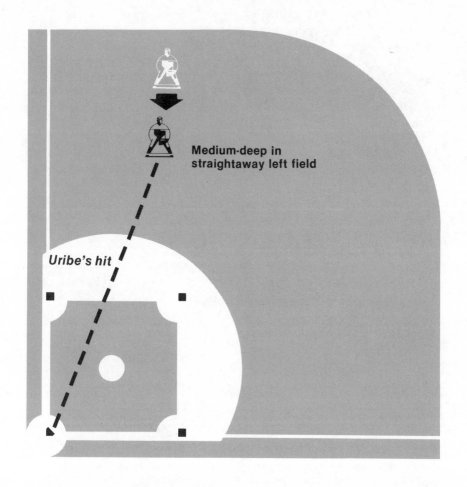

Medium-deep in straightaway left field

Uribe's hit

**Jose Uribe    Batting Right-Handed
Against All Left-Handed Pitchers All Teams**

Fastball Average .312

|      | Inside | Middle | Outside |
|------|--------|--------|---------|
| High | 6/<br>333 / 2 | 25/<br>200 / 5 | 11/<br>90 / 1 |
| Med  | 14/<br>428 / 6 | 8/<br>500 / 4 | 25/<br>440 / 11 |
| Low  | 11/<br>545 / 6 | 15/<br>200 / 3 | 13/<br>153 / 2 |

## Preventing The Extra Base

The fielding strategy of the BARS System allows fielders to be positioned so precisely that many extra-base hits could be cut off in time to hold the hitter to fewer bases. In addition, the proper positioning of fielders could allow them to reach a base hit more quickly and relay the ball to the infield to prevent runs.

The following extra-base hit illustrates both points.

On July 3, 1987, St. Louis was playing at Atlanta. With no score in the game, St. Louis switch-hitter Willie McGee (batting LH) came to bat in the top of the fourth, facing Charlie Puleo (RH). There were two outs and Jack Clark was on first base.

On the 3-2 pitch, McGee slapped a high-inside fastball down the third base line for a double, driving in Clark from first with the game-winning RBI.

The Atlanta left fielder, Ken Griffey, was playing medium-deep and shifted toward center field. He had a long run to the ball and couldn't reach it in time to prevent the run.

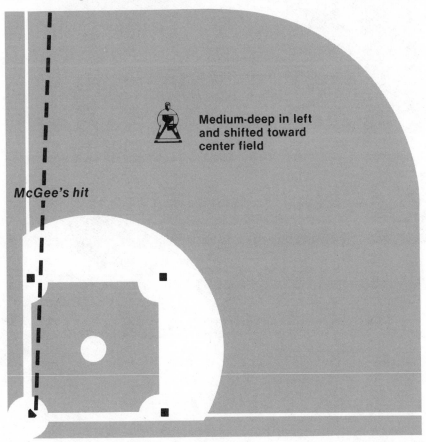

Medium-deep in left and shifted toward center field

McGee's hit

Griffey could not have caught the ball in any case, but if he had been positioned in short left field and shifted toward the left field line, he possibly could have fielded the ball in time to prevent Clark from scoring.

**BARS: LEFTFIELDER  Short and shifted toward the left field line**

The BARS System fielding strategy would have positioned Griffey short in left and shifted toward the left field line, allowing him to possibly cut the ball off in time to prevent the run.

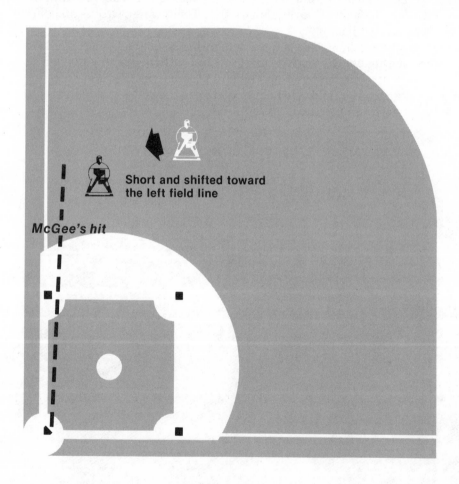

Short and shifted toward
the left field line

*McGee's hit*

If Griffey had not wanted to play McGee short in left field, he could at least have been aware that McGee has a tendency to hit high-inside fastballs to short left field. Griffey could have played medium-deep while anticipating McGee's hit. In this way he could have gotten a jump on the ball.

The base hits and charts shown in this chapter are examples of line-drive base hits, fly-ball base hits, bloop base hits and ground-ball base hits that could be prevented by positioning each fielder according to an overall coordinated fielding strategy on every pitch.

By properly positioning fielders on a pitch-by-pitch basis, infielders and outfielders could prevent an average of two to three base hits per game, cut off many extra base hits and prevent many runs.

## *Personal Comments*

In the Super Summary fielding strategy we position the shortstop, the second baseman and the three outfielders. We didn't include the first baseman because he has to hold the runner on first so often. And we didn't include the third baseman because his territory is smaller than the other fielders. But when we were testing the strategy, we found that the third baseman is out of position much more than we thought he would be.

There has been a debate in baseball for many years about whether it's better to have the third baseman play near the bag in tight situations to prevent an extra base hit down the line, or to play in his regular position to cut off ground balls through the hole. But accurate fielding strategy doesn't depend on theory. It requires a fielder to be positioned according to the past performance of a batter. The required fielding strategy changes for different types of pitches, different locations of a pitch in the strike zone, and even when the ball-and -strike count changes.

For this reason we're contemplating putting the third baseman in the BARS fielding strategy. This would take the guesswork out of positioning him correctly. The third baseman's two suggested positions would be 'Shifted toward third base' and 'Normal position.'

Baseball is unlike other sports in that the team on defense initiates the play by pitching the ball. The defensive team in football can only guess what a play is going to be and where it's going to go, but in baseball the defensive team could align itself correctly for every pitch by following the suggested fielding strategy for the type and location of pitch to the particular batter. We've had 90 percent accuracy for the other fielders, and we hope to do the same for the third baseman as well.

# Chapter Five

## Preventable Hits: Three Games

Every game played contains base hits that are allowed because the defensive alignment is not as accurate as possible.

These unnecessary hits may occur at the beginning or end of a game. They may occur when the score is close or when the game has already been wrapped up. They may drive in a run (even the winning run), start or sustain a run-producing rally, or be isolated hits that do not produce any runs.

No matter what the circumstances, in every game there are instances in which base hits could have been prevented if the fielders had been correctly positioned.

The BARS System fielding strategy allows a team to align itself properly in the field in all situations, thereby maximizing the chances for fielders to be in the right place at the right time — preventing base hits, intercepting base hits that would have gone for extra bases, and holding runners to fewer bases.

The following illustrations show how important these hits can be in terms of runs saved.

### New York at Boston, October 4, 1986
### New York 5, Boston 3

In this game, five of the eight runs scored were the direct result of hits that could have been prevented by each team positioning its fielders according to the BARS System fielding strategy. This included the hit that produced the game-winning RBI for the Yankees in the top of the seventh inning.

In all, New York had five hits that could have been prevented and Boston had two. Boston also had one instance in which a runner could have been held to fewer bases.

1. In the bottom of the second inning, with two outs and the bases loaded,

Boston batter Spike Owen (batting LH) came to the plate against Yankee pitcher Bob Tewksbury (RH). The count went to 1-1 and Owen slowly grounded a medium-high outside fastball over the second base bag into center field. The shortstop could have fielded the slow grounder if he had been playing shifted more toward second base. Two runs scored on the hit.

### Spike Owen   Left-Handed Hitter
### Against All Right-Handed Pitchers All Teams

Fastball Average .282

| | Outside | Middle | Inside |
|---|---|---|---|
| High | 16/<br>187 / 3 | 25/<br>320 / 8 | 8/<br>375 / 3 |
| Med | 68/<br>338 / 23 | 19/<br>473 / 9 | 32/<br>187 / 6 |
| Low | 10/<br>200 / 2 | 38/<br>236 / 9 | 18/<br>166 / 3 |

The following fielding strategy is taken from the BARS System Super Summary chart. It shows the best position for each fielder based on the trends found by computer from the many medium-high outside fastballs that Owen has hit during the past several seasons.

**BARS SYSTEM SUPER SUMMARY:**

MEDIUM-HIGH OUTSIDE FASTBALLS
(THROWN TO OWEN WITH THE COUNT EVEN)

BATTING AVERAGE .338
   *PLAY*
LEFTFIELDER          Medium-deep in straightaway left field
CENTERFIELDER    Medium-deep in straightaway center field
RIGHTFIELDER       Deep and shifted toward center field
**SHORTSTOP**        **Up middle (shifted toward second base)**
SECOND                   Shifted toward first base

In this instance, if the Yankee fielders had been positioned according to the BARS System fielding strategy, the shortstop would have been playing shifted toward second base.

In this position, he could have fielded the ground ball and either forced the runner at second or thrown Owen out at first, ending the inning and preventing the two runs that scored on the base hit.

In the actual game, the Yankee shortstop was playing in his normal fielding position and couldn't reach the ball, which went through into center field, driving in the two runners.

2. In the bottom of the third, Boston batter Bill Buckner (LH) came to bat against Tewksbury. With the count 2-2, Buckner hit a low-over-the-middle curveball into medium-deep right-center field.

The Yankee center fielder, Rickey Henderson, was playing in straight-away center and just missed catching the ball. He could have caught it if he had been playing shifted toward right field.

**BARS: CENTERFIELDER Deep and shifted toward right field**

Henderson could have caught the ball if he had been positioned shifted toward right field, as suggested by the BARS System fielding strategy. In the game, Henderson was playing straightaway in center and couldn't reach the ball, which dropped in for a single.

### Bill Buckner   Left-Handed Hitter
### Against All Right-Handed Pitchers All Teams

Curve Average .284

|  | Outside | Middle | Inside |
|---|---|---|---|
| High | 9 / 444 / 4 | 11 / 454 / 5 | 3 / 0 / 0 |
| Med | 31 / 193 / 6 | 10 / 500 / 5 | 14 / 285 / 4 |
| Low | 14 / 285 / 4 | 24 / 166 / 4 | 14 / 357 / 5 |

The above batting chart shows that a low-over-the-midle curve ball is an excellent pitch to throw Buckner. His .166 average in the location is very low. But if the fielders are not positioned properly, even a pitcher's best pitch will be wasted.

3. In the top of the fifth, Dave Winfield (RH) came to bat for the Yankees, facing Boston right-hander Dennis Boyd. The count went to 1-2, and Winfield hit a medium-high outside fastball to deep right-center.

The Boston right fielder, who was playing medium-deep and shifted toward the right field line, couldn't quite get to the ball. Two more steps and he would have had it.

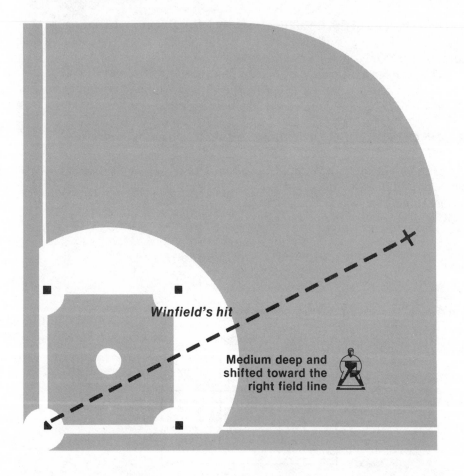

Winfield's hit

Medium deep and
shifted toward the
right field line

If the right fielder had been playing shifted toward center field, he would have been able to catch the ball easily.

## BARS: RIGHTFIELDER Deep and shifted toward center field

The Boston right fielder could have caught the ball if he had been shifted more toward center field, as suggested by the Super Summary fielding strategy.

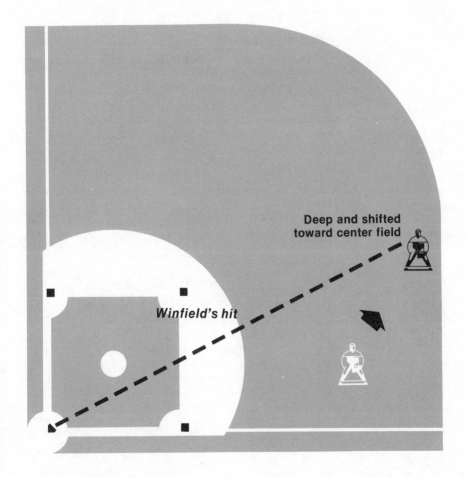

**Dave Winfield   Right-Handed Hitter**
**Against All Right-Handed Pitchers All Teams**

Fastball Average .311

|  | Inside | Middle | Outside |
|------|--------|--------|---------|
| High | 15 / 200 / 3 | 31 / 483 / 15 | 14 / 357 / 5 |
| Med | 43 / 302 / 13 | 34 / 352 / 12 | 108 / 314 / 34 |
| Low | 19 / 105 / 2 | 44 / 318 / 14 | 39 / 256 / 10 |

Winfield's hit in this instance resulted from a medium-high outside fastball.  It is interesting to compare the BARS System fielding strategy required for a medium-high outside fastball with the strategy required for a medium-high inside fastball.

MEDIUM-HIGH OUTSIDE FASTBALLS

BATTING AVERAGE .314
   *PLAY*
LEFTFIELDER          Deep and shifted toward the left field line
CENTERFIELDER        Deep  in straightaway center field
RIGHTFIELDER         Deep and shifted toward center field
SHORTSTOP            Up middle (shifted toward second base)
SECOND               Normal position


MEDIUM-HIGH INSIDE FASTBALLS

BATTING AVERAGE .302
   *PLAY*
LEFTFIELDER          Deep and shifted toward the left field line
CENTERFIELDER        Deep and shifted toward left field
RIGHTFIELDER         Medium-deep in straightaway right field
SHORTSTOP            Shifted toward third base
SECOND               Normal position

The center fielder, the right fielder and the shortstop would be required to position themselves differently for fastballs to these two pitch locations.

4. In the top of the fifth, Yankee Joel Skinner (RH) came to bat against Boyd. On the 1-2 pitch Skinner hit a medium-high inside fastball to short right field. The pop-up fell in for a single.

The Boston right fielder, Dwight Evans, was playing very deep in straightaway right and couldn't get to the ball. If he had been playing medium-deep instead of deep, he could have caught it.

**BARS: RIGHTFIELDER Medium-deep in straightaway right field**

The Boston right fielder was playing very deep in right field and couldn't reach this pop-up. If he had been playing medium-deep, as suggested by the BARS System, he could have caught the ball, preventing the hit.

### Joel Skinner   Right-Handed Hitter
### Against All Right-Handed Pitchers All Teams

Fastball Average .227

|  | Inside | Middle | Outside |
|---|---|---|---|
| High | 7/ 0 / 0 | 3/ 0 / 0 | 1/ 0 / 0 |
| Med | 9/ 333 / 3 | 11/ 363 / 4 | 32/ 250 / 8 |
| Low | 8/ 0 / 0 | 12/ 416 / 5 | 5/ 0 / 0 |

5. In the top of the sixth, Yankee batter Mike Easler (LH) came to the plate against Steve Crawford (RH). Easler hit the 2-1 pitch, a low-outside fastball, on the ground to the first-base side of second.

The second baseman was playing shifted toward first and couldn't reach the ball, which went through into center field, driving in Don Mattingly to tie the score at 3-3. The second baseman could have fielded the ball if he had been playing in his normal straightaway position, rather than shifted toward first base.

**BARS: SECOND Normal position**

Both the hit and the RBI could have been prevented if the second baseman had been positioned according to the BARS Super Summary.

## Mike Easler   Left-Handed Hitter
## Against All Right-Handed Pitchers All Teams

Fastball Average .297

| | Outside | Middle | Inside |
|---|---|---|---|
| High | 15/<br>66 / 1 | 33/<br>212 / 7 | 11/<br>181 / 2 |
| Med | 61/<br>229 / 14 | 31/<br>580 / 18 | 38/<br>394 / 15 |
| Low | 17/<br>352 / 6 | 52/<br>384 / 20 | 31/<br>96 / 3 |

6. In the top of the seventh, right-handed Yankee hitter Willie Randolph came to the plate against Crawford. With two outs and Rickey Henderson on second, the count went to 3-2. Crawford then threw a low-over-the-middle fastball which Randolph hit on the ground toward the shortstop's normal fielding position.

The shortstop was playing shifted toward second; he would have been able to field the ball if he had been playing in his normal position.

**BARS: SHORTSTOP Normal position**

The shortstop would have been able to get to the ball and prevent the hit (thereby stopping Henderson from scoring the game's winning run) if he had been positioned according to the BARS System fielding strategy.

It is interesting to note that if Randolph had been behind in the count instead of even, the shortstop would have been required by the BARS System to be shifted toward second base for this particular type and location of pitch thrown by a right-handed pitcher. This shows the importance of following the BARS fielding strategy on every pitch.

**Willie Randolph   Right-Handed Hitter**
**Against All Right-Handed Pitchers All Teams**

Fastball Average .245

|  | Inside | Middle | Outside |
|---|---|---|---|
| High | 5/<br>200 / 1 | 33/<br>303 / 10 | 7/<br>142 / 1 |
| Med | 46/<br>260 / 12 | 30/<br>333 / 10 | 101/<br>227 / 23 |
| Low | 10/<br>200 / 2 | 68/<br>279 / 19 | 34/<br>117 / 4 |

7. In the top of the seventh, with two outs and runners on first and second, Yankee batter Mike Easler came to the plate. On the first pitch, a low-inside fastball, Easler blooped a soft fly to short left center.

The center fielder was playing deep and shifted toward right field. He just missed catching the ball after a frantic run. He would have been able to catch it if he had been playing more straightaway.

**BARS: CENTERFIELDER Deep in straightaway center field**

The center fielder just missed getting to the ball. He was positioned in deep center shifted toward right. If he had been playing in straightaway center, he could have caught the ball for the out, preventing the hit and the RBI.

**Mike Easler    Left-Handed Hitter**
**Against All Right-Handed Pitchers All Teams**

Fastball Average .297

|  | Outside | Middle | Inside |
|---|---|---|---|
| High | 15/<br>66 / 1 | 33/<br>212 / 7 | 11/<br>181 / 2 |
| Med | 61/<br>229 / 14 | 31/<br>580 / 18 | 38/<br>394 / 15 |
| Low | 17/<br>352 / 6 | 52/<br>384 / 20 | 31/<br>96 / 3 |

8. In the bottom of the ninth, Boston batter Jim Rice (RH) faced Yankee pitcher Dave Righetti (LH). The 2-1 pitch was a medium-high inside fastball that Rice hit to shallow left field down the line for a double.

The Yankee left fielder was playing shaded toward center. The ball would have been a base hit in any case, but if the Yankee left fielder had been playing in straightaway left, rather than shifted toward center field, he could have fielded the ball in time to hold Rice to a single.

**BARS: LEFTFIELDER Deep in straightaway left field**

This is an instance in which positioning fielders according to the BARS System fielding strategy would not have actually prevented the hit, but would have allowed a fielder to be more properly positioned to cut off a hit ball, preventing the runner from taking an extra base.

As will be shown in many upcoming examples, preventing a runner from taking extra bases can be just as important as preventing base hits.

### Jim Rice     Right-Handed Hitter
### Against All Left-Handed Pitchers All Teams

Fastball Average .298

|  | Inside | Middle | Outside |
|---|---|---|---|
| High | 5/<br>**0** / 0 | 15/<br>**533** / 8 | 4/<br>**250** / 1 |
| Med | 30/<br>**366** / 11 | 13/<br>**307** / 4 | 55/<br>**236** / 13 |
| Low | 8/<br>**250** / 2 | 27/<br>**296** / 8 | 17/<br>**294** / 5 |

**Game Summary:**

New York had five hits that could have been prevented by Boston.

Boston had two hits that could have been prevented by New York, plus one instance (Rice's double in the bottom of the ninth) in which a runner could have been held to fewer bases.

**Chicago at St. Louis, June 14, 1987**
**St. Louis 3, Chicago 2**

In this relatively low-scoring game, St. Louis had four hits that could have been prevented and Chicago had three. Both Chicago runs resulted directly from hits that could have been prevented, as did the game-winning run by St. Louis.

1. In the bottom of the fourth with two outs and no runners on base, St. Louis' Tony Pena (RH) came to the plate against Scott Sanderson (RH). Pena went ahead in the count 2-0, then hit a high-over-the-middle fastball to left field (approximately 270 feet) which fell in front of Cubs' left fielder Jerry Mumphrey, who was playing deep in straightaway left.

If Mumphrey had been playing shorter in left, he could have caught this line drive for the out.

**BARS: LEFTFIELDER Short in straightaway left field**

Mumphrey could have caught this ball if he had been playing short in left. Line drive singles of 250-275 feet could often be caught if outfielders positioned themselves medium-deep or even short when called for by the BARS System.

If outfielders are hesitant to play certain hitters short, even when called for by the BARS System, they could position themselves medium-deep and guard against deep drives, while still covering the shorter area.

**Tony Pena    Right-Handed Hitter**
**Against All Right-Handed Pitchers All Teams**

Fastball Average .346

|  | Inside | Middle | Outside |
|---|---|---|---|
| High | 11 / 181 / 2 | 29 / 379 / 11 | 8 / 375 / 3 |
| Med | 27 / 185 / 5 | 11 / 454 / 5 | 29 / 517 / 15 |
| Low | 7 / 142 / 1 | 38 / 342 / 13 | 13 / 384 / 5 |

2. Vince Coleman led off the bottom of the fifth for St. Louis. He was batting left-handed against the right-handed Sanderson. The 0-1 pitch was a change-up, low-over-the-middle part of the plate, which Coleman blooped into center field.

Dave Martinez, the Cubs' center fielder, was playing straightaway and deep in center. He needed to be straightaway and medium-deep to make the catch.

### BARS: CENTERFIELDER Medium-deep in straightaway center field

Martinez would have had to come in on the ball to make the catch, but he could have reached it if he had been playing medium-deep. As it was, he was playing about ten feet too deep, and caught the ball on the hop.

### Vince Coleman  Left-Handed Hitter
### Against All Right-Handed Pitchers All Teams

Change-Up Average .300

|  | Outside | Middle | Inside |
|---|---|---|---|
| High | 1/ 0 / 0 | 1/ 0 / 0 | 0/ 0 / 0 |
| Med | 2/ 0 / 0 | 3/ 0 / 0 | 3/ 666 / 2 |
| Low | 5/ 0 / 0 | 3/ 666 / 2 | 2/ 1000 / 2 |

3. In the top of the sixth, with two outs and a runner on first, Chicago's Jerry Mumphrey (LH) came to bat against St. Louis right-hander Danny Cox. On the 2-1 pitch, a low-outside change-up, Mumphrey hit a bloop single to left field down the line.

St. Louis left fielder Vince Coleman was playing straight and deep, but the ball was blooped so softly that he almost caught it. If he had been playing medium-deep and near the line, he would have had no trouble making the catch.

**BARS: LEFTFIELDER    Medium-deep and shifted
toward the left field line**

Coleman would have been perfectly positioned to make the catch.

**Jerry Mumphrey    Left-Handed Hitter
Against All Right-Handed Pitchers All Teams**

Change-Up Average .176

|  | Outside | Middle | Inside |
|---|---|---|---|
| **High** | 1 / 0 / 0 | 3 / 0 / 0 | 1 / 1000 / 1 |
| **Med** | 4 / 250 / 1 | 3 / 0 / 0 | 3 / 0 / 0 |
| **Low** | 5 / 400 / 2 | 11 / 90 / 1 | 3 / 333 / 1 |

4. In the bottom of the sixth, Jack Clark (RH) came up for St. Louis to face Sanderson. The 1-2 pitch was a medium-high outside curve ball that Clark hit to left for a single. The ball went about 280 feet and was pulled along the line.

The Cubs' left fielder, Jerry Mumphrey, was playing straight and deep. If he had been playing toward the line, he could have caught the ball.

**BARS: LEFTFIELDER  Deep and shifted toward the left field line**

Even playing straight and deep, Mumphrey fielded the ball about ten feet from where it landed. If he had been playing shifted toward the line, he should have had no trouble making the catch.

This hit was costly because Clark scored later in the inning to give the Cards a 3-0 lead. They won 3-2.

### Jack Clark    Right-Handed Hitter
### Against All Right-Handed Pitchers All Teams

Curve Average .166

|  | Inside | Middle | Outside |
|------|--------|--------|---------|
| High | 1/<br>**0** / 0 | 2/<br>**0** / 0 | 1/<br>**0** / 0 |
| Med | 4/<br>**500** / 2 | 4/<br>**0** / 0 | 8/<br>**125** / 1 |
| Low | 2/<br>**0** / 0 | 6/<br>**333** / 2 | 14/<br>**142** / 2 |

5. The next batter in the bottom of the sixth, Willie McGee (batting LH against Sanderson), hit the 1-0 pitch, a high-inside fastball, into short center field for a single. Clark went from first to third on the hit.

The Cubs' center fielder, Dave Martinez, was playing straight and deep. If he had been playing medium-deep, he could have made the catch and held Clark on first base.

### BARS: CENTERFIELDER Medium-deep in straightaway center field

The hit could have been prevented and the eventual winning run (Clark) could have been held on first if Martinez had been positioned as suggested by the BARS System fielding strategy.

### Willie McGee    Left-Handed Hitter
### Against All Right-Handed Pitchers All Teams

Fastball Average .330

|  | Outside | Middle | Inside |
|------|---------|--------|--------|
| High | 7/<br>**142** / 1 | 23/<br>**304** / 7 | 21/<br>**238** / 5 |
| Med | 43/<br>**325** /14 | 14/<br>**428** / 6 | 49/<br>**306** /15 |
| Low | 17/<br>**235** / 4 | 37/<br>**459** /17 | 25/<br>**360** / 9 |

6. Jim Sundberg led off the top of the eighth for the Cubs. He hit the first pitch, a medium-high outside fastball, on the ground between the second and first basemen.

The St. Louis second baseman, Tom Herr, was playing shifted toward second base and couldn't reach the ball. If he had been playing shifted toward first base, he could have fielded the ball and thrown Sundberg out.

**BARS: SECOND  Shifted toward first base**

Herr could have fielded the ball easily if he had been shifted toward first as suggested.

### Jim Sundberg     Right-Handed Hitter
### Against All Right-Handed Pitchers All Teams

Fastball Average .275

|  | Inside | Middle | Outside |
|---|---|---|---|
| **High** | 12/<br>166 / 2 | 25/<br>120 / 3 | 3/<br>0 / 0 |
| **Med** | 56/<br>303 / 17 | 37/<br>459 / 17 | 69/<br>275 / 19 |
| **Low** | 8/<br>250 / 2 | 55/<br>236 / 13 | 18/<br>277 / 5 |

7. In the top of the ninth, with two outs and runners on second and third, Manny Trillo (RH) came to the plate for the Cubs, facing St. Louis right-hander Todd Worrell. With the count 2-2, Trillo lined a medium-high outside fastball between the shortstop and third baseman for a single, driving in both runners (Mumphrey and Durham).

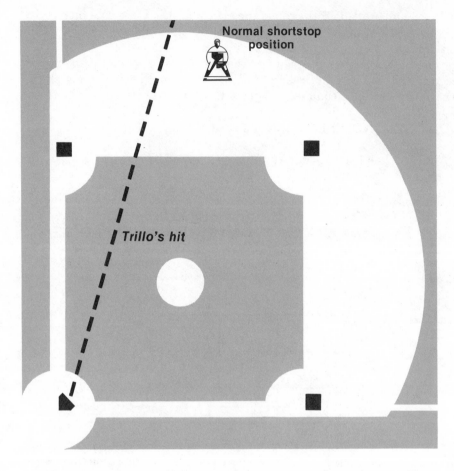

The Cards' shortstop, Ozzie Smith, was playing at the normal shortstop position. If he had been playing shifted toward third base, he could have caught this line drive to end the game.

### BARS: SHORTSTOP  Shifted toward third base

Smith could have caught this ball for the game's final out if he had been positioned as suggested.

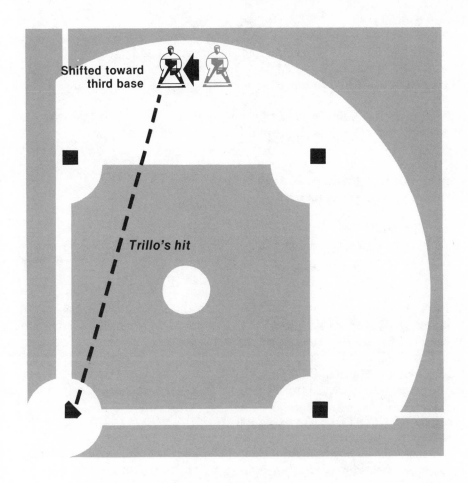

**Manny Trillo     Right-Handed Hitter**
**Against All Right-Handed Pitchers All Teams**

Fastball Average .293

|  | Inside | Middle | Outside |
|---|---|---|---|
| High | 10/<br>**200** / 2 | 12/<br>**0** / 0 | 9/<br>**222** / 2 |
| Med | 18/<br>**277** / 5 | 6/<br>**666** / 4 | 39/<br>**333** /13 |
| Low | 7/<br>**428** / 3 | 26/<br>**384** /10 | 16/<br>**187** / 3 |

**Game Summary:**

St. Louis had four hits that could have been prevented by Chicago.

Chicago had three hits that could have been prevented by St. Louis.

Three of the five runs scored in the game, including the game-winner, were direct results of hits that could have been prevented.

**Chicago at San Francisco, July 9, 1986**
**Chicago 4, San Francisco 3**

In this game, three of the Cubs' four runs resulted directly from hits that could have been prevented using the BARS System fielding strategy. In the game, the Cubs and the Giants each had four hits that could have been prevented.

1. In the bottom of the fourth, with two outs and no runners on base, Jeff Leonard (RH) of the Giants came to bat against Ed Lynch (RH). On the 1-0 pitch, Leonard hit a medium-high outside curve into short left center field that the Cubs' shortstop, Shawon Dunston, could have caught if he had been playing his normal fielding position. As it was, Dunston was playing in the hole (shifted toward third base) and could not reach the bloop single.

**BARS: SHORTSTOP Normal position**

Dunston could have caught the short pop-up if he had been in his normal straightaway shortstop position, as suggested by the BARS System fielding strategy.

**Jeff Leonard     Right-Handed Hitter**
**Against All Right-Handed Pitchers All Teams**

Curve Average .246

|  | Inside | Middle | Outside |
|---|---|---|---|
| High | 1/ 0 / 0 | 4/ 500 / 2 | 2/ 500 / 1 |
| Med | 4/ 750 / 3 | 5/ 200 / 1 | 18/ 277 / 5 |
| Low | 0/ 0 / 0 | 12/ 166 / 2 | 19/ 105 / 2 |

2. In the bottom of the fifth, San Francisco's Chris Brown (RH) came up to face Lynch. There were no outs and a runner was on first base. Brown hit the 1-1 pitch, a medium-high outside curve, on a line into left center, about 320 feet from the plate.

Chicago center fielder Jerry Mumphrey could have caught the ball if he had been deep and shifted toward left.

**BARS: CENTERFIELDER  Deep and shifted toward left field**

Mumphrey would have been perfectly positioned to catch the ball if he had been deep in center and shifted toward left field, as suggested by the BARS System fielding strategy.

**Chris Brown     Right-Handed Hitter**
**Against All Right-Handed Pitchers All Teams**

Curve Average .464

|  | Inside | Middle | Outside |
|---|---|---|---|
| High | 0/ 0 / 0 | 3/ 0 / 0 | 1/ 1000 / 1 |
| Med | 2/ 500 / 1 | 2/ 500 / 1 | 6/ 666 / 4 |
| Low | 0/ 0 / 0 | 4/ 750 / 3 | 10/ 300 / 3 |

3. Davey Lopes led off for the Cubs in the top of the sixth, facing San Francisco right-hander Mike LaCoss. Lopes worked the count full (3-2), then hit a medium-high inside fastball on a line into right field for a single.

The Giants' right fielder Chili Davis could have caught the ball if he had been playing medium-deep in right and straightaway.

**BARS: RIGHTFIELDER  Medium-deep in straightaway right field**

If he had been positioned correctly, Davis would have had to run in only a short way to catch this line drive.

### Davey Lopes     Right-Handed Hitter
### Against All Right-Handed Pitchers All Teams

Fastball Average .328

| | Inside | Middle | Outside |
|---|---|---|---|
| High | 4/<br>250 / 1 | 23/<br>217 / 5 | 5/<br>600 / 3 |
| Med | 20/<br>350 / 7 | 9/<br>333 / 3 | 67/<br>343 /23 |
| Low | 8/<br>250 / 2 | 42/<br>404 /17 | 29/<br>241 / 7 |

4. With one out in the top of the sixth, Keith Moreland (RH) came to bat for the Cubs against LaCoss with Davey Lopes on second and Ryne Sandberg on first. Moreland went ahead in the count 2-1, then hit a low-over-the-middle fastball to deep straightaway left field for a double, driving in both runners.

If San Francisco left fielder Jeff Leonard had been playing deep in straightaway left, he would have had no trouble making the catch for the out.

**BARS: LEFTFIELDER  Deep in straightaway left field**

Leonard, the San Francisco left fielder, could have caught the ball if he had been positioned deep in straightaway left. If he had caught the ball, it is doubtful that either runner could have advanced. As it was, the ball went past him and both runners scored.

**Keith Moreland     Right-Handed Hitter**
**Against All Right-Handed Pitchers All Teams**

Fastball Average .309

|  | Inside | Middle | Outside |
|------|--------|--------|---------|
| High | 39/179 / 7 | 94/265 / 25 | 43/302 / 13 |
| Med | 100/430 / 43 | 37/324 / 12 | 182/329 / 60 |
| Low | 35/314 / 11 | 198/338 / 67 | 99/181 / 18 |

5.  In the bottom of the sixth, the Giants' Harry Spilman (LH pinch hitter) came up to face Lynch with one out and a runner on first. The first pitch was a ball. Spilman hit the second pitch, a high fastball over the middle part of the plate, on the ground between the first and second basemen, advancing the runner to second.

If Ryne Sandberg, the Cubs' second baseman, had been playing shifted toward first, he could have fielded the ball and possibly started a double play. In any case, he could have thrown Spilman out at first. As it happened in the game, Sandberg could not get to the ball, and it went through into right field.

**BARS: SECOND Shifted toward first base**

Sandberg was playing too far toward second and could not field the ball. If he had been positioned more toward first base as suggested by the BARS System fielding strategy, he could have reached the ball and possibly started an inning-ending double play.

### Harry Spilman     Left-Handed Hitter
### Against All Right-Handed Pitchers All Teams

Fastball Average .213

| | Outside | Middle | Inside |
|---|---|---|---|
| High | 7/<br>142 / 1 | 15/<br>333 / 5 | 5/<br>0 / 0 |
| Med | 14/<br>214 / 3 | 10/<br>400 / 4 | 13/<br>307 / 4 |
| Low | 4/<br>250 / 1 | 12/<br>0 / 0 | 9/<br>111 / 1 |

6. Two batters later in the Giants' bottom of the sixth, Jeff Leonard (RH) came to the plate. There were two outs and runners at first and second. On the 2-1 pitch, Lynch threw a medium-high curveball over the outside part of the plate. Leonard hit a short fly ball into right-center field. The ball fell for a single, driving in Randy Kutcher from second.

If the Cubs' right fielder, Keith Moreland, had been shifted toward center field, he could have caught the ball, ending the inning.

### BARS: RIGHTFIELDER  Deep and shifted toward center field

Moreland would have had to come in on the ball, but he could have caught it to end the inning, preventing the hit and the run.

### Jeff Leonard     Right-Handed Hitter
### Against All Right-Handed Pitchers All Teams

Curve Average .246

| | Inside | Middle | Outside |
|---|---|---|---|
| High | 1/<br>0 / 0 | 4/<br>500 / 2 | 2/<br>500 / 1 |
| Med | 4/<br>750 / 3 | 5/<br>200 / 1 | 18/<br>277 / 5 |
| Low | 0/<br>0 / 0 | 12/<br>166 / 2 | 19/<br>105 / 2 |

7. Joel Youngblood (RH pinch hitter) led off the Giants' bottom of the eighth, facing Cubs' right-hander Dave Gumpert. Youngblood fell behind 1-2, then hit a medium-high outside fastball into medium-deep right center field.

If the Cub's right fielder, Keith Moreland, had been medium-deep in right and shifted toward center, the ball would have been hit almost directly to him.

**BARS: RIGHTFIELDER  Medium-deep and shifted toward center field**

Moreland could have caught the ball and prevented the hit if he had been positioned as suggested.

**Joel Youngblood     Right-Handed Hitter**
**Against All Right-Handed Pitchers All Teams**

Fastball Average .320

|  | Inside | Middle | Outside |
|---|---|---|---|
| High | 4/<br>250 / 1 | 15/<br>400 / 6 | 5/<br>200 / 1 |
| Med | 28/<br>321 / 9 | 17/<br>352 / 6 | 28/<br>321 / 9 |
| Low | 6/<br>333 / 2 | 19/<br>315 / 6 | 12/<br>250 / 3 |

8. In the top of the ninth, with two outs and no runners on base, Cubs' batter Thad Bosley (LH) came up to face Giants' right-hander Juan Berenguer. Bosley hit the 0-1 pitch, a low-inside curve, into right field between the first and second basemen.

If Giants' second baseman Joel Youngblood had been shifted more toward first base, he could have fielded the ball and thrown Bosley out.

**BARS: SECOND  Shifted toward first base**

Youngblood could have ended the game if he had been positioned according the BARS System fielding strategy.

## Thad Bosley     Left-Handed Hitter
## Against All Right-Handed Pitchers All Teams

Curve Average .323

|  | Outside | Middle | Inside |
|---|---|---|---|
| High | 7 / 0 | 33 / 303 / 10 | 21 / 333 / 7 |
| Med | 25 / 120 / 3 | 13 / 461 / 6 | 44 / 386 / 17 |
| Low | 10 / 300 / 3 | 58 / 379 / 22 | 33 / 333 / 11 |

**Game Summary:**

Chicago had four hits that could have been prevented by San Francisco.

San Francisco had four hits that could have been prevented by Chicago.

Three of the Cubs' runs resulted directly from hits that the Giants could have prevented by positioning their fielders according to the BARS System fielding strategy.

**Additional games in which hits could be prevented are described in Chapter Nineteen.**

# *Personal Comments*

Managers tell their players that a game won in April is as important in the final standings as a game won in October. The same holds true for RBIs in a game; a run prevented early is as important as a run prevented late.

In many ways, preventing an early run could be even more important because if a team falls behind it could have trouble catching up. Early runs scored against a team can be demoralizing. By the time the eighth or ninth inning rolls around, a game could be over.

That's the reason the BARS fielding strategy needs to be used throughout a game, not just in tight spots or in the late innings. Since more fastballs are thrown than all other types of pitches combined, teams could start by using the BARS fielding strategy only when fastballs are thrown. This would simplify the system and, since pitchers are most accurate with their fastballs, using the fielding strategy when fastballs are thrown would bring the most immediate results.

Preventing two or three hits per game and holding runners to fewer bases can make a big difference in the number of runs scored. It's hard to say exactly how many runs per game would be prevented, but over an entire season the savings would be significant.

The next chapter discusses game-winning RBIs that could have been prevented by using the BARS System fielding strategy. The chapter contains 29 game-winning RBIs. It is interesting to note that for the purpose of finding hits that could have been prevented by using the BARS System, about 150 random games were studied. This means that almost 20 percent of the games studied had game-winning RBIs that could have been prevented.

At first this high percentage surprised me, but now I realize that I should have expected it. The average number of base hits is about nine per team each game. The BARS fielding strategy would allow two to three of these nine to be prevented — that's 20 to 33 percent.Since these preventable hits can occur at any time during a game, it's not surprising that some of them produce game-winning RBIs.

# Chapter Six

# Game-Winning RBIs

The preventable hits described in the previous chapters were not categorized by importance to the eventual outcome of the game in which they occurred. Some led to runs, some did not. Each hit described in this chapter produced a game-winning RBI.

When the score of a game is tied in late innings or in extra innings, it is obviously important to pitch carefully to a batter's weaknesses and to position fielders correctly.

But not all game-winning RBIs occur in the late innings. Any hit can lead to the game-winning RBI, whether in the first inning with no one on base, or in the bottom of the ninth with the winning run in scoring position. This emphasizes the importance of using the BARS System fielding strategy on every pitch throughout a game.

The hits in this chapter are examples of the hundreds of preventable hits that produce game-winning RBIs each season.

## Pittsburgh at St. Louis, July 31, 1987
## St. Louis 4, Pittsburgh 3

In the bottom of the ninth, with the score tied 3-3, St. Louis' Vince Coleman (batting LH) came up to hit against Barry Jones (RH). There were two outs and Jose Oquendo was on first base.

The first pitch to Coleman was a low-over-the-middle fastball He lined it about 290 feet into the right-center gap, driving in Oquendo with the winning run. Pittsburgh's right fielder Bobby Bonilla was playing fairly deep in straightaway right and could not reach the ball.

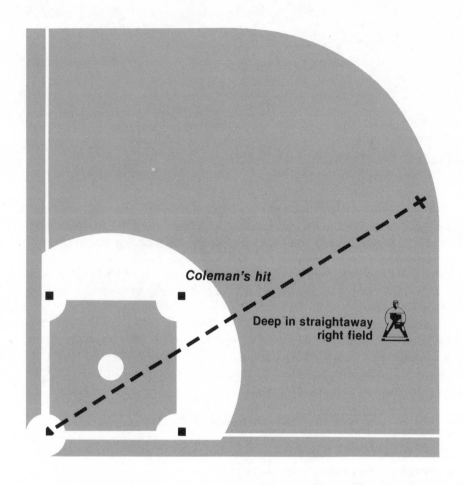

If Bonilla had been playing shifted toward center field, he could have cut the ball off, preventing Oquendo from scoring from first base.

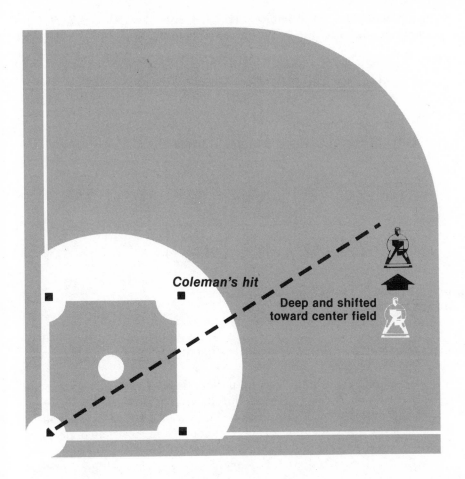

Coleman's hit

Deep and shifted
toward center field

This line drive could not have been caught, but if Bonilla had been playing as suggested, he could have cut it off in time to prevent Oquendo from scoring from first base.

As it was, Oquendo circled the bases to score, giving the Cardinals a 4-3 win.

The BARS System Super Summary shows that the best position for the right fielder on a low-over-the-middle fastball to Coleman with the count even (0-0) is deep and shifted toward center field.

## BARS: RIGHTFIELDER  Deep and shifted toward center field

By following the BARS Fielding strategy, the game-winning RBI could have been prevented, and Coleman held to a single.

The following Super Summary batting chart shows Coleman's overall record against fastballs thrown by right-handed pitchers.

### Vince Coleman    Batting Left-Handed
### Against All Right-Handed Pitchers All Teams

Fastball Average .289

|      | Outside | Middle | Inside |
|------|---------|--------|--------|
| High | 9/ 111 / 1 | 27/ 296 / 8 | 15/ 266 / 4 |
| Med  | 23/ 478 / 11 | 6/ 500 / 3 | 31/ 322 / 10 |
| Low  | 7/ 285 / 2 | 30/ 300 / 9 | 25/ 80 / 2 |

## Cincinnati at Chicago, August 22, 1986
## Chicago 3, Cincinnati 2

In the bottom of the fourth inning, with two outs and the bases loaded, Chicago switch-hitter Jerry Mumphrey (batting LH) came to the plate against Ted Power (RH).

The 0-1 pitch was a high-over-the-middle fastball that Mumphrey hit 370 feet into the left-center gap for a triple, driving in Terry Francona, Mike Martin and Jamie Moyer for all three of the Cubs' runs in their 3-2 win.

Eric Davis, the Cincinnati center fielder, was positioned deep in straightaway center field and could not reach the ball.

The BARS System Super Summary shows that for a high-over-the-middle fastball thrown by a right-handed pitcher to Mumphrey with the count 0-1, the center fielder should be positioned deep and shifted toward left field. This would have prevented the hit and the three runs.

### Jerry Mumphrey    Batting Left-Handed
### Against All Right-Handed Pitchers All Teams

Fastball Average .348

|      | Outside | Middle | Inside |
|------|---------|--------|--------|
| High | 18/ 111 / 2 | 39/ 435 / 17 | 18/ 166 / 3 |
| Med  | 51/ 372 / 19 | 30/ 333 / 10 | 51/ 392 / 20 |
| Low  | 16/ 62 / 1 | 69/ 376 / 26 | 49/ 428 / 21 |

**Atlanta at Houston, April 21, 1987**
**Houston 7, Atlanta 6**

With two outs and the score tied 6-6 in the bottom of the ninth, Houston loaded the bases against Atlanta right-handed pitcher Gene Garber. Denny Walling (LH) came to the plate and drew a ball on the first pitch. The next pitch was a curve, low over the middle of the plate, which Walling grounded into center field.

The Atlanta second baseman, Glenn Hubbard, was playing shifted toward first against the left-handed hitter. The ground ball was hit approximately 15 feet to the first-base side of second.

If Hubbard had been playing in his normal position, he could have fielded the ball and tossed to second for the force out, ending the inning. Instead, the ball rolled into center field and the runner scored from third with the game-winning run.

**BARS: SECOND Normal position**

If Hubbard had been playing in his normal position, as suggested by the BARS System in this instance, he could have fielded the ball and prevented the game-winning RBI.

**Denny Walling    Left-Handed Hitter**
**Against All Right-Handed Pitchers All Teams**

Curve Average .261

|  | Outside | Middle | Inside |
|---|---|---|---|
| High | 2/<br>500 / 1 | 6/<br>166 / 1 | 2/<br>0 / 0 |
| Med | 15/<br>466 / 7 | 4/<br>500 / 2 | 10/<br>200 / 2 |
| Low | 5/<br>200 / 1 | 16/<br>187 / 3 | 5/<br>0 / 0 |

**New York at Philadelphia, June 27, 1987**
**New York 5, Philadelphia 4**

In the top of the fifth, Mets batter Kevin McReynolds (RH) came to the plate against Doug Bair (RH). With two outs, there were runners on first and third. The count went to 3-0, and McReynolds hit a low-outside fastball on the ground up the middle, driving in the runner from third with the game-winning RBI.

Luis Aguayo, the Philadelphia shortstop, was playing in his normal position. If he had been playing up middle (shifted toward second base), he could have fielded the ball and ended the inning by either forcing the runner at second or throwing the batter out at first.

**BARS : SHORTSTOP Up middle (shifted toward second base)**

The Philadelphia shortstop would have been able to field the ball and end the inning if he had been positioned as suggested.

### Kevin McReynolds    Right-Handed Hitter
### Against All Right-Handed Pitchers All Teams

Fastball Average .280

|  | Inside | Middle | Outside |
|---|---|---|---|
| High | 11/90 / 1 | 28/178 / 5 | 9/333 / 3 |
| Med | 19/157 / 3 | 10/900 / 9 | 37/297 / 11 |
| Low | 7/428 / 3 | 45/244 / 11 | 23/304 / 7 |

**Oakland at New York, August 23, 1986**
**Oakland 2, New York 1**

In the top of the ninth inning, with the score tied 1-1, Jose Canseco (RH) came to the plate for Oakland to face New York pitcher Dave Righetti (LH). There was one out and a runner (Alfredo Griffin) on second.

On the 1-0 pitch, a low-over-the-middle fastball, Canseco lined a double into right center field, driving in Griffin to give the A's a 2-1 lead, which they held to win the game.

The ball was hit about 330 feet into the right-center gap. If New York's right fielder Dave Winfield had been positioned deep in right and shifted toward center, he could have caught the ball, holding Griffin on second and preventing the run.

**BARS: RIGHTFIELDER Deep and shifted toward center field**

Winfield would have been perfectly positioned to make the catch if he had been deep and shifted toward center field, as suggested by the BARS System fielding strategy. Please see Canseco's batting chart on the following page.

### Jose Canseco    Right-Handed Hitter
### Against All Left-Handed Pitchers All Teams

Fastball Average .295

|  | Inside | Middle | Outside |
|---|---|---|---|
| High | 5/ **0** / 0 | 10/ **200** / 2 | 3/ **0** / 0 |
| Med | 12/ **166** / 2 | 6/ **666** / 4 | 15/ **533** / 8 |
| Low | 3/ **333** / 1 | 12/ **333** / 4 | 5/ **0** / 0 |

## Atlanta at San Diego, August 5, 1986
## Atlanta 3, San Diego 2

In the top of the fifth, with one out and a runner on third base (Andres Thomas), Glenn Hubbard (RH) came to bat against the Padres' Ed Whitson (RH). On the 1-1 pitch, Hubbard hit a high-inside fastball into short center field, about 150 feet from home plate.

The San Diego shortstop could have caught this blooped pop-up if he had been playing up middle (shifted toward second).

### BARS: SHORTSTOP Up middle (shifted toward second base)

Gary Templeton, the San Diego shortstop, could have caught this short pop-up if he had been positioned correctly. The ball fell in, driving in the runner from third to give Atlanta a 1-0 lead which they never relinquished.

### Glenn Hubbard    Batting Right-Handed
### Against All Right-Handed Pitchers All Teams

Fastball Average .277

|  | Inside | Middle | Outside |
|---|---|---|---|
| High | 21/ **142** / 3 | 34/ **176** / 6 | 16/ **62** / 1 |
| Med | 74/ **351** / 26 | 49/ **367** / 18 | 90/ **288** / 26 |
| Low | 28/ **214** / 6 | 108/ **333** / 36 | 52/ **173** / 9 |

**Toronto at Kansas City, April 12, 1986**
**Kansas City 1, Toronto 0**

In the bottom of the eighth, with no score in the game, Jorge Orta (LH) came to bat for Kansas City. There were two outs and a runner (Buddy Biancalana) on second base.

The 1-2 pitch was a high-over-the-middle fastball that Orta hit to deep right center field for a double, driving in Biancalana with the game's only run.

If Jesse Barfield, Toronto's right fielder, had been positioned deep in right and shifted toward center, he could have caught the ball, ending the inning and preventing the run.

**BARS: RIGHTFIELDER Deep and shifted toward center field**

The ball was hit approximately 350 feet. If Barfield had been positioned as suggested, he would have been able to make the catch, preventing the hit and the run.

**Jorge Orta     Left-Handed Hitter**
**Against All Right-Handed Pitchers All Teams**

Fastball Average .296

|  | Outside | Middle | Inside |
|---|---|---|---|
| High | 17/<br>176 / 3 | 40/<br>350 / 14 | 4/<br>250 / 1 |
| Med | 98/<br>275 / 27 | 53/<br>433 / 23 | 45/<br>244 / 11 |
| Low | 21/<br>95 / 2 | 62/<br>338 / 21 | 31/<br>258 / 8 |

**Philadelphia at Chicago, September 10, 1986**
**Chicago 8, Philadelphia 7**

In the bottom of the sixth, Chicago at bat, Jody Davis (RH) came up to face Kent Tekulve (RH) with one out and Leon Durham on second. The count went to 2-2 and Davis hit a medium-high outside slider deep into left center field, about 350 feet from the plate.

Milt Thompson, the Philadelphia center fielder, was playing deep in straightaway center and couldn't reach the ball, which fell in for a double. If Thompson had been playing deep in center and shifted toward left field, he could have caught the ball for the out, preventing both the hit and the game-winning RBI.

## BARS: CENTERFIELDER Deep and shifted toward left field

If the Phillies' center fielder had been positioned as suggested, he could have caught the ball, preventing the run that gave the Cubs a 6-5 lead. They never trailed after this, winning 8-7.

### Jody Davis    Right-Handed Hitter
### Against All Right-Handed Pitchers All Teams

Slider Average .236

|  | Inside | Middle | Outside |
|---|---|---|---|
| High | 0 / 0 **0** | 3 / 1 **333** | 6 / 2 **333** |
| Med | 4 / 2 **500** | 3 / 1 **333** | 52 / 14 **269** |
| Low | 2 / 0 **0** | 17 / 5 **294** | 57 / 9 **157** |

## Kansas City at Toronto, July 12, 1987
## Toronto 3, Kansas City 2

With two outs in the bottom of the seventh inning, Jesse Barfield (RH) came to the plate for the Blue Jays, facing Kansas City right-hander Steve Farr. The game was tied 2-2. There were two outs and a runner was on third base.

On the 2-2 pitch, a low fastball over the middle of the plate , Barfield hit a ground ball to the normal shortstop position that went through for a single, driving in the game-winning RBI from third.

Angel Salazar, the Royals' shortstop, was playing shifted toward third. If he had been playing in his normal position, he could have fielded the ball and thrown Barfield out at first, ending the inning and preventing the run.

## BARS: SHORTSTOP  Normal position

The infield was playing Barfield to pull, but he hit a grounder that could have been fielded if the Kansas City shortstop had been playing in his normal fielding position.

### Jesse Barfield      Right-Handed Hitter
### Against All Right-Handed Pitchers All Teams

Fastball Average .316

|  | Inside | Middle | Outside |
|---|---|---|---|
| High | 7/ 142 /1 | 13/ 153 /2 | 6/ 333 /2 |
| Med | 19/ 315 /6 | 22/ 590 /13 | 45/ 355 /16 |
| Low | 12/ 416 /5 | 17/ 235 /4 | 17/ 58 /1 |

## Los Angeles at New York, May 23, 1987
## Los Angeles 4, New York 2

With two outs in the top of the seventh, New York right-hander Ron Darling faced Steve Sax (RH) with runners on first and second. The first pitch was a medium-high inside fastball that Sax bounced up the middle into center field, driving in the runner from second to give the Dodgers a 3-2 lead. They eventually won the game 4-2.

The ground ball was hit to the shortstop-side of second. Lenny Dykstra, the Met's center fielder, was playing deep in straightaway center. He had to run in to field the ground ball, and his throw to the plate was not in time to catch the runner scoring from second.

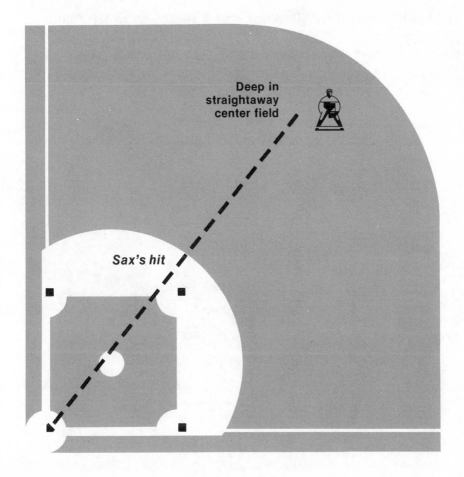

If Dykstra had been playing shorter in center, and shifted slightly toward left, he could possibly have fielded the ball in time to keep the runner from scoring. Please see the diagram on the following page.

**BARS: CENTERFIELDER** Short and shifted toward left field

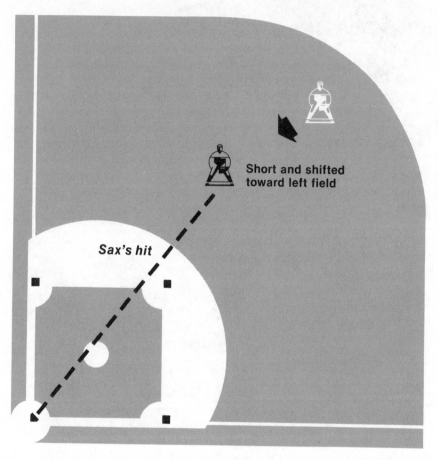

Short and shifted
toward left field

Sax's hit

The hit could not have been prevented, but proper positioning of the center fielder could possibly have prevented the run.

This particular game-winning RBI illustrates the overall importance of the Super Summary fielding strategy. Preventing actual hits is only one of the benefits that comes from correctly positioning all fielders.

When fielders are positioned correctly, they can get to the ball quickly, preventing runners from advancing and thereby directly reducing the number of runs scored.

In this instance, the Mets' center fielder could not have prevented the hit. But if he had been positioned as suggested by the BARS System fielding strategy, he would have had a chance to field the ball in time to prevent the run.

**Steve Sax    Right-Handed Hitter**
**Against All Right-Handed Pitchers All Teams**

Fastball Average .355

|  | Inside | Middle | Outside |
|---|---|---|---|
| High | 23 / 260 / 6 | 48 / 270 / 13 | 12 / 166 / 2 |
| Med | 45 / 422 / 19 | 22 / 318 / 7 | 54 / 370 / 20 |
| Low | 17 / 411 / 7 | 58 / 482 / 28 | 30 / 266 / 8 |

## Atlanta at Cincinnati, June 14, 1987
## Cincinnati 4, Atlanta 3

In the bottom of the eighth, with two outs and runners on first and second, Gene Garber (RH) faced Cincinnati hitter Dave Concepcion (RH). On the 2-1 pitch Concepcion hit a sinking line drive over the shortstop's head into short left center field, driving in the runner from second with the game-winning RBI. The pitch was a low-over-the-middle fastball.

Ken Griffey, the Atlanta left fielder, was playing deep in left field. He could not have caught the line drive in any case, but if he had been playing medium-deep and shifted toward center, he could possibly have fielded the ball in time to prevent the runner on second from scoring.

**BARS: LEFTFIELDER  Medium-deep and shifted**
**toward center field**

**Dave Concepcion    Right-Handed Hitter**
**Against All Right-Handed Pitchers All Teams**

Fastball Average .259

|  | Inside | Middle | Outside |
|---|---|---|---|
| High | 14 / 428 / 6 | 23 / 217 / 5 | 5 / 200 / 1 |
| Med | 40 / 325 / 13 | 16 / 187 / 3 | 30 / 233 / 7 |
| Low | 14 / 285 / 4 | 31 / 258 / 8 | 16 / 125 / 2 |

## New York at Cleveland, August 2, 1986
## Cleveland 6, New York 5

In the bottom of the tenth inning, with the score tied 5-5, Cory Snyder (RH) came to the plate against Yankee reliever Dave Righetti (LH). There were runners on first and second with one out.

Snyder fell behind in the count 1-2. Righetti then threw a high-inside fastball that Snyder blooped into short left field for a single, driving in Joe Carter from second with the game-winning RBI.

If the Yankee left fielder had been playing short in left, he could have caught the blooped pop-up, preventing the run.

**BARS: LEFTFIELDER Short and shifted toward center field**

The Yankee outfielders were playing Snyder too deep for this particular type and location of pitch. If the left fielder had been playing as suggested, this short pop fly could have been caught.

### Cory Snyder     Right-Handed Hitter
### Against All Left-Handed Pitchers All Teams

Fastball Average .296

|       | Inside    | Middle    | Outside   |
|-------|-----------|-----------|-----------|
| High  | 500 2/1   | 0 3/0     | 333 3/1   |
| Med   | 166 6/1   | 500 2/1   | 800 5/4   |
| Low   | 0 1/0     | 0 3/0     | 0 2/0     |

## Chicago at St. Louis, April 8, 1986
## St. Louis 2, Chicago 1

With no outs and no score in the game, Andy Van Slyke (LH) came to bat against Rick Sutcliffe (RH) in the bottom of the fourth inning. Tommy Herr was on third base and Jack Clark on second.

The 1-2 pitch was a medium-high outside curveball, which Van Slyke lined into right field for a single, driving in both runners. The Cardinals eventually won 2-1.

The ball was hit about 220 feet into right field toward the line. The Cubs' right fielder, Keith Moreland, probably could not have caught this ball in any case, but if he had been been positioned medium-deep and shifted toward the line, he could possibly have cut the ball off in time to prevent the second runner from scoring.

**BARS: RIGHTFIELDER  Medium-deep and shifted
toward the right field line**

The runner on third would have scored on the hit, but the runner on second possibly could have been prevented from scoring if Moreland had been positioned as suggested.

It is interesting to note here the different fielding positions required when Van Slyke is ahead and behind in the count.

In the actual situation, when Van Slyke was behind in the count 1-2, the BARS System fielding strategy calls for the right fielder to be positioned medium-deep and shifted toward the line, as described above. When Van Slyke is ahead in the count, the strategy calls for the right fielder to be positioned deep and straightaway in right field.

This shows how exacting the computer analysis of the BARS System can be, allowing fielders to take their best-possible positions in every situation.

**Andy Van Slyke    Left-Handed Hitter
Against All Right-Handed Pitchers All Teams**

Curve Average .200

|  | Outside | Middle | Inside |
|---|---|---|---|
| High | 2/<br>**0** / 0 | 4/<br>**250** / 1 | 0/<br>**0** / 0 |
| Med | 10/<br>**400** / 4 | 1/<br>**1000**/ 1 | 7/<br>**142** / 1 |
| Low | 8/<br>**0** / 0 | 5/<br>**200** / 1 | 3/<br>**0** / 0 |

**California at Detroit, May 13, 1987
Detroit 10, California 7**

In the bottom of the first inning, with two outs and runners on first and second, Larry Herndon (RH) came to the plate for the Tigers, facing

California left-hander John Candelaria. Herndon fell behind in the count 1-2, then hit a medium-outside fastball deep to left center between the center fielder and left fielder for a double, driving in Mike Heath from second base with the game-winning RBI. This gave Detroit a 1-0 lead and they never trailed.

The California center fielder, Gary Pettis, was playing medium-deep in straightaway center. If he had been playing deep and shifted toward left field (in the gap), he could have caught the ball, preventing the run.

**BARS: CENTERFIELDER Deep and shifted toward left field**

This ball could have been caught by Pettis if he had been positioned as suggested by the BARS System Super Summary. This would have prevented the game-winning RBI.

Although the final score was 10-7 Detroit, this first-inning game-winning RBI highlights the importance of using the best possible fielding strategy at all times.

**Larry Herndon      Right-Handed Hitter**
**Against All Left-Handed Pitchers All Teams**

Fastball Average .258

|  | Inside | Middle | Outside |
|---|---|---|---|
| High | 8/<br>125 / 1 | 7/<br>571 / 4 | 12/<br>333 / 4 |
| Med | 13/<br>153 / 2 | 13/<br>461 / 6 | 37/<br>108 / 4 |
| Low | 12/<br>333 / 4 | 22/<br>318 / 7 | 15/<br>266 / 4 |

**Atlanta at Houston, April 22, 1987**
**Houston 6, Atlanta 0**

In the bottom of the first inning, Bill Doran (batting LH) came to the plate for the Astros against Atlanta pitcher Dave Palmer (RH). On the 1-0 pitch, Palmer threw a high-over-the-middle fastball that Doran hit to deep right center field.

Both Albert Hall, the Atlanta center fielder, and Dale Murphy, the right fielder, were playing deep and straightaway in their respective positions.

Neither could get to the ball. Murphy threw himself headlong for it, missed, then got up and chased it to the wall.

By the time the ball was relayed back to the infield, Doran had circled the bases for an inside-the-park home run, which turned out to be the game-winning RBI.

The ball could have been caught if either of the two fielders had been playing deep in right center. The BARS System would have positioned the right fielder deep and shifted toward center field.

**BARS: RIGHTFIELDER Deep and shifted toward center field**

The ball could have been caught by Murphy if he had been positioned according to the BARS System Super Summary. That would have prevented this first inning game-winning RBI.

**Bill Doran    Left-Handed Hitter**
**Against All Right-Handed Pitchers All Teams**

Fastball Average .303

|      | Outside | Middle | Inside |
|------|---------|--------|--------|
| High | 27/259 / 7 | 45/200 / 9 | 7/0 / 0 |
| Med  | 60/316 / 19 | 34/382 / 13 | 32/312 / 10 |
| Low  | 22/227 / 5 | 48/437 / 21 | 28/285 / 8 |

**St. Louis at Atlanta, July 3, 1987**
**St. Louis 9, Atlanta 1**

With no score in the game, Willie McGee (batting LH) came to bat in the top of the fourth, facing Atlanta right-hander Charlie Puleo. With a runner on first base (Jack Clark) and two outs, McGee worked the count to 3-2, then lashed a high-inside fastball down the third base line, driving in Clark.

The ball could not have been caught, but if Ken Griffey, the Atlanta left fielder, had been playing medium-deep or short along the line, he could have cut off the ball and kept Clark from scoring.

As it was, Griffey was playing medium-deep and shifted toward center and could not reach the ball in time to prevent the run.

**BARS: LEFTFIELDER Short and shifted toward the left field line**

### Willie McGee    Batting Left-Handed
### Against All Right-Handed Pitchers All Teams

Fastball Average .330

|  | Outside | Middle | Inside |
|---|---|---|---|
| High | 7 / 142 / 1 | 23 / 304 / 7 | 21 / 238 / 5 |
| Med | 43 / 325 / 14 | 14 / 428 / 6 | 49 / 306 / 15 |
| Low | 17 / 235 / 4 | 37 / 459 / 17 | 25 / 360 / 9 |

If Griffey had been playing as suggested by the BARS System fielding strategy, he could have fielded the ball in time to prevent Clark from scoring from first base.

As an added note in this instance, the Atlanta third baseman was playing away from the line and could not stop McGee's hit. If he had been playing toward the line, he possibly could have caught the ball or knocked it down, keeping it in the infield. This would have held Clark at second.

While reviewing existing information, BARS System analysts have noticed that third basemen are out of position quite often.

The BARS System is now preparing fielding strategy for third basemen. When the strategy is completed, correct fielding positioning for third basemen will be available for each batter, based on type and location of pitch, as well as variations in the count. This will allow exact fielding positioning for all fielders.

Unlike the second baseman and the shortstop, which each have three suggested fielding positions in the BARS System fielding strategy, the third baseman will have two suggested positions: SHIFTED TOWARD THE LINE and NORMAL POSITION.


**St. Louis at Atlanta, July 5, 1987**
**St. Louis 4, Atlanta 1**

In the top of the seventh, Ozzie Smith (batting LH) came up to face Doyle Alexander (RH) with two outs and the bases loaded. The score was tied

1-1. On the first pitch, a high-over-the-middle change-up, Smith hit a grounder up the middle into center field.

Andres Thomas, the Atlanta shortstop, was playing at his normal position. If he had been playing up middle (shifted toward second base), he could have fielded the ball and forced the runner at second to end the inning.

**BARS: SHORTSTOP Up middle (shifted toward second base)**

If the Atlanta shortstop had been positioned more toward second base, he could have gotten to the ground and made a force out to end the inning, preventing the game-winning RBI.

As it was, the ball went into center field and two runs scored, giving St. Louis a 3-1 lead. St. Louis eventually won 4-1.

### Ozzie Smith    Batting Left-Handed
### Against All Right-Handed Pitchers All Teams

Change-Up Average .375

|  | Outside | Middle | Inside |
|---|---|---|---|
| High | 1/ 0 / 0 | 4/ 250 / 1 | 0/ 0 / 0 |
| Med | 4/ 500 / 2 | 2/ 500 / 1 | 2/ 500 / 1 |
| Low | 2/ 0 / 0 | 1/ 1000 / 1 | 0/ 0 / 0 |

**Los Angeles at Atlanta, June 9, 1987**
**Los Angeles 5, Atlanta 3**

In the top of the seventh, with two outs and a runner on second, Steve Sax (RH) came to the plate against Atlanta left-hander Zane Smith. On the 0-1 pitch, Smith threw a medium-high inside fastball that Sax popped-up to left center.

Ken Griffey, the Atlanta left fielder, was playing deep in straightaway left and couldn't get to the ball. It fell in front of him, allowing the runner to score from second. If Griffey had been playing medium-deep instead of deep, he could have caught this pop-up, preventing the RBI.

## BARS: LEFTFIELDER  Medium-deep in straightaway left field

Griffey would have had little trouble catching this ball if he had been positioned as suggested.

### Steve Sax    Right-Handed Hitter
### Against All Left-Handed Pitchers All Teams

Fastball Average .322

|  | Inside | Middle | Outside |
|---|---|---|---|
| High | $^{4}/_{250 \quad 1}$ | $^{13}/_{307 \quad 4}$ | $^{10}/_{100 \quad 1}$ |
| Med | $^{15}/_{533 \quad 8}$ | $^{1}/_{0 \quad 0}$ | $^{39}/_{487 \quad 19}$ |
| Low | $^{5}/_{0 \quad 0}$ | $^{22}/_{272 \quad 6}$ | $^{18}/_{111 \quad 2}$ |

## Chicago at Atlanta, May 30, 1987
## Chicago 11, Atlanta 6

In the top of the sixth, with two outs and runners on first and second, Chicago batter Shawon Dunston (RH) came up to face Atlanta right-hander Jim Acker. On the 1-0 pitch, Dunston hit a low-outside slider to short right field for a double, driving in the runner from second. The RBI made the score 4-3 Chicago, and the Cubs never trailed again.

The hit was a blooper over the second baseman's head. The ball could not have been caught, but if the Atlanta right fielder, Dale Murphy, who was playing in straightaway right, had been playing short or medium-deep and shifted toward center, he could possibly have fielded the ball in time to keep the runner on second from scoring.

## BARS: RIGHTFIELDER  Short and shifted toward center field

Murphy could not have caught the ball, but he could possibly have fielded the ball in time to cut off the game-winning RBI if he had been positioned as suggested by the BARS System fielding strategy.

If he had not wanted to play short in right field, he could have played medium-deep while anticipating that a ball could be hit to short right field.

## Shawon Dunston    Right-Handed Hitter
## Against All Right-Handed Pitchers All Teams

Slider Average .300

|  | Inside | Middle | Outside |
|---|---|---|---|
| High | $1000 \Big/ \begin{smallmatrix}1\\1\end{smallmatrix}$ | $0 \Big/ \begin{smallmatrix}1\\0\end{smallmatrix}$ | $200 \Big/ \begin{smallmatrix}5\\1\end{smallmatrix}$ |
| Med | $500 \Big/ \begin{smallmatrix}2\\1\end{smallmatrix}$ | $500 \Big/ \begin{smallmatrix}2\\1\end{smallmatrix}$ | $303 \Big/ \begin{smallmatrix}33\\10\end{smallmatrix}$ |
| Low | $1000 \Big/ \begin{smallmatrix}1\\1\end{smallmatrix}$ | $700 \Big/ \begin{smallmatrix}10\\7\end{smallmatrix}$ | $177 \Big/ \begin{smallmatrix}45\\8\end{smallmatrix}$ |

## Chicago at Atlanta, May 31, 1987
## Atlanta 2, Chicago 1

In the previous game, Chicago drove in the game-winning RBI with a hit that could have been prevented by positioning fielders as suggested by the BARS System fielding strategy. The next day, Atlanta returned the favor.

In the bottom of the tenth, with the score tied 1-1, Atlanta batter Gerald Perry (LH) faced Chicago right-hander Ed Lynch. There were two outs and Ken Oberkfell was on second. Perry fell behind in the count one ball to two strikes, then hit a high-inside fastball to medium-deep center field.

Chicago center fielder Dave Martinez was playing deep in straightaway center and couldn't get to the ball. It fell in, driving in Oberkfell with the winning run. If Martinez had been playing less deep, he could have caught the ball.

## BARS:  CENTERFIELDER  Medium-deep and shifted
## toward left field

Martinez could have caught the ball to end the inning, preventing the run.

### Gerald Perry     Left-Handed Hitter
### Against All Right-Handed Pitchers All Teams

Fastball Average .262

|  | Outside | Middle | Inside |
|---|---|---|---|
| High | 7/<br>285 / 2 | 40/<br>350 / 14 | 15/<br>400 / 6 |
| Med | 45/<br>266 / 12 | 18/<br>388 / 7 | 37/<br>243 / 9 |
| Low | 3/<br>0 / 0 | 45/<br>200 / 9 | 19/<br>52 / 1 |

## Kansas City at California, June 18, 1987
## Kansas City 10, California 4

In the top of the third inning, with two outs and runners on second and third, Royals' rookie Bo Jackson (RH) came to the plate against California right-hander Willie Frazier.

Jackson quickly fell behind 0-2, but when Frazier threw a low-outside fastball, Jackson bounced it up the middle into center field.

The California shortstop, Dick Schofield, was playing in his normal position. If he had been playing up middle (shifted toward second), the ball would have been hit right at him and he could have thrown Jackson out at first, ending the inning and preventing the runner on third from scoring what turned out to be the game-winning RBI.

## BARS:  SHORTSTOP  Up middle (shifted toward second base)

If the California shortstop had been playing as suggested, he could have fielded the ball and thrown Jackson out at first, ending the inning.

### Bo Jackson    Right-Handed Hitter
### Against All Right-Handed Pitchers All Teams

Fastball Average .266

|      | Inside | Middle | Outside |
|------|--------|--------|---------|
| High | 200 $5/1$ | 250 $4/1$ | 0 $3/0$ |
| Med  | 125 $8/1$ | 333 $3/1$ | 272 $11/3$ |
| Low  | 500 $2/1$ | 500 $4/2$ | 400 $5/2$ |

**Toronto at New York, September 30, 1986**
**New York 5, Toronto 2**

In the bottom of the first, with one out and runners on first and third, Dan Pasqua (LH) came to the plate for the Yankees. The first pitch was a low-over-the-middle fastball, which Pasqua hit to very deep left center field, scoring both runners. The second run was the game-winning RBI.

The Toronto center fielder was playing medium-deep in right center and couldn't reach the ball. Please see the diagram on the next page.

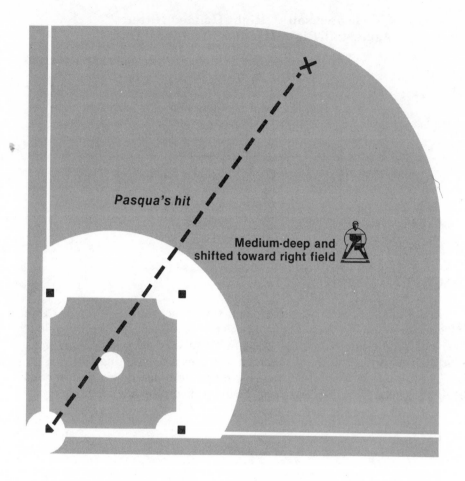

Pasqua's hit

Medium-deep and
shifted toward right field

The center fielder could have caught the ball if he had been playing deeper and more straightaway. Please see the diagram on the following page.

**BARS: CENTERFIELDER** Deep in straightaway center field

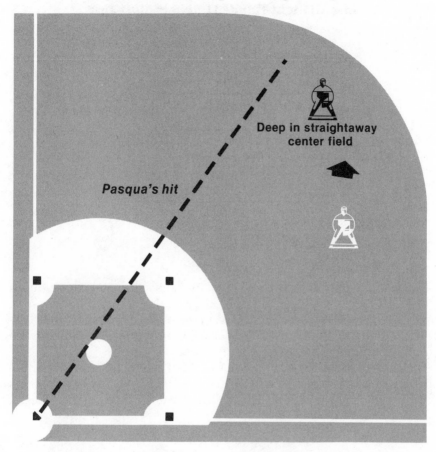

The center fielder could have caught the ball if he had been positioned according to the BARS System fielding strategy. The runner on third would have scored on the sacrifice fly, but the hit and the second run (the game-winning RBI) could have been prevented.

**Dan Pasqua    Left-Handed Hitter**
**Against All Right-Handed Pitchers All Teams**

Fastball Average .255

| | Outside | Middle | Inside |
|---|---|---|---|
| High | 11/272 / 3 | 6/166 / 1 | 1/0 / 0 |
| Med | 49/265 / 13 | 14/428 / 6 | 12/166 / 2 |
| Low | 9/222 / 2 | 19/263 / 5 | 8/125 / 1 |

## St. Louis at Atlanta, May 20, 1987
## St. Louis 5, Atlanta 4

In the top of the ninth with no outs, St. Louis shortstop Ozzie Smith (batting LH) came to bat against Gene Garber, Atlanta right-hander. With runners on first and second, the count went to 0-2. Garber then threw a low-outside fastball that Smith grounded between the first and second basemen for a single, driving in the game-winning run.

The Atlanta second baseman (Ken Oberkfell) was playing in his normal straightaway position and couldn't reach the ball. If he had been playing toward first, he could have fielded the ball and thrown Smith out at first base, preventing the game-winning RBI.

## BARS: SECOND  Shifted toward first base

The ball wasn't hit hard enough for a double play, but if the Atlanta second baseman had been shifted toward first base, he could have fielded the ball, preventing the run.

**Ozzie Smith    Batting Left-Handed**
**Against All Right-Handed Pitchers All Teams**

Fastball Average .316

| | Outside | Middle | Inside |
|---|---|---|---|
| High | 11 / 181 / 2 | 43 / 348 / 15 | 15 / 400 / 6 |
| Med | 42 / 309 / 13 | 31 / 322 / 10 | 49 / 265 / 13 |
| Low | 16 / 375 / 6 | 46 / 347 / 16 | 22 / 272 / 6 |

**San Francisco at St. Louis, May 4, 1987**
**San Francisco 10, St. Louis 7**

With one out and runners on first and second in the top of the eighth, San Francisco's Jose Uribe (batting RH) came to the plate to face St. Louis left-hander Ricky Horton.

The first pitch to Uribe was a high-over-the-middle fastball that he lined into left field for a single, driving in Candy Maldonado from second with the game's winning run.

The ball was hit to medium-deep left field. St. Louis left fielder Vince Coleman was playing deep in straightaway left and couldn't reach the ball. If he had been playing medium-deep, he could have made the catch and held the runners at first and second.

**BARS: LEFTFIELDER Medium-deep and straightaway in left field**

If Coleman had been playing medium-deep in left as suggested, he could have made the catch and prevented the run.

### Jose Uribe    Batting Right-Handed
### Against All Left-Handed Pitchers All Teams

Fastball Average .341

|  | Inside | Middle | Outside |
|---|---|---|---|
| High | 1 / <br> 0 / 0 | 6 / <br> 500 / 3 | 2 / <br> 0 / 0 |
| Med | 3 / <br> 0 / 0 | 2 / <br> 1000 / 2 | 7 / <br> 428 / 3 |
| Low | 4 / <br> 500 / 2 | 11 / <br> 272 / 3 | 5 / <br> 200 / 1 |

## St. Louis at Los Angeles, May 10, 1987
## Los Angeles 7, St. Louis 6

In the bottom of the eighth, Ken Landreaux (LH) came to bat for the Dodgers, facing Pat Perry (LH). There was one out and a runner (Mike Ramsey) on first base.

The first pitch was a fastball, low and inside, which Landreaux hit directly down the right field line. By the time the right fielder reached the ball and got it back to the infield, Ramsey had scored from first to give Los Angeles a 7-6 lead, which remained as the final score.

It is doubtful that the hit could have been prevented, but if the St. Louis right fielder had been playing medium-deep and shifted toward the right field line, he could have cut the ball off and had time to prevent the runner from scoring.

**BARS: RIGHTFIELDER    Medium-deep and shifted
toward the right field line**

The St. Louis right fielder would have been perfectly positioned to field the ball if he had been positioned as suggested. This would not have prevented the hit, but it could have enabled him to prevent the game-winning run.

**Ken Landreaux     Left-Handed Hitter**
**Against All Left-Handed Pitchers All Teams**

Fastball Average .416

| | Outside | Middle | Inside |
|---|---|---|---|
| High | 0 / 0 | 5 / 200 / 1 | 3 / 666 / 2 |
| Med | 5 / 400 / 2 | 4 / 500 / 2 | 2 / 500 / 1 |
| Low | 1 / 0 / 0 | 12 / 416 / 5 | 4 / 500 / 2 |

## Montreal at Philadelphia, June 6, 1987
## Philadelphia 4, Montreal 3

In the bottom of the first inning, with two outs and the bases loaded, Philadelphia batter Rick Schu (RH) came up to face Bob Sebra (RH). Schu fell behind in the count 1-2, then hit a low-over-the-middle fastball on the ground between the first and second basemen, driving in two runs.

Montreal second baseman Vance Law was playing shifted toward second base and couldn't reach the ball. If he had been playing in his normal position, he could have fielded the ball and thrown Schu out at first, ending the inning.

### BARS: SECOND BASEMAN Normal Position

The Montreal second baseman was playing the right-handed Schu to pull the ball. If the second baseman had been playing in his normal straightaway position, he could have fielded the ball, preventing Von Hayes and Mike Easler from scoring (Easler with the eventual game-winning run).

### Rick Schu    Right-Handed Hitter
### Against All Right-Handed Pitchers All Teams

Fastball Average .245

Inside    Middle    Outside

|       | Inside | Middle | Outside |
|-------|--------|--------|---------|
| High  | 4/ 250 / 1 | 10/ 200 / 2 | 4/ 500 / 2 |
| Med   | 7/ 285 / 2 | 5/ 200 / 1 | 11/ 181 / 2 |
| Low   | 1/ 0 / 0 | 8/ 250 / 2 | 3/ 333 / 1 |

## Montreal at San Francisco, August 25, 1986
## Montreal 6, San Francisco 5

In the top of the first inning, with one out and the bases loaded, Montreal's Mitch Webster (batting LH) came up to face Mike LaCoss (RH). Webster worked the count to 3-2, then hit a medium-high outside fastball on a low line into right center field, driving in Wallace Johnson and Tim Raines.

The San Francisco second baseman, Rob Thompson, was playing shifted too far toward first base. If he had been playing at his normal position, he could have caught this low line drive, preventing the hit and the runs.

## BARS: SECOND  Normal position

This hit gave Montreal a 2-0 lead and they went on to score five runs in the first inning. The final score was 6-5. If the San Francisco second baseman had been positioned as suggested by the BARS System fielding strategy, he could have caught the line drive.

### Mitch Webster  Batting Left-Handed
### Against All Right-Handed Pitchers All Teams

Fastball Average .302

|      | Outside | Middle | Inside |
|------|---------|--------|--------|
| High | 10/ 200 / 2 | 18/ 277 / 5 | 4/ 0 / 0 |
| Med  | 27/ 222 / 6 | 8/ 250 / 2 | 9/ 444 / 4 |
| Low  | 7/ 142 / 1 | 23/ 391 / 9 | 13/ 538 / 7 |

## Boston at New York, June 16, 1986
## Boston 10, New York 1

In the top of the first, Jim Rice (RH) came to bat against Yankee left-hander Ron Guidry. There was one out and runners were on second and third. On the 1-0 pitch, a low over-the-middle slider, Rice hit a ground ball to the shortstop-side of second base that skipped through for a single, driving in both runners.

New York shortstop Ivan DeJesus was playing shifted toward third base and couldn't reach the ball. If he had been playing at his normal shortstop position, he could have fielded the ball, keeping it in the infield.

This would at least have prevented the second, game-winning run from scoring. Possibly it would also have prevented the runner on third from scoring.

## BARS: SHORTSTOP  Normal Position

This is yet another example of a game-winning RBI that occurred in the first inning.

The Yankee shortstop could have prevented the RBI if he had been playing in his normal position, as suggested by the BARS System. These runs gave the Red Sox a 2-0 lead and they never trailed thereafter. The final score was 10-1.

### Jim Rice      Right-Handed Hitter
### Against All Left-Handed Pitchers All Teams

Slider Average .303

|       | Inside | Middle | Outside |
|-------|--------|--------|---------|
| High  | 500 $\diagup$ $^2\!/_1$ | 0 $\diagup$ $^1\!/_0$ | 1000 $\diagup$ $^1\!/_1$ |
| Med   | 500 $\diagup$ $^4\!/_2$ | 500 $\diagup$ $^4\!/_2$ | 250 $\diagup$ $^4\!/_1$ |
| Low   | 250 $\diagup$ $^4\!/_1$ | 111 $\diagup$ $^9\!/_1$ | 250 $\diagup$ $^4\!/_1$ |

## Philadelphia at Chicago, July 31, 1987
## Philadelphia 8, Chicago 5

In the top of the eighth, with the score tied 5-5, Philadelphia's Rick Schu (RH) came to the plate to hit against Scott Sanderson (RH). There was one out and runners were at first (Kent Tekulve) and second (Juan Samuel).

The 1-1 pitch was a low-over-the-middle fastball that Schu hit hard between the center and right fielders for a triple, driving in both runners.

The Cubs' center fielder, Bob Dernier, was playing medium-deep and shifted toward left field. The ball was hit about 360 feet to right center. If Dernier had been playing deep in straightaway center, he could have caught this long drive for the out, preventing the hit and holding the runners at first and second.

## BARS: CENTERFIELDER  Deep in straightaway center field

This ball was hit hard, but if Dernier had been positioned correctly he could have made the catch for the out, preventing the hit and both runs.

**Rick Schu     Right-Handed Hitter**
**Against All Right-Handed Pitchers All Teams**

Fastball Average .245

|  | Inside | Middle | Outside |
|---|---|---|---|
| High | 250 $^4\!/_1$ | 200 $^{10}\!/_2$ | 500 $^4\!/_2$ |
| Med | 285 $^7\!/_2$ | 200 $^5\!/_1$ | 181 $^{11}\!/_2$ |
| Low | 0 $^1\!/_0$ | 250 $^8\!/_2$ | 333 $^3\!/_1$ |

**Pittsburgh at Chicago, June 19, 1987**
**Pittsburgh 4, Chicago 0**

With one out and a runner on third base in the top of the first inning, Pittsburgh's Johnny Ray (batting LH) came up to face Dickie Noles (RH). There was no score in the game.

Ray fell behind in the count 1-2, then hit a medium-high inside slider on the ground to the shortstop-side of second base. The ball went through into center field for a single, driving in Barry Bonds from third. That made the score 1-0 and Pittsburgh never trailed.

The Cubs' shortstop, Mike Brumley, was playing shifted toward third base and couldn't reach the ball. Please see the diagram on the following page.

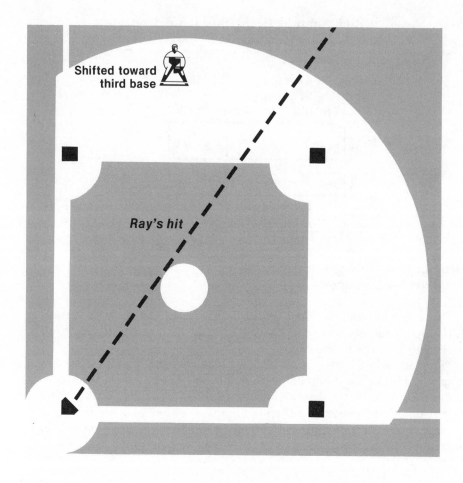

If the Cubs' shortstop had been playing shifted toward second, he would have been perfectly positioned to field the ball, holding the runner on third and throwing Ray out at first.

**BARS: SHORTSTOP Up middle (shifted toward second base)**

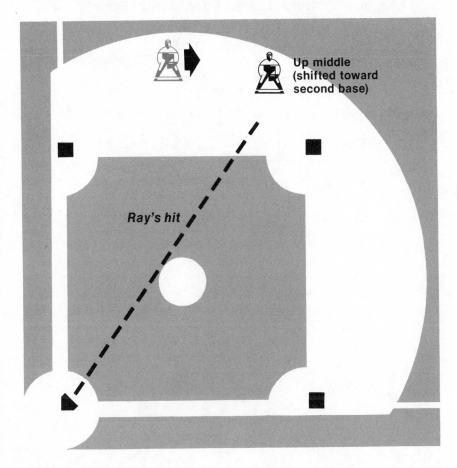

Brumley would have had to charge this ground ball, but if he had been shifted more toward second he could have fielded it, held the runner at third and thrown the batter out at first. Ray's batting chart is shown on the following page.

### Johnny Ray     Batting Left-Handed
### Against All Right-Handed Pitchers All Teams

Slider Average .206

|  | Outside | Middle | Inside |
|---|---|---|---|
| High | $0/$ **0** $/$ 0 | $0/$ **0** $/$ 0 | $0/$ **0** $/$ 0 |
| Med | $1/$ **0** $/$ 0 | $0/$ **0** $/$ 0 | $8/$ **125** $/$ 1 |
| Low | $2/$ **500** $/$ 1 | $8/$ **250** $/$ 2 | $10/$ **200** $/$ 2 |

## Personal Comments

It's going to be a lot easier for a team to start using the BARS System than most people think. When I first started gathering information and planning how the system might be used, everyone thought we'd need one computer in the manager's office, one in the dugout, one in the locker room and so on, just so everyone could have the information instantaneously. All kinds of computer people gave me advice. They said that everyone would need split-second information and that the computer would have to be right there during the game. But that's not right.

Actually, the BARS information — the Super Summary, the pitching charts, the Batting Order Report and so on — needs to be on paper so the manager and ballplayers can digest the details before the game starts. The information needs to be laid out so that it can be studied before the game and easily implemented during the game.

The time will come when a baseball team takes the first step and starts using the ideas in this book. Teams need to come up with innovative ideas. When a team does, they have an advantage for maybe two or three years, until everyone catches up with them. That was the case with Vince Lombardi, the football coach. He coached football just a little bit differently than anyone else and had great success until his assistant coaches went out and started doing the same thing he did. After that, he lost his advantage. Landry's probably the same way at Dallas.

That's what'll happen with the BARS System. The first team that uses it will have an advantage for a few years, until others catch up. After the 1988 season, the BARS System will have six full years of information. It would take quite a bit of time, effort and expense for another system to become competitive.

I think baseball fans will be amazed in the next few years at the communication between fielders. Each fielder might have a microphone and an earphone right in his cap so he can talk with the other fielders and the dugout. The whole game will change. Each fielder will become part of a tightly knit unit, like in football. They might move into the best position before each pitch, or break toward it as the pitch is thrown. They might try to fake out the batter or confuse him. That will change baseball considerably. And it will make the game even more interesting.

Some people will argue that positioning fielders by computer will change the game too much. But even now fielders always try to get in the best position for each batter. The BARS fielding strategy will give them more information to go on. This will make their fielding decisions more accurate and will allow them to be in the right position for each pitch.

# Chapter Seven

# How To Implement The Fielding Strategy In Actual Play

It would be easy to implement the coordination of fielders on a pitch-by-pitch basis as suggested in the BARS System. Signals could be given to the outfielders and infielders so they could move to their optimal positions for each pitch.

Rather than have the fielders go to the trouble of memorizing their positions (which would vary considerably for different types of pitches and pitch locations among batters), a simplified approach could be taken.

Each outfielder has only nine possible fielding locations:

Deep shifted left          Deep shifted right          Deep straightaway
Medium shifted left     Medium shifted right     Medium straightaway
Short shifted left          Short shifted right          Short straightaway

Each infielder currently involved — the shortstop and second baseman — has three locations. The shortstop can be positioned shifted toward third base, in his normal straightaway shortstop position or shifted toward second base (up middle). The second baseman can be positioned shifted toward second base (up middle), in his normal straightaway second baseman position or shifted toward first base.

Before each pitch, a signal could be given to each fielder, indicating his optimal fielding position. Numbers one through nine would be signalled to each outfielder, and numbers one through three to the two infielders.

For example, the designated fielding positions for the left fielder would be:

1. Deep toward the left line
2. Deep in straightaway left
3. Deep shifted toward center
4. Medium-deep toward the left line
5. Medium-deep in straightaway left
6. Medium-deep shifted toward center

7. Short toward the left line
8. Short in straightaway left
9 Short shifted toward center

Similar designations could be given for the other fielders.

## Mechanics On A Pitch-By-Pitch Basis

Before each pitch, the catcher or pitcher would signal the location and type of pitch to the dugout. Coaches or players in the dugout would interpret the optimal fielding locations and signal the fielders, indicating the fielding location each should move to.

Since there is a short amount of time between pitches, it would not be possible for one coach to signal all five fielders involved. Each fielder would have a separate coach or player signalling from the dugout. The coaches or players in the dugout would be versed in the system used, assuring speed and accuracy. The signals could be changed inning by inning, and could be hidden or disguised so the opposing team would not pick them up.

Once the fielders know their optimal fielding positions for a pitch, they could either move to that position immediately or wait and break toward that position with the pitch. This is common in football, a sport in which the defensive players position themselves in the best alignment for the type of play they feel is coming, and often adjust at the line of scrimmage or even after the ball has been snapped to confuse the opponent.

Such defensive coordination could be even more effective in baseball, because if the expected type of pitch is delivered to the expected location, there is close to a 90 percent probability that any hit ball will go exactly where anticipated.

To make the fielding strategy as simple as possible when implementing the BARS System, a team could elect to adjust fielders only when fastballs are thrown. Pitchers are most accurate with their fastballs and throw more of them than any other type of pitch, so this would be the most effective way to implement the system. Then, as coaches and players gain familiarity with the system, fielding adjustments could be made for curves, sliders and change-ups.

## Electronic Communication With Fielders

Another possibility that would greatly facilitate the positioning of fielders on each pitch would be to install an electronic system that would allow instantaneous communication between the players and the dugout.

Since there is always at least 30 to 45 seconds between pitches, there would be plenty of time to position each fielder. Signals could be given audibly via the electronic system from the dugout to each player, and the players could either assume their optimum positions before the pitch or break toward their positions with the pitch.

Sophisticated electronic systems are available to serve this purpose, and during the next few years the continuing advancement in electronics will provide even more effective communication systems.

## Such Coordination Would Be Simpler Than In Other Sports

Although such defensive coordination would be more complicated than the present defensive strategy in baseball, it would be simpler than the strategy used in other major sports.

College and professional football is based on exacting coordination between players. The exact position and assignment of every player is diagrammed for every play.

In modern football it would be unthinkable for a team to go to the line of scrimmage without an exact assignment for every member of the team. The sum total of the coordinated effort of all players is what makes or breaks a play. Missed assignments are the worst form of error.

Spectacular individual efforts — such as an intercepted pass or an open-field tackle — are the heart and soul of the game; but the more successful teams rate highest in the fundamentals, which include the basic coordination between players.

Coordinating the defensive alignment in baseball would be more effective than in football, because in football the defense merely guesses on any particular down what the play will be. When the offense comes to the line of scrimmage, the defensive team can align itself with great exactness, but it is not sure if the play will be a pass or a run. When the quarterback drops into shotgun formation, the defensive team knows that the play will very likely be a pass, but it does not know where the pass is going.

In baseball a much greater degree of accuracy is possible for the defense, because the defense (the pitcher) initiates each play. In baseball the defense can know with 90 percent probability where any hit ball will go by using the BARS System fielding strategy. By aligning itself with 90 percent probability, great defensive accuracy can be attained by any baseball team.

## *Personal Comments*

There's another thing that got me started on the BARS System. It has to do with golf. Putting is the best part of my golf game, and most people think that I'm a better than average putter. But I was such a poor putter when I was in my teens that Bill Stewart, two-time Missouri Amateur Champion and father of now-famous golf pro Payne Stewart, advised me to go out on the practice green and just putt, putt, putt — which is what I did one hour a day for a week.

After that I could at least keep the ball on line, but Bill Stewart said, "Bill, you always have the ball on line but you're always short." So I kept practicing. Whenever I got on the golf course and missed a putt inside ten feet, I'd get irritated because I wanted to make them all.

After I graduated from college, Bill stopped at Chillicothe every six weeks to play golf with me. We'd play for a little money so I could help finance him as he travelled around the country selling furniture. He could see that my game was improving, and he told me to start keeping track of each of my putts, especially putts that broke sharply one way or another. After that I made a mental note of each putt and wrote it down after the round. I kept a record of how many I missed on the high side, how many on the low side, how many I left short, how many I hit long.

As a result, when I came to certain types of putts I'd line them up differently than I normally would have. Say a putt broke left to right, and I had a mental note that I'd been missing a certain percentage of this type of putt on the low side. In that case, I'd force myself to line the putt up a little more above the hole. It didn't take long before my putts started dropping. It's hard to describe how much my game improved.

They say that as a person gets older he doesn't putt as well. But I think that if a person would really keep track of his putts, he would be a better putter. He could force himself to putt in a certain way, even if his eyes told him something different.

When I had success with that system, the thought crossed my mind that if being systematic turned my putting from the worst part of my golf game to the best, I could do something similar with baseball. It's funny how one thing leads to another, but I think that's one of the things that encouraged me to get started with the BARS System.

# Chapter Eight

---

# Computers In Sports

The preceding chapters present a unique approach to baseball strategy. Until now computers have been used for scouting and analysis only on the most limited basis. The BARS System, with its easily understood and practical reports, makes implementing computers into baseball easier and more dramatic than most baseball people have thought possible.

But the use of computers is not new in many other sports. The best example in team sports is football. Nearly every aspect of college and professional football has come under the scrutiny of computers, even to the point of scouting and anticipating the opposing team's offensive and defensive capabilities on a play-by-play basis.

When Dick Vermeil, who took the Philadelphia Eagles to the 1981 Super Bowl, was head coach at UCLA, he used computers to engineer a stunning upset of Ohio State in the 1976 Rose Bowl.

"I gave Vermeil computer reports on every conceivable Ohio State tendency," said Joe Guardino, who provides computerized scouting reports to professional and college teams. "Afterward, Dick said it was the easiest defensive game he ever played. He said it was never in doubt because he knew exactly what Ohio State was going to do." [1]

Over the last decade, most professional and many college teams have begun using computers to analyze individual and team performances.

"We've learned that a team gets the ball an average of 68 plays per game," said Hank Stram, former head coach of the Kansas City Chiefs who after retiring worked as a consultant for a California computer company that supplies many professional clubs. "These plays break down to a certain number of first-, second- and third-down situations. Every time a play takes place, we can compare its performance and execution not only to how that play worked in the past, but to the needs of our entire game plan...The game has become so complex that if you wait for halftime to adjust, you've already lost." [2]

No pro team has used the computer more extensively than the Dallas Cowboys, who have been in the National Football League playoffs more often than any other team. Cowboy president Tex Schramm was first impressed with the possibilities of computers when working for CBS-TV at the 1960 Winter Olympics in Squaw Valley.

"At first everyone laughed at us," recalls Gil Brandt, who set up the system for Schramm. "But only three years later Vince Lombardi asked if he and the Packers could join in our computerized scouting."[3]

## Use of Computers In Skiing, Golf, Auto Racing And Other Sports

Many sports that involve individual performance, such as skiing, golf, tennis and automobile racing, have utilized the computer to refine individual techniques.

In skiing, computers have been used to determine the most efficient body-tuck positions to minimize wind resistance. Computers have also been used to help design ski equipment for maximum effectiveness in different events and varying conditions of weather and terrain.

In golf, computers have been used to determine which muscles are used during different parts of the swing, and extensive research has been done with computers in designing golf clubs, balls and even golf courses.

The computer has found great inroads into track and field and other Olympic events. Extensive studies have been done to maximize the mechanical techniques used in different aspects of running, jumping, putting the shot and throwing the javelin. Many dramatic developments have resulted.

For example, computers have shown the best ways for shot putters to cross the ring and position themselves at the moment of releasing the shot, for javelin throwers to release the javelin, and for high jumpers to approach and clear the bar. In one interesting study, computers showed that U.S. world-class cyclists were pulling up on their handlebars while driving down on the pedals; the more successful European cyclists were found to be pushing down on both.

The computer has probably been used in automobile racing more than in any other sport. This is due in part to the extensive use of computers by the large commercial manufacturers (GM, Ford, Chrysler, Mercedes Benz, BMW, Toyota, etc.).

Successful drivers and their teams have experimented with computers to perfect every aspect of equipment and track performance. This includes not only determining the optimal speed and positioning at key points on a track, but lateral and longitudinal acceleration, fuel use, weight on each tire, and cylinder temperatures, among hundreds of other indicators of performance.

"This can give precise readings of what the car is doing and take a lot of the guesswork out of preparing and running a car," says Jim Mastro, who developed the computer equipment used on Chuck Needham's rocket car which broke the sound barrier on land in 1979.

## Baseball And Computers

No sport offers greater potential for dramatic growth through the use of computers than baseball. In part, this is because the same basic event occurs repetitively in baseball: a pitcher throws a ball to a stationary batter who either swings or does not, and who either hits the ball or misses.

This is unlike football, basketball, soccer or hockey, in which each play involves the complex jostling for position of every player on the field. Even though the inner game of baseball — the mental preparation of the players and the psychological momentum inning by inning — is as complex as in any sport, each separate play has a more similar, repetitive beginning.

Because of this repetitiveness, computers can analyze many key aspects of a hitter's past performance and find trends that can be used as the basis for strategy in actual pitch-by-pitch situations.

For example, if a manager could know that during the preceeding five seasons an opposing hitter had only a .100 average against high-outside fastballs, in comparison to a .200 average against waist-high outside fastballs and a .300 average against low-outside fastballs, a new exactness for strategy would come into play.

Such exactness would be a more powerful analytic tool than scouting reports saying that a hitter "has trouble with outside fastballs." Knowing that a hitter has more trouble with high-outside fastballs than with low-outside fastballs (and the opposite may easily be the case), appropriate pitching strategy could be taken.

Extending the example even further, if a manager could know the best possible position for his fielders on each of these pitches, an overall coordination could be developed in baseball as it has in other sports.

Winning baseball is an ongoing accumulation of small advantages. Almost every year we see division races decided by one or two games. Considering how many games are won and lost over the course of a season because of one misplayed pitch or because one fielder was out of position and could not reach a ball, it can be seen how important it is to take advantage of every strategic edge possible.

1. Robert S. Lyons, Jr., "Coaching by Computers", The Saturday Evening Post, September 1983

2. Stephen Kindel, "Plugged in Pigskin", Forbes, November 1983

3. Robert S. Lyons, Jr., "Coaching by Computers", The Saturday Evening Post, September 1983

## *Personal Comments*

The following chapter talks about how a sports psychologist would work with the BARS System to help baseball players improve their performance. Frank Boehm, the sports expert interviewed in the chapter, also works with players of other sports, such as basketball, football and golf.

I went to Frank a few times to improve my golf game. One of the many valuable tips he gave me was to get a picture of where I want to hit the ball each time I get ready for a shot. He advised me to address the ball and pick out a very small spot in the fairway where I'd like the ball to go. I'd always thought that I should pick out a big target so I would be more relaxed. But he said to focus on a very small target, and it worked well for me.

When it came to putting, he had me examine the hole and notice how large it is in comparison to the golf ball. Actually, the diameter of a golf hole is three golf balls across, and when you place a golf ball right by the hole, the hole looks large in comparison. Sometimes when you have a tricky putt, the hole can look awfully small. He told me to line three balls up by the hole so I could realize that if all three could fit into the hole at one time, one could fit in very easily.

I bought a practice golf cup the exact size of a golf hole and put it on my desk next to a golf ball, so I could continually refresh my thoughts of the ball fitting easily into the hole. I still have them on my desk, and it's helped my game quite a bit.

One time I was playing golf in Bermuda. My friends and I had played 18 holes in the morning and were going to play 9 more in the afternoon. We had a wait at the first tee, so I went to the practice green with some balls and my putter, but I didn't putt a single ball. I just stood there looking at the hole. I'd look at it and once in awhile reach down and put three balls by it to see how small the balls were in comparison.

People must have thought it was strange for me to just stand there looking at the hole, but I'll be darned if I didn't go out and tie the course record on those nine holes — four under par.

# Chapter Nine

# A Sports Psychologist Looks At The BARS System

It is well known that two athletes with comparable physical ability for a given sport may not perform equally well in actual competition. One may greatly excel the other. This is most commonly caused by a difference in attitude. Motivation, maintaining a positive self-image, and being willing to work on improving shortcomings are vitally important for sports success.

Frank Boehm is a psychologist who lives and works in Columbia, Missouri. Since his college days at the University of Arkansas he has been interested in helping athletes improve their performances by working with them on the fundamental psychological skills required for excellence in sports.

Frank has successfully worked with athletes in many different sports and has found that there are certain fundamental inner skills necessary for success in any athletic endeavor. In this chapter he talks about these inner skills and how he would use the BARS System information to assist in his work with professional baseball players.

**Q.** (Interviewer) *Over the years you've worked with athletes in many different sports. How did you first get started?*

**A.** (Frank Boehm) I first worked with a field goal kicker when I was at the University of Arkansas. He was having a problem duplicating in games what he could do in practice.

**Q.** *That's a common problem for kickers, isn't it?*

**A.** It is. They put themselves under a lot of pressure. They tend to think of themselves as being responsible for winning or losing a game.

**Q.** *How did you help him with the problem?*

**A.** A sports psychologist has best results by helping a person focus on the actual task that's performed. Kicking a field goal really means kicking the ball between two upright poles; scoring is only secondary.

So by helping a kicker to focus on the performance of what he is actually doing — moving his leg and kicking the ball in a desired direction — it takes the pressure away and allows the best chance for positive results.

That's how I started, and it was very successful.

**Q.** *Did you continue working with kickers?*

**A.** Yes, and with other football players as well.

I worked with several running backs who had problems with fumbling. Their coach had given them instructions about proper techniques for holding the ball, but no one had presented it to them on the basis of attitude.

I believe that they were thinking incorrectly. As they ran they were thinking about the details of how to hold the ball, when they should have just been focussing on the specific task — on the fact that the ball is in their possession and that no one can have it as long as they do.

I encouraged them to do something specifically to key themselves into a success mode of thinking — slap themselves on the leg or step on the sideline as they went in — something like that.

That helped each player adjust his mind, his mental computer, to tell himself, "Here I am in a game, I'm going to use the techniques I've been taught but I'm not going to think about them. I'm going to hold onto the ball because it's mine and no one is going to take it from me."

**Q.** *And that proved successful?*

**A.** Dramatically.

**Q.** *Just like that?*

**A.** An attitude is so fundamental to everything an athlete does on the field that once it improves, everything improves.

**Q.** *What other players have you worked with?*

**A.** I worked with an end who was having trouble catching the ball. It turned out that he was trying to think about the techniques of catching the ball even as he was catching it.

If someone walked in the room right now and threw you something, you'd probably catch it. That's because you're not thinking about it. Catching something is a straightforward act of mind/body coordination. It doesn't require thinking. The more you think about it, the harder it is to do.

That's the problem the end was having. By working to help him focus on the primary task — watching the ball and catching it — it took the pressure away from him and he started performing much better.

I also worked with a lineman who kept getting his legs banged up.

**Q.** *How could you work psychologically on something like that?*

**A.** It turned out that he would plant his feet instead of keeping his legs churning. As a result he'd take a hit and his knees would get hurt. If he'd kept his legs moving, when he took a hit his feet would slide and he wouldn't have a problem.

**Q.** *That sounds more like a mechanical adjustment.*

**A.** It's psychological to keep his feet moving. If his mental computer tells him to keep moving, he will.

When you work with athletes, the end results are always mechanical — holding onto the ball is mechanical — but it's the mental process controlling the mechanical activity that's important.

An athlete can't think about how he's doing something at the same time he's doing it. To be successful he has to just let his on-board system, his mental computer, know what he wants to do, then without aiming or trying to steer, he'll accomplish what he wants.

**Q.** *What other sports have you worked with?*

**A.** Quite a bit with basketball — golf, both amateur and professional — tennis — and, of course, baseball.

**Q.** *What difference do you find working with athletes in different sports?*

**A.** Actually, it's more of a similarity. I work with gifted athletes; I'm not a teacher. The people who come to me have already had many years of training. So when they're having some problem with their performance, it's usually a mental thing, an attitude thing.

What I've found is that each of us has an amazing computer inside that is capable of taking instruction and coordinating extremely refined and delicate physical movement. This coordination is the basis of everything in athletics — hitting a baseball, returning a serve, catching a pass, anything.

I don't focus as much on the psychology of an athlete as on his attitude. There have been a lot of top-quality, successful athletes — even on the professional level — who really weren't physically good enough to have the success they had.

The thing is that they didn't know they weren't good enough. They had the attitude to be successful and that carried them beyond any physical shortcomings. Mostly it's on the conscious level of attitude. It's not a mysterious or subconscious thing.

**Q.** *The BARS System is primarily a computerized scouting system for baseball. In what other sports have you experienced computers being widely used?*

**A.** Computers are used a lot in basketball. They use computers to graphically show individual players where on the floor they shoot best, and where they shoot worst.

**Q.** *The team charts each of its players?*

**A.** Right. The charts can be very exact and helpful. When a player sees a computer demonstration of what areas he shoots best from, he'll become more patient to get to his areas and not take poor shots.

He can become aware of his least-effective areas of shooting and either avoid shooting there — or better still — work on improving in those areas.

**Q.** *Is there an actual graph printed out that the player can study?*

**A.** That's right. I've seen them in different colors, or crosshatched, or with little boxes representing a player's best areas. The printouts are a graphic representation of a basketball court.

It's done somewhat like the BARS System: scouts watch a game and indicate where on the floor each shot is taken. They indicate whether a shot is made or missed, and the computer takes it from there.

**Q.** *Is the idea to gather information over a number of games?*

**A.** That's the purpose. Like the BARS System, the teams want to chart a player's trends over a long period.

**Q.** *Do many pro basketball teams do this?*

**A.** I'm not aware of any that don't.

**Q.** *How about college?*

**A.** I think most do.

**Q.** *For every shot in every game?*

**A.** Yes.

**Q.** *Do teams gather information like this on their opponents?*

**A.** Professional teams do, but not college as much. It would be too expensive for a college in California to scout a team from Florida.

That's what's so good about the BARS System. All the teams have been scouted so intensively.

**Q.** *Do professional basketball teams always scout their opponents like this?*

**A.** Always. They have the scouts right there at the games.

You'll notice pro players giving their opponents shots from certain locations on the floor. That's based on charts.

**Q.** *How do you use a basketball player's charts to improve his performance?*

**A.** One thing to realize is that charts can also limit a player. When a player feels that he can't hit from a particular spot, that guarantees he can't. What I'd have him do is re-examine that.

The important thing is to help him realize that physically it is possible for him to make baskets from the locations he's having trouble with. You work to take away the negative stigma of shooting from those areas. You get him to realize that it's the same physical act of shooting, whatever area of the court it is.

Once you get a player to focus on the actual task — the shooting of a basketball — the pressure and negative reinforcement he's had become secondary.

**Q.** *Have you had good results with this?*

**A.** Excellent results. When a player starts hitting from new spots on the floor, he'll go on a real streak until opposing teams adjust to him.

**Q.** *You mentioned that the charts used in basketball are similar in ways to those used in the BARS System.*

**A.** Similar in that teams chart the strengths and weaknesses of individual players, like the BARS System does.

**Q.** *And you could work with players the same way using the BARS charts?*

**A.** It would be very similar. If a baseball player feels that he can't hit a low-outside pitch, for instance, then he'll automatically have trouble with low-outside pitches. It's a self-fulfilling prophecy.

When a player believes that he can't do something, then he'll start acting as if he can't do it. If you ask him to change his belief and attitude, then you can start improving his performance.

**Q.** *What would you do if a professional baseball player came to you for help with his hitting?*

**A.** The first thing I'd do is examine his BARS batting charts, if the charts were available. Weaknesses are obvious when the charts show a player is hitting .400 in one location and .150 in another. Studying the BARS charts could save weeks of research.

**Q.** *After determining strengths and weaknesses, what then?*

**A.** I'd ask the player to be more patient for awhile and not swing at specific pitches that he has trouble with. The next step is to ask the player if there's anything physically wrong with him that makes him unable to hit these pitches. I'd ask him if his arms were too short or if his elbows didn't work right — or whatever.

But of course there wouldn't be anything physically preventing him from hitting these pitches. When he sees that he has the same number of fingers as other hitters and his eyes are 20-20 and his arms are long enough, I would hope to be able to convince him that it's not a physical thing causing him to have trouble.

That leaves only one thing: the mental aspect. It always gets back to the fact that when you think you can't do something, you can't.

**Q.** *So the player would realize that he has every physical capability of hitting that kind of pitch, but there's some mental block that's causing the difficulty?*

**A.** Or some knowledge block. Maybe he needs to learn something about how to hit those pitches.

But the first step is to get him to realize that it is possible to hit those pitches. I'll show him other players' BARS charts, showing that other people can hit fairly well in that area. If they can do it, he can do it. All he has to do is believe he can and then learn how.

**Q.** *What then? Send him to a coach?*

**A.** For the technical part, I would send him to a coach. But a lot depends on a player. What I'd suggest is to have someone throw to him. Have them throw whatever pitch he's having trouble with. But I'd have the player not think about trying to hit the ball. I'd only have him think about what direction he wants to hit the ball.

By getting a player away from worrying and thinking about trying to make contact, and by encouraging him to think only about what direction he wants to hit the ball, his mental computer will take him back to the task at hand. And he'll start hitting the ball.

**Q.** *Do players respond quickly to this?*

**A.** It's really much simpler than people think. It's usually a quick "Ah-ha" experience and the player starts doing better.

**Q.** *What about when a player's BARS charts show that he hits better in a particular situation — like when ahead or behind in the count?*

**A.** Most players hit better when ahead, I'd imagine. But some probably do hit better when behind.

**Q.** *That's what some BARS charts show.*

**A.** It's what drives a person. Some people respond differently to pressure, although everyone can learn to respond.

Great players learn how to use pressure, others let pressure use them. So a player who responds well in situations like that might hit better when behind in the count.

---

Note: the following two players, Frank White and Dave Winfield, hit better when behind in the count than when ahead, as indicated by the BARS System batting charts. These two players are among the many who hit better when behind than when ahead in the count.

### Frank White, Kansas City Royals    Right-Handed Hitter
### Against All Right-Handed Pitchers All Teams
### Average When Behind In The Count .297

| | Fastball Average .351 | | | Curve Average .280 | | |
|---|---|---|---|---|---|---|
| | Inside | Middle | Outside | Inside | Middle | Outside |
| High | 2 / 0 / 0 | 10 / 400 / 4 | 4 / 250 / 1 | 4 / 250 / 1 | 9 / 444 / 4 | 0 / 0 / 0 |
| Med | 14 / 428 / 6 | 16 / 437 / 7 | 21 / 285 / 6 | 4 / 0 / 0 | 7 / 285 / 2 | 15 / 400 / 6 |
| Low | 6 / 166 / 1 | 11 / 363 / 4 | 7 / 428 / 3 | 0 / 0 / 0 | 8 / 125 / 1 | 3 / 0 / 0 |

### Frank White     Right-Handed Hitter
### Against All Right-Handed Pitchers All Teams
### Average When Ahead In The Count .261

Fastball Average .300

|       | Inside | Middle | Outside |
|-------|--------|--------|---------|
| High  | 9 / 333 / 3 | 29 / 344 / 10 | 9 / 222 / 2 |
| Med   | 35 / 257 / 9 | 42 / 357 / 15 | 60 / 316 / 19 |
| Low   | 13 / 153 / 2 | 45 / 311 / 14 | 14 / 214 / 3 |

Curve Average .229

|       | Inside | Middle | Outside |
|-------|--------|--------|---------|
| High  | 1 / 0 / 0 | 8 / 500 / 4 | 1 / 0 / 0 |
| Med   | 8 / 250 / 2 | 10 / 500 / 5 | 18 / 0 / 0 |
| Low   | 1 / 1000 / 1 | 12 / 166 / 2 | 2 / 0 / 0 |

### Dave Winfield, New York Yankees     Right-Handed Hitter
### Against All Right-Handed Pitchers All Teams
### Average When Behind In The Count .333

Fastball Average .333

|       | Inside | Middle | Outside |
|-------|--------|--------|---------|
| High  | 2 / 500 / 1 | 8 / 250 / 2 | 3 / 333 / 1 |
| Med   | 9 / 333 / 3 | 5 / 800 / 4 | 25 / 360 / 9 |
| Low   | 6 / 0 / 0 | 11 / 272 / 3 | 3 / 333 / 1 |

Curve Average .322

|       | Inside | Middle | Outside |
|-------|--------|--------|---------|
| High  | 1 / 0 / 0 | 1 / 1000 / 1 | 1 / 0 / 0 |
| Med   | 5 / 600 / 3 | 2 / 0 / 0 | 11 / 363 / 4 |
| Low   | 0 / 0 / 0 | 2 / 0 / 0 | 8 / 250 / 2 |

### Dave Winfield     Right-Handed Hitter
### Against All Right-Handed Pitchers All Teams
### Average When Ahead In The Count .296

Fastball Average .326

|       | Inside | Middle | Outside |
|-------|--------|--------|---------|
| High  | 10 / 100 / 1 | 13 / 538 / 7 | 4 / 500 / 2 |
| Med   | 22 / 318 / 7 | 16 / 250 / 4 | 43 / 325 / 14 |
| Low   | 5 / 400 / 2 | 23 / 217 / 5 | 17 / 470 / 8 |

Curve Average .458

|       | Inside | Middle | Outside |
|-------|--------|--------|---------|
| High  | 1 / 1000 / 1 | 2 / 500 / 1 | 0 / 0 / 0 |
| Med   | 2 / 500 / 1 | 2 / 1000 / 2 | 8 / 250 / 2 |
| Low   | 0 / 0 / 0 | 3 / 333 / 1 | 6 / 500 / 3 |

**Q.** *But it would still be better for a player if he could hit as well when ahead as when behind. How would you work with him to improve?*

**A.** First I would ask him why he's limiting himself. He may feel that he can't hit until he has to, so he might be taking a couple of strikes to get into a position where he's behind, when he feels it's now or never. But that cuts down his chances.

You have to be very careful when you work with someone — as you help improve weaknesses, you don't want to take away from strengths. It's ticklish. You never want to take anything away from a person.

I would never trifle with a person's attitude to the point that he would lose the ability to hit when behind.

**Q.** *What would you do for him?*

**A.** I would show him that he does respond well to pressure. I'd use the BARS charts to show him that he hits well when behind in the count. But I'd also show him that he doesn't need that kind of pressure to hit. He probably hits well in batting practice, when there's very little pressure.

I'd reinforce his strengths. I'd tell him, "You do a great job under pressure, but you're also capable of doing a great job when you're under a little less pressure."

Then I'd work with him so that he would focus on the task at hand when he's ahead in the count. That means, focussing on hitting the ball in the direction he wants, rather than worrying about whether he can make contact with the ball.

If he can physically hit the ball when he's behind in the count, he can hit it when he's ahead. And the same is true in reverse. It's a matter of showing the player that he physically can do it, then allowing him to prove it to himself.

**Q.** *And he would improve in that area?*

**A.** Very quickly. Surprisingly quickly in most cases.

In looking at BARS charts for many teams, I've noticed that there are players who hit best in locations that are normally considered the most difficult — like low-outside or low-inside. They're best in those locations because they've worked at them and are confident that they can hit in those areas. So they wait for those pitches.

When they swing at pitches in other locations they only half believe they can hit them, so they seldom do. What they don't know is that they're perfectly capable of hitting all locations just as well as they do their best.

---

Note: The following two players, among many others in the major leagues, hit low-outside pitches very well, as indicated by their BARS System batting charts.

### Dave Parker     Left-Handed Hitter
### Against All Right-Handed Pitchers All Teams

Fastball Average .320

|  | Outside | Middle | Inside |
|---|---|---|---|
| High | 15/466 / 7 | 27/333 / 9 | 18/166 / 3 |
| Med | 42/309 / 13 | 18/388 / 7 | 41/317 / 13 |
| Low | 10/500 / 5 | 40/275 / 11 | 29/310 / 9 |

### Don Mattingly     Left-Handed Hitter
### Against All Right-Handed Pitchers All Teams

Fastball Average .366

|  | Outside | Middle | Inside |
|---|---|---|---|
| High | 37/432 / 16 | 32/343 / 11 | 14/571 / 8 |
| Med | 115/286 / 33 | 39/435 / 17 | 31/290 / 9 |
| Low | 35/457 / 16 | 70/400 / 28 | 23/304 / 7 |

On the other hand, some very fine players have difficulty hitting low-outside pitches. Wade Boggs and Ryne Sandberg are examples.

### Wade Boggs    Left-Handed Hitter
### Against All Right-Handed Pitchers All Teams

Fastball Average .348

| | Outside | Middle | Inside |
|---|---|---|---|
| High | 28/<br>**178** / 5 | 33/<br>**333** / 11 | 19/<br>**526** / 10 |
| Med | 173/<br>**341** / 59 | 57/<br>**438** / 25 | 84/<br>**404** / 34 |
| Low | 20/<br>**150** / 3 | 47/<br>**340** / 16 | 41/<br>**292** / 12 |

### Ryne Sandberg    Right-Handed Hitter
### Against All Right-Handed Pitchers All Teams

Fastball Average .358

| | Inside | Middle | Outside |
|---|---|---|---|
| High | 47/<br>**404** / 19 | 99/<br>**373** / 37 | 58/<br>**275** / 16 |
| Med | 91/<br>**384** / 35 | 53/<br>**547** / 29 | 210/<br>**371** / 78 |
| Low | 33/<br>**272** / 9 | 189/<br>**354** / 67 | 140/<br>**235** / 33 |

**Q.** *How would you use the BARS charts with a hitter in very specific situations, such as a pinch hitter preparing to face a particular pitcher?*

**A.** I don't think it would be any different for a pinch hitter than a regular hitter. He could study a pitcher and be more prepared for what and where the pitcher throws.

I can see how the BARS charts could help a coach pick a pinch hitter. Normally there would be several hitters on the bench. The coach could look at the BARS chart of the pitcher to see what he throws, then look at the BARS charts to see which hitter would be best against him.

**Q.** *What about pitchers? How do you see the BARS System helping them?*

**A.** If a pitcher or a catcher had an opposing batter's BARS chart, I think he could take the hitter apart. I think the pitcher could take a batting lineup apart.

If a team's pitching staff had an opposing team's batting charts, they could have a field day.

At the same time, if they had their own pitching charts, they could learn to break their own habits.

**Q.** *The BARS pitching reports show that pitchers actually tend to throw more to their own strengths than to batters' weaknesses.*

**A.** Each pitcher has pitches he feels best with. And usually the type of pitch and the favorite location of a pitch go together. For example, a pitcher may consistently try to catch the outside corner with a slider, but not the inside corner.

If catchers let pitchers pick their pitches, most pitchers would fall into terrible habits.

**Q.** *Why do you think baseball has been slower than other sports in starting to use computers?*

**A.** Knowing what I know about athletic performance, I don't understand why someone isn't using the BARS System already. I do know it's just a matter of time. The right people in an organization have to understand the advantages the BARS System would give them.

For the cost each year of not even the salary of one player — not even a utility infielder — a whole team could turn around.

If I were the owner of a team that I felt could be doing better, I'd look seriously at using computers, simply because the potential for improvement is so great.

**Q.** *A lot of baseball people are of the old school. They like to trust their own experience and intuition.*

**A.** I can see how a manager might feel that using computers to help make decisions could take something away from using his experience and instincts.

But computers won't take anything away. Baseball people should think of computers as tools. And I think they will. I think the time is coming.

There's not a team that can't improve and there's not a player who can't improve — in some way, at least. If you use the BARS System to help some of the players on a team, the whole team will improve.

**Q.** *What excites you most about working with baseball players using the BARS System?*

**A.** I think the potential for improvement of individual players is the most exciting aspect.

I'd like to take the BARS charts to spring camp. It wouldn't take any longer than that to effect the changes I've been talking about. It's not a year-long or even a month-long process. If a hitter did what was necessary, he'd improve very quickly in his weak areas.

It would be exciting for me to go to spring training and work with some marginal players, some players that the team had labeled: "fields OK, can't hit" or "can't hit the breaking pitch."

Even working with marginal players, I know I could improve them so that they'd become valuable to the team. There's nothing for the team to lose; those players aren't likely to make the team anyway. I'd use the BARS System and work with each player individually.

**Q.** *But you could use the BARS charts to work with established players as well, couldn't you?*

**A.** Every player has room to improve. Look at the BARS charts of even the top hitters. They have areas of weakness. Some of them might be surprised that they're only hitting .150 in a certain location. But they could improve in that location, and their overall performance would be the better for it.

**Q.** *If a team wanted you to help them implement the BARS System, what would you do?*

**A.** I'd work with the coaches, most likely. The hitting, pitching and fielding coaches.

**Q.** *How would you work with a hitting coach?*

**A.** The first thing would be to let the coach realize that I'm aware he knows more about hitting than I'll ever know. I would not be telling him how to do his job. All I'd be doing would be to give him a tool to help him define where a batter is having trouble. And I'd help him use that tool.

He knows how to help hitters get better, and if I can increase the coach's productivity, he'll be a better batting coach.

**Q.** *And with the pitching and fielding coaches?*

**A.** They have years of experience in their field. I would never begin to tell them what to do. All I'd bring in would be how they could work with the statistical information that the BARS System supplies.

I could help a team implement the BARS System with all their coaches. Knowing that the BARS System would be easy to use would probably make a team more likely to start with BARS.

**Q.** *What about the fielding aspect of the BARS System? We haven't talked about that.*

**A.** If a team could prevent an average of two or three hits a game, it would be phenomenal. If they could prevent even one hit a game, that would be phenomenal.

When pitchers and fielders work in tandem, it has to cut down the effectiveness of opposing hitters. And it's never been done before like it could be done using the BARS System.

The batting charts allow pitchers to know what a batter has trouble with. And since the fielders can know where a batter is likely to hit the ball, they can adjust as soon as he comes up.

Even if a batter saw the fielders adjusting and knew what they were doing, the only thing he could do would be to try something different. And if you can get a player to do something different, you've already got him.

There are so many different things involved in hitting and pitching and fielding that having a tool like the BARS System could help players and teams improve very quickly.

It's like bringing a science to the art, and helping the art get better.

## *Personal Comments*

Most people think the BARS System is a good idea, but they just don't want to take the time to study it, to get involved with it. A lot of people think computers are complicated, but they're really not. Computers just do the same thing over and over once you program them. That's why I designed it so the computer does all the work in the BARS System. I've done everything I could so that no one has to think.

Before the Super Summary program was worked out, there was so much information that it was almost impossible to figure out where the fielders should play for each pitch. We have five or more years of information, and it's just too much for a human being to work with. At this point in the BARS System, the computer takes the information and automatically positions each fielder in the best possible location. The computer prints it out in black and white, and it's accurate 90 percent of the time.

You don't need a high school education to understand the BARS System. I tried it out with my secretary's boy when he was in the seventh grade. He was a baseball player in little league. He brought some of his friends over to the house, and they were intrigued by the system. They followed the program as they watched a few games on TV. When they saw that the program could predict where a fastball to such and such a spot would be hit, or where a curveball would be hit, they got excited. These young kids understood it and had fun with it, so it can't be too hard to understand.

One day I was talking about the BARS System with a good friend of mine, Julien Thompson, who was my baseball coach and history teacher at the Lawrenceville School in Lawrenceville, New Jersey. He said, "Bill, the BARS System has to be simple because if it weren't you couldn't have thought of it!"

# Chapter Ten

# Examining Batting Weaknesses Using The BARS System Batting Charts

It is not the purpose of this book to focus unnecessarily on the specific weaknesses of individual players. The BARS System does, however, bring an exactness to baseball reporting that has not been available before. When looking at a player's batting charts, strengths and weaknesses are clearly shown.

In the preceding chapter, Frank Boehm, a sports psychologist, offered tips for players to improve their hitting by first using the BARS batting charts. Once players know exactly what their weaknesses are, they can hold off on those pitches until they have two strikes. By focussing on strengths, and by ultimately working to improve specific weaknesses, players can improve their overall effectiveness.

Most good hitters have learned to hold off on pitches to their weak locations. Poor hitters would do better by realizing their weaknesses and holding off on pitches that they have problems with until they have to swing.

This chapter begins with an examination of weaknesses within the charts of several players who have had trouble hitting with consistency. Later in the chapter, weaknesses are examined in the charts of several of the top hitters in the game.

## Mariano Duncan, Los Angeles Dodgers

Players often have ongoing difficulty with certain types and locations of pitches. The players and their coaches may know what these pitches are, but the BARS System pinpoints problem areas with great accuracy.

Switch-hitting Mariano Duncan of the Los Angeles Dodgers has difficulty with many different types of pitches. But he also has definite areas of strength.

Examining Duncan's fastball and curve charts against right-handed pitchers is interesting:

### Mariano Duncan    Batting Left-Handed
### Against All Right-Handed Pitchers All Teams
### Overall Batting Average .193

**Fastball Average .233**

|  | Outside | Middle | Inside |
|---|---|---|---|
| High | 21 / 142 / 3 | 25 / 320 / 8 | 8 / 250 / 2 |
| Med | 32 / 156 / 5 | 3 / 0 / 0 | 22 / 318 / 7 |
| Low | 12 / 166 / 2 | 25 / 280 / 7 | 15 / 266 / 4 |

**Curve Average .230**

|  | Outside | Middle | Inside |
|---|---|---|---|
| High | 0 / 0 / 0 | 3 / 666 / 2 | 0 / 0 / 0 |
| Med | 7 / 285 / 2 | 1 / 0 / 0 | 4 / 250 / 1 |
| Low | 3 / 0 / 0 | 3 / 0 / 0 | 5 / 200 / 1 |

Notice that Duncan has several strong fastball locations. His .318 in the medium-high inside location and his .320 in the high-over-the-middle location show that he can hit the ball. His .280 in low-over-the-middle and .266 against low-inside are also respectable.

His fastball problems are primarily with the outside locations. Adding up the numbers in his three outside fastball locations shows that Duncan has only ten hits in 65 at-bats ended by pitches to the outside locations. This is a definite weakness that gives pitchers too much of an advantage.

By laying off outside pitches until he has two strikes, Duncan could concentrate on his strong locations. By working to improve his performance against outside fastballs, he could become a more effective overall hitter.

Fewer recorded instances are available in Duncan's curveball chart, but it is apparent that he has difficulty with low curves.

When ahead in the count against right-handed pitchers, Duncan hits fastballs very well overall.

**Mariano Duncan   Batting Left-Handed**
**Against All Right-Handed Pitchers When Ahead In The Count**
**Overall Batting Average .245**

Fastball Average .289

|  | Outside | Middle | Inside |
|---|---|---|---|
| High | 6/<br>166 / 1 | 11/<br>363 / 4 | 6/<br>166 / 1 |
| Med | 11/<br>272 / 3 | 3/<br>0 / 0 | 10/<br>500 / 5 |
| Low | 6/<br>166 / 1 | 12/<br>250 / 3 | 11/<br>363 / 4 |

His difficulties in the high-outside and low-outside fastball locations persist, but he hits medium-high outside fastballs well when ahead in the count. He has high averages in several other locations also.

This increased ability when ahead in the count shows that Duncan has the ability to hit well when he has an advantage on the pitcher.

Against left-handed pitchers, the switch-hitting Duncan has similar BARS System batting patterns.

**Mariano Duncan   Batting Right-Handed**
**Against All Left-Handed Pitchers All Teams**
**Overall Batting Average .179**

Fastball Average .200

|  | Inside | Middle | Outside |
|---|---|---|---|
| High | 6/<br>0 / 0 | 11/<br>363 / 4 | 1/<br>0 / 0 |
| Med | 12/<br>250 / 3 | 2/<br>500 / 1 | 19/<br>157 / 3 |
| Low | 5/<br>0 / 0 | 19/<br>263 / 5 | 5/<br>0 / 0 |

Curve Average .250

|  | Inside | Middle | Outside |
|---|---|---|---|
| High | 2/<br>500 / 1 | 3/<br>666 / 2 | 1/<br>0 / 0 |
| Med | 1/<br>0 / 0 | 0/<br>0 / 0 | 5/<br>200 / 1 |
| Low | 1/<br>0 / 0 | 4/<br>250 / 1 | 7/<br>142 / 1 |

Duncan's fastball difficulties are primarily in the outside locations, as they were against right-handers. He hits medium-high inside fastballs fairly well (.250), but has problems with high-inside and low-inside fastballs. His only consistently strong fastball location against left-handers is high-over-the-middle (.363).

Duncan's weaknesses persist against both right- and left-handed pitchers. By becoming aware of the obvious weaknesses that his BARS charts indicate, Duncan could work to improve his overall performance.

### Steve Balboni, Seattle Mariners

Steve Balboni, a right-handed hitter, has great power but strikes out often. His BARS charts clearly indicate his problem locations.

First, against right-handed pitchers:

### Steve Balboni   Right-Handed Hitter
### Against All Right-Handed Pitchers All Teams
### Overall Batting Average .225

**Fastball Average .237**

|  | Inside | Middle | Outside |
|---|---|---|---|
| High | 24/ 0 / 0 | 39/ 256 /10 | 20/ 100 / 2 |
| Med | 72/ 194 /14 | 51/ 411 /21 | 95/ 210 /20 |
| Low | 25/ 80 / 2 | 80/ 337 /27 | 36/ 250 / 9 |

**Curve Average .202**

|  | Inside | Middle | Outside |
|---|---|---|---|
| High | 5/ 200 / 1 | 15/ 533 / 8 | 3/ 0 / 0 |
| Med | 15/ 400 / 6 | 22/ 454 /10 | 40/ 150 / 6 |
| Low | 8/ 125 / 1 | 26/ 115 / 3 | 39/ 0 / 0 |

**Slider Average .244**

|  | Inside | Middle | Outside |
|---|---|---|---|
| High | 3/ 0 / 0 | 8/ 375 / 3 | 4/ 500 / 2 |
| Med | 14/ 285 / 4 | 13/ 461 / 6 | 26/ 307 / 8 |
| Low | 2/ 0 / 0 | 18/ 277 / 5 | 39/ 76 / 3 |

**Change-Up Average .307**

|  | Inside | Middle | Outside |
|---|---|---|---|
| High | 2/ 1000/ 2 | 10/ 300 / 3 | 3/ 666 / 2 |
| Med | 2/ 1000/ 2 | 4/ 500 / 2 | 4/ 0 / 0 |
| Low | 1/ 0 / 0 | 6/ 0 / 0 | 7/ 142 / 1 |

Balboni's fastball chart is a study in contrasts. His medium-over-the-middle (.411) and low-over-the-middle (.337) averages are excellent. But his weaknesses in the high-inside (.000 on 0 for 24), low-inside (.080) and high-outside (.100) locations lower his overall effectiveness. His .210 in the medium-high outside location is also weak. This is his most highly pitched location and brings his overall average down considerably.

A great part of Balboni's fastball problems can be traced to his extreme weaknesses in several curve locations. His inability to hit low-outside curves (.000 on 0 for 39) and his problems in general with low curves and outside curves allow pitchers to completely disrupt his rhythm. By holding off on outside curves until he has two strikes, and by ultimately improving against these pitches, Balboni can improve his overall hitting.

This weakness extends to low-outside sliders (.076). With the exception of that single location, Balboni hits sliders fairly well.

When behind in the count, Balboni has more trouble with fastballs than when he is ahead in the count. When behind, he looks for curves and hits them fairly well overall. For simplicity's sake, only his fastball and curve charts will be shown.

### Steve Balboni    Right-Handed Hitter
### Against Right-Handed Pitchers When Behind In The Count
### Overall Batting Average .281

Fastball Average .225          Curve Average .409

|  | Inside | Middle | Outside | Inside | Middle | Outside |
|------|--------|--------|---------|--------|--------|---------|
| High | 4 / 0 / 0 | 3 / 333 / 1 | 4 / 0 / 0 | 2 / 0 / 0 | 5 / 600 / 3 | 1 / 0 / 0 |
| Med | 16 / 187 / 3 | 11 / 545 / 6 | 22 / 181 / 4 | 8 / 625 / 5 | 8 / 625 / 5 | 7 / 428 / 3 |
| Low | 3 / 0 / 0 | 14 / 214 / 3 | 3 / 333 / 1 | 3 / 0 / 0 | 7 / 285 / 2 | 3 / 0 / 0 |

The above charts show that against curveballs he has weaknesses in the four corner locations, but hits well in the other locations. His fastball averages are generally low. His inside fastball locations are weak; he has only three hits in 23 at-bats ended by pitches to the inside fastball locations.

When ahead in the count against right-handers his fastball average soars and his curve average falls. Again, only his fastball and curve charts are shown.

## Steve Balboni   Right-Handed Hitter
### Against Right-Handed Pitchers When Ahead In The Count
### Overall Batting Average .319

### Fastball Average .343

|      | Inside      | Middle       | Outside      |
|------|-------------|--------------|--------------|
| High | 4 / 0 / 0   | 11 / 636 / 7 | 2 / 1000 / 2 |
| Med  | 26 / 192 / 5 | 24 / 375 / 9 | 38 / 315 / 12 |
| Low  | 7 / 142 / 1 | 35 / 400 / 14 | 16 / 375 / 6 |

### Curve Average .243

|      | Inside       | Middle       | Outside      |
|------|--------------|--------------|--------------|
| High | 2 / 0 / 0    | 6 / 500 / 3  | 2 / 0 / 0    |
| Med  | 3 / 0 / 0    | 6 / 500 / 3  | 13 / 153 / 2 |
| Low  | 1 / 1000 / 1 | 6 / 166 / 1  | 2 / 0 / 0    |

Except for the inside fastball locations, Balboni's fastball averages are superb when ahead in the count.  His curve averages are generally weak.

Even though Balboni's medium-high inside fastball average does not rise significantly when he is ahead in the count compared to when he is behind, he hits the ball with much greater authority, pulling it deep to all fields.

MEDIUM-HIGH INSIDE FASTBALLS
(THROWN TO BALBONI WHEN HE IS AHEAD IN THE COUNT)

BATTING AVERAGE .192
   *PLAY*
LEFTFIELDER        Deep and shifted toward the left field line
CENTERFIELDER      Deep and shifted toward left field
RIGHTFIELDER       Deep and shifted toward center field
SHORTSTOP          Shifted toward third base
SECOND             Normal position

MEDIUM-HIGH INSIDE FASTBALLS
(THROWN TO BALBONI WHEN HE IS BEHIND IN THE COUNT)

BATTING AVERAGE .187
   *PLAY*
LEFTFIELDER        Deep and shifted toward the left field line
CENTERFIELDER      Medium-deep in straightaway center field
RIGHTFIELDER       Short and shifted toward center field
SHORTSTOP          Up middle (shifted toward second base)
SECOND             No recorded instances

## Balboni Against Left-Handed Pitchers

Against left-handed pitchers Balboni's fastball and curve averages are higher than against right-handers.

### Steve Balboni  Right-Handed Hitter
### Against All Left-Handed Pitchers All Teams
### Overall Batting Average .270

**Fastball Average .299**

| | Inside | Middle | Outside |
|---|---|---|---|
| **High** | 11/ <br> 0 / 0 | 17/ <br> 176 / 3 | 11/ <br> 90 / 1 |
| **Med** | 16/ <br> 250 / 4 | 24/ <br> 541 / 13 | 52/ <br> 365 / 19 |
| **Low** | 12/ <br> 333 / 4 | 38/ <br> 368 / 14 | 16/ <br> 62 / 1 |

**Curve Average .323**

| | Inside | Middle | Outside |
|---|---|---|---|
| **High** | 1/ <br> 0 / 0 | 7/ <br> 428 / 3 | 3/ <br> 666 / 2 |
| **Med** | 9/ <br> 333 / 3 | 10/ <br> 300 / 3 | 12/ <br> 333 / 4 |
| **Low** | 6/ <br> 166 / 1 | 13/ <br> 384 / 5 | 7/ <br> 142 / 1 |

**Slider Average .156**

| | Inside | Middle | Outside |
|---|---|---|---|
| **High** | 1/ <br> 0 / 0 | 2/ <br> 0 / 0 | 1/ <br> 0 / 0 |
| **Med** | 3/ <br> 333 / 1 | 4/ <br> 500 / 2 | 5/ <br> 400 / 2 |
| **Low** | 4/ <br> 0 / 0 | 6/ <br> 0 / 0 | 6/ <br> 0 / 0 |

**Change-Up Average .241**

| | Inside | Middle | Outside |
|---|---|---|---|
| **High** | 1/ <br> 0 / 0 | 5/ <br> 0 / 0 | 1/ <br> 0 / 0 |
| **Med** | 3/ <br> 333 / 1 | 0/ <br> 0 / 0 | 8/ <br> 125 / 1 |
| **Low** | 0/ <br> 0 / 0 | 10/ <br> 500 / 5 | 1/ <br> 0 / 0 |

Against left-handed pitchers, Balboni has several very strong fastball locations, but his performance against fastballs to the high locations and to the low-outside location brings down his overall average. He hits curves much better against left-handers than against right-handers, and this in itself may contribute to his better fastball average against left-handers.

When ahead in the count against left-handed pitchers, Balboni hits fastballs and curves very strongly.

### Steve Balboni    Right-Handed Hitter
### Against All Left-Handed Pitchers When Ahead In The Count
### Overall Batting Average .364

Fastball Average .393

|      | Inside | Middle | Outside |
|------|--------|--------|---------|
| High | 0 / 0 / 0 | 2 / 0 / 0 | 2 / 500 / 1 |
| Med  | 7 / 285 / 2 | 10 / 800 / 8 | 14 / 357 / 5 |
| Low  | 2 / 500 / 1 | 18 / 388 / 7 | 6 / 0 / 0 |

Curve Average .523

|      | Inside | Middle | Outside |
|------|--------|--------|---------|
| High | 0 / 0 / 0 | 5 / 400 / 2 | 0 / 0 / 0 |
| Med  | 3 / 666 / 2 | 4 / 250 / 1 | 4 / 750 / 3 |
| Low  | 1 / 1000 / 1 | 3 / 666 / 2 | 1 / 0 / 0 |

There is no question that Balboni can hit well against left-handed pitchers, especially when he is ahead in the count.  By improving his noticeable weaknesses against curves  and inside fastballs when facing right-handers, he could become a much more effective overall hitter.

## Jim Presley,  Seattle Mariners

Right-handed Jim Presley of the Seattle Mariners is a fairly good fastball hitter whose problems with curves bring down his overall effectiveness.

### Jim Presley    Right-Handed Hitter
### Against All Right-Handed Pitchers All Teams
### Overall Batting Average .219

Fastball Average .286

|      | Inside | Middle | Outside |
|------|--------|--------|---------|
| High | 11 / 0 / 0 | 15 / 400 / 6 | 10 / 300 / 3 |
| Med  | 25 / 320 / 8 | 9 / 333 / 3 | 50 / 260 / 13 |
| Low  | 11 / 272 / 3 | 28 / 392 / 11 | 12 / 166 / 2 |

Curve Average .086

|      | Inside | Middle | Outside |
|------|--------|--------|---------|
| High | 1 / 0 / 0 | 1 / 0 / 0 | 2 / 500 / 1 |
| Med  | 3 / 333 / 1 | 4 / 250 / 1 | 14 / 0 / 0 |
| Low  | 1 / 0 / 0 | 10 / 0 / 0 | 22 / 90 / 2 |

Slider Average .239      Change-Up Average .111

| | Inside | Middle | Outside | Inside | Middle | Outside |
|---|---|---|---|---|---|---|
| High | 0/0   0 | 1/0   0 | 1/0   0 | 0/0   0 | 1/1000   1 | 1/0   0 |
| Med | 2/0   0 | 3/0   0 | 14/285   4 | 1/0   0 | 0/0   0 | 2/0   0 |
| Low | 0/0   0 | 7/571   4 | 18/166   3 | 0/0   0 | 2/0   0 | 2/0   0 |

It is obvious that Presley hits fastballs fairly well overall. His .392 average in the low-over-the-middle fastball location, his .400 in the high-over-the middle location and his .320 in the medium-high inside location are first rate. His .260 in the highly pitched medium-high outside fastball location, however, is only fair. His .166 in low-outside and .000 in high-inside (on 0 for 11) present specific weaknesses to pitchers and definite areas for Presley to work on.

His overall curve average of .086 is extremely weak. He has difficulty with curves in the low and the outside locations. This inability to hit curves keeps him off balance and hinders his ability to hit fastballs. By working on improving his performance against curves, Presley's overall performance could improve.

It is interesting to look at the direction and distance Presley tends to hit pitches in his key locations. He hits low-outside curves and low-outside fastballs weakly.


LOW-OUTSIDE CURVEBALLS

BATTING AVERAGE .090
    *PLAY*
LEFTFIELDER      Medium-deep and shifted toward the left field line
CENTERFIELDER      No recorded instances
RIGHTFIELDER      Medium-deep and shifted toward the right field line
SHORTSTOP      Normal position
SECOND      No recorded instances

LOW-OUTSIDE FASTBALLS

BATTING AVERAGE .166
  *PLAY*
LEFTFIELDER          No recorded instances
CENTERFIELDER        Medium-deep and shifted toward left field
RIGHTFIELDER         Medium-deep in straightaway right field
SHORTSTOP            Up middle (shifted toward second base)
SECOND               No recorded instances

The above records are in complete contrast to the way Presley drives low-over-the-middle fastballs deep to all fields.

LOW-OVER-THE-MIDDLE FASTBALLS

BATTING AVERAGE .392
  *PLAY*
LEFTFIELDER          Deep in straightaway left field
CENTERFIELDER        Deep and shifted toward left field
RIGHTFIELDER         Deep and shifted toward center field
SHORTSTOP            Up middle (shifted toward second base)
SECOND               Normal position

## Presley Against Left-Handed Pitchers

Against left-handed pitchers, Presley hits fastballs extremely well:

### Jim Presley    Right-Handed Hitter
### Against All Left-Handed Pitchers All Teams
### Overall Batting Average .291

Fastball Average .388                Curve Average .200

|       | Inside | Middle | Outside |   | Inside | Middle | Outside |
|-------|--------|--------|---------|---|--------|--------|---------|
| High  | 2/ 500 / 1 | 4/ 250 / 1 | 4/ 0 / 0 |   | 0/ 0 / 0 | 0/ 0 / 0 | 2/ 500 / 1 |
| Med   | 7/ 428 / 3 | 3/ 666 / 2 | 16/ 375 / 6 |   | 3/ 0 / 0 | 2/ 0 / 0 | 5/ 600 / 3 |
| Low   | 5/ 400 / 2 | 15/ 466 / 7 | 11/ 363 / 4 |   | 5/ 0 / 0 | 2/ 0 / 0 | 1/ 0 / 0 |

Against left-handed pitchers, Presley has no weak fastball locations. His 0-for-4 against high-outside fastballs is a possible weakness, but there are too few instances to make an accurate determination.

He has difficulty with curveballs against lefties. His 3-for-5 record against medium-high outside curves is a good indication, but his weak performances against inside and against low curves show that he has room for improvement.

## Bob Boone, California Angels

Bob Boone, catcher for the Angels, is known more for his defensive than offensive ability. A right-handed hitter, Boone has trouble against both right- and left-handed pitchers.

First, against right-handers:

### Bob Boone  Right-Handed Hitter
### Against All Right-Handed Pitchers All Teams
### Overall Batting Average .205

#### Fastball Average .246

|      | Inside | Middle | Outside |
|------|--------|--------|---------|
| High | 11 / 181 / 2 | 23 / 391 / 9 | 6 / 666 / 4 |
| Med  | 44 / 272 / 12 | 18 / 166 / 3 | 51 / 215 / 11 |
| Low  | 5 / 400 / 2 | 27 / 111 / 3 | 10 / 200 / 2 |

#### Curve Average .185

|      | Inside | Middle | Outside |
|------|--------|--------|---------|
| High | 1 / 1000 / 1 | 6 / 333 / 2 | 2 / 500 / 1 |
| Med  | 10 / 200 / 2 | 3 / 0 / 0 | 19 / 52 / 1 |
| Low  | 0 / 0 / 0 | 7 / 285 / 2 | 6 / 166 / 1 |

#### Slider Average .179

|      | Inside | Middle | Outside |
|------|--------|--------|---------|
| High | 0 / 0 / 0 | 2 / 0 / 0 | 2 / 0 / 0 |
| Med  | 5 / 400 / 2 | 0 / 0 / 0 | 12 / 166 / 2 |
| Low  | 1 / 0 / 0 | 6 / 333 / 2 | 11 / 90 / 1 |

#### Change-Up Average .090

|      | Inside | Middle | Outside |
|------|--------|--------|---------|
| High | 0 / 0 / 0 | 2 / 0 / 0 | 0 / 0 / 0 |
| Med  | 2 / 500 / 1 | 0 / 0 / 0 | 2 / 0 / 0 |
| Low  | 1 / 0 / 0 | 1 / 0 / 0 | 3 / 0 / 0 |

The above charts show that Boone has difficulty with all types of pitches. His .246 overall fastball average is low, but he does have high averages in a few fastball locations. His .272 against medium-high inside fastballs is adequate, and his .391 against high-over-the-middle fastballs is excellent. Several other locations also have high averages, but they are less significant because the averages are based on fewer recorded instances. His good locations show that he can hit fastballs, and with added work could improve his overall performance.

Boone's weakest area in his fastball chart is in the four locations bordering the low-outside location: low-outside (.200), medium-high outside (.215), low-over-the-middle (.111) and medium-over-the-middle (.166). Improvement in these four locations, which are within the same general area of the strike zone, could greatly improve his overall average.

Boone's curve chart clearly defines his problems with breaking balls: he hits high curves well but hits medium-high and low curves poorly. His difficulties with low-outside pitches extend into his slider and change-up charts.

Boone has no recorded hit balls to left field in the low-outside fastball, curve or change-up charts. He tends to hit the ball short or medium-deep to center and right.

LOW-OUTSIDE FASTBALLS

BATTING AVERAGE .200
> PLAY

| | |
|---|---|
| LEFTFIELDER | No recorded instances |
| CENTERFIELDER | Medium-deep in straightaway center field |
| RIGHTFIELDER | Medium-deep and shifted toward the right field line |
| SHORTSTOP | Normal position |
| SECOND | No recorded instances |

LOW-OUTSIDE CURVEBALLS

BATTING AVERAGE .166
> PLAY

| | |
|---|---|
| LEFTFIELDER | No recorded instances |
| CENTERFIELDER | No recorded instances |
| RIGHTFIELDER | Short and shifted toward the right field line |
| SHORTSTOP | No recorded instances |
| SECOND | No recorded instances |

LOW-OUTSIDE SLIDERS

BATTING AVERAGE .090
*PLAY*
LEFTFIELDER          No recorded instances
CENTERFIELDER        Medium-deep in straightaway center field
RIGHTFIELDER         Medium-deep and shifted toward center field
SHORTSTOP            Up middle (shifted toward second base)
SECOND               Shifted toward first base

## Boone Against Left-Handed Pitchers

Against left-handed pitchers, Boone has several strong fastball locations and his overall fastball average is higher than against right-handed pitchers.

### Bob Boone  Right-Handed Hitter
### Against All Left-Handed Pitchers All Teams
### Overall Batting Average .241

Fastball Average .262                    Curve Average .153

| | Inside | Middle | Outside | Inside | Middle | Outside |
|---|---|---|---|---|---|---|
| High | 8/125 / 1 | 7/142 / 1 | 11/272 / 3 | 1/0 / 0 | 0/0 / 0 | 0/0 / 0 |
| Med | 15/333 / 5 | 14/357 / 5 | 23/304 / 7 | 0/0 / 0 | 3/333 / 1 | 1/0 / 0 |
| Low | 3/0 / 0 | 26/269 / 7 | 15/200 / 3 | 1/0 / 0 | 3/333 / 1 | 4/0 / 0 |

All three of Boone's medium-high fastball locations are strong against left-handers. His low-over-the-middle (.269) and high-outside (.272) averages are adequate.  But his other fastball locations bring his overall performance down.

He hits some low-outside fastballs against left-handers to left field.

LOW-OUTSIDE FASTBALLS
(THROWN TO BOONE BY LEFT-HANDED PITCHERS)

BATTING AVERAGE .200
*PLAY*

| | |
|---|---|
| LEFTFIELDER | Medium-deep in straightaway left field |
| CENTERFIELDER | Deep in straightaway center field |
| RIGHTFIELDER | Deep in straightaway right field |
| SHORTSTOP | Up middle (shifted toward second base) |
| SECOND | No recorded instances |

He hits medium-high outside fastballs strongly against left-handers.

MEDIUM-HIGH OUTSIDE FASTBALLS
(THROWN TO BOONE BY LEFT-HANDED PITCHERS)

BATTING AVERAGE .304
*PLAY*

| | |
|---|---|
| LEFTFIELDER | Deep in straightaway left field |
| CENTERFIELDER | Deep and shifted toward left field |
| RIGHTFIELDER | Deep in straightaway right field |
| SHORTSTOP | Normal position |
| SECOND | Normal position |

Boone's high average against medium-over-the-middle fastballs (.357), could be partly due to fielders being out of position for the unusual way he hits these pitches.

MEDIUM-OVER-THE-MIDDLE FASTBALLS
(THROWN TO BOONE BY LEFT-HANDED PITCHERS)

BATTING AVERAGE .357
*PLAY*

| | |
|---|---|
| LEFTFIELDER | Medium-deep in straightaway left field |
| CENTERFIELDER | Medium-deep and shifted toward right field |
| RIGHTFIELDER | Short in straightaway right field |
| SHORTSTOP | Normal position |
| SECOND | No recorded instances |

There are fewer recorded instances in Boone's curve charts against left-handers, but the general trend is clear: difficulty with low-outside pitches.

If Boone could improve his obvious weaknesses, his hitting could become more effective.

# Weaknesses in Very Strong Hitters

### Willie Upshaw, Toronto Blue Jays

Even the strongest hitters have weaknesses. Left-handed hitter Willie Upshaw of the Toronto Blue Jays is a good example. He hits fastballs and breaking balls well overall, but could improve by strengthening himself in certain areas.

### Willie Upshaw     Left-Handed Hitter
### Against All Right-Handed Pitchers All Teams
### Overall Batting Average .311

Fastball Average .346

| | Outside | Middle | Inside |
|---|---|---|---|
| High | 24/ 291 / 7 | 35/ 228 / 8 | 8/ 125 / 1 |
| Med | 85/ 364 / 31 | 23/ 652 / 15 | 33/ 363 / 12 |
| Low | 17/ 176 / 3 | 38/ 421 / 16 | 11/ 181 / 2 |

Curve Average .295

| | Outside | Middle | Inside |
|---|---|---|---|
| High | 5/ 200 / 1 | 6/ 500 / 3 | 3/ 0 / 0 |
| Med | 12/ 416 / 5 | 5/ 600 / 3 | 5/ 600 / 3 |
| Low | 3/ 333 / 1 | 15/ 133 / 2 | 7/ 0 / 0 |

Slider Average .125

| | Outside | Middle | Inside |
|---|---|---|---|
| High | 1/ 0 / 0 | 0/ 0 / 0 | 0/ 0 / 0 |
| Med | 3/ 333 / 1 | 3/ 333 / 1 | 7/ 0 / 0 |
| Low | 4/ 0 / 0 | 4/ 0 / 0 | 2/ 500 / 1 |

Change-Up Average .241

| | Outside | Middle | Inside |
|---|---|---|---|
| High | 4/ 250 / 1 | 3/ 333 / 1 | 1/ 0 / 0 |
| Med | 5/ 200 / 1 | 1/ 0 / 0 | 5/ 400 / 2 |
| Low | 2/ 500 / 1 | 4/ 0 / 0 | 4/ 250 / 1 |

Upshaw's .346 overall fastball average is excellent. It is supported by a strong .295 overall curve average. Even so, there are definite areas of weakness that Upshaw could work on to improve his total performance.

Upshaw is strong against waist-high pitches: his three medium-high fastball locations are first-rate. His .652 average against medium-over-the-middle fastballs is exceptional, as is his .421 against low-over-the-middle fastballs.

Before examining the obvious weak locations in Upshaw's fastball chart, it is interesting to note how he hits low-over-the-middle fastballs. His high average in this location is almost certainly due to fielders being out of position for pitches to this location.

LOW-OVER-THE-MIDDLE FASTBALLS

BATTING AVERAGE .421
   *PLAY*
LEFTFIELDER        Short and shifted toward center field
CENTERFIELDER      Deep and shifted toward left field
RIGHTFIELDER       Deep in straightaway right field
SHORTSTOP          Normal position
SECOND             Shifted toward first base

The above chart shows that there is a corridor in left-center that must be guarded when defending against Upshaw. He also hits to this corridor when thrown medium-high outside and medium-over-the-middle fastballs.

Turning to the areas Upshaw could improve, he has four weak fastball locations: low-inside (.181), low-outside (.176), high-inside (.125) and high-over-the-middle (.228). Improvement in the high-over-the-middle area would seem to be the best place for Upshaw to start, because he is thrown so many of these pitches. Many good hitters know their weaknesses and are experienced at laying off pitches to those locations until they have two strikes. It is obvious, however, that pitchers are taking advantage of Upshaw by throwing him many high-over-the-middle fastballs, which he hits poorly.

Upshaw's curve chart is good overall. His most noticeable weaknesses are in the low-inside (.000 on 0 for 7) and the low-over-the-middle (.133) locations.

## Upshaw Against Left-Handed Pitchers

Against left-handed pitchers, Upshaw's curve average falls off sharply. He has difficulties with low-inside and low-outside fastballs against left-handers, as he does against right-handers.

## Willie Upshaw   Left-Handed Hitter
## Against All Left-Handed Pitchers All Teams
## Overall Batting Average .230

### Fastball Average .309

|       | Outside | Middle | Inside |
|-------|---------|--------|--------|
| High  | 1 / 0 / 0 | 10 / 300 / 3 | 4 / 500 / 2 |
| Med   | 37 / 297 / 11 | 11 / 363 / 4 | 16 / 312 / 5 |
| Low   | 10 / 100 / 1 | 15 / 466 / 7 | 9 / 222 / 2 |

### Curve Average .108

|       | Outside | Middle | Inside |
|-------|---------|--------|--------|
| High  | 3 / 0 / 0 | 2 / 500 / 1 | 2 / 0 / 0 |
| Med   | 7 / 0 / 0 | 5 / 400 / 2 | 3 / 333 / 1 |
| Low   | 9 / 0 / 0 | 5 / 0 / 0 | 1 / 0 / 0 |

### Slider Average .250

|       | Outside | Middle | Inside |
|-------|---------|--------|--------|
| High  | 1 / 0 / 0 | 4 / 0 / 0 | 1 / 0 / 0 |
| Med   | 8 / 500 / 4 | 4 / 500 / 2 | 4 / 250 / 1 |
| Low   | 7 / 0 / 0 | 6 / 333 / 2 | 1 / 0 / 0 |

### Change-Up Average .000

|       | Outside | Middle | Inside |
|-------|---------|--------|--------|
| High  | 0 / 0 / 0 | 1 / 0 / 0 | 0 / 0 / 0 |
| Med   | 1 / 0 / 0 | 0 / 0 / 0 | 0 / 0 / 0 |
| Low   | 2 / 0 / 0 | 0 / 0 / 0 | 0 / 0 / 0 |

As against right-handed pitchers, Upshaw's fastball charts are generally solid. By improving several key weaknesses, his overall performance could be enhanced.

## Tim Raines,  Montreal Expos

Tim Raines is one of the most consistent hitters in the game, yet he has definite areas that could be improved.

## Tim Raines   Batting Left-Handed
## Against All Right-Handed Pitchers All Teams
## Overall Batting Average .317

### Fastball Average .350

|  | Outside | Middle | Inside |
|---|---|---|---|
| High | 13/ 307 / 4 | 50/ 340 / 17 | 18/ 111 / 2 |
| Med | 53/ 396 / 21 | 20/ 350 / 7 | 62/ 338 / 21 |
| Low | 21/ 285 / 6 | 57/ 421 / 24 | 31/ 387 / 12 |

### Curve Average .183

|  | Outside | Middle | Inside |
|---|---|---|---|
| High | 3/ 0 / 0 | 2/ 500 / 1 | 1/ 0 / 0 |
| Med | 9/ 0 / 0 | 6/ 666 / 4 | 8/ 250 / 2 |
| Low | 2/ 500 / 1 | 11/ 0 / 0 | 7/ 142 / 1 |

### Slider Average .317

|  | Outside | Middle | Inside |
|---|---|---|---|
| High | 0/ 0 / 0 | 3/ 666 / 2 | 5/ 600 / 3 |
| Med | 3/ 333 / 1 | 0/ 0 / 0 | 16/ 312 / 5 |
| Low | 1/ 0 / 0 | 7/ 285 / 2 | 6/ 0 / 0 |

### Change-Up Average .403

|  | Outside | Middle | Inside |
|---|---|---|---|
| High | 1/ 1000 / 1 | 1/ 1000 / 1 | 0/ 0 / 0 |
| Med | 3/ 333 / 1 | 1/ 0 / 0 | 4/ 500 / 2 |
| Low | 3/ 333 / 1 | 6/ 166 / 1 | 3/ 666 / 2 |

Notice the weak locations in Raines' curveball chart. His 0-for-11 against low-over-the-middle curves, 0-for-9 against medium-high outside curves and 1-for-7 against low-outside curves show that Raines must work on improving his performance in these locations. The BARS System has not recorded a medium-high outside curve or a low-inside curve thrown by a right-handed pitcher that Raines has hit out of the infield.

Raines' strengths are in his fastball, slider and change-up charts. His only fastball weakness is in the high-inside location (.111). His average in this location is so much lower than in his other fastball locations that an improvement would remove the only chink in his armor. It is nearly impossible, however, for a hitter to hit well in every location. Laying off these pitches until he has two strikes could improve his effectiveness.

## Raines Against Left-Handed Pitchers

The switch-hitting Raines has similar overall percentages against left-handed pitchers.

### Tim Raines  Batting Right-Handed
### Against All Left-Handed Pitchers All Teams
### Overall Batting Average .327

Fastball Average .345          Curve Average .173

| | Inside | Middle | Outside | | Inside | Middle | Outside |
|---|---|---|---|---|---|---|---|
| High | 1 / <br> 0 / 0 | 11 / <br> 272 / 3 | 7 / <br> 428 / 3 | | 0 / <br> 0 / 0 | 1 / <br> 0 / 0 | 1 / <br> 0 / 0 |
| Med | 10 / <br> 400 / 4 | 7 / <br> 428 / 3 | 30 / <br> 233 / 7 | | 5 / <br> 0 / 0 | 2 / <br> 500 / 1 | 7 / <br> 285 / 2 |
| Low | 5 / <br> 600 / 3 | 27 / <br> 370 / 10 | 9 / <br> 444 / 4 | | 0 / <br> 0 / 0 | 2 / <br> 500 / 1 | 5 / <br> 0 / 0 |

Raines has a general overall weakness against curves thrown by left-handers, although there are fewer instances recorded against left-handers than against right-handers.

His fastball chart is solid, except for the highly pitched medium-high outside location (.233). This low average is in contrast to the .396 Raines hits in the medium-high outside location against right-handers.

By working on his weaknesses, as spotted by the BARS System, Raines could improve his overall average. Already one of the best hitters in the game, he could become even more exceptional.

## Gary Carter, New York Mets

Right-handed Gary Carter of the Mets hits fastballs and curves well. Although he hits for a consistent average, he has numerous specific weaknesses that bring down his overall effectiveness.

He hits better against left-handed than right-handed pitchers. First against right-handers:

## Gary Carter    Right-Handed Hitter
## Against All Right-Handed Pitchers All Teams
## Overall Batting Average .256

### Fastball Average .283

|       | Inside | Middle | Outside |
|-------|--------|--------|---------|
| High  | 18 / 111 / 2 | 34 / 294 / 10 | 20 / 200 / 4 |
| Med   | 35 / 514 / 18 | 17 / 235 / 4 | 81 / 234 / 19 |
| Low   | 15 / 133 / 2 | 41 / 390 / 16 | 35 / 257 / 9 |

### Curve Average .307

|       | Inside | Middle | Outside |
|-------|--------|--------|---------|
| High  | 1 / 1000 / 1 | 7 / 428 / 3 | 5 / 200 / 1 |
| Med   | 3 / 333 / 1 | 3 / 333 / 1 | 35 / 314 / 11 |
| Low   | 0 / 0 / 0 | 8 / 375 / 3 | 16 / 187 / 3 |

### Slider Average .217

|       | Inside | Middle | Outside |
|-------|--------|--------|---------|
| High  | 3 / 333 / 1 | 4 / 500 / 2 | 4 / 500 / 2 |
| Med   | 4 / 0 / 0 | 3 / 666 / 2 | 27 / 111 / 3 |
| Low   | 4 / 0 / 0 | 10 / 300 / 3 | 19 / 210 / 4 |

### Change-Up Average .363

|       | Inside | Middle | Outside |
|-------|--------|--------|---------|
| High  | 0 / 0 / 0 | 2 / 1000 / 2 | 1 / 0 / 0 |
| Med   | 0 / 0 / 0 | 1 / 0 / 0 | 3 / 333 / 1 |
| Low   | 0 / 0 / 0 | 0 / 0 / 0 | 4 / 250 / 1 |

Carter's overall fastball average of .283 is above average, but notice the weak locations within his fastball chart. Carter's high-inside (.111), low-inside (.133) and high-outside (.200) locations are weak. Surprisingly, Carter does not hit medium-over-the-middle fastballs well (.235). His medium-high outside average of .234 is also low.

His main strengths are in the medium-high inside and low-over-the-middle locations (.514 and .390 respectively). In fact, these two locations sustain his relatively high overall fastball average of .283. His .514 average in the medium-high inside location is so much higher than the averages in his two other inside locations that Carter should determine the causes of the difference. Improvement in either of the two weak inside locations could increase his effectiveness significantly.

His difficulties against high-inside fastballs are clear.

HIGH-INSIDE FASTBALLS

BATTING AVERAGE .111
   *PLAY*
LEFTFIELDER       Deep in straightaway left field
CENTERFIELDER   Short in straightaway center field
RIGHTFIELDER    Short and shifted toward center field
SHORTSTOP       Up middle (shifted toward second base)
SECOND          Normal position

Carter's average in the medium-high outside curve location (.314) sustains his overall curve average. His main curve weakness is in the low-outside location (.187).

Carter's key slider locations (medium-high outside and low-outside) are weak. By focussing on these two locations and raising his averages, he could raise his overall slider average and remove this weakness from his charts.

## Carter Against Left-Handed Pitchers

Against left-handers, Carter hits fastballs exceptionally well overall.

**Gary Carter    Right-Handed Hitter**
**Against All Left-Handed Pitchers All Teams**
**Overall Batting Average .294**

Fastball Average .346         Curve Average .250

| | Inside | Middle | Outside | Inside | Middle | Outside |
|------|--------|--------|---------|--------|--------|---------|
| High | 2/ 0/0 | 4/ 250/1 | 17/ 235/4 | 0/ 0/0 | 4/ 500/2 | 0/ 0/0 |
| Med | 5/ 0/0 | 2/ 500/1 | 43/ 395/17 | 2/ 0/0 | 3/ 0/0 | 2/ 500/1 |
| Low | 5/ 400/2 | 22/ 409/9 | 24/ 375/9 | 4/ 250/1 | 2/ 500/1 | 3/ 0/0 |

### Slider Average .263      Change-Up Average .210

| | Inside | Middle | Outside | | Inside | Middle | Outside |
|------|--------|--------|---------|--|--------|--------|---------|
| High | 1/ **0** / 0 | 1/ **1000** / 1 | 0/ **0** / 0 | | 0/ **0** / 0 | 0/ **0** / 0 | 2/ **500** / 1 |
| Med | 3/ **0** / 0 | 2/ **500** / 1 | 2/ **500** / 1 | | 0/ **0** / 0 | 1/ **0** / 0 | 4/ **0** / 0 |
| Low | 5/ **200** / 1 | 4/ **250** / 1 | 1/ **0** / 0 | | 1/ **0** / 0 | 2/ **500** / 1 | 9/ **222** / 2 |

Carter's medium-high outside (.395), low-outside (.375) and low-over-the-middle (.409) fastball locations are outstanding. Only his .235 in the high-outside fastball location is weak. By improving in this location, his one weakness could be removed.

Notice how few inside fastballs left-handed pitchers throw to Carter. They might do well by throwing him more. This is an example of how studying a hitter's BARS batting charts could benefit pitchers.

Left-handers throw Carter so few curves, sliders and change-ups in comparison to fastballs that his averages in these charts are not as significant as in his fastball chart.

## Jose Cruz, Houston Astros

Jose Cruz of the Houston Astros is a good hitter overall with several definite areas that could be improved.

### Jose Cruz    Left-Handed Hitter
### Against All Right-Handed Pitchers All Teams
### Overall Average .285

### Fastball Average .326      Curve Average .285

| | Outside | Middle | Inside | | Outside | Middle | Inside |
|------|---------|--------|--------|--|---------|--------|--------|
| High | 38/ **421** / 16 | 54/ **407** / 22 | 21/ **238** / 5 | | 13/ **384** / 5 | 14/ **357** / 5 | 5/ **400** / 2 |
| Med | 122/ **245** / 30 | 38/ **368** / 14 | 41/ **365** / 15 | | 21/ **333** / 7 | 8/ **625** / 5 | 11/ **272** / 3 |
| Low | 23/ **217** / 5 | 51/ **372** / 19 | 23/ **347** / 8 | | 8/ **0** / 0 | 26/ **269** / 7 | 13/ **0** / 0 |

Slider Average .173          Change-Up Average .230

| | Outside | Middle | Inside |
|---|---|---|---|
| High | 1/ 0 / 0 | 2/ 0 / 0 | 6/ 0 / 0 |
| Med | 5/ 400 / 2 | 4/ 250 / 1 | 9/ 333 / 3 |
| Low | 3/ 333 / 1 | 7/ 0 / 0 | 9/ 111 / 1 |

| | Outside | Middle | Inside |
|---|---|---|---|
| High | 3/ 666 / 2 | 11/ 272 / 3 | 1/ 0 / 0 |
| Med | 8/ 125 / 1 | 2/ 500 / 1 | 4/ 250 / 1 |
| Low | 8/ 375 / 3 | 10/ 100 / 1 | 5/ 0 / 0 |

Cruz's overall fastball average of .326 is excellent, and he has several very strong locations in his fastball chart. But notice the weaknesses. His .245 in the highly pitched medium-high outside location is low, as are the .217 in the low-outside and .238 in the high-inside fastball locations.

Working to improve his performance in his low-outside and medium-high outside locations would be the first place for Cruz to start. These are his two primary weaknesses, and any improvement would strengthen his overall performance. His main concern would be to not sacrifice his high averages against medium-high inside and low-inside fastballs.

Cruz's curve weaknesses are evident. The low-inside (.000 on 0 for 13) and low-outside (.000 on 0 for 8) locations offer ample targets for pitchers.

Cruz's low-inside and low-over-the-middle slider and change-up locations are also weak.

### Cruz Against Left-Handed Pitchers

Against left-handers, Cruz has several pronounced weaknesses:

## Jose Cruz    Left-Handed Hitter
## Against All Left-Handed Pitchers All Teams
## Overall Batting Average .273

### Fastball Average .285

|      | Outside | Middle | Inside |
|------|---------|--------|--------|
| High | 17 / **58** / 1 | 33 / **303** / 10 | 25 / **160** / 4 |
| Med  | 35 / **285** / 10 | 15 / **533** / 8 | 29 / **344** / 10 |
| Low  | 9 / **0** / 0 | 21 / **428** / 9 | 16 / **312** / 5 |

### Curve Average .295

|      | Outside | Middle | Inside |
|------|---------|--------|--------|
| High | 4 / **750** / 3 | 13 / **538** / 7 | 3 / **666** / 2 |
| Med  | 25 / **200** / 5 | 8 / **375** / 3 | 11 / **363** / 4 |
| Low  | 19 / **157** / 3 | 14 / **71** / 1 | 1 / **1000** / 1 |

### Slider Average .244

|      | Outside | Middle | Inside |
|------|---------|--------|--------|
| High | 2 / **500** / 1 | 10 / **200** / 2 | 1 / **0** / 0 |
| Med  | 11 / **181** / 2 | 0 / **0** / 0 | 6 / **500** / 3 |
| Low  | 6 / **0** / 0 | 7 / **285** / 2 | 2 / **500** / 1 |

### Change-Up Average .500

|      | Outside | Middle | Inside |
|------|---------|--------|--------|
| High | 0 / **0** / 0 | 0 / **0** / 0 | 1 / **1000** / 1 |
| Med  | 0 / **0** / 0 | 0 / **0** / 0 | 0 / **0** / 0 |
| Low  | 0 / **0** / 0 | 0 / **0** / 0 | 1 / **0** / 0 |

Notice Cruz's three weak fastball locations: low-outside (.000 on 0 for 9), high-outside (.058) and high-inside (.160).

Cruz has many strong curve locations, but his three lowest locations bring down his overall curve average. His low-over-the-middle (.071), low-outside (.157) and medium-high outside (.200) curve locations present a definite area for Cruz to work on.

Cruz has fewer recorded instances in his slider and change-up charts, but his low-outside and medium-high outside slider locations are weak.

In general, Cruz is weak against low-outside pitches. He is a strong hitter overall, and improving this area of weakness would make him extremely effective.

## Willie Wilson, Kansas City Royals

Switch-hitting Willie Wilson of the Kansas City Royals is a good overall fastball hitter with a few weak locations.

### Willie Wilson   Batting Left-Handed
### Against All Right-Handed Pitchers All Teams
### Overall Batting Average .269

Fastball Average .304

|  | Outside | Middle | Inside |
|------|---------|--------|--------|
| High | 18 / 611 / 11 | 55 / 363 / 20 | 29 / 310 / 9 |
| Med  | 130 / 292 / 38 | 107 / 327 / 35 | 176 / 312 / 55 |
| Low  | 25 / 80 / 2 | 142 / 302 / 43 | 93 / 247 / 23 |

Curve Average .298

|  | Outside | Middle | Inside |
|------|---------|--------|--------|
| High | 8 / 500 / 4 | 7 / 142 / 1 | 2 / 500 / 1 |
| Med  | 35 / 257 / 9 | 17 / 352 / 6 | 34 / 411 / 14 |
| Low  | 11 / 363 / 4 | 33 / 212 / 7 | 24 / 208 / 5 |

Slider Average .222

|  | Outside | Middle | Inside |
|------|---------|--------|--------|
| High | 0 / 0 / 0 | 0 / 0 / 0 | 4 / 0 / 0 |
| Med  | 2 / 0 / 0 | 6 / 500 / 3 | 35 / 228 / 8 |
| Low  | 2 / 500 / 1 | 16 / 437 / 7 | 34 / 88 / 3 |

Change-Up Average .136

|  | Outside | Middle | Inside |
|------|---------|--------|--------|
| High | 2 / 0 / 0 | 8 / 250 / 2 | 2 / 0 / 0 |
| Med  | 13 / 153 / 2 | 1 / 1000 / 1 | 3 / 333 / 1 |
| Low  | 6 / 0 / 0 | 5 / 0 / 0 | 4 / 0 / 0 |

Wilson's fastball averages are solid across the high and medium-high locations. But his low-outside (.080) and low-inside (.247) fastball locations bring down his overall average. Simply by concentrating on improving or holding off on low-outside fastballs, Wilson could remove a considerable part of any hitting difficulty he experiences.

Wilson has several weak curve locations. His .212 low-over-the-middle average and .208 low-inside average bring down his effectiveness against curves. His .411 against medium-high inside curves, however, is excellent.

Wilson's difficulties with sliders are easy to describe. The .088 in his low-inside and .228 in his medium-high inside slider locations present targets for pitchers. Wilson hits low-over-the-middle sliders extremely well (.437), and by working on low-inside sliders he should be able to improve his overall performance.

### Wilson Against Left-Handed Pitchers

Wilson hits better overall against left-handed than against right-handed pitchers.

#### Willie Wilson    Batting Right-Handed
#### Against All Left-Handed Pitchers All Teams
#### Overall Batting Average .303

Fastball Average .323

| | Inside | Middle | Outside |
|---|---|---|---|
| High | 8 / 375 / 3 | 21 / 571 / 12 | 10 / 100 / 1 |
| Med | 37 / 405 / 15 | 31 / 258 / 8 | 57 / 350 / 20 |
| Low | 21 / 142 / 3 | 65 / 353 / 23 | 19 / 105 / 2 |

Curve Average .337

| | Inside | Middle | Outside |
|---|---|---|---|
| High | 1 / 0 / 0 | 0 / 0 / 0 | 4 / 750 / 3 |
| Med | 7 / 714 / 5 | 8 / 375 / 3 | 17 / 294 / 5 |
| Low | 1 / 0 / 0 | 31 / 290 / 9 | 8 / 125 / 1 |

Slider Average .204

| | Inside | Middle | Outside |
|---|---|---|---|
| High | 4 / 250 / 1 | 3 / 333 / 1 | 2 / 0 / 0 |
| Med | 11 / 90 / 1 | 4 / 250 / 1 | 3 / 0 / 0 |
| Low | 10 / 300 / 3 | 10 / 200 / 2 | 2 / 500 / 1 |

Change-Up Average .296

| | Inside | Middle | Outside |
|---|---|---|---|
| High | 0 / 0 / 0 | 3 / 0 / 0 | 4 / 500 / 2 |
| Med | 2 / 0 / 0 | 3 / 333 / 1 | 4 / 250 / 1 |
| Low | 1 / 1000 / 1 | 5 / 200 / 1 | 5 / 400 / 2 |

Wilson's fastball, curve and slider weaknesses against left-handers are apparent. His overall fastball average is very good (.323), with excellent averages in his medium-high inside (.405), high-inside (.375) and high-over-the-middle (.571) locations. His difficulties in three of the four corner locations, however, reduce his overall performance. His low-outside (.105), high-outside (.100) and low-inside (.142) fastball locations are weak.

Wilson's only significant curve weakness is in his low-outside location (.125). By removing or holding off on this one weakness, he could become very strong against curves thrown by left-handed pitchers.

Few sliders are thrown to Wilson, but his need for improvement is evident. In particular, the .200 in his low-over-the-middle and the .090 in his medium-high inside slider locations bring down his overall slider average.

Wilson is a fine hitter overall. By improving several key areas of difficulty, he could bring his average up to the .300 level consistently.

### Larry Parrish, Texas Rangers

Right-handed Larry Parrish of the Texas Rangers hits much better overall against right-handed than against left-handed pitchers. Against right-handers his overall fastball average of .330 tells only half the story. He has weak fastball locations that are offset by very strong locations.

**Larry Parrish    Right-Handed Hitter**
**Against All Right-Handed Pitchers All Teams**
**Overall Batting Average .303**

Fastball Average .330

| | Inside | Middle | Outside |
|---|---|---|---|
| High | 14/ 142 / 2 | 14/ 214 / 3 | 7/ 428 / 3 |
| Med | 36/ 222 / 8 | 35/ 542 / 19 | 100/ 340 / 34 |
| Low | 21/ 190 / 4 | 46/ 478 / 22 | 30/ 166 / 5 |

Curve Average .318

| | Inside | Middle | Outside |
|---|---|---|---|
| High | 0/ 0 / 0 | 7/ 857 / 6 | 2/ 0 / 0 |
| Med | 9/ 333 / 3 | 14/ 571 / 8 | 44/ 431 / 19 |
| Low | 5/ 0 / 0 | 16/ 312 / 5 | 41/ 73 / 3 |

Slider Average .283          Change-Up Average .263

|  | Inside | Middle | Outside |
|---|---|---|---|
| High | $0/0$ | $1/1$ 1000 | $5/2$ 400 |
| Med | $6/0$ | $7/2$ 285 | $23/11$ 478 |
| Low | $0/0$ | $10/2$ 200 | $29/5$ 172 |

|  | Inside | Middle | Outside |
|---|---|---|---|
| High | $1/0$ | $4/3$ 750 | $1/1$ 1000 |
| Med | $1/0$ | $4/1$ 250 | $4/0$ |
| Low | $0/0$ | $1/0$ | $3/0$ |

Parrish has four excellent fastball locations: medium-over-the-middle (.542), low-over-the-middle (.478), high-outside (.428) and medium-high outside (.340). These four locations buoy up his entire fastball chart.

His low-outside (.166) and high-over-the-middle (.214) locations are like islands of weakness in the midst of great strength. But his three inside fastball locations present a solid area of weakness that Parrish must improve if he is to remain an effective hitter.

Parrish does not have a recorded instance in which he has hit a high-inside fastball to left field. He has trouble getting around on these pitches, punching them to center and right.

HIGH-INSIDE FASTBALLS

BATTING AVERAGE .142
   *PLAY*
LEFTFIELDER          No recorded instances
CENTERFIELDER        Deep in straightaway center field
RIGHTFIELDER         Medium-deep and shifted toward the right field line
SHORTSTOP            Up middle (shifted toward second base)
SECOND               Normal position

Parrish undoubtedly knows that he has trouble with inside pitches, but the low BARS System averages in these locations might surprise him. It is difficult to hold off inside fastballs altogether, but as much as possible, he should try. By working on this area of weakness, he could improve his effectiveness.

His curve chart also has contrasting locations. The .857 of his high-over-the-middle, the .571 of his medium-over-the-middle and the .431 of his medium-high outside curve locations bring his overall curve average above .300. But his .073 against low-outside curves gives a target for pitchers that keeps Parrish continually off balance. This weak curve location may help explain his difficulty with inside fastballs.

Parrish's low-outside slider location is weak (.172). But his medium-high outside slider location is extremely high (.478). The contrast of these two locations is similar to his curve chart.

In general, Parrish has difficulty with low-outside pitches. By improving just this one area of weakness, he would be stronger against every type of pitch. In addition, his weakness against inside fastballs should be worked on.

### Parrish Against Left-Handed Pitchers

Parrish does not hit as well overall against left-handers.

**Larry Parrish    Right-Handed Hitter**
**Against All Left-Handed Pitchers All Teams**
**Overall Batting Average .254**

Fastball Average .290

| | Inside | Middle | Outside |
|---|---|---|---|
| High | 142 / 1 (7) | 0 / 0 (4) | 142 / 1 (7) |
| Med | 250 / 3 (12) | 428 / 9 (21) | 309 / 13 (42) |
| Low | 428 / 3 (7) | 277 / 5 (18) | 230 / 3 (13) |

Curve Average .250

| | Inside | Middle | Outside |
|---|---|---|---|
| High | 0 / 0 (1) | 500 / 1 (2) | 0 / 0 (0) |
| Med | 0 / 0 (3) | 200 / 1 (5) | 375 / 3 (8) |
| Low | 0 / 0 (0) | 250 / 1 (4) | 200 / 1 (5) |

Slider Average .129

| | Inside | Middle | Outside |
|---|---|---|---|
| High | 0 / 0 (1) | 0 / 0 (1) | 0 / 0 (0) |
| Med | 0 / 0 (6) | 0 / 0 (3) | 0 / 0 (3) |
| Low | 0 / 0 (7) | 571 / 4 (7) | 0 / 0 (3) |

Change-Up Average .352

| | Inside | Middle | Outside |
|---|---|---|---|
| High | 0 / 0 (0) | 0 / 0 (0) | 0 / 0 (1) |
| Med | 0 / 0 (1) | 1000 / 2 (2) | 250 / 2 (8) |
| Low | 0 / 0 (1) | 0 / 0 (0) | 500 / 2 (4) |

Parrish has problems with low-outside fastballs against left-handers, as he does against right-handers. In contrast to his performance against right-handers, Parrish has trouble with high-outside fastballs thrown by lefties. He hits fastballs over the heart of the plate very well (.428). Notice that the contrast between Parrish's low-outside and medium-high outside fastball locations is almost as pronounced against left-handers as it is against right-handers.

He has fewer recorded instances in his curve, slider and change-up charts against left-handers, but his strengths and weaknesses emerge. He has difficulty with low-outside curves and with outside and inside sliders.

Parrish, like most good hitters, could become extremely effective by working on and improving several key areas of weakness.

## Personal Comments

A lot of players and managers helped me design the BARS System over the years. It's been a lot of fun. Dick Howser had some good ideas, and Lou Pinella helped me when he was with the Royals. I talked with Lou back when he was playing and he admitted he was kind of a guess hitter. He said he guessed about the pitch even when he had two strikes on him. The main thing he wanted to know from the BARS System was what the first pitch from a pitcher was likely to be — whether it would be a fastball or a curveball. Lou wasn't a great first-pitch hitter, but he was one of the best two-strike hitters I've ever seen.

I've talked to various players and they think the BARS System is awfully good. I sure haven't heard anybody put it down. When I set up my various BARS System booths at the baseball meetings, the owners I talk with think the system's a good idea. Of course they're businessmen and work with computers all the time, so they're used to them. John McMullen, owner of the Astros, said that all successful businesses today use computers and that baseball should also start.

One thing that really made me feel good was when I talked with Davey Johnson a few years ago at a baseball meeting in Nashville. Davey was probably one of the first to use a computer, so I thought he might be interested in my system. One evening I ran into him in the hotel lobby and asked him to come down to my BARS booth the next day. He jumped at the idea.

"Look," he said, "I know a lot about computers and I guarantee you one thing, I'm gonna be down there in the morning, and I'm gonna just cut your system up and down." I said that's fine, the booth opens at nine o'clock. "I'll be there at 8:30," he said.

He showed up right at 8:30 and I was pretty scared, because I figured that he probably knew much more about computers than I did. I took him from one end of my booth to the other, and he didn't say a word. He sat down for a while and started asking questions. He didn't say one critical word as long as he was there. I think that he was impressed. He left just before nine o'clock, and I know the reason he came down at 8:30 was because he didn't want any of the baseball people in the hotel to know he was looking at the system.

After that he and I kind of kept up to date. One time he asked me how I get all my information. I said, "Well, I've got this satellite dish. I watch all this on TV." I told him I had four scouts working full time. "You can't watch games on TV," he said. "You can't tell where these pitches are thrown on TV." I told him, "Davey, I believe you can."

One week later, I saw a picture in a publication. It showed Davey Johnson's dish on top of Shea Stadium.

# Chapter Eleven

# Large Batting-Average Gains

When a player has a significant gain or decline in his batting average from one year to the next, it is often difficult to pinpoint exactly what caused the difference. The BARS System, with its analysis of many hitting variables, can pin down the exact changes in a player's batting results.

The BARS System Super Summary Report gives an analysis of how a player performs against left-handed and right-handed pitchers, how he performs against certain types of pitches thrown in each of nine locations around the strike zone, how he performs when ahead and when behind in the count, and the distance and direction he tends to hit specific pitches.

BY EXAMINING AND COMPARING A PLAYER'S SUPER SUMMARY REPORTS FROM ONE YEAR TO THE NEXT, IT CAN READILY BE SEEN HOW HIS PERFORMANCE DIFFERED.

The main points to examine in such a comparison are:

(1) Overall average against right-handed pitchers in the two years
(2) Overall average against left-handed pitchers in the two years
(3) Performance against certain types of pitches in the two years (fastballs, curves, etc.)
(4) Comparison of particular weaknesses in the two years
(5) Comparison of performance when ahead and behind in the count
(6) Comparison of direction and distance the player hit certain types of pitches (Did he get around better on fastballs in one of the years? Did he hit with the pitch in one of the years? etc.)
(7) Differences in where pitchers threw their pitches in the two years
(8) Differences in pitch selection (fastball, curve, etc.)

When comparing a player's reports from one year to the next, the 90 percent accuracy of the BARS System fielding charts remains consistent.

Players tend to hit the same way year after year, and it is usually difficult to find significant differences.

Nonetheless, when examining the charts of a player who had a large gain or decline in his batting average, instances can be found in which particular types and locations of pitches were hit differently. The fielding strategy for the majority of a player's pitching locations will show that he hit similarly both years, but the few significant differences can shed light on what caused his gain or decline.

When making a comparison between two seasons, each player has four separate Super Summary Reports: one for each year's performance against left-handed pitchers and one for each year's performance against right-handed pitchers. For this reason the quantity of information available for examination is large. Space requirements permit only the most significant information to be highlighted.

It should also be noted that Super Summary records for single years are being used; therefore, the number of instances in the individual pitching locations are fewer than in Super Summaries that are composites of information gained over five seasons or more. The overall BARS averages reflect all types of pitches that a player receives (fastballs, curves, sliders, change-ups, etc.), but in this chapter only BARS System fastball and curve charts are shown.

In this chapter, the records of players who had large batting average gains are examined. The following chapter examines players with large declines.

## LARGEST GAINS

| Player | '87 Club | '86 Average | '87 Average | Gain |
|---|---|---|---|---|
| V. Coleman | Cardinals | .232 | .289 | 57 |
| W. Randolph | Yankees | .276 | .305 | 29 |

| Player | '86 Club | '85 Average | '86 Average | Gain |
|---|---|---|---|---|
| Mike Easler | Yankees | .262 | .302 | 40 |
| K. Puckett | Twins | .288 | .328 | 40 |
| Joe Carter | Indians | .262 | .302 | 40 |
| George Bell | Blue Jays | .275 | .309 | 34 |

| Player | '87 Club | '85 Average | '86 Average | '87 Average |
|---|---|---|---|---|
| Steve Sax | Dodgers | .279 | .332 | .280 |
| M. Marshall | Dodgers | .293 | .233 | .294 |

## Vince Coleman, St. Louis Cardinals

Switch-hitting Vince Coleman of the Cardinals raised his official average 57 points in 1987. In 1986 he hit .232; in 1987 he hit .289. Coleman's BARS System averages reflect this increase.

### Vince Coleman Against Right-Handed Pitchers 1986
### Overall Batting Average .265

Fastball Average .259

| | Outside | Middle | Inside |
|---|---|---|---|
| High | 5/ 0 / 0 | 17/ 411 / 7 | 4/ 250 / 1 |
| Med | 12/ 333 / 4 | 0/ 0 / 0 | 16/ 187 / 3 |
| Low | 4/ 250 / 1 | 7/ 285 / 2 | 12/ 166 / 2 |

Curve Average .500

| | Outside | Middle | Inside |
|---|---|---|---|
| High | 0/ 0 / 0 | 0/ 0 / 0 | 0/ 0 / 0 |
| Med | 0/ 0 / 0 | 0/ 0 / 0 | 1/ 1000 / 1 |
| Low | 2/ 500 / 1 | 5/ 400 / 2 | 2/ 500 / 1 |

### Vince Coleman Against Right-Handed Pitchers 1987
### Overall Batting Average .346

Fastball Average .361

| | Outside | Middle | Inside |
|---|---|---|---|
| High | 7/ 428 / 3 | 14/ 285 / 4 | 11/ 272 / 3 |
| Med | 11/ 363 / 4 | 3/ 1000 / 3 | 17/ 352 / 6 |
| Low | 4/ 0 / 0 | 17/ 470 / 8 | 10/ 300 / 3 |

Curve Average .363

| | Outside | Middle | Inside |
|---|---|---|---|
| High | 1/ 0 / 0 | 0/ 0 / 0 | 0/ 0 / 0 |
| Med | 2/ 0 / 0 | 0/ 0 / 0 | 2/ 500 / 1 |
| Low | 3/ 666 / 2 | 0/ 0 / 0 | 3/ 333 / 1 |

Coleman hit 102 points higher against fastballs in 1987 than in 1986. His two main improvements were in the medium-high inside location (.187 in 1986, .352 in 1987) and in the low-over-the-middle location (.285 in 1986, .470 in 1987). He also improved against high-outside fastballs, low-inside fastballs and high-inside fastballs. But he declined in two fastball locations: high-over-the-middle and low-outside.

Batting left-handed against right-handed pitchers, Coleman pulled medium-high inside fastballs down the right field line and to the right side of the infield in 1986, hitting .187. He hit medium-high inside fastballs more to all fields in 1987, with a resulting .352 average.

MEDIUM-HIGH INSIDE
(FASTBALLS THROWN BY RIGHT-HANDED PITCHERS 1986)

BATTING AVERAGE .187
    *PLAY*

| | |
|---|---|
| LEFTFIELDER | Deep in straightaway left field |
| CENTERFIELDER | Medium-deep in straightaway center field |
| RIGHTFIELDER | Medium-deep and shifted toward the right field line |
| SHORTSTOP | Up middle (shifted toward second base) |
| SECOND | Shifted toward first base |

MEDIUM-HIGH INSIDE
(FASTBALLS THROWN BY RIGHT-HANDED PITCHERS 1987)

BATTING AVERAGE .352
    *PLAY*

| | |
|---|---|
| LEFTFIELDER | Medium-deep in straightaway left field |
| CENTERFIELDER | Deep and shifted toward left field |
| RIGHTFIELDER | Deep in straightaway right field |
| SHORTSTOP | Shifted toward third base |
| SECOND | Shifted toward first base |

He hit medium-high outside fastballs similarly both years.

MEDIUM-HIGH OUTSIDE
(FASTBALLS THROWN BY RIGHT-HANDED PITCHERS 1986)

BATTING AVERAGE .333
    *PLAY*

| | |
|---|---|
| LEFTFIELDER | Deep and shifted toward the left field line |
| CENTERFIELDER | Medium-deep in straightaway center field |
| RIGHTFIELDER | Medium-deep and shifted toward center field |
| SHORTSTOP | Up middle (shifted toward second base) |
| SECOND | Normal position |

MEDIUM-HIGH OUTSIDE
(FASTBALLS THROWN BY RIGHT-HANDED PITCHERS 1987)

BATTING AVERAGE .363
*PLAY*

| | |
|---|---|
| LEFTFIELDER | Medium-deep and shifted toward the left field line |
| CENTERFIELDER | Medium-deep and shifted toward left field |
| RIGHTFIELDER | Medium-deep and shifted toward center field |
| SHORTSTOP | Up middle (shifted toward second base) |
| SECOND | Normal position |

Coleman's .470 low-over-the-middle fastball average in 1987 was excellent.

LOW-OVER-THE-MIDDLE
(FASTBALLS THROWN BY RIGHT-HANDED PITCHERS 1986)

BATTING AVERAGE .285
*PLAY*

| | |
|---|---|
| LEFTFIELDER | No recorded instances |
| CENTERFIELDER | Medium-deep in straightaway center field |
| RIGHTFIELDER | Deep in straightaway right field |
| SHORTSTOP | Up middle (shifted toward second base) |
| SECOND | Normal position |

LOW-OVER-THE-MIDDLE
(FASTBALLS THROWN BY RIGHT-HANDED PITCHERS 1987)

BATTING AVERAGE .470
*PLAY*

| | |
|---|---|
| LEFTFIELDER | Medium-deep and shifted toward the left field line |
| CENTERFIELDER | Deep and shifted toward right field |
| RIGHTFIELDER | Medium-deep in straightaway right field |
| SHORTSTOP | Up middle (shifted toward second base) |
| SECOND | Shifted toward first base |

When ahead in the count, Coleman hit much better in 1987.

### Vince Coleman Ahead In The Count
### Against Right-Handed Pitchers 1986
### Batting Average .224

Fastball Average .243

| | Outside | Middle | Inside |
|---|---|---|---|
| High | 2 / 0 / 0 | 11 / 363 / 4 | 2 / 500 / 1 |
| Med | 4 / 0 / 0 | 0 / 0 / 0 | 8 / 125 / 1 |
| Low | 2 / 500 / 1 | 3 / 333 / 1 | 5 / 200 / 1 |

Curve Average 1.000

| | Outside | Middle | Inside |
|---|---|---|---|
| High | 0 / 0 / 0 | 0 / 0 / 0 | 0 / 0 / 0 |
| Med | 0 / 0 / 0 | 0 / 0 / 0 | 0 / 0 / 0 |
| Low | 0 / 0 / 0 | 0 / 0 / 0 | 1 / 1000 / 1 |

### Vince Coleman Ahead In The Count
### Against Right-Handed Pitchers 1987
### Batting Average .461

Fastball Average .516

| | Outside | Middle | Inside |
|---|---|---|---|
| High | 1 / 0 / 0 | 4 / 500 / 2 | 6 / 166 / 1 |
| Med | 1 / 1000 / 1 | 1 / 1000 / 1 | 6 / 666 / 4 |
| Low | 2 / 0 / 0 | 6 / 833 / 5 | 4 / 500 / 2 |

Curve Average .500

| | Outside | Middle | Inside |
|---|---|---|---|
| High | 0 / 0 / 0 | 0 / 0 / 0 | 0 / 0 / 0 |
| Med | 0 / 0 / 0 | 0 / 0 / 0 | 1 / 1000 / 1 |
| Low | 0 / 0 / 0 | 0 / 0 / 0 | 1 / 0 / 0 |

The fastball increase from .243 to .516 when ahead in the count is the foundation of Coleman's higher overall 1987 average. What immediately catches the eye in his 1986 charts is Coleman's weakness against outside fastballs, his strong .363 against high-over-the-middle fastballs and his weak .125 against medium-high inside fastballs.

His 1987 fastball chart shows an excellent .833 against low-over-the-middle fastballs, a weak .166 against high-inside fastballs and a strong .666 against medium-high inside fastballs.

## Coleman Against Left-Handed Pitchers

Although Coleman's total average went up in 1987, his BARS averages indicate that he hit slightly better against left-handed pitchers in 1986.

### Vince Coleman Against Left-Handed Pitchers 1986
### Overall Batting Average .222

Fastball Average .205

|  | Inside | Middle | Outside |
|---|---|---|---|
| High | 1 / 1000 / 1 | 7 / 142 / 1 | 2 / 0 / 0 |
| Med | 10 / 300 / 3 | 1 / 0 / 0 | 8 / 0 / 0 |
| Low | 2 / 500 / 1 | 6 / 166 / 1 | 2 / 500 / 1 |

Curve Average .384

|  | Inside | Middle | Outside |
|---|---|---|---|
| High | 1 / 0 / 0 | 2 / 1000 / 2 | 0 / 0 / 0 |
| Med | 0 / 0 / 0 | 1 / 0 / 0 | 2 / 0 / 0 |
| Low | 2 / 1000 / 2 | 5 / 200 / 1 | 0 / 0 / 0 |

### Vince Coleman Against Left-Handed Pitchers 1987
### Overall Batting Average .188

Fastball Average .166

|  | Inside | Middle | Outside |
|---|---|---|---|
| High | 0 / 0 / 0 | 2 / 500 / 1 | 4 / 500 / 2 |
| Med | 3 / 0 / 0 | 0 / 0 / 0 | 8 / 250 / 2 |
| Low | 3 / 0 / 0 | 8 / 0 / 0 | 2 / 0 / 0 |

Curve Average .250

|  | Inside | Middle | Outside |
|---|---|---|---|
| High | 0 / 0 / 0 | 0 / 0 / 0 | 2 / 500 / 1 |
| Med | 0 / 0 / 0 | 0 / 0 / 0 | 0 / 0 / 0 |
| Low | 1 / 0 / 0 | 0 / 0 / 0 | 1 / 0 / 0 |

Fewer instances are recorded against left-handers than right-handers, but it is evident that against left-handers Coleman had difficulty with low fastballs in '87 and with medium-high outside fastballs both years.

### Willie Randolph, New York Yankees

Willie Randolph, right-handed hitter for the Yankees, raised his official average 29 points, from .276 in 1986 to .305 in 1987. Randolph's improvement was due mainly to his stronger performance against fastballs in 1987. His BARS System record shows that he hit better against both right- and left-handed pitchers in 1987.

First against right-handers:

### Willie Randolph Against Right-Handed Pitchers 1986
### Overall Batting Average .226

Fastball Average .205

| | Inside | Middle | Outside |
|---|---|---|---|
| High | 1/ 0 / 0 | 13/ 384 / 5 | 2/ 0 / 0 |
| Med | 15/ 200 / 3 | 4/ 500 / 2 | 51/ 137 / 7 |
| Low | 1/ 0 / 0 | 14/ 357 / 5 | 11/ 90 / 1 |

Curve Average .173

| | Inside | Middle | Outside |
|---|---|---|---|
| High | 0/ 0 / 0 | 1/ 0 / 0 | 0/ 0 / 0 |
| Med | 2/ 0 / 0 | 1/ 0 / 0 | 7/ 428 / 3 |
| Low | 0/ 0 / 0 | 3/ 333 / 1 | 9/ 0 / 0 |

### Willie Randolph Against Right-Handed Pitchers 1987
### Overall Batting Average .290

Fastball Average .338

| | Inside | Middle | Outside |
|---|---|---|---|
| High | 4/ 250 / 1 | 15/ 333 / 5 | 4/ 500 / 2 |
| Med | 14/ 500 / 7 | 10/ 700 / 7 | 38/ 289 / 11 |
| Low | 1/ 0 / 0 | 14/ 357 / 5 | 18/ 111 / 2 |

Curve Average .117

| | Inside | Middle | Outside |
|---|---|---|---|
| High | 0/ 0 / 0 | 1/ 0 / 0 | 0/ 0 / 0 |
| Med | 1/ 0 / 0 | 4/ 0 / 0 | 5/ 400 / 2 |
| Low | 0/ 0 / 0 | 2/ 0 / 0 | 4/ 0 / 0 |

Randolph's curve average fell in 1987, but it was more than compensated for by the 133 point increase in his fastball average.

Randolph improved in the highly pitched medium-high outside fastball location, hitting .137 in 1986 and .289 in 1987.

The following comparison shows that Coleman hit medium-high outside fastballs deeper to left field and more down the right field line in 1987.

MEDIUM-HIGH OUTSIDE
(FASTBALLS THROWN BY RIGHT-HANDED PITCHERS 1986)

BATTING AVERAGE .137
*PLAY*

| | |
|---|---|
| LEFTFIELDER | Medium-deep and shifted toward center field |
| CENTERFIELDER | Deep in straightaway center field |
| RIGHTFIELDER | Deep in straightaway right field |
| SHORTSTOP | Up middle (shifted toward second base) |
| SECOND | Normal position |

MEDIUM-HIGH OUTSIDE
(FASTBALLS THROWN BY RIGHT-HANDED PITCHERS 1987)

BATTING AVERAGE .289
*PLAY*

| | |
|---|---|
| LEFTFIELDER | Deep and shifted toward center field |
| CENTERFIELDER | Deep in straightaway center field |
| RIGHTFIELDER | Medium-deep and shifted toward the right field line |
| SHORTSTOP | Up middle (shifted toward second base) |
| SECOND | Normal position |

He also went more to the opposite field with inside pitches in 1987. This resulted in a much higher average in his medium-high inside average.

MEDIUM-HIGH INSIDE
(FASTBALLS THROWN BY RIGHT-HANDED PITCHERS 1986)

BATTING AVERAGE .200
*PLAY*

| | |
|---|---|
| LEFTFIELDER | Deep and shifted toward the left field line |
| CENTERFIELDER | Deep in straightaway center field |
| RIGHTFIELDER | No recorded instances |
| SHORTSTOP | Up middle (shifted toward second base) |
| SECOND | Normal position |

MEDIUM-HIGH INSIDE
(FASTBALLS THROWN BY RIGHT-HANDED PITCHERS 1987)

BATTING AVERAGE .500
  *PLAY*
LEFTFIELDER      Deep and shifted toward the left field line
CENTERFIELDER    Medium-deep in straightaway center field
RIGHTFIELDER     Medium-deep and shifted toward the right field line
SHORTSTOP        Up middle (shifted toward second base)
SECOND           Shifted toward first base

Randolph's overall curve average went down in 1987, but he continued to hit medium-high outside curves well. Notice Randolph's weakness against low-outside curves both years.

When ahead in the count, Randolph's average jumped in 1987. His fastball average more than doubled.

Notice how many more fastballs than curves Randolph was thrown when ahead in the count.

**Willie Randolph Ahead In The Count
Against Right-Handed Pitchers 1986
Batting Average .260**

Fastball Average .207

| | Inside | Middle | Outside |
|---|---|---|---|
| High | 1 / 0 / 0 | 5 / 600 / 3 | 2 / 0 / 0 |
| Med | 4 / 0 / 0 | 1 / 1000 / 1 | 31 / 161 / 5 |
| Low | 0 / 0 / 0 | 5 / 400 / 2 | 4 / 0 / 0 |

Curve Average .500

| | Inside | Middle | Outside |
|---|---|---|---|
| High | 0 / 0 / 0 | 0 / 0 / 0 | 0 / 0 / 0 |
| Med | 0 / 0 / 0 | 0 / 0 / 0 | 2 / 500 / 1 |
| Low | 0 / 0 / 0 | 1 / 1000 / 1 | 1 / 0 / 0 |

## Willie Randolph Ahead In The Count
## Against Right-Handed Pitchers 1987
## Batting Average .447

Fastball Average .476          Curve Average .000

| | Inside | Middle | Outside | Inside | Middle | Outside |
|---|---|---|---|---|---|---|
| High | 0/0 0 | 10/400 4 | 2/500 1 | 0/0 0 | 0/0 0 | 0/0 0 |
| Med | 7/714 5 | 8/875 7 | 17/470 8 | 0/0 0 | 1/0 0 | 1/0 0 |
| Low | 1/0 0 | 9/333 3 | 9/222 2 | 0/0 0 | 0/0 0 | 0/0 0 |

When ahead in the count in 1987, Randolph hit medium-high outside fastballs with great authority to all fields.

MEDIUM-HIGH OUTSIDE
(FASTBALLS THROWN BY RIGHT-HANDED PITCHERS 1986)

BATTING AVERAGE .161
    *PLAY*
LEFTFIELDER        Medium-deep and shifted toward center field
CENTERFIELDER    Deep in straightaway center field
RIGHTFIELDER     Deep in straightaway right field
SHORTSTOP         Normal position
SECOND            Normal position

MEDIUM-HIGH OUTSIDE
(FASTBALLS THROWN BY RIGHT-HANDED PITCHERS 1987)

BATTING AVERAGE .470
    *PLAY*
LEFTFIELDER        Deep and shifted toward the left field line
CENTERFIELDER    Deep and shifted toward left field
RIGHTFIELDER     Deep and shifted toward the right field line
SHORTSTOP         Normal position
SECOND            Normal position

## Randolph Against Left-Handed Pitchers

Randolph's average also rose significantly against left-handers in 1987.

### Willie Randolph Against Left-Handed Pitchers 1986
### Overall Batting Average .259

Fastball Average .305

|  | Inside | Middle | Outside |
|---|---|---|---|
| High | 1/ 1000/1 | 7/ 285/2 | 0/ 0/0 |
| Med | 3/ 333/1 | 3/ 666/2 | 21/ 238/5 |
| Low | 1/ 0/0 | 16/ 250/4 | 7/ 428/3 |

Curve Average .181

|  | Inside | Middle | Outside |
|---|---|---|---|
| High | 0/ 0/0 | 1/ 0/0 | 1/ 0/0 |
| Med | 0/ 0/0 | 2/ 500/1 | 3/ 333/1 |
| Low | 2/ 0/0 | 2/ 0/0 | 0/ 0/0 |

### Willie Randolph Against Left-Handed Pitchers 1987
### Overall Batting Average .355

Fastball Average .375

|  | Inside | Middle | Outside |
|---|---|---|---|
| High | 1/ 0/0 | 3/ 666/2 | 4/ 500/2 |
| Med | 4/ 250/1 | 2/ 1000/2 | 9/ 333/3 |
| Low | 2/ 0/0 | 3/ 333/1 | 4/ 250/1 |

Curve Average .500

|  | Inside | Middle | Outside |
|---|---|---|---|
| High | 0/ 0/0 | 0/ 0/0 | 0/ 0/0 |
| Med | 1/ 1000/1 | 0/ 0/0 | 1/ 0/0 |
| Low | 0/ 0/0 | 0/ 0/0 | 2/ 500/1 |

Fewer instances were recorded in 1987 for Randolph against left-handed pitchers, but the indications are clear. Randolph's improved performance against medium-high outside fastballs accounted for much of his increase. He hit medium-high inside fastballs almost exactly the same both years, driving the ball deep down both lines and to center field.

### Steve Sax, Los Angeles Dodgers

During the '85, '86 and '87 seasons, Steve Sax, right-handed hitter for the Dodgers, was on a batting-average roller coaster. In 1985, he officially hit .279. He raised his average 53 points in 1986, hitting .332. Then his average fell 52 points to .280 in 1987.

This rise and fall is unusual, and makes for an interesting BARS System examination. Sax's overall BARS batting averages against right-handed pitchers were recorded at .241 in 1985, .354 in 1986 and .235 in 1987. These correspond well with his official yearly averages.

Notice how few medium-over-the-middle fastballs Sax was thrown each of the three years. This shows how carefully he was pitched.

### Steve Sax Against Right-Handed Pitchers 1985
### Overall Batting Average .241

Fastball Average .301

| | Inside | Middle | Outside |
|---|---|---|---|
| High | 7/<br>285 / 2 | 14/<br>142 / 2 | 2/<br>0 / 0 |
| Med | 16/<br>312 / 5 | 0/<br>0 / 0 | 14/<br>428 / 6 |
| Low | 2/<br>0 / 0 | 8/<br>500 / 4 | 10/<br>300 / 3 |

Curve Average .083

| | Inside | Middle | Outside |
|---|---|---|---|
| High | 1/<br>0 / 0 | 1/<br>0 / 0 | 1/<br>0 / 0 |
| Med | 0/<br>0 / 0 | 2/<br>0 / 0 | 2/<br>500 / 1 |
| Low | 1/<br>0 / 0 | 4/<br>0 / 0 | 0/<br>0 / 0 |

### Steve Sax Against Right-Handed Pitchers 1986
### Overall Batting Average .354

Fastball Average .400

| | Inside | Middle | Outside |
|---|---|---|---|
| High | 6/<br>500 / 3 | 18/<br>388 / 7 | 5/<br>200 / 1 |
| Med | 16/<br>500 / 8 | 3/<br>333 / 1 | 27/<br>407 / 11 |
| Low | 3/<br>0 / 0 | 17/<br>470 / 8 | 5/<br>200 / 1 |

Curve Average .304

| | Inside | Middle | Outside |
|---|---|---|---|
| High | 1/<br>1000 / 1 | 2/<br>0 / 0 | 1/<br>0 / 0 |
| Med | 2/<br>500 / 1 | 1/<br>1000 / 1 | 9/<br>333 / 3 |
| Low | 0/<br>0 / 0 | 3/<br>333 / 1 | 4/<br>0 / 0 |

## Steve Sax Against Right-Handed Pitchers 1987
## Overall Batting Average .235

Fastball Average .288                Curve Average .400

| | Inside | Middle | Outside | Inside | Middle | Outside |
|---|---|---|---|---|---|---|
| High | 500 $^2/_1$ | 428 $^7/_3$ | 200 $^5/_1$ | 0 $^1/_0$ | 0 $^1/_0$ | 0 $^0/_0$ |
| Med | 200 $^5/_1$ | 0 $^0/_0$ | 285 $^{14}/_4$ | 0 $^0/_0$ | 0 $^0/_0$ | 600 $^5/_3$ |
| Low | 0 $^5/_0$ | 500 $^8/_4$ | 166 $^6/_1$ | 0 $^1/_0$ | 0 $^0/_0$ | 500 $^2/_1$ |

Sax is a good fastball hitter. His fastball average of .301 in 1985 rose nearly 100 points to an even .400 in 1986. It fell to .288 in 1987.

The most significant differences in Sax's fastball locations between the years were in his medium-high inside location. His rising and falling average in this location most closely mirrored his overall changes. In 1985 he recorded a .312 average, but did not hit the ball with great authority. In 1986 he hit .500, hitting the ball deep to center and down the left field line. Then in 1987 he hit .200, pushing the ball down the right field line.

MEDIUM-HIGH INSIDE
(FASTBALLS THROWN BY RIGHT-HANDED PITCHERS 1985)

BATTING AVERAGE .312
   *PLAY*
LEFTFIELDER        Medium-deep in straightaway left field
CENTERFIELDER      Short and shifted toward left field
RIGHTFIELDER       No recorded instances
SHORTSTOP          Normal position
SECOND             Normal position

MEDIUM-HIGH INSIDE
(FASTBALLS THROWN BY RIGHT-HANDED PITCHERS 1986)

BATTING AVERAGE .500
*PLAY*
LEFTFIELDER      Deep and shifted toward the left field line
CENTERFIELDER    Deep in straightaway center field
RIGHTFIELDER     No recorded instances
SHORTSTOP        Up middle (shifted toward second base)
SECOND           Normal position


MEDIUM-HIGH INSIDE
(FASTBALLS THROWN BY RIGHT-HANDED PITCHERS 1987)

BATTING AVERAGE .200
*PLAY*
LEFTFIELDER      No recorded instances
CENTERFIELDER    No recorded instances
RIGHTFIELDER     Medium-deep and shifted toward the right field line
SHORTSTOP        Normal position
SECOND           Normal position

Between the 1985 and 1986 seasons, Sax had a significant increase in his high-over-the-middle fastball average (.142 to .388). His average in this location remained high (.428) in 1987, even though his overall average fell that year.

Sax's medium-high outside fastball average was .428 in 1985. It remained high at .407 in 1986, but fell to .285 in 1987. Sax went strongly to right field with medium-high outside fastballs during his successful 1986 season.

It is interesting that not one hit ball to left or center fields was recorded in Sax's medium-high outside location in 1986, even though a fairly large number of instances and base hits were recorded. This location does not reflect the rise and fall of his overall average, but the direction and distance he hit these pitches show much about his performance. Please see Sax's chart on the following page.

MEDIUM-HIGH OUTSIDE
(FASTBALLS THROWN BY RIGHT-HANDED PITCHERS 1985)

BATTING AVERAGE .428
*PLAY*
LEFTFIELDER     No recorded instances
CENTERFIELDER    Short and shifted toward right field
RIGHTFIELDER    Deep in straightaway right field
SHORTSTOP    Normal position
SECOND    Normal position


MEDIUM-HIGH OUTSIDE
(FASTBALLS THROWN BY RIGHT-HANDED PITCHERS 1986)

BATTING AVERAGE .407
*PLAY*
LEFTFIELDER     No recorded instances
CENTERFIELDER    No recorded instances
RIGHTFIELDER    Deep and shifted toward the right field line
SHORTSTOP    Normal position
SECOND    Normal position


MEDIUM-HIGH OUTSIDE
(FASTBALLS THROWN BY RIGHT-HANDED PITCHERS 1987)

BATTING AVERAGE .285
*PLAY*
LEFTFIELDER     Deep and shifted toward center field
CENTERFIELDER    Deep in straightaway center field
RIGHTFIELDER    Deep in straightaway right field
SHORTSTOP    Normal position
SECOND    Normal position

Sax hit low-over-the-middle fastballs well all three years (.500 in '85, .470 in '86 and .500 in '87). This location seems to be one of his ongoing strengths (see Sax's record in Chapter Two). But notice that he did not have a recorded hit in the low-inside location. Only a few low-inside instances were recorded each year, but he seems to have a weakness against these pitches.

## Sax Against Left-Handed Pitchers

Sax's BARS averages against left-handed pitchers also rose and fell over the three seasons: In 1985 he hit .214 overall against left-handed pitchers. In 1986 he hit .388, and in 1987 he hit .342. His average in the 1987 season did not fall significantly, but there were fewer recorded instances to go on.

In 1986, Sax hit fastballs very well against left-handers. In the chart below, notice his strong .555 average against medium-high outside fastballs. His .166 against low-outside fastballs indicates a possible weakness.

### Steve Sax Against Left-Handed Pitchers 1986
### Overall Batting Average .388

Fastball Average .434       Curve Average .416

|  | Inside | Middle | Outside |  | Inside | Middle | Outside |
|---|---|---|---|---|---|---|---|
| High | 1/ 0 / 0 | 4/ 500 / 2 | 3/ 0 / 0 |  | 3/ 333 / 1 | 1/ 0 / 0 | 1/ 0 / 0 |
| Med | 6/ 833 / 5 | 0/ 0 / 0 | 18/ 555 /10 |  | 0/ 0 / 0 | 1/ 1000/ 1 | 3/ 666 / 2 |
| Low | 0/ 0 / 0 | 8/ 250 / 2 | 6/ 166 / 1 |  | 2/ 500 / 1 | 1/ 0 / 0 | 0/ 0 / 0 |

It is interesting to examine how Sax hit medium-high outside and low-outside fastballs against left-handers in his excellent 1986 season. He went with low-outside fastballs, hitting them medium-deep to straightaway center and right. He hit medium-high outside fastballs deep down both lines and to right-center field.

LOW OUTSIDE
(FASTBALLS THROWN BY LEFT-HANDED PITCHERS 1986)

BATTING AVERAGE .166
    *PLAY*
LEFTFIELDER      No recorded instances
CENTERFIELDER    Medium-deep in straightaway center field
RIGHTFIELDER     Medium-deep in straightaway right field
SHORTSTOP        Normal position
SECOND            Normal position

MEDIUM-HIGH OUTSIDE
(FASTBALLS THROWN BY LEFT-HANDED PITCHERS 1986)

BATTING AVERAGE .555
   *PLAY*
LEFTFIELDER      Deep and shifted toward the left field line
CENTERFIELDER    Deep and shifted toward right field
RIGHTFIELDER     Deep and shifted toward the right field line
SHORTSTOP        Up middle (shifted toward second base)
SECOND           Normal position

These charts again emphasize the importance of fielders adjusting on a pitch-by-pitch basis. If the fielders took positions against Sax and held them through all the pitches to him, they would be badly out of position for at least one of these pitches.

### Mike Marshall, Los Angeles Dodgers

Right-handed Mike Marshall, Sax's teammate on the Dodgers, also was on a batting-average roller coaster during the '85, '86 and '87 seasons, but in directions opposite to Sax.

In 1985, Marshall officially hit .293. His average declined 60 points to .233 in 1986, then rose 61 points to .294 in 1987. His BARS averages against right-handed pitchers closely mirror his official averages. His BARS average was .297 in '85, .193 in '86 and .301 in '87.

Like Sax, Marshall was carefully pitched each year. He was thrown few medium-over-the-middle fastballs or curves.

### Mike Marshall Against Right-Handed Pitchers 1985
### Overall Batting Average .297

Fastball Average .416

|      | Inside | Middle | Outside |
|------|--------|--------|---------|
| High | 4 / 250 / 1 | 9 / 444 / 4 | 5 / 200 / 1 |
| Med  | 4 / 500 / 2 | 0 / 0 / 0 | 17 / 529 / 9 |
| Low  | 6 / 666 / 4 | 9 / 333 / 3 | 6 / 166 / 1 |

Curve Average .181

|      | Inside | Middle | Outside |
|------|--------|--------|---------|
| High | 0 / 0 / 0 | 2 / 500 / 1 | 1 / 0 / 0 |
| Med  | 0 / 0 / 0 | 1 / 1000 / 1 | 4 / 250 / 1 |
| Low  | 3 / 0 / 0 | 2 / 0 / 0 | 9 / 111 / 1 |

### Mike Marshall Against Right-Handed Pitchers 1986
### Overall Batting Average .193

Fastball Average .205

| | Inside | Middle | Outside |
|---|---|---|---|
| High | **0** 3/0 | **200** 5/1 | **0** 1/0 |
| Med | **0** 5/0 | **1000** 2/2 | **272** 11/3 |
| Low | **0** 1/0 | **181** 11/2 | **0** 0/0 |

Curve Average .277

| | Inside | Middle | Outside |
|---|---|---|---|
| High | **0** 0/0 | **0** 0/0 | **0** 1/0 |
| Med | **500** 2/1 | **0** 1/0 | **333** 3/1 |
| Low | **0** 1/0 | **666** 3/2 | **142** 7/1 |

### Mike Marshall Against Right-Handed Pitchers 1987
### Overall Batting Average .301

Fastball Average .333

| | Inside | Middle | Outside |
|---|---|---|---|
| High | **333** 3/1 | **0** 3/0 | **333** 3/1 |
| Med | **333** 6/2 | **0** 2/0 | **416** 12/5 |
| Low | **1000** 1/1 | **333** 3/1 | **333** 3/1 |

Curve Average .312

| | Inside | Middle | Outside |
|---|---|---|---|
| High | **0** 0/0 | **0** 1/0 | **0** 1/0 |
| Med | **1000** 1/1 | **0** 2/0 | **500** 4/2 |
| Low | **0** 0/0 | **0** 0/0 | **285** 7/2 |

Marshall's medium-high outside fastball location was a key to his performance each year because so many of these pitches were thrown to him. He hit .529 in this location in '85, .272 in '86 and .416 in '87.

Notice Marshall's difficulty with inside fastballs in his weak 1986 season. He hit inside fastballs well in 1985 and 1987.

During 1985 and 1986, Marshall hit low-outside curves very poorly (.111 in 1985 and .142 in 1986). In 1987 he hit .285, but that is still only adequate. This weakness could be linked to his difficulty with inside fastballs.

Few BARS instances were recorded for Marshall against left-handed pitchers, so his charts against lefties are not shown here.

### Mike Easler, New York Yankees

Easler, a left-handed batter, improved his average 40 points against right-handed pitchers in 1986. Both his fastball and curve averages rose. His BARS averages against right-handed pitchers of .248 in 1985 and .291 in 1986 closely mirror his official averages of .262 and .302 respectively in those two years.

### Mike Easler Against Right-Handed Pitchers 1985
### Overall Batting Average .248

**Fastball Average .271**

|      | Outside | Middle | Inside |
|------|---------|--------|--------|
| High | 5 / 0 / 0 | 15 / 266 / 4 | 9 / 111 / 1 |
| Med  | 27 / 259 / 7 | 8 / 625 / 5 | 12 / 333 / 4 |
| Low  | 3 / 333 / 1 | 18 / 277 / 5 | 10 / 200 / 2 |

**Curve Average .212**

|      | Outside | Middle | Inside |
|------|---------|--------|--------|
| High | 1 / 0 / 0 | 3 / 0 / 0 | 0 / 0 / 0 |
| Med  | 8 / 250 / 2 | 3 / 666 / 2 | 2 / 500 / 1 |
| Low  | 5 / 0 / 0 | 6 / 166 / 1 | 5 / 200 / 1 |

### Mike Easler Against Right-Handed Pitchers 1986
### Overall Batting Average .291

**Fastball Average .330**

|      | Outside | Middle | Inside |
|------|---------|--------|--------|
| High | 11 / 181 / 2 | 10 / 300 / 3 | 1 / 1000 / 1 |
| Med  | 52 / 307 / 16 | 10 / 600 / 6 | 13 / 230 / 3 |
| Low  | 7 / 285 / 2 | 21 / 476 / 10 | 11 / 181 / 2 |

**Curve Average .240**

|      | Outside | Middle | Inside |
|------|---------|--------|--------|
| High | 1 / 0 / 0 | 4 / 250 / 1 | 4 / 250 / 1 |
| Med  | 3 / 666 / 2 | 0 / 0 / 0 | 2 / 0 / 0 |
| Low  | 5 / 200 / 1 | 5 / 200 / 1 | 1 / 0 / 0 |

Easler raised his fastball average nearly 60 points in 1986. Two of his weakest fastball locations in 1985 — high-outside and low-inside — continued to be weak in 1986; but his medium-high outside average jumped to .307 in 1986, up from .259 in 1985.

One of the major factors in the improvement of his fastball average was his ability to go with the pitch and hit more to all fields in 1986. The following charts show that the left-handed hitting Easler tended to pull the ball less in 1986. The result was a higher average in 1986.

MEDIUM-HIGH OUTSIDE
(FASTBALLS THROWN BY RIGHT-HANDED PITCHERS 1985)

BATTING AVERAGE .259
    *PLAY*

| | |
|---|---|
| LEFTFIELDER | Deep and shifted toward the left field line |
| CENTERFIELDER | Deep and shifted toward right field |
| RIGHTFIELDER | Deep and shifted toward the right field line |
| SHORTSTOP | Normal position |
| SECOND | Normal position |

MEDIUM-HIGH OUTSIDE
(FASTBALLS THROWN BY RIGHT-HANDED PITCHERS 1986)

BATTING AVERAGE .307
    *PLAY*

| | |
|---|---|
| LEFTFIELDER | Deep and shifted toward the left field line |
| CENTERFIELDER | Medium deep in straightaway center field |
| RIGHTFIELDER | Deep and shifted toward center field |
| SHORTSTOP | Normal position |
| SECOND | Normal position |

LOW-OVER-THE-MIDDLE
(FASTBALLS THROWN BY RIGHT-HANDED PITCHERS 1985)

BATTING AVERAGE .277
    *PLAY*

| | |
|---|---|
| LEFTFIELDER | Medium-deep in straightaway left field |
| CENTERFIELDER | Deep in straightaway center field |
| RIGHTFIELDER | Deep and shifted toward the right field line |
| SHORTSTOP | Normal position |
| SECOND | Shifted toward first base |

LOW-OVER-THE-MIDDLE
(FASTBALLS THROWN BY RIGHT-HANDED PITCHERS 1986)

BATTING AVERAGE .476
   *PLAY*
LEFTFIELDER      Medium-deep and shifted toward the left field line
CENTERFIELDER   Deep and shifted toward right field
RIGHTFIELDER    Deep in straightaway right field
SHORTSTOP       Normal position
SECOND          Normal position

To remind the reader, the Super Summary fielding strategy for a particular player remains basically the same over the years. Dramatic changes in a hitter's performance sometimes cause significant differences in the distance and direction of hit balls from one year to the next, but for the most part the distance and direction remain constant. This allows the BARS System fielding strategy to maintain its 90 percent accuracy year in and year out.

Right-handed pitchers threw Easler more outside fastballs in 1986 than in 1985. He responded well by hitting medium-high outside fastballs for a .307 average in 1986.

His curve average went up slightly in 1986. He still had trouble with low curves, but he hit better against high curves and outside curves.

In 1985, Easler hit 100 points higher against right-handed pitchers when he was ahead in the count than when behind. He was looking for fastballs and hitting them well.

### Mike Easler Behind In The Count
### Against Right-Handed Pitchers 1985
### Batting Average .250

Fastball Average .285            Curve Average .300

|  | Outside | Middle | Inside | Outside | Middle | Inside |
|---|---|---|---|---|---|---|
| High | 1/ 0 / 0 | 4/ 500 / 2 | 2/ 0 / 0 | 0/ 0 / 0 | 1/ 0 / 0 | 0/ 0 / 0 |
| Med | 4/ 0 / 0 | 0/ 0 / 0 | 4/ 500 / 2 | 4/ 500 / 2 | 0/ 0 / 0 | 0/ 0 / 0 |
| Low | 1/ 1000/ 1 | 4/ 0 / 0 | 1/ 1000/ 1 | 2/ 0 / 0 | 2/ 0 / 0 | 1/ 1000/ 1 |

### Mike Easler Ahead In The Count
### Against Right-Handed Pitchers 1985
### Batting Average .358

Fastball Average .382

| | Outside | Middle | Inside |
|---|---|---|---|
| High | 1 / 0 / 0 | 7 / 285 / 2 | 2 / 500 / 1 |
| Med | 12 / 500 / 6 | 5 / 400 / 2 | 4 / 500 / 2 |
| Low | 1 / 0 / 0 | 8 / 500 / 4 | 7 / 142 / 1 |

Curve Average .333

| | Outside | Middle | Inside |
|---|---|---|---|
| High | 1 / 0 / 0 | 0 / 0 / 0 | 0 / 0 / 0 |
| Med | 2 / 0 / 0 | 1 / 1000 / 1 | 1 / 1000 / 1 |
| Low | 0 / 0 / 0 | 0 / 0 / 0 | 1 / 0 / 0 |

In 1986, he hit well both when ahead and behind in the count, but overall he hit better when behind.

### Mike Easler Behind In The Count
### Against Right-Handed Pitchers 1986
### Batting Average .392

Fastball Average .448

| | Outside | Middle | Inside |
|---|---|---|---|
| High | 4 / 250 / 1 | 3 / 333 / 1 | 1 / 1000 / 1 |
| Med | 8 / 500 / 4 | 1 / 1000 / 1 | 2 / 0 / 0 |
| Low | 3 / 333 / 1 | 3 / 666 / 2 | 4 / 500 / 2 |

Curve Average .400

| | Outside | Middle | Inside |
|---|---|---|---|
| High | 0 / 0 / 0 | 3 / 333 / 1 | 1 / 0 / 0 |
| Med | 1 / 1000 / 1 | 0 / 0 / 0 | 1 / 0 / 0 |
| Low | 3 / 333 / 1 | 1 / 1000 / 1 | 0 / 0 / 0 |

## Mike Easler Ahead In The Count
## Against Right-Handed Pitchers 1986
## Batting Average .300

Fastball Average .352

|  | Outside | Middle | Inside |
|---|---|---|---|
| High | 333 3/1 | 166 6/1 | 0 0/0 |
| Med | 357 28/10 | 500 8/4 | 400 5/2 |
| Low | 333 3/1 | 400 15/6 | 0 3/0 |

Curve Average .000

|  | Outside | Middle | Inside |
|---|---|---|---|
| High | 0 0/0 | 0 0/0 | 0 1/0 |
| Med | 0 1/0 | 0 0/0 | 0 1/0 |
| Low | 0 1/0 | 0 1/0 | 0 1/0 |

## Easler Against Left-Handed Pitchers

Against left-handed pitchers, Easler hit better in 1986.

## Mike Easler Against Left-Handed Pitchers 1985
## Overall Batting Average .247

Fastball Average .323

|  | Outside | Middle | Inside |
|---|---|---|---|
| High | 500 2/1 | 125 8/1 | 0 5/0 |
| Med | 333 15/5 | 400 10/4 | 250 12/3 |
| Low | 0 2/0 | 600 10/6 | 500 4/2 |

Curve Average .117

|  | Outside | Middle | Inside |
|---|---|---|---|
| High | 0 0/0 | 1000 1/1 | 0 1/0 |
| Med | 0 4/0 | 0 3/0 | 500 2/1 |
| Low | 0 2/0 | 0 1/0 | 0 3/0 |

## Mike Easler Against Left-Handed Pitchers 1986
## Overall Batting Average .275

### Fastball Average .321

| | Outside | Middle | Inside |
|---|---|---|---|
| High | ²/ 500 / 1 | ²/ 0 / 0 | ²/ 0 / 0 |
| Med | ⁵/ 600 / 3 | ³/ 0 / 0 | ⁷/ 571 / 4 |
| Low | ¹/ 0 / 0 | ⁴/ 250 / 1 | ²/ 0 / 0 |

### Curve Average .285

| | Outside | Middle | Inside |
|---|---|---|---|
| High | ⁰/ 0 / 0 | ²/ 500 / 1 | ¹/ 0 / 0 |
| Med | ²/ 0 / 0 | ¹/ 0 / 0 | ⁵/ 400 / 2 |
| Low | ⁶/ 166 / 1 | ¹/ 1000 / 1 | ³/ 333 / 1 |

Easler's two problem spots against fastballs thrown by left-handers in 1985 — high-inside and high-over-the-middle — persisted in 1986. Overall he hit fastballs thrown by left-handers about the same both years, but he hit curves much better in 1986.

Overall, Easler's Super Summary shows that he improved against fastballs and curves in 1986. Against right-handed pitchers he hit much better when behind in the count in 1986 than he did when behind in 1985. This could have been due to increased confidence, and to the fact that he stopped trying to pull the ball and went more with the pitch in 1986.

## Kirby Puckett, Minnesota Twins

Kirby Puckett's 40 point gain from .288 in 1985 to .328 gave him one of the highest 1986 American League averages. A right-handed hitter, his average soared against right-handed pitchers in 1986 compared to 1985. Please see his charts on the following page.

### Kirby Puckett Against Right-Handed Pitchers 1985
### Overall Batting Average .224

**Fastball Average .274**

| | Inside | Middle | Outside |
|---|---|---|---|
| High | 2 / 0 / 0 | 8 / 125 / 1 | 2 / 500 / 1 |
| Med | 11 / 454 / 5 | 6 / 666 / 4 | 10 / 200 / 2 |
| Low | 2 / 0 / 0 | 5 / 200 / 1 | 5 / 0 / 0 |

**Curve Average .208**

| | Inside | Middle | Outside |
|---|---|---|---|
| High | 1 / 0 / 0 | 0 / 0 / 0 | 0 / 0 / 0 |
| Med | 2 / 500 / 1 | 2 / 0 / 0 | 8 / 250 / 2 |
| Low | 0 / 0 / 0 | 4 / 250 / 1 | 7 / 142 / 1 |

### Kirby Puckett Against Right-Handed Pitchers 1986
### Overall Batting Average .355

**Fastball Average .373**

| | Inside | Middle | Outside |
|---|---|---|---|
| High | 4 / 250 / 1 | 6 / 500 / 3 | 0 / 0 / 0 |
| Med | 9 / 444 / 4 | 5 / 200 / 1 | 29 / 344 / 10 |
| Low | 7 / 285 / 2 | 9 / 333 / 3 | 6 / 666 / 4 |

**Curve Average .458**

| | Inside | Middle | Outside |
|---|---|---|---|
| High | 1 / 1000 / 1 | 2 / 1000 / 2 | 0 / 0 / 0 |
| Med | 1 / 1000 / 1 | 1 / 1000 / 1 | 7 / 714 / 5 |
| Low | 0 / 0 / 0 | 2 / 0 / 0 | 10 / 100 / 1 |

Puckett's fastball average rose nearly 100 points. In 1985, he had problems with low fastballs and some high fastballs. In 1986, he hit solidly in all these locations.

His Super Summary Reports show that he pulled low pitches more in 1986 and hit them deeper. He hit low-outside and medium-high outside fastballs for much higher averages in 1986. He pulled medium-high outside fastballs more in 1986.

MEDIUM-HIGH OUTSIDE
(FASTBALLS THROWN BY RIGHT-HANDED PITCHERS 1985)

BATTING AVERAGE .200
*PLAY*
LEFTFIELDER            No instances recorded
CENTERFIELDER         Deep in straightaway center field
RIGHTFIELDER          Medium-deep in straightaway right field
SHORTSTOP            Up middle (shifted toward second base)
SECOND              Normal position


MEDIUM-HIGH OUTSIDE
(FASTBALLS THROWN BY RIGHT-HANDED PITCHERS 1986)

BATTING AVERAGE .344
*PLAY*
LEFTFIELDER            Medium-deep in straightaway left field
CENTERFIELDER         Deep in straightaway center field
RIGHTFIELDER          Medium-deep in straightaway right field
SHORTSTOP            Normal position
SECOND              Normal position

In 1986, right-handed pitchers threw him a higher percentage of outside fastballs, with the majority of these in the medium-high outside location. Puckett responded strongly, hitting .344 in this location.

Puckett's curve average also soared in 1986, although he continued to have trouble with low curves. His Super Summary shows that in 1986 he pulled almost every curve to left field and center field, while in 1985 he hit most curves to center and right. He hit curves deeper in 1986 than in 1985. The shortstop and second baseman play normal in both these charts.

MEDIUM-HIGH OUTSIDE
(CURVES THROWN BY RIGHT-HANDED PITCHERS 1985)

BATTING AVERAGE .250
*PLAY*
LEFTFIELDER            No instances recorded
CENTERFIELDER         Medium-deep and shifted toward left field
RIGHTFIELDER          Medium-deep and shifted toward the right field line

MEDIUM-HIGH OUTSIDE
(CURVES THROWN BY RIGHT-HANDED PITCHERS 1986)

BATTING AVERAGE .714
   *PLAY*
LEFTFIELDER      Deep in straightaway left field
CENTERFIELDER   Deep in straightaway center field
RIGHTFIELDER    Deep and shifted toward center field

In 1985, Puckett hit better against right-handed pitchers when he was behind in the count.

**Kirby Puckett Behind In The Count**
**Against Right-Handed Pitchers 1985**
**Batting Average .296**

Fastball Average .363

| | Inside | Middle | Outside |
|---|---|---|---|
| High | 1/ 0 / 0 | 1/ 0 / 0 | 1/ 0 / 0 |
| Med | 0/ 0 / 0 | 3/ 666 / 2 | 3/ 666 / 2 |
| Low | 0/ 0 / 0 | 0/ 0 / 0 | 2/ 0 / 0 |

Curve Average .500

| | Inside | Middle | Outside |
|---|---|---|---|
| High | 0/ 0 / 0 | 0/ 0 / 0 | 0/ 0 / 0 |
| Med | 1/ 1000 / 1 | 0/ 0 / 0 | 0/ 0 / 0 |
| Low | 0/ 0 / 0 | 0/ 0 / 0 | 3/ 333 / 1 |

**Kirby Puckett Ahead In The Count**
**Against Right-Handed Pitchers 1985**
**Batting Average .250**

Fastball Average .222

| | Inside | Middle | Outside |
|---|---|---|---|
| High | 0/ 0 / 0 | 7/ 142 / 1 | 0/ 0 / 0 |
| Med | 9/ 444 / 4 | 2/ 500 / 1 | 3/ 0 / 0 |
| Low | 1/ 0 / 0 | 4/ 0 / 0 | 1/ 0 / 0 |

Curve Average .200

| | Inside | Middle | Outside |
|---|---|---|---|
| High | 1/ 0 / 0 | 0/ 0 / 0 | 0/ 0 / 0 |
| Med | 1/ 0 / 0 | 1/ 0 / 0 | 4/ 500 / 2 |
| Low | 0/ 0 / 0 | 1/ 0 / 0 | 2/ 0 / 0 |

In 1986, he hit better when ahead in the count.

### Kirby Puckett Behind In The Count
### Against Right-Handed Pitchers 1986
### Batting Average .333

Fastball Average .230

| | Inside | Middle | Outside |
|------|--------|--------|---------|
| High | 0 / **0** / 0 | 1 / **0** / 0 | 0 / **0** / 0 |
| Med | 2 / **0** / 0 | 2 / **500** / 1 | 4 / **250** / 1 |
| Low | 2 / **0** / 0 | 2 / **500** / 1 | 0 / **0** / 0 |

Curve Average .500

| | Inside | Middle | Outside |
|------|--------|--------|---------|
| High | 0 / **0** / 0 | 0 / **0** / 0 | 0 / **0** / 0 |
| Med | 0 / **0** / 0 | 1 / **1000** / 1 | 3 / **666** / 2 |
| Low | 0 / **0** / 0 | 0 / **0** / 0 | 2 / **0** / 0 |

### Kirby Puckett Ahead In The Count
### Against Right-Handed Pitchers 1986
### Batting Average .446

Fastball Average .473

| | Inside | Middle | Outside |
|------|--------|--------|---------|
| High | 4 / **250** / 1 | 4 / **750** / 3 | 0 / **0** / 0 |
| Med | 4 / **750** / 3 | 2 / **0** / 0 | 10 / **400** / 4 |
| Low | 4 / **500** / 2 | 7 / **285** / 2 | 3 / **1000** / 3 |

Curve Average .666

| | Inside | Middle | Outside |
|------|--------|--------|---------|
| High | 0 / **0** / 0 | 2 / **1000** / 2 | 0 / **0** / 0 |
| Med | 1 / **1000** / 1 | 0 / **0** / 0 | 4 / **750** / 3 |
| Low | 0 / **0** / 0 | 1 / **0** / 0 | 1 / **0** / 0 |

## Puckett Against Left-handed Pitchers

Puckett hit left-handed pitchers better in 1985 than in 1986. He hit curves better in 1986, but had more trouble with fastballs.

### Kirby Puckett Against Left-Handed Pitchers 1985
### Overall Batting Average .295

| Fastball Average .323 | | | | Curve Average .142 | | |
| --- | --- | --- | --- | --- | --- | --- |
| | Inside | Middle | Outside | Inside | Middle | Outside |
| High | 2 / 500 / 1 | 1 / 1000 / 1 | 2 / 500 / 1 | 1 / 0 / 0 | 0 / 0 / 0 | 0 / 0 / 0 |
| Med | 4 / 250 / 1 | 4 / 750 / 3 | 10 / 300 / 3 | 0 / 0 / 0 | 0 / 0 / 0 | 1 / 0 / 0 |
| Low | 2 / 0 / 0 | 4 / 250 / 1 | 5 / 0 / 0 | 0 / 0 / 0 | 4 / 250 / 1 | 1 / 0 / 0 |

### Kirby Puckett Against Left-Handed Pitchers 1986
### Overall Batting Average .267

| Fastball Average .266 | | | | Curve Average .333 | | |
| --- | --- | --- | --- | --- | --- | --- |
| | Inside | Middle | Outside | Inside | Middle | Outside |
| High | 1 / 1000 / 1 | 3 / 333 / 1 | 2 / 0 / 0 | 0 / 0 / 0 | 0 / 0 / 0 | 1 / 1000 / 1 |
| Med | 8 / 125 / 1 | 0 / 0 / 0 | 6 / 333 / 2 | 1 / 0 / 0 | 0 / 0 / 0 | 1 / 0 / 0 |
| Low | 1 / 0 / 0 | 7 / 285 / 2 | 2 / 500 / 1 | 0 / 0 / 0 | 1 / 1000 / 1 | 5 / 200 / 1 |

## Joe Carter, Cleveland Indians

Joe Carter, a right-handed hitter, raised his average 40 points from .262 in 1985 to .302 in 1986. Carter's BARS averages mirror this rise.

### Joe Carter Against Right-Handed Pitchers 1985
### Overall Batting Average .261

Fastball Average .185

| | Inside | Middle | Outside |
|---|---|---|---|
| **High** | 2 / 0 / 0 | 2 / 1000 / 2 | 0 / 0 / 0 |
| **Med** | 3 / 333 / 1 | 6 / 166 / 1 | 7 / 0 / 0 |
| **Low** | 1 / 0 / 0 | 4 / 250 / 1 | 2 / 0 / 0 |

Curve Average .428

| | Inside | Middle | Outside |
|---|---|---|---|
| **High** | 0 / 0 / 0 | 0 / 0 / 0 | 0 / 0 / 0 |
| **Med** | 1 / 0 / 0 | 1 / 1000 / 1 | 0 / 0 / 0 |
| **Low** | 0 / 0 / 0 | 1 / 0 / 0 | 4 / 500 / 2 |

### Joe Carter Against Right-Handed Pitchers 1986
### Overall Batting Average .349

Fastball Average .416

| | Inside | Middle | Outside |
|---|---|---|---|
| **High** | 5 / 400 / 2 | 8 / 250 / 2 | 2 / 500 / 1 |
| **Med** | 9 / 666 / 6 | 4 / 1000 / 4 | 27 / 296 / 8 |
| **Low** | 7 / 571 / 4 | 10 / 400 / 4 | 12 / 333 / 4 |

Curve Average .318

| | Inside | Middle | Outside |
|---|---|---|---|
| **High** | 1 / 0 / 0 | 3 / 333 / 1 | 0 / 0 / 0 |
| **Med** | 0 / 0 / 0 | 0 / 0 / 0 | 11 / 545 / 6 |
| **Low** | 1 / 0 / 0 | 0 / 0 / 0 | 6 / 0 / 0 |

Carter's 1985 average of .262 was close to his official lifetime average of .260 (lifetime through the 1985 season). His gain to .302 can be traced mainly to his performance against fastballs thrown by right-handed pitchers in 1986.

There is a greater total of recorded fastballs in Carter's 1986 Super Summary, but the distribution of pitches around the fastball grid is about the same as in 1985. There are fewer medium-over-the-middle pitches in 1986, indicating that Carter was pitched with greater care in 1986.

Notice how poorly he hit outside fastballs in 1985. Carter's Super Summary shows that most of his outside fastballs in 1985 were strikeouts, with a few infield outs and pop-ups to right field. In 1986, however, he hit strongly in all outside fastball categories, driving the ball deeper and more straightaway.

MEDIUM-HIGH OUTSIDE
(FASTBALLS THROWN BY RIGHT-HANDED PITCHERS 1985)

BATTING AVERAGE .000
> *PLAY*

| | |
|---|---|
| LEFTFIELDER | No instances recorded |
| CENTERFIELDER | No instances recorded |
| RIGHTFIELDER | Medium-deep and straightaway in right field |

MEDIUM-HIGH OUTSIDE
(FASTBALLS THROWN BY RIGHT-HANDED PITCHERS 1986)

BATTING AVERAGE .296
> *PLAY*

| | |
|---|---|
| LEFTFIELDER | Deep and shifted toward center field |
| CENTERFIELDER | Deep in straightaway center field |
| RIGHTFIELDER | Deep and shifted toward center field |

Overall, Carter hit curves for a higher percentage in 1985 than in 1986. Notice the very high percentage of curves that were in the outside locations in 1986. That season he hit medium-high outside curves very well, but he hit low-outside curves poorly.

LOW OUTSIDE
(CURVES THROWN BY RIGHT-HANDED PITCHERS 1986)

BATTING AVERAGE .000
> *PLAY*

| | |
|---|---|
| LEFTFIELDER | Medium-deep and shifted toward center field |
| CENTERFIELDER | Deep in straightaway center field |
| RIGHTFIELDER | Medium-deep in straightaway right field |

MEDIUM-HIGH OUTSIDE
(CURVES THROWN BY RIGHT-HANDED PITCHERS 1986)

BATTING AVERAGE .545
> *PLAY*

| | |
|---|---|
| LEFTFIELDER | Deep and shifted toward the left field line |
| CENTERFIELDER | Medium-deep in straightaway center field |
| RIGHTFIELDER | Deep and shifted toward center field |

In 1986 Carter hit better when he was behind in the count. Little information is available for his ahead- and behind-in-the-count performances in 1985, so it is not included here.

### Joe Carter Behind In The Count
### Against Right-Handed Pitchers 1986
### Batting Average .461

Fastball Average .500              Curve Average .600

| | Inside | Middle | Outside |
|---|---|---|---|
| High | 0 / 0 / 0 | 3 / 333 / 1 | 1 / 1000 / 1 |
| Med | 3 / 1000 / 3 | 1 / 1000 / 1 | 9 / 333 / 3 |
| Low | 0 / 0 / 0 | 0 / 0 / 0 | 1 / 0 / 0 |

| | Inside | Middle | Outside |
|---|---|---|---|
| High | 0 / 0 / 0 | 2 / 500 / 1 | 0 / 0 / 0 |
| Med | 0 / 0 / 0 | 0 / 0 / 0 | 7 / 714 / 5 |
| Low | 0 / 0 / 0 | 0 / 0 / 0 | 1 / 0 / 0 |

### Joe Carter Ahead In The Count
### Against Right-Handed Pitchers 1986
### Batting Average .400

Fastball Average .468              Curve Average .200

| | Inside | Middle | Outside |
|---|---|---|---|
| High | 1 / 1000 / 1 | 1 / 1000 / 1 | 1 / 0 / 0 |
| Med | 2 / 500 / 1 | 1 / 1000 / 1 | 12 / 333 / 4 |
| Low | 4 / 1000 / 4 | 4 / 250 / 1 | 6 / 333 / 2 |

| | Inside | Middle | Outside |
|---|---|---|---|
| High | 1 / 0 / 0 | 1 / 0 / 0 | 0 / 0 / 0 |
| Med | 0 / 0 / 0 | 0 / 0 / 0 | 2 / 500 / 1 |
| Low | 0 / 0 / 0 | 0 / 0 / 0 | 1 / 0 / 0 |

Note that Carter's ahead and behind averages of .400 and .461 for 1986 are much higher than his .349 overall BARS System 1986 average against right-handers. The difference is accounted for in his performance when even in the count.

## Carter Against Left-Handed Pitchers

Carter's average against left-handed pitchers doubled in 1986. His .274 average in 1986 included a strong performance against fastballs (.387) and a curve average 89 points higher than in 1985.

### Joe Carter Against Left-Handed Pitchers 1985
### Overall Batting Average .137

Fastball Average .178

| | Inside | Middle | Outside |
|------|--------|--------|---------|
| High | 0/ 0 0 | 2/ 0 0 | 6/ 333 2 |
| Med | 4/ 250 1 | 1/ 0 0 | 7/ 142 1 |
| Low | 1/ 0 0 | 4/ 250 1 | 3/ 0 0 |

Curve Average .111

| | Inside | Middle | Outside |
|------|--------|--------|---------|
| High | 0/ 0 0 | 0/ 0 0 | 0/ 0 0 |
| Med | 1/ 0 0 | 0/ 0 0 | 2/ 0 0 |
| Low | 1/ 0 0 | 1/ 1000 1 | 4/ 0 0 |

### Joe Carter Against Left-Handed Pitchers 1986
### Overall Batting Average .274

Fastball Average .387

| | Inside | Middle | Outside |
|------|--------|--------|---------|
| High | 1/ 0 0 | 5/ 400 2 | 6/ 500 3 |
| Med | 5/ 600 3 | 0/ 0 0 | 5/ 400 2 |
| Low | 0/ 0 0 | 3/ 333 1 | 6/ 166 1 |

Curve Average .200

| | Inside | Middle | Outside |
|------|--------|--------|---------|
| High | 0/ 0 0 | 0/ 0 0 | 0/ 0 0 |
| Med | 0/ 0 0 | 0/ 0 0 | 3/ 333 1 |
| Low | 1/ 0 0 | 0/ 0 0 | 1/ 0 0 |

**George Bell, Toronto Blue Jays**

George Bell, a right-handed hitter, raised his official average 34 points between 1985 and 1986. His official averages of .275 in 1985 and .309 in 1986 are well-represented by his BARS averages of .271 and .359 against right-handed pitchers those two years.

**George Bell Against Right-Handed Pitchers 1985**
**Overall Batting Average .271**

Fastball Average .257          Curve Average .423

|  | Inside | Middle | Outside | Inside | Middle | Outside |
|---|---|---|---|---|---|---|
| High | 3/ 0 / 0 | 1/ 0 / 0 | 3/ 333 / 1 | 0/ 0 / 0 | 1/ 0 / 0 | 1/ 0 / 0 |
| Med | 6/ 166 / 1 | 8/ 375 / 3 | 23/ 217 / 5 | 1/ 1000 / 1 | 4/ 500 / 2 | 10/ 500 / 5 |
| Low | 3/ 0 / 0 | 11/ 363 / 4 | 12/ 333 / 4 | 0/ 0 / 0 | 2/ 500 / 1 | 7/ 285 / 2 |

**George Bell Against Right-Handed Pitchers 1986**
**Overall Batting Average .359**

Fastball Average .409          Curve Average .277

|  | Inside | Middle | Outside | Inside | Middle | Outside |
|---|---|---|---|---|---|---|
| High | 6/ 0 / 0 | 8/ 250 / 2 | 3/ 666 / 2 | 1/ 0 / 0 | 1/ 0 / 0 | 0/ 0 / 0 |
| Med | 14/ 285 / 4 | 4/ 750 / 3 | 28/ 571 / 16 | 1/ 0 / 0 | 1/ 1000 / 1 | 7/ 428 / 3 |
| Low | 1/ 0 / 0 | 14/ 500 / 7 | 5/ 0 / 0 | 0/ 0 / 0 | 2/ 500 / 1 | 5/ 0 / 0 |

In 1986 Bell doubled his percentages in several locations that were relatively high even in 1985, but his problem locations persisted.

He had trouble both years with high-inside and low-inside fastballs, and although he hit low-outside fastballs well in 1985, he had trouble with them in 1986.

Bell's Super Summary fielding charts indicate that in 1985 he tended to pop-up high-inside fastballs to right field. In 1986, he still was hitless in that location, but he hit to left field along the line and to deep left-center, as well as popping to right.

HIGH INSIDE
(FASTBALLS THROWN BY RIGHT-HANDED PITCHERS IN 1985)

BATTING AVERAGE .000
   *PLAY*
LEFTFIELDER        No instances recorded
CENTERFIELDER    No instances recorded
RIGHTFIELDER     Short in straightaway right field

HIGH INSIDE
(FASTBALLS THROWN BY RIGHT-HANDED PITCHERS IN 1986)

BATTING AVERAGE .000
   *PLAY*
LEFTFIELDER        Medium-deep and shifted toward the left field line
CENTERFIELDER    Deep and shifted toward left field
RIGHTFIELDER     Short and shifted toward the right field line

The number of fastballs thrown medium-over-the-middle decreased in 1986, indicating that pitchers were pitching him more carefully, but the distribution of inside, middle and outside pitches stayed about the same. In 1986, most pitches to Bell were outside, and he hit them well.

Bell's curve average against right-handed pitchers fell in 1986. He had trouble with inside curves and low-outside curves. He hit low-outside curves to the right side of the infield in 1986. In 1985, he got them out of the infield, although all were hit to right field.

Against right-handers, Bell hit slightly better when he was behind in the count, both in 1985 and 1986.

Bell's lower average against fastballs when ahead in the count in 1985 indicates the difficulty he had with fastballs during the year. He must have been expecting fastballs when ahead in the count, but he still could not hit them.

## George Bell Behind In The Count
## Against Right-Handed Pitchers 1985
## Batting Average .351

### Fastball Average .352

|       | Inside | Middle | Outside |
|-------|--------|--------|---------|
| High  | 0 / 0 / 0 | 0 / 0 / 0 | 2 / 0 / 0 |
| Med   | 1 / 0 / 0 | 2 / 500 / 1 | 7 / 285 / 2 |
| Low   | 0 / 0 / 0 | 4 / 500 / 2 | 1 / 1000 / 1 |

### Curve Average .571

|       | Inside | Middle | Outside |
|-------|--------|--------|---------|
| High  | 0 / 0 / 0 | 0 / 0 / 0 | 0 / 0 / 0 |
| Med   | 1 / 1000 / 1 | 0 / 0 / 0 | 4 / 500 / 2 |
| Low   | 0 / 0 / 0 | 1 / 0 / 0 | 1 / 1000 / 1 |

## George Bell Ahead In The Count
## Against Right-Handed Pitchers 1985
## Batting Average .311

### Fastball Average .230

|       | Inside | Middle | Outside |
|-------|--------|--------|---------|
| High  | 3 / 0 / 0 | 1 / 0 / 0 | 0 / 0 / 0 |
| Med   | 4 / 250 / 1 | 1 / 1000 / 1 | 8 / 250 / 2 |
| Low   | 2 / 0 / 0 | 4 / 250 / 1 | 3 / 333 / 1 |

### Curve Average .625

|       | Inside | Middle | Outside |
|-------|--------|--------|---------|
| High  | 0 / 0 / 0 | 1 / 0 / 0 | 0 / 0 / 0 |
| Med   | 0 / 0 / 0 | 3 / 666 / 2 | 3 / 666 / 2 |
| Low   | 0 / 0 / 0 | 1 / 1000 / 1 | 0 / 0 / 0 |

In 1986, his fastball average when behind was .578. When ahead, it was .432. Please see his charts on the following page.

## George Bell Behind In The Count
## Against Right-Handed Pitchers 1986
## Batting Average .409

### Fastball Average .578

| | Inside | Middle | Outside |
|---|---|---|---|
| **High** | 1 / 0 / 0 | 1 / 1000 / 1 | 2 / 1000 / 2 |
| **Med** | 6 / 500 / 3 | 1 / 1000 / 1 | 5 / 400 / 2 |
| **Low** | 0 / 0 / 0 | 2 / 1000 / 2 | 1 / 0 / 0 |

### Curve Average .375

| | Inside | Middle | Outside |
|---|---|---|---|
| **High** | 1 / 0 / 0 | 0 / 0 / 0 | 0 / 0 / 0 |
| **Med** | 1 / 0 / 0 | 0 / 0 / 0 | 3 / 666 / 2 |
| **Low** | 0 / 0 / 0 | 1 / 1000 / 1 | 2 / 0 / 0 |

## George Bell Ahead In The Count
## Against Right-Handed Pitchers 1986
## Batting Average .396

### Fastball Average .432

| | Inside | Middle | Outside |
|---|---|---|---|
| **High** | 2 / 0 / 0 | 4 / 250 / 1 | 0 / 0 / 0 |
| **Med** | 6 / 166 / 1 | 2 / 500 / 1 | 14 / 714 / 10 |
| **Low** | 1 / 0 / 0 | 6 / 500 / 3 | 2 / 0 / 0 |

### Curve Average .400

| | Inside | Middle | Outside |
|---|---|---|---|
| **High** | 0 / 0 / 0 | 1 / 0 / 0 | 0 / 0 / 0 |
| **Med** | 0 / 0 / 0 | 1 / 1000 / 1 | 3 / 333 / 1 |
| **Low** | 0 / 0 / 0 | 0 / 0 / 0 | 0 / 0 / 0 |

## Bell Against Left-Handed Pitchers

Bell also hit considerably better against left-handed pitchers in 1986.

## George Bell Against Left-Handed Pitchers 1985
## Overall Batting Average .242

### Fastball Average .235

| | Inside | Middle | Outside |
|---|---|---|---|
| **High** | 2 / 0 / 0 | 4 / 0 / 0 | 1 / 0 / 0 |
| **Med** | 8 / 125 / 1 | 8 / 375 / 3 | 14 / 142 / 2 |
| **Low** | 2 / 500 / 1 | 9 / 444 / 4 | 3 / 333 / 1 |

### Curve Average .250

| | Inside | Middle | Outside |
|---|---|---|---|
| **High** | 0 / 0 / 0 | 0 / 0 / 0 | 0 / 0 / 0 |
| **Med** | 1 / 0 / 0 | 1 / 0 / 0 | 5 / 200 / 1 |
| **Low** | 1 / 1000 / 1 | 5 / 400 / 2 | 3 / 0 / 0 |

## George Bell Against Left-Handed Pitchers 1986
## Overall Batting Average .327

Fastball Average .285          Curve Average .625

|      | Inside | Middle | Outside |
|------|--------|--------|---------|
| High | 2/<br>0 / 0 | 4/<br>500 / 2 | 2/<br>500 / 1 |
| Med  | 2/<br>500 / 1 | 2/<br>500 / 1 | 10/<br>300 / 3 |
| Low  | 3/<br>0 / 0 | 3/<br>0 / 0 | 7/<br>285 / 2 |

|      | Inside | Middle | Outside |
|------|--------|--------|---------|
| High | 0/<br>0 / 0 | 0/<br>0 / 0 | 0/<br>0 / 0 |
| Med  | 1/<br>1000/ 1 | 1/<br>0 / 0 | 3/<br>666 / 2 |
| Low  | 1/<br>1000/ 1 | 2/<br>500 / 1 | 0/<br>0 / 0 |

Bell got around better on fastballs thrown by left-handers in 1986. He pulled outside pitches more to deep center and deep left field.

MEDIUM-HIGH OUTSIDE
(FASTBALLS THROWN BY LEFT-HANDED PITCHERS IN 1985)

BATTING AVERAGE .142
    PLAY
LEFTFIELDER         Deep and shifted toward center field
CENTERFIELDER    Deep in straightaway center field
RIGHTFIELDER     Deep in straightaway right field


MEDIUM-HIGH OUTSIDE
(FASTBALLS THROWN BY LEFT-HANDED PITCHERS IN 1986)

BATTING AVERAGE .300
    PLAY
LEFTFIELDER         Deep and shifted toward the left field line
CENTERFIELDER    Medium-deep in straightaway center field
RIGHTFIELDER     Deep and shifted toward center field

## *Personal Comments*

Individual players sometimes change their batting styles from one year to the next. This can result in a gain or decline in their batting averages and overall effectiveness. But large gains or declines do not happen only to players who try new methods. Sometimes the pitchers catch on to weaknesses a player has. Once pitchers find a hitter's weaknesses, the hitter's average will fall.

The next chapter talks about players who had large declines in their batting averages from one year to the next. The BARS System doesn't show how a player changed his stance, swing or any other physical characteristic that may have contributed to his gain or decline. The BARS System does, however, clearly show the changes in a player's batting percentages in the nine locations of the batting grid. The BARS System also shows if a player tended to hit the ball different distances and directions from one year to the next. The BARS fielding strategy is accurate 90 percent of the time, and maintains that accuracy from season to season. But when a player has a significant change in his performance, differences in how he hits the ball can sometimes be found.

You'll notice in the next chapter that the batting grids contain less information because a single-year's record is used, not the cumulative BARS averages of many seasons. I'm looking forward to the time when every team uses the BARS System — or a similar system — to chart every pitch of every game. When that happens, the records will be complete, and the accuracy of the batting, fielding and pitching reports will be very high.

# Chapter Twelve

# Large Batting-Average Declines

In this chapter, large batting average declines are examined for the 1985-1986 and 1986-1987 seasons.

## LARGEST DECLINES

| Player | '87 Club | '86 Average | '87 Average | Decline |
|---|---|---|---|---|
| Gary Ward | Yankees | .316 | .248 | 68 |
| T. Bernazard | Athletics | .301 | .250 | 51 |

| Player | '86 Club | '85 Average | '86 Average | Decline |
|---|---|---|---|---|
| George Brett | Royals | .335 | .290 | 45 |
| R. Henderson | Yankees | .314 | .263 | 51 |
| Willie McGee | Cardinals | .353 | .256 | 97 |
| Dave Parker | Reds | .312 | .273 | 39 |

**Gary Ward, New York Yankees**

Gary Ward, right-handed hitter for the New York Yankees, experienced the largest batting-average decline in the American League from 1986 to 1987. Ward's average with the Rangers in 1986 was .316. He declined 68 points to .248 with the Yankees in 1987.

Ward's official averages were accurately represented by his BARS averages of .308 in 1986 and .222 in 1987.

### Gary Ward Against Right-Handed Pitchers 1986
### Overall Batting Average .308

| | Fastball Average .362 | | | Curve Average .312 | | |
|---|---|---|---|---|---|---|
| | Inside | Middle | Outside | Inside | Middle | Outside |
| High | 3 / 0 / 0 | 8 / 125 / 1 | 5 / 600 / 3 | 0 / 0 / 0 | 2 / 0 / 0 | 0 / 0 / 0 |
| Med | 14 / 500 / 7 | 5 / 800 / 4 | 24 / 291 / 7 | 0 / 0 / 0 | 1 / 1000 / 1 | 6 / 166 / 1 |
| Low | 6 / 166 / 1 | 8 / 375 / 3 | 7 / 428 / 3 | 0 / 0 / 0 | 1 / 1000 / 1 | 6 / 333 / 2 |

### Gary Ward Against Right-Handed Pitchers 1987
### Overall Batting Average .222

| | Fastball Average .229 | | | Curve Average .263 | | |
|---|---|---|---|---|---|---|
| | Inside | Middle | Outside | Inside | Middle | Outside |
| High | 4 / 0 / 0 | 7 / 0 / 0 | 4 / 250 / 1 | 0 / 0 / 0 | 1 / 0 / 0 | 1 / 0 / 0 |
| Med | 11 / 272 / 3 | 1 / 1000 / 1 | 29 / 241 / 7 | 1 / 1000 / 1 | 1 / 1000 / 1 | 9 / 333 / 3 |
| Low | 12 / 166 / 2 | 13 / 307 / 4 | 6 / 333 / 2 | 0 / 0 / 0 | 1 / 0 / 0 | 5 / 0 / 0 |

Ward's fastball average declined over 100 points in 1987. He hit fastballs very well overall in 1986 (.362), but very poorly in 1987 (.229).

One item of interest is the reduced number of pitches thrown medium-over-the-middle to Ward in 1987. The total number of instances in his other locations is about the same both years, but only one-fifth as many pitches were thrown medium-over-the-middle in 1987. This indicates that pitchers were more careful with him, giving him many pitches on the corners or perhaps slightly off the corners. He may have been anxious to hit the ball after his excellent 1986 season and gone after bad pitches in 1987, with a resulting drop in his average.

He declined 50 points in his medium-high outside location. His BARS Super Summary shows that he hit pitches in this location similarly both years. Many of his long hits were fly-ball outs in 1987.

MEDIUM-HIGH OUTSIDE
(FASTBALLS THROWN BY RIGHT-HANDED PITCHERS 1986)

BATTING AVERAGE .291
*PLAY*

| | |
|---|---|
| LEFTFIELDER | Deep and shifted toward the left field line |
| CENTERFIELDER | Deep and shifted toward right field |
| RIGHTFIELDER | Medium-deep in straightaway right field |
| SHORTSTOP | Normal position |
| SECOND | Shifted toward first base |

MEDIUM-HIGH OUTSIDE
(FASTBALLS THROWN BY RIGHT-HANDED PITCHERS 1987)

BATTING AVERAGE .241
*PLAY*

| | |
|---|---|
| LEFTFIELDER | Deep and shifted toward the left field line |
| CENTERFIELDER | Deep in straightaway center field |
| RIGHTFIELDER | Deep in straightaway right field |
| SHORTSTOP | Up middle (shifted toward second base) |
| SECOND | Normal position |

Ward also fell sharply in the medium-inside location (.500 in 1986, .272 in 1987) and the low-over-the-middle location (.375 in 1986, .307 in 1987).

Ward's poor performance against high-over-the-middle fastballs both years indicates a weakness. He mostly hit these pitches deep to the outfield or grounded out to the shortstop.

Ward's overall curve average also dropped in 1987. He hit medium-high outside curves well (.333 in 1987), but was hitless (0 for 5) in the low-outside location.

It is noteworthy that Ward hit better when behind in the count during his fine 1986 season (.414 behind, .385 ahead) but better when ahead in 1987 (.222 behind, .294 ahead).

## Ward Against Left-Handed Pitchers

Ward's overall BARS average fell about 20 points against left-handed pitchers in 1987. His charts are on the following page.

## Gary Ward Against Left-Handed Pitchers 1986
## Overall Batting Average .310

### Fastball Average .405

|      | Inside | Middle | Outside |
|------|--------|--------|---------|
| High | 0 / **0** / 0 | 3 / **0** / 0 | 4 / **250** / 1 |
| Med  | 6 / **500** / 3 | 2 / **500** / 1 | 13 / **384** / 5 |
| Low  | 3 / **666** / 2 | 4 / **500** / 2 | 2 / **500** / 1 |

### Curve Average .000

|      | Inside | Middle | Outside |
|------|--------|--------|---------|
| High | 1 / **0** / 0 | 0 / **0** / 0 | 0 / **0** / 0 |
| Med  | 0 / **0** / 0 | 0 / **0** / 0 | 3 / **0** / 0 |
| Low  | 3 / **0** / 0 | 1 / **0** / 0 | 1 / **0** / 0 |

## Gary Ward Against Left-Handed Pitchers 1987
## Overall Batting Average .291

### Fastball Average .325

|      | Inside | Middle | Outside |
|------|--------|--------|---------|
| High | 2 / **0** / 0 | 0 / **0** / 0 | 2 / **0** / 0 |
| Med  | 3 / **333** / 1 | 1 / **1000** / 1 | 19 / **263** / 5 |
| Low  | 6 / **500** / 3 | 4 / **750** / 3 | 6 / **166** / 1 |

### Curve Average .444

|      | Inside | Middle | Outside |
|------|--------|--------|---------|
| High | 0 / **0** / 0 | 1 / **1000** / 1 | 1 / **1000** / 1 |
| Med  | 0 / **0** / 0 | 1 / **1000** / 1 | 1 / **0** / 0 |
| Low  | 3 / **333** / 1 | 1 / **0** / 0 | 1 / **0** / 0 |

Notice his decline against medium-high outside fastballs (.384 in 1986, .263 in 1987). He hit these pitches deeper and pulled them slightly more in 1986.

MEDIUM-HIGH OUTSIDE
(FASTBALLS THROWN BY LEFT-HANDED PITCHERS 1986)

BATTING AVERAGE .384
*PLAY*
LEFTFIELDER        Deep in straightaway left field
CENTERFIELDER      Deep in straightaway center field
RIGHTFIELDER       Deep and shifted toward center field
SHORTSTOP          Shifted toward third base
SECOND             Normal position


MEDIUM-HIGH OUTSIDE
(FASTBALLS THROWN BY LEFT-HANDED PITCHERS 1987)

BATTING AVERAGE .263
*PLAY*
LEFTFIELDER        Medium-deep in straightaway left field
CENTERFIELDER      Deep in straightaway center field
RIGHTFIELDER       Deep in straightaway right field
SHORTSTOP          Up middle (shifted toward second base)
SECOND             Shifted toward first base


**Tony Bernazard, Oakland A's**

Switch-hitting Tony Bernazard of the Athletics dropped from .301 in 1986 (playing with the Cleveland Indians) to .250 in 1987. His 51-point drop was the third largest in the American League. Batting left-handed, Bernazard's overall BARS average dropped 56 points in 1987 against right-handed pitchers. Please see his charts on the following page.

## Tony Bernazard Against Right-Handed Pitchers 1986
### Overall Batting Average .261

Fastball Average .280                    Curve Average .210

| | Outside | Middle | Inside | | Outside | Middle | Inside |
|------|---------|--------|--------|---|---------|--------|--------|
| High | 3/0 / 0 | 3/333 / 1 | 3/333 / 1 | | 1/0 / 0 | 2/0 / 0 | 0/0 / 0 |
| Med | 24/250 / 6 | 4/750 / 3 | 17/235 / 4 | | 2/500 / 1 | 1/0 / 0 | 5/200 / 1 |
| Low | 2/0 / 0 | 12/250 / 3 | 7/428 / 3 | | 1/0 / 0 | 3/333 / 1 | 4/250 / 1 |

## Tony Bernazard Against Right-Handed Pitchers 1987
### Overall Batting Average .205

Fastball Average .195                    Curve Average .750

| | Outside | Middle | Inside | | Outside | Middle | Inside |
|------|---------|--------|--------|---|---------|--------|--------|
| High | 3/0 / 0 | 5/400 / 2 | 4/0 / 0 | | 1/1000 / 1 | 2/1000 / 2 | 0/0 / 0 |
| Med | 18/111 / 2 | 1/1000 / 1 | 6/333 / 2 | | 1/0 / 0 | 0/0 / 0 | 0/0 / 0 |
| Low | 0/0 / 0 | 5/200 / 1 | 4/250 / 1 | | 0/0 / 0 | 0/0 / 0 | 0/0 / 0 |

Bernazard's BARS fastball average dropped 85 points in 1987. He dropped nearly 140 points in the medium-high outside location. He did not hit the ball very differently in the two years, although several fielders would have been required to shift.

MEDIUM-HIGH OUTSIDE
(FASTBALLS THROWN BY RIGHT-HANDED PITCHERS 1986)

BATTING AVERAGE .250
*PLAY*
LEFTFIELDER         Deep in straightaway left field
CENTERFIELDER       Deep and shifted toward left field
RIGHTFIELDER        Medium-deep in straightaway right field
SHORTSTOP           Up middle (shifted toward second base)
SECOND              Normal position


MEDIUM-HIGH OUTSIDE
(FASTBALLS THROWN BY RIGHT-HANDED PITCHERS 1987)

BATTING AVERAGE .111
*PLAY*
LEFTFIELDER         Medium-deep in straightaway left field
CENTERFIELDER       Deep in straightaway center field
RIGHTFIELDER        Deep and shifted toward center field
SHORTSTOP           Normal position
SECOND              Shifted toward first base

Bernazard's curve average rose in 1987, but it is based on very few instances and should not be considered accurate.

Bernazard's overall BARS average against left-handed pitchers fell 49 points in 1987. (His charts are not shown here.) Batting right-handed against lefties, his average fell significantly in the medium-high outside fastball location. Also, he had difficulty both years with medium-high inside fastballs. His 1986 medium-high inside fastball Super Summary shows that that he punched many inside fastballs to right field.

MEDIUM-HIGH INSIDE
(FASTBALLS THROWN BY LEFT-HANDED PITCHERS 1986)

BATTING AVERAGE .142
*PLAY*
LEFTFIELDER         Deep and shifted toward the left field line
CENTERFIELDER       Short and shifted toward right field
RIGHTFIELDER        Short in straightaway right field
SHORTSTOP           Shifted toward third base
SECOND              Normal position

## George Brett, Kansas City Royals

Left-handed hitting George Brett's average declined against both right- and left-handed pitchers in 1986. His fastball averages did not fall significantly, but he had more trouble with curves in 1986. First against right-handed pitchers:

### George Brett Against Right-Handed Pitchers 1985
### Overall Batting Average .355

**Fastball Average .362**

| | Outside | Middle | Inside |
|---|---|---|---|
| High | 6/ 166 / 1 | 17/ 294 / 5 | 5/ 400 / 2 |
| Med | 33/ 454 / 15 | 33/ 515 / 17 | 16/ 375 / 6 |
| Low | 8/ 0 / 0 | 28/ 250 / 7 | 3/ 333 / 1 |

**Curve Average .309**

| | Outside | Middle | Inside |
|---|---|---|---|
| High | 2/ 500 / 1 | 2/ 500 / 1 | 1/ 0 / 0 |
| Med | 7/ 428 / 3 | 5/ 400 / 2 | 8/ 375 / 3 |
| Low | 2/ 0 / 0 | 11/ 181 / 2 | 4/ 250 / 1 |

### George Brett Against Right-Handed Pitchers 1986
### Overall Batting Average .311

**Fastball Average .358**

| | Outside | Middle | Inside |
|---|---|---|---|
| High | 6/ 166 / 1 | 18/ 222 / 4 | 0/ 0 / 0 |
| Med | 32/ 375 / 12 | 5/ 400 / 2 | 12/ 250 / 3 |
| Low | 15/ 466 / 7 | 26/ 384 / 10 | 3/ 1000 / 3 |

**Curve Average .300**

| | Outside | Middle | Inside |
|---|---|---|---|
| High | 2/ 0 / 0 | 0/ 0 / 0 | 0/ 0 / 0 |
| Med | 8/ 375 / 3 | 2/ 0 / 0 | 4/ 500 / 2 |
| Low | 1/ 0 / 0 | 1/ 0 / 0 | 2/ 500 / 1 |

Even though Brett's fastball average stayed about the same in 1986, a brief examination is valuable, because it helps illustrate his overall decline.

Notice that fewer fastballs were thrown medium-over-the-middle to Brett in 1986. The same trend will be found when examining his record against left-handed pitchers.

Brett did not have a strong cleanup hitter following him in 1986. In fact, the Royals' fourth batting position accounted for the second-lowest RBI total of any cleanup position in the American League in 1986. Because of this, Brett was probably pitched as carefully as any hitter in the league during the 1986 season.

A higher percentage of fastballs were thrown outside to Brett in 1986 than in 1985. Almost twice as many pitches were thrown to the low-outside location in 1986. Brett responded to this by hitting low-outside fastballs for a .466 average.

His average fell in the highly pitched medium-high outside location. His one continuing weakness was in the high-outside location, where he hit .166 both years.

In Brett's power fastball location, medium-high outside, his average dropped, but his swing stayed the same both years.

MEDIUM-HIGH OUTSIDE
(FASTBALLS THROWN IN 1985 AND 1986)

BATTING AVERAGE .454 IN 1985; .375 IN 1986
   *PLAY*

| | |
|---|---|
| LEFTFIELDER | Deep and shifted toward the left field line |
| CENTERFIELDER | Deep in straightaway center field |
| RIGHTFIELDER | Deep and shifted toward center field |
| SHORTSTOP | Up middle (shifted toward second base) |
| SECOND | Normal position |

In the high-over-the-middle location, he pulled the ball more in 1986. This resulted in many easy fly balls and a lower batting percentage in that location.

HIGH-OVER-THE-MIDDLE
(FASTBALLS THROWN BY RIGHT-HANDED PITCHERS 1985)

BATTING AVERAGE .294
   *PLAY*

| | |
|---|---|
| LEFTFIELDER | Deep in straightaway left field |
| CENTERFIELDER | Deep in straightaway center field |
| RIGHTFIELDER | Deep in straightaway right field |

HIGH-OVER-THE-MIDDLE
(FASTBALLS THROWN BY RIGHT-HANDED PITCHERS 1986)

BATTING AVERAGE .222
*PLAY*
LEFTFIELDER        Deep and shifted toward center field
CENTERFIELDER    Deep and shifted toward right field
RIGHTFIELDER      Deep in straightaway right field

The left-handed hitting Brett didn't get around on inside fastballs as well in 1986, hitting more to left and center.

MEDIUM-HIGH INSIDE
(FASTBALLS THROWN BY RIGHT-HANDED PITCHERS 1985)

BATTING AVERAGE .375
*PLAY*
LEFTFIELDER        Medium-deep in straightaway left field
CENTERFIELDER    Medium-deep in straightaway center field
RIGHTFIELDER      Deep and shifted toward the right field line

MEDIUM-HIGH INSIDE
(FASTBALLS THROWN BY RIGHT-HANDED PITCHERS 1986)

BATTING AVERAGE .250
*PLAY*
LEFTFIELDER        Medium-deep and shifted toward the left field line
CENTERFIELDER    Deep in straightaway center field
RIGHTFIELDER      Deep and shifted toward center field

In 1985, Brett hit better when ahead in the count against right-handed pitchers. Notice how strongly he hit fastballs when ahead.

## George Brett Behind In The Count
## Against Right-Handed Pitchers 1985
## Batting Average .365

Fastball Average .304

| | Outside | Middle | Inside |
|---|---|---|---|
| High | 1 / 0 / 0 | 4 / 0 / 0 | 0 / 0 / 0 |
| Med | 5 / 800 / 4 | 5 / 200 / 1 | 2 / 500 / 1 |
| Low | 1 / 0 / 0 | 5 / 200 / 1 | 0 / 0 / 0 |

Curve Average .266

| | Outside | Middle | Inside |
|---|---|---|---|
| High | 0 / 0 / 0 | 1 / 1000 / 1 | 0 / 0 / 0 |
| Med | 3 / 0 / 0 | 1 / 0 / 0 | 5 / 400 / 2 |
| Low | 1 / 0 / 0 | 4 / 250 / 1 | 0 / 0 / 0 |

## George Brett Ahead In The Count
## Against Right-Handed Pitchers 1985
## Batting Average .398

Fastball Average .410

| | Outside | Middle | Inside |
|---|---|---|---|
| High | 2 / 500 / 1 | 5 / 400 / 2 | 3 / 0 / 0 |
| Med | 17 / 529 / 9 | 19 / 684 / 13 | 13 / 307 / 4 |
| Low | 3 / 0 / 0 | 15 / 200 / 3 | 1 / 0 / 0 |

Curve Average .461

| | Outside | Middle | Inside |
|---|---|---|---|
| High | 1 / 1000 / 1 | 0 / 0 / 0 | 1 / 0 / 0 |
| Med | 2 / 500 / 1 | 2 / 500 / 1 | 2 / 500 / 1 |
| Low | 0 / 0 / 0 | 4 / 250 / 1 | 1 / 1000 / 1 |

In 1986, he also hit better when ahead in the count.

## George Brett Behind In The Count
## Against Right-Handed Pitchers 1986
## Batting Average .333

Fastball Average .333

| | Outside | Middle | Inside |
|---|---|---|---|
| High | 0 / **0** / 0 | 2 / **0** / 0 | 0 / **0** / 0 |
| Med | 4 / **500** / 2 | 0 / **0** / 0 | 1 / **0** / 0 |
| Low | 0 / **0** / 0 | 5 / **400** / 2 | 0 / **0** / 0 |

Curve Average .400

| | Outside | Middle | Inside |
|---|---|---|---|
| High | 2 / **0** / 0 | 0 / **0** / 0 | 0 / **0** / 0 |
| Med | 2 / **500** / 1 | 0 / **0** / 0 | 0 / **0** / 0 |
| Low | 0 / **0** / 0 | 0 / **0** / 0 | 1 / **1000** / 1 |

## George Brett Ahead In The Count
## Against Right-Handed Pitchers 1986
## Batting Average .368

Fastball Average .394

| | Outside | Middle | Inside |
|---|---|---|---|
| High | 4 / **250** / 1 | 11 / **272** / 3 | 0 / **0** / 0 |
| Med | 20 / **450** / 9 | 4 / **500** / 2 | 9 / **333** / 3 |
| Low | 8 / **500** / 4 | 18 / **333** / 6 | 2 / **1000** / 2 |

Curve Average .250

| | Outside | Middle | Inside |
|---|---|---|---|
| High | 0 / **0** / 0 | 0 / **0** / 0 | 0 / **0** / 0 |
| Med | 1 / **0** / 0 | 2 / **0** / 0 | 1 / **1000** / 1 |
| Low | 0 / **0** / 0 | 0 / **0** / 0 | 0 / **0** / 0 |

### Brett Against Left-Handed Pitchers

Brett's average fell nearly 80 points in 1986 against left-handed pitchers.

## George Brett Against Left-Handed Pitchers 1985
### Overall Batting Average .344

#### Fastball Average .342

| | Outside | Middle | Inside |
|---|---|---|---|
| High | 0/ 0 / 0 | 7/ 1000 / 7 | 6/ 500 / 3 |
| Med | 18/ 166 / 3 | 13/ 384 / 5 | 14/ 214 / 3 |
| Low | 3/ 0 / 0 | 11/ 272 / 3 | 4/ 500 / 2 |

#### Curve Average .379

| | Outside | Middle | Inside |
|---|---|---|---|
| High | 3/ 666 / 2 | 4/ 750 / 3 | 2/ 0 / 0 |
| Med | 2/ 0 / 0 | 3/ 666 / 2 | 8/ 250 / 2 |
| Low | 3/ 333 / 1 | 4/ 250 / 1 | 0/ 0 / 0 |

## George Brett Against Left-Handed Pitchers 1986
### Overall Batting Average .266

#### Fastball Average .322

| | Outside | Middle | Inside |
|---|---|---|---|
| High | 4/ 500 / 2 | 7/ 285 / 2 | 3/ 333 / 1 |
| Med | 24/ 250 / 6 | 2/ 500 / 1 | 10/ 500 / 5 |
| Low | 2/ 500 / 1 | 6/ 166 / 1 | 4/ 250 / 1 |

#### Curve Average .320

| | Outside | Middle | Inside |
|---|---|---|---|
| High | 0/ 0 / 0 | 5/ 0 / 0 | 1/ 1000 / 1 |
| Med | 8/ 750 / 6 | 2/ 500 / 1 | 3/ 0 / 0 |
| Low | 2/ 0 / 0 | 3/ 0 / 0 | 1/ 0 / 0 |

Again, notice how few fastballs were thrown to Brett over the heart of the plate in 1986. Left-handers, like right-handers, pitched Brett more carefully in 1986, seemingly content to walk him and face the next batter.

Brett's medium-high outside average increased in 1986, but it did not make up for the overall decline resulting from having fewer fastballs thrown in the medium-over-the-middle location.

Brett's curve average against left-handers fell 59 points in 1986. He had trouble with low curves, inside curves and high-over-the-middle curves.

Against left-handers, Brett hit better when behind in the count both years.

### George Brett Behind In The Count
### Against Left-Handed Pitchers 1986
### Batting Average .315

Fastball Average .444

| | Outside | Middle | Inside |
|---|---|---|---|
| High | 1 / 1000 / 1 | 2 / 0 / 0 | 0 / 0 / 0 |
| Med | 5 / 400 / 2 | 1 / 1000 / 1 | 0 / 0 / 0 |
| Low | 0 / 0 / 0 | 0 / 0 / 0 | 0 / 0 / 0 |

Curve Average .285

| | Outside | Middle | Inside |
|---|---|---|---|
| High | 0 / 0 / 0 | 2 / 0 / 0 | 0 / 0 / 0 |
| Med | 2 / 1000 / 2 | 0 / 0 / 0 | 2 / 0 / 0 |
| Low | 0 / 0 / 0 | 1 / 0 / 0 | 0 / 0 / 0 |

### George Brett Ahead In The Count
### Against Left-Handed Pitchers 1986
### Batting Average .294

Fastball Average .303

| | Outside | Middle | Inside |
|---|---|---|---|
| High | 1 / 0 / 0 | 3 / 666 / 2 | 2 / 500 / 1 |
| Med | 13 / 153 / 2 | 0 / 0 / 0 | 7 / 571 / 4 |
| Low | 1 / 0 / 0 | 2 / 0 / 0 | 4 / 250 / 1 |

Curve Average .400

| | Outside | Middle | Inside |
|---|---|---|---|
| High | 0 / 0 / 0 | 3 / 0 / 0 | 1 / 1000 / 1 |
| Med | 3 / 666 / 2 | 2 / 500 / 1 | 0 / 0 / 0 |
| Low | 0 / 0 / 0 | 0 / 0 / 0 | 1 / 0 / 0 |

## Rickey Henderson, New York Yankees

Rickey Henderson, a right-handed hitter, had the second-largest decline in the American League from 1985 to 1986. His average fell against both right- and left-handed pitchers.

Predominately a fastball hitter, Henderson's decline can be traced to his lower fastball average in 1986, although his 1986 fastball averages of .344 against right-handed pitchers and .288 against left-handers were still very respectable.

## Rickey Henderson Against Right-Handed Pitchers 1985
### Overall Batting Average .324

**Fastball Average .391**

|      | Inside | Middle | Outside |
|------|--------|--------|---------|
| High | 5 / 400 / 2 | 7 / 428 / 3 | 3 / 333 / 1 |
| Med  | 20 / 300 / 6 | 22 / 454 / 12 | 19 / 368 / 7 |
| Low  | 2 / 0 / 0 | 24 / 458 / 11 | 13 / 230 / 3 |

**Curve Average .058**

|      | Inside | Middle | Outside |
|------|--------|--------|---------|
| High | 1 / 0 / 0 | 1 / 0 / 0 | 0 / 0 / 0 |
| Med  | 3 / 0 / 0 | 1 / 0 / 0 | 4 / 0 / 0 |
| Low  | 0 / 0 / 0 | 1 / 1000 / 1 | 6 / 0 / 0 |

## Rickey Henderson Against Right-Handed Pitchers 1986
### Overall Average .265

**Fastball Average .344**

|      | Inside | Middle | Outside |
|------|--------|--------|---------|
| High | 3 / 0 / 0 | 6 / 666 / 4 | 1 / 0 / 0 |
| Med  | 11 / 272 / 3 | 16 / 437 / 7 | 48 / 333 / 16 |
| Low  | 7 / 142 / 1 | 21 / 476 / 10 | 9 / 111 / 1 |

**Curve Average .137**

|      | Inside | Middle | Outside |
|------|--------|--------|---------|
| High | 0 / 0 / 0 | 2 / 500 / 1 | 2 / 0 / 0 |
| Med  | 2 / 0 / 0 | 2 / 500 / 1 | 9 / 111 / 1 |
| Low  | 1 / 1000 / 1 | 6 / 0 / 0 | 5 / 0 / 0 |

Henderson's fastball average against right-handers dropped 47 points in 1986. Right-handers threw him more outside fastballs in 1986 (mostly medium-high outside), with slightly fewer inside and over-the-middle pitches.

Henderson was thrown a lower percentage of medium-over-the-middle fastballs in 1986. This indicates that he was pitched very carefully.

His .333 average against medium-high outside fastballs in 1986 was down from his .368 in the same location in 1985; but there were over twice as many instances in 1986, and the decline (with such a large number of instances) probably represented a retreat toward a normal average for Henderson.

Henderson's weakest fastball locations in 1986 were low-outside, high-inside, and low-inside.  In 1985 he hit low-outside fastballs to left field and to center.  In 1986, he did not have a recorded hit ball to left or center fields in the low-outside location.  Going with the pitch like this usually results in a better performance.  Since it didn't, he may not have been aggressive enough, trying too much to merely slap low-outside pitches to the opposite field.

LOW-OUTSIDE
(FASTBALLS THROWN BY RIGHT-HANDED PITCHERS 1985)

BATTING AVERAGE .230
    *PLAY*
LEFTFIELDER       Medium-deep and shifted toward the left field line
CENTERFIELDER    Deep in straightaway center field
RIGHTFIELDER     Deep and shifted toward center field

LOW-OUTSIDE
(FASTBALLS THROWN BY RIGHT-HANDED PITCHERS 1986)

BATTING AVERAGE .111
    *PLAY*
LEFTFIELDER       No instances recorded
CENTERFIELDER    No instances recorded
RIGHTFIELDER     Deep and shifted toward the right field line

Henderson did not hit curveballs well against right-handed pitchers. He improved slightly in 1986, but his average was still low (.137).  Both years he had trouble with outside curves.  In 1985, he pulled outside curves to left and center.  In 1986 it seemed that he tried to go with outside curves and hit them more to right, but he still had difficulty getting base hits.

Both years, Henderson hit better when ahead in the count against right-handers.

### Rickey Henderson Behind In The Count
### Against Right-Handed Pitchers 1985
### Batting Average .324

Fastball Average .692                    Curve Average .071

| | Inside | Middle | Outside |
|---|---|---|---|
| High | 2 / 1000 / 2 | 1 / 1000 / 1 | 0 / 0 / 0 |
| Med | 1 / 1000 / 1 | 2 / 1000 / 2 | 1 / 1000 / 1 |
| Low | 0 / 0 / 0 | 3 / 333 / 1 | 3 / 333 / 1 |

| | Inside | Middle | Outside |
|---|---|---|---|
| High | 1 / 0 / 0 | 1 / 0 / 0 | 0 / 0 / 0 |
| Med | 2 / 0 / 0 | 1 / 0 / 0 | 4 / 0 / 0 |
| Low | 0 / 0 / 0 | 1 / 1000 / 1 | 4 / 0 / 0 |

### Rickey Henderson Ahead In The Count
### Against Right-Handed Pitchers 1985
### Batting Average .369

Fastball Average .338                    Curve Average .000

| | Inside | Middle | Outside |
|---|---|---|---|
| High | 0 / 0 / 0 | 4 / 250 / 1 | 1 / 1000 / 1 |
| Med | 11 / 181 / 2 | 13 / 384 / 5 | 8 / 250 / 2 |
| Low | 0 / 0 / 0 | 20 / 450 / 9 | 2 / 0 / 0 |

| | Inside | Middle | Outside |
|---|---|---|---|
| High | 0 / 0 / 0 | 0 / 0 / 0 | 0 / 0 / 0 |
| Med | 0 / 0 / 0 | 0 / 0 / 0 | 0 / 0 / 0 |
| Low | 0 / 0 / 0 | 0 / 0 / 0 | 1 / 0 / 0 |

## Rickey Henderson Behind In The Count
## Against Right-Handed Pitchers 1986
## Batting Average .243

Fastball Average .250 | Curve Average .200

**Fastball**

| | Inside | Middle | Outside |
|---|---|---|---|
| High | 2/ ; 0 / 0 | 0/ ; 0 / 0 | 0/ ; 0 / 0 |
| Med | 2/ ; 0 / 0 | 0/ ; 0 / 0 | 4/ ; 750 / 3 |
| Low | 3/ ; 333 / 1 | 3/ ; 0 / 0 | 2/ ; 0 / 0 |

**Curve**

| | Inside | Middle | Outside |
|---|---|---|---|
| High | 0/ ; 0 / 0 | 1/ ; 1000 / 1 | 1/ ; 0 / 0 |
| Med | 1/ ; 0 / 0 | 0/ ; 0 / 0 | 3/ ; 333 / 1 |
| Low | 0/ ; 0 / 0 | 3/ ; 0 / 0 | 1/ ; 0 / 0 |

## Rickey Henderson Ahead In The Count
## Against Right-Handed Pitchers 1986
## Batting Average .365

Fastball Average .450 | Curve Average .200

**Fastball**

| | Inside | Middle | Outside |
|---|---|---|---|
| High | 1/ ; 0 / 0 | 4/ ; 750 / 3 | 0/ ; 0 / 0 |
| Med | 5/ ; 400 / 2 | 10/ ; 500 / 5 | 23/ ; 347 / 8 |
| Low | 1/ ; 0 / 0 | 13/ ; 615 / 8 | 3/ ; 333 / 1 |

**Curve**

| | Inside | Middle | Outside |
|---|---|---|---|
| High | 0/ ; 0 / 0 | 0/ ; 0 / 0 | 0/ ; 0 / 0 |
| Med | 1/ ; 0 / 0 | 1/ ; 1000 / 1 | 2/ ; 0 / 0 |
| Low | 0/ ; 0 / 0 | 1/ ; 0 / 0 | 0/ ; 0 / 0 |

Notice how carefully pitchers placed the ball on the corners of the plate when Henderson was behind in the count in 1986. When he was ahead, they pitched him outside as well as they could, but many pitches came in over the middle. He was waiting for fastballs when ahead, no matter what location, and he hit them well.

## Henderson Against Left-Handed Pitchers

Henderson's average also declined against left-handed pitchers in 1986.

### Rickey Henderson Against Left-Handed Pitchers 1985
### Overall Batting Average .371

Fastball Average .409

| | Inside | Middle | Outside |
|------|--------|--------|---------|
| High | 1 / 0 / 0 | 3 / 666 / 2 | 0 / 0 / 0 |
| Med | 10 / 400 / 4 | 10 / 400 / 4 | 21 / 380 / 8 |
| Low | 3 / 333 / 1 | 6 / 500 / 3 | 7 / 428 / 3 |

Curve Average .250

| | Inside | Middle | Outside |
|------|--------|--------|---------|
| High | 0 / 0 / 0 | 0 / 0 / 0 | 1 / 1000 / 1 |
| Med | 4 / 750 / 3 | 0 / 0 / 0 | 6 / 166 / 1 |
| Low | 5 / 0 / 0 | 1 / 0 / 0 | 3 / 0 / 0 |

### Rickey Henderson Against Left-Handed Pitchers 1986
### Overall Batting Average .234

Fastball Average .288

| | Inside | Middle | Outside |
|------|--------|--------|---------|
| High | 0 / 0 / 0 | 5 / 400 / 2 | 0 / 0 / 0 |
| Med | 6 / 0 / 0 | 2 / 500 / 1 | 22 / 227 / 5 |
| Low | 4 / 750 / 3 | 8 / 375 / 3 | 5 / 200 / 1 |

Curve Average .230

| | Inside | Middle | Outside |
|------|--------|--------|---------|
| High | 0 / 0 / 0 | 1 / 0 / 0 | 0 / 0 / 0 |
| Med | 1 / 0 / 0 | 0 / 0 / 0 | 2 / 1000 / 2 |
| Low | 2 / 0 / 0 | 1 / 1000 / 1 | 6 / 0 / 0 |

Although his .288 fastball average in 1986 was respectable, it dropped over 120 points from his 1985 fastball average against left-handers.

Left-handed pitchers threw him a higher percentage of outside fastballs in 1986. Fewer inside fastballs and medium-over-the-middle fastballs were thrown.

The percentages in his outside locations fell sharply in 1986. Henderson's performance in the heavily pitched, medium-high outside location fell over 150 points.

Henderson's curve average dropped only slightly in 1986 against left-handers. Notice his trouble with low curves, especially with low-outside curves. In 1986, he had no hits in that location against curveballs.

LOW OUTSIDE
(CURVES THROWN BY LEFT-HANDED PITCHERS 1986)

BATTING AVERAGE .000 (0 FOR 6)
   *PLAY*
| | |
|---|---|
| LEFTFIELDER | No instances recorded |
| CENTERFIELDER | Medium-deep in straightaway center field |
| RIGHTFIELDER | Short in straightaway right field |
| SHORTSTOP | Shifted toward third base |
| SECOND | Shifted toward first base |

Henderson hit better against left-handed pitchers when ahead in the count than when behind in 1985.

**Rickey Henderson Behind In The Count**
**Against Left-Handed Pitchers 1985**
**Batting Average .409**

Fastball Average .500

| | Inside | Middle | Outside |
|---|---|---|---|
| High | 0 — 0/0 | 1 — 1000/1 | 0 — 0/0 |
| Med | 3 — 1000/3 | 2 — 0/0 | 4 — 0/0 |
| Low | 1 — 0/0 | 2 — 1000/2 | 1 — 1000/1 |

Curve Average .200

| | Inside | Middle | Outside |
|---|---|---|---|
| High | 0 — 0/0 | 0 — 0/0 | 1 — 1000/1 |
| Med | 1 — 0/0 | 0 — 0/0 | 3 — 0/0 |
| Low | 0 — 0/0 | 0 — 0/0 | 0 — 0/0 |

### Rickey Henderson Ahead In The Count
### Against Left-Handed Pitchers 1985
### Batting Average .466

Fastball Average .437               Curve Average .666

|      | Inside | Middle | Outside | Inside | Middle | Outside |
|------|--------|--------|---------|--------|--------|---------|
| High | 0/0 0  | 1/0 0  | 0/0 0   | 0/0 0  | 0/0 0  | 0/0 0   |
| Med  | 6/166 1 | 4/750 3 | 12/500 6 | 1/1000 1 | 0/0 0 | 1/1000 1 |
| Low  | 2/500 1 | 3/333 1 | 4/500 2 | 0/0 0  | 1/0 0  | 0/0 0   |

In 1986 against left-handers, Henderson's average was three times higher when ahead in the count than when behind. This was almost completely a result of his fastball performance.

### Rickey Henderson Behind In The Count
### Against Left-Handed Pitchers 1986
### Batting Average .142

Fastball Average .111               Curve Average .166

|      | Inside | Middle | Outside | Inside | Middle | Outside |
|------|--------|--------|---------|--------|--------|---------|
| High | 0/0 0  | 0/0 0  | 0/0 0   | 0/0 0  | 0/0 0  | 0/0 0   |
| Med  | 2/0 0  | 0/0 0  | 5/200 1 | 1/0 0  | 0/0 0  | 1/1000 1 |
| Low  | 0/0 0  | 2/0 0  | 0/0 0   | 0/0 0  | 0/0 0  | 4/0 0   |

## Rickey Henderson Ahead In The Count
## Against Left-Handed Pitchers 1986
## Batting Average .444

Fastball Average .523              Curve Average .500

|      | Inside | Middle | Outside | Inside | Middle | Outside |
|------|--------|--------|---------|--------|--------|---------|
| High | $0/$ **0** $/$ 0 | $2/$ **500** $/$ 1 | $0/$ **0** $/$ 0 | $0/$ **0** $/$ 0 | $0/$ **0** $/$ 0 | $0/$ **0** $/$ 0 |
| Med  | $1/$ **0** $/$ 0 | $1/$ **1000** $/$ 1 | $9/$ **333** $/$ 3 | $0/$ **0** $/$ 0 | $0/$ **0** $/$ 0 | $1/$ **1000** $/$ 1 |
| Low  | $3/$ **1000** $/$ 3 | $3/$ **666** $/$ 2 | $2/$ **500** $/$ 1 | $0/$ **0** $/$ 0 | $0/$ **0** $/$ 0 | $1/$ **0** $/$ 0 |

Henderson did not have a weak fastball location when ahead in the count against left-handers. He was waiting for fastballs when ahead, timing his swing and hitting the ball deep to all fields.

The following charts show that when ahead in the count, Henderson hit the ball with greater authority than when behind.

MEDIUM-HIGH OUTSIDE
(FASTBALLS THROWN BY LEFT-HANDED PITCHERS
WHEN HENDERSON WAS BEHIND IN THE COUNT 1986)

BATTING AVERAGE .200
    *PLAY*
LEFTFIELDER         Medium-deep and shifted toward the left field line
CENTERFIELDER       Short in straightaway center field
RIGHTFIELDER        No instances recorded


MEDIUM-HIGH OUTSIDE
(FASTBALLS THROWN BY LEFT-HANDED PITCHERS
WHEN HENDERSON WAS AHEAD IN THE COUNT 1986)

BATTING AVERAGE .333
    *PLAY*
LEFTFIELDER         Deep in straightaway left field
CENTERFIELDER       Deep in straightaway center field
RIGHTFIELDER        Deep and shifted toward center field

## Willie McGee, St. Louis Cardinals

Willie McGee, switch hitter for the St. Louis Cardinals, had the largest batting decline of any major league player from the 1985 to 1986 season. After leading the National League in hitting in 1985 with a .353 average, McGee fell to .256 in 1986.

### Willie McGee Against Right-Handed Pitchers 1983-1985
### Overall Batting Average .302

Fastball Average .355

| | Outside | Middle | Inside |
|---|---|---|---|
| High | 6/ **166** /1 | 14/ **285** /4 | 18/ **222** /4 |
| Med | 28/ **428** /12 | 13/ **461** /6 | 32/ **343** /11 |
| Low | 13/ **307** /4 | 30/ **466** /14 | 23/ **304** /7 |

Curve Average .289

| | Outside | Middle | Inside |
|---|---|---|---|
| High | 2/ **0** /0 | 4/ **250** /1 | 3/ **0** /0 |
| Med | 10/ **400** /4 | 6/ **500** /3 | 11/ **181** /2 |
| Low | 6/ **0** /0 | 21/ **476** /10 | 13/ **153** /2 |

### Willie McGee Against Right-Handed Pitchers 1986
### Overall Batting Average .211

Fastball Average .254

| | Outside | Middle | Inside |
|---|---|---|---|
| High | 1/ **0** /0 | 9/ **333** /3 | 3/ **333** /1 |
| Med | 15/ **133** /2 | 1/ **0** /0 | 17/ **235** /4 |
| Low | 4/ **0** /0 | 7/ **428** /3 | 2/ **1000** /2 |

Curve Average .269

| | Outside | Middle | Inside |
|---|---|---|---|
| High | 1/ **0** /0 | 3/ **0** /0 | 1/ **0** /0 |
| Med | 4/ **250** /1 | 1/ **0** /0 | 7/ **571** /4 |
| Low | 2/ **500** /1 | 4/ **0** /0 | 3/ **333** /1 |

Notice that the first chart is for McGee against right-handed pitchers in the years 1983-1985, in which he hit .302 overall in games scouted by the BARS System. The second is for the year 1986, in which he hit .211 overall.

Many of McGee's difficulties in 1986 can be traced to his trouble with fastballs. Batting left-handed against right-handed pitchers, McGee declined over 100 points in 1986 against fastballs.

He had three strong locations against fastballs in 1986: high-over-the-middle, high-inside, and low-over-the-middle. In all other locations he declined significantly.

Notice how few medium-over-the-middle pitches McGee was thrown in 1986. This indicates that pitchers pitched McGee extremely carefully after his spectacular year in 1985. McGee's lower average also indicates that he may have gone after many bad pitches in 1986.

McGee's overall average against curveballs stayed about the same, but he had considerable problems against curves over the middle of the plate.

McGee's average declined significantly when behind in the count.

### Willie McGee Behind In The Count
### Against Right-Handed Pitchers 1983-1985
### Batting Average .333

| | Fastball Average .315 | | | Curve Average .310 | | |
|---|---|---|---|---|---|---|
| | Outside | Middle | Inside | Outside | Middle | Inside |
| High | 1/ 0 / 0 | 3/ 333 / 1 | 5/ 0 / 0 | 2/ 0 / 0 | 1/ 0 / 0 | 1/ 0 / 0 |
| Med | 3/ 333 / 1 | 5/ 400 / 2 | 7/ 285 / 2 | 4/ 250 / 1 | 1/ 1000 / 1 | 2/ 0 / 0 |
| Low | 4/ 500 / 2 | 5/ 600 / 3 | 5/ 200 / 1 | 4/ 0 / 0 | 12/ 500 / 6 | 2/ 500 / 1 |

## Willie McGee Behind In The Count
## Against Right-Handed Pitchers 1986
## Batting Average .206

Fastball Average .214

| | Outside | Middle | Inside |
|------|---------|--------|--------|
| High | 0 / 0 <br> 0 | 1 / 0 <br> 0 | 1 / 0 <br> 0 |
| Med | 4 / 0 <br> 0 | 0 / 0 <br> 0 | 6 / 333 <br> 2 |
| Low | 0 / 0 <br> 0 | 2 / 500 <br> 1 | 0 / 0 <br> 0 |

Curve Average .333

| | Outside | Middle | Inside |
|------|---------|--------|--------|
| High | 0 / 0 <br> 0 | 2 / 0 <br> 0 | 0 / 0 <br> 0 |
| Med | 3 / 333 <br> 1 | 0 / 0 <br> 0 | 1 / 1000 <br> 1 |
| Low | 1 / 1000 <br> 1 | 1 / 0 <br> 0 | 1 / 0 <br> 0 |

## Willie McGee Ahead In The Count
## Against Right-Handed Pitchers 1983-1985
## Batting Average .337

Fastball Average .392

| | Outside | Middle | Inside |
|------|---------|--------|--------|
| High | 2 / 500 <br> 1 | 9 / 222 <br> 2 | 9 / 333 <br> 3 |
| Med | 16 / 437 <br> 7 | 6 / 500 <br> 3 | 14 / 214 <br> 3 |
| Low | 2 / 500 <br> 1 | 14 / 500 <br> 7 | 12 / 500 <br> 6 |

Curve Average .333

| | Outside | Middle | Inside |
|------|---------|--------|--------|
| High | 0 / 0 <br> 0 | 1 / 1000 <br> 1 | 1 / 0 <br> 0 |
| Med | 2 / 500 <br> 1 | 4 / 250 <br> 1 | 6 / 333 <br> 2 |
| Low | 0 / 0 <br> 0 | 6 / 500 <br> 3 | 7 / 142 <br> 1 |

## Willie McGee Ahead In The Count
## Against Right-Handed Pitchers 1986
## Batting Average .343

### Fastball Average .473

|  | Outside | Middle | Inside |
|---|---|---|---|
| High | 0/ 0 / 0 | 3/ 666 / 2 | 1/ 1000/ 1 |
| Med | 4/ 250 / 1 | 0/ 0 / 0 | 4/ 250 / 1 |
| Low | 1/ 0 / 0 | 4/ 500 / 2 | 2/ 1000/ 2 |

### Curve Average .333

|  | Outside | Middle | Inside |
|---|---|---|---|
| High | 0/ 0 / 0 | 1/ 0 / 0 | 0/ 0 / 0 |
| Med | 1/ 0 / 0 | 0/ 0 / 0 | 3/ 666 / 2 |
| Low | 0/ 0 / 0 | 1/ 0 / 0 | 0/ 0 / 0 |

## McGee Against Left-Handed Pitchers

McGee's average also dropped sharply against left-handed pitchers. Batting right-handed against lefties, McGee's fastball average dropped 75 points.

## Willie McGee Against Left-Handed Pitchers 1983-1985
## Overall Batting Average .277

### Fastball Average .275

|  | Inside | Middle | Outside |
|---|---|---|---|
| High | 3/ 0 / 0 | 3/ 333 / 1 | 3/ 333 / 1 |
| Med | 14/ 357 / 5 | 3/ 666 / 2 | 17/ 470 / 8 |
| Low | 7/ 0 / 0 | 12/ 83 / 1 | 7/ 142 / 1 |

### Curve Average .275

|  | Inside | Middle | Outside |
|---|---|---|---|
| High | 0/ 0 / 0 | 4/ 250 / 1 | 0/ 0 / 0 |
| Med | 2/ 1000/ 2 | 2/ 0 / 0 | 6/ 333 / 2 |
| Low | 5/ 0 / 0 | 7/ 285 / 2 | 3/ 333 / 1 |

### Willie McGee Against Left-Handed Pitchers 1986
### Overall Batting Average .192

Fastball Average .200

| | Inside | Middle | Outside |
|---|---|---|---|
| High | 2 / 0 / 0 | 4 / 250 / 1 | 2 / 0 / 0 |
| Med | 2 / 0 / 0 | 0 / 0 / 0 | 10 / 300 / 3 |
| Low | 2 / 0 / 0 | 5 / 400 / 2 | 3 / 0 / 0 |

Curve Average .000

| | Inside | Middle | Outside |
|---|---|---|---|
| High | 1 / 0 / 0 | 0 / 0 / 0 | 0 / 0 / 0 |
| Med | 1 / 0 / 0 | 0 / 0 / 0 | 1 / 0 / 0 |
| Low | 0 / 0 / 0 | 2 / 0 / 0 | 1 / 0 / 0 |

Notice his weakness against outside fastballs in 1986, and his weakness in general against low fastballs in all years.

### Dave Parker, Cincinnati Reds

In 1986, left-handed hitting Dave Parker's average dropped nearly 100 points against right-handed pitchers in games recorded by the BARS System.

### Dave Parker Against Right-Handed Pitchers 1985
### Overall Batting Average .366

Fastball Average .426

| | Outside | Middle | Inside |
|---|---|---|---|
| High | 7 / 285 / 2 | 6 / 666 / 4 | 6 / 333 / 2 |
| Med | 10 / 400 / 4 | 7 / 428 / 3 | 12 / 333 / 4 |
| Low | 4 / 1000 / 4 | 14 / 285 / 4 | 9 / 555 / 5 |

Curve Average .428

| | Outside | Middle | Inside |
|---|---|---|---|
| High | 1 / 0 / 0 | 4 / 500 / 2 | 0 / 0 / 0 |
| Med | 4 / 250 / 1 | 1 / 0 / 0 | 2 / 1000 / 2 |
| Low | 1 / 0 / 0 | 4 / 750 / 3 | 4 / 250 / 1 |

## Dave Parker Against Right-Handed Pitchers 1986
## Overall Batting Average .268

### Fastball Average .277

|  | Outside | Middle | Inside |
|---|---|---|---|
| High | 8/ 625 / 5 | 14/ 214 / 3 | 8/ 125 / 1 |
| Med | 13/ 307 / 4 | 2/ 1000/ 2 | 13/ 76 / 1 |
| Low | 2/ 0 / 0 | 8/ 375 / 3 | 4/ 250 / 1 |

### Curve Average .214

|  | Outside | Middle | Inside |
|---|---|---|---|
| High | 2/ 0 / 0 | 4/ 750 / 3 | 0/ 0 / 0 |
| Med | 4/ 0 / 0 | 0/ 0 / 0 | 0/ 0 / 0 |
| Low | 0/ 0 / 0 | 0/ 0 / 0 | 4/ 0 / 0 |

Right-handed pitchers threw Parker about the same number of inside, middle and outside fastballs each year, but note that a lower number of fastballs were thrown medium-over-the-middle in 1986. This indicates that Parker, who is always carefully pitched, was given even less to hit in 1986 after his strong .312 season in 1985. As a result, he might have chased bad pitches in 1986.

His averages dropped in the medium-high outside and medium-high inside fastball locations. His .076 in medium-high inside, along with his .125 in high-inside and .250 in low-inside, gave pitchers ample targets in 1986.

Parker hit the ball more from line to line in 1986. This spraying to all fields could have helped his average; since it didn't, it indicates that he may have been hitting many pop flies that were easy outs.

MEDIUM-HIGH INSIDE
(FASTBALLS THROWN BY RIGHT-HANDED PITCHERS 1985)

BATTING AVERAGE .333
 *PLAY*

| | |
|---|---|
| LEFTFIELDER | Deep and shifted toward the left field line |
| CENTERFIELDER | Deep in straightaway center field |
| RIGHTFIELDER | Deep in straightaway right field |
| SHORTSTOP | Normal position |
| SECOND | Normal position |

MEDIUM-HIGH INSIDE
(FASTBALLS THROWN BY RIGHT-HANDED PITCHERS 1986)

BATTING AVERAGE .076
*PLAY*

| | |
|---|---|
| LEFTFIELDER | Medium-deep and shifted toward the left field line |
| CENTERFIELDER | Deep and shifted toward left field |
| RIGHTFIELDER | Deep and shifted toward the right field line |
| SHORTSTOP | Shifted toward third |
| SECOND | Shifted toward first |

Parker tended to hit medium-high outside pitches more to left field in 1986 than in 1985.

MEDIUM-HIGH OUTSIDE
(FASTBALLS THROWN BY RIGHT-HANDED PITCHERS IN 1985)

BATTING AVERAGE .400
*PLAY*

| | |
|---|---|
| LEFTFIELDER | Deep in straightaway left field |
| CENTERFIELDER | Medium-deep and shifted toward left field |
| RIGHTFIELDER | Deep in straightaway right field |
| SHORTSTOP | Up middle (shifted toward second base) |
| SECOND | Shifted toward first |

MEDIUM-HIGH OUTSIDE
(FASTBALLS THROWN BY RIGHT-HANDED PITCHERS IN 1986)

BATTING AVERAGE .307
*PLAY*

| | |
|---|---|
| LEFTFIELDER | Deep and shifted toward the left field line |
| CENTERFIELDER | Deep and shifted toward left field |
| RIGHTFIELDER | Deep and shifted toward center field |
| SHORTSTOP | Normal position |
| SECOND | Shifted toward first |

Parker's curve average was cut in half in 1986. The only location in which he hit with authority was high-over-the-middle.

Parker hit better when ahead in the count against right-handers both years.

## Dave Parker Behind In The Count
## Against Right-Handed Pitchers 1985
## Batting Average .333

Fastball Average .384                Curve Average .500

|  | Outside | Middle | Inside |
|------|---------|--------|--------|
| High | 1 / 0 / 0 | 1 / 1000 / 1 | 2 / 0 / 0 |
| Med | 1 / 0 / 0 | 2 / 500 / 1 | 2 / 500 / 1 |
| Low | 1 / 1000 / 1 | 1 / 1000 / 1 | 2 / 0 / 0 |

|  | Outside | Middle | Inside |
|------|---------|--------|--------|
| High | 0 / 0 / 0 | 0 / 0 / 0 | 0 / 0 / 0 |
| Med | 1 / 0 / 0 | 0 / 0 / 0 | 0 / 0 / 0 |
| Low | 0 / 0 / 0 | 1 / 1000 / 1 | 0 / 0 / 0 |

## Dave Parker Ahead In The Count
## Against Right-Handed Pitchers 1985
## Batting Average .530

Fastball Average .542                Curve Average .800

|  | Outside | Middle | Inside |
|------|---------|--------|--------|
| High | 1 / 1000 / 1 | 4 / 750 / 3 | 2 / 500 / 1 |
| Med | 4 / 500 / 2 | 2 / 500 / 1 | 4 / 500 / 2 |
| Low | 2 / 1000 / 2 | 10 / 200 / 2 | 6 / 833 / 5 |

|  | Outside | Middle | Inside |
|------|---------|--------|--------|
| High | 0 / 0 / 0 | 0 / 0 / 0 | 0 / 0 / 0 |
| Med | 1 / 1000 / 1 | 1 / 0 / 0 | 2 / 1000 / 2 |
| Low | 0 / 0 / 0 | 0 / 0 / 0 | 1 / 1000 / 1 |

## Dave Parker Behind In The Count
## Against Right-Handed Pitchers 1986
## Batting Average .250

### Fastball Average .333

| | Outside | Middle | Inside |
|---|---|---|---|
| High | 750 ⁴/3 | 0 ⁴/0 | 250 ⁴/1 |
| Med | 0 ¹/0 | 0 ⁰/0 | 0 ³/0 |
| Low | 0 ¹/0 | 750 ⁴/3 | 0 ⁰/0 |

### Curve Average .000

| | Outside | Middle | Inside |
|---|---|---|---|
| High | 0 ²/0 | 0 ⁰/0 | 0 ⁰/0 |
| Med | 0 ¹/0 | 0 ⁰/0 | 0 ⁰/0 |
| Low | 0 ⁰/0 | 0 ⁰/0 | 0 ⁰/0 |

## Dave Parker Ahead In The Count
## Against Right-Handed Pitchers 1986
## Batting Average .297

### Fastball Average .310

| | Outside | Middle | Inside |
|---|---|---|---|
| High | 1000 ¹/1 | 500 ⁴/2 | 0 ²/0 |
| Med | 375 ⁸/3 | 1000 ¹/1 | 200 ⁵/1 |
| Low | 0 ¹/0 | 0 ⁴/0 | 333 ³/1 |

### Curve Average .333

| | Outside | Middle | Inside |
|---|---|---|---|
| High | 0 ⁰/0 | 500 ²/1 | 0 ⁰/0 |
| Med | 0 ¹/0 | 0 ⁰/0 | 0 ⁰/0 |
| Low | 0 ⁰/0 | 0 ⁰/0 | 0 ⁰/0 |

## Parker Against Left-Handed Pitchers

Parker hit slightly better against left-handed pitchers in 1986 than in 1985, but the gain was small and was not enough to offset the large drop against right-handers.

## *Personal Comments*

Davey Johnson helped me design the pitching charts. He wanted to know how pitchers throw when there are no runners on base, when there is a runner on first and when a runner or runners are in scoring position. Davey said that he thought a pitcher would probably throw differently in those situations, and the information we've gathered shows that he was right. The BARS pitching charts are the subject of the next chapter.

Pitchers feel that they are most accurate with their fastballs. This can be seen by examining the pitching charts to find out what pitchers throw when they are behind in the count 3-0 or 3-1. Most pitchers throw fastballs nearly 100 percent of the time on these counts.

Almost without exception, pitchers throw more fastballs than all other types of pitches combined. Even a control pitcher like Fernando Valenzuela, who throws four or five types of pitches well, depends on his fastball in tight situations. Overall, 54 percent of Valenzuela's pitches are fastballs. Jack Morris throws fastballs 60 percent of the time; Dwight Gooden, 77 percent; and Roger Clemens, 81 percent.

Pitchers develop patterns that they feel comfortable with, and they don't vary these patterns very much. The BARS pitching charts can predict with 75 percent accuracy what type of pitch will be thrown. The location of pitches can be predicted with 65 percent accuracy.

On almost all occasions, pitchers throw to their own strengths, rather than to the batter's weaknesses. When batters realize this, they can study these charts and learn a lot about a particular pitcher. And pitchers can look at their own charts, so they don't get stuck in a rut.

# Chapter Thirteen

# The Pitchers

*"While you shouldn't get into guessing games with the pitcher, you should use your head about what he can throw and what he's likely to throw. What is his best pitch, and where does he usually put it?"*

Willie Mays

The BARS System has two separate reports for pitchers: the Pitch Information Report, which charts the types of pitches (fastball, curve, slider, etc.) that a pitcher throws; and the Pitch Location Report, which charts where in the strike zone the pitcher throws.

Taken together, these two reports allow hitters to study past performances of individual pitchers. The study of a pitcher's past performance can tell a hitter what type of pitch the pitcher is likely to throw in a particular situation, and where he is likely to throw it. Also, pitchers can benefit by studying their own charts. Pitchers often develop patterns of pitching that they are not aware of. Batters become familiar with these patterns and begin expecting certain types of pitches in certain situations. Studying the BARS System Pitching Charts allows a pitcher to spot patterns he has fallen into. The BARS Pitch Information Report has been proven accurate 70 percent of the time. The Pitch Location Report has been proven accurate 65 percent of the time.

Two separate Pitch Information and Pitch Location Reports are generated for each pitcher: one for pitches made when facing right-handed batters, one for when facing left-handed batters. Each Report is divided into four categories: when no runners are on base, when a runner is on first, when a runner or runners are in scoring position, and 'All Situations,' which is a composite of the three other categories.

### Fernando Valenzuela, Los Angeles Dodgers

As an example, the 'All Situations' Pitch Information Report for left-handed pitcher Fernando Valenzuela of the Los Angeles Dodgers is shown on the following page. Note that the chart shows only Valenzuela's performance against right-handed batters.

**BASE SITUATION:** All Situations

| *Various Counts on Batter* | | **Ahead In The Count** | | | | | **Even Count** | | | |
|---|---|---|---|---|---|---|---|---|---|---|
| | Balls | 0 | 0 | 1 | 2 | | 0 | 1 | 3 | |
| | Strikes | 1 | 2 | 2 | 2 | | 0 | 1 | 2 | |
| Total Pitches On Each Count | | 368 | 158 | 299 | 287 | 1112 | 981 | 381 | 216 | 1578 |
| **Fast** | Balls | 25 | 41 | 24 | 18 | 25 | 25 | 20 | 12 | 22 |
| | Strikes | 24 | 22 | 26 | 32 | 26 | 23 | 31 | 50 | 29 |
| **Curve** | Balls | 5 | 3 | 6 | 5 | 5 | 11 | 7 | 1 | 9 |
| | Strikes | 14 | 4 | 10 | 11 | 11 | 13 | 12 | 7 | 12 |
| **Slider** | Balls | 2 | 4 | 2 | 2 | 2 | 2 | 2 | 1 | 2 |
| | Strikes | 3 | 3 | 4 | 3 | 3 | 2 | 3 | 4 | 3 |
| **Knuckleball** | Balls | | | | | | | | | |
| | Strikes | | | | | | | | | |
| **Screwball** | Balls | 11 | 13 | 13 | 9 | 12 | 11 | 7 | 5 | 9 |
| | Strikes | 14 | 9 | 13 | 18 | 14 | 11 | 15 | 19 | 13 |
| **Sinker** | Balls | | | | | | | | | |
| | Strikes | | | | | | | | | |
| **Change-Up** | Balls | 1 | | | 1 | 1 | 1 | 1 | | 1 |
| | Strikes | 1 | 2 | 1 | 2 | 1 | 1 | 2 | | 1 |

| *Various Counts on Batter* | | **Behind In The Count** | | | | | |
|---|---|---|---|---|---|---|---|
| | Balls | 1 | 2 | 2 | 3 | 3 | |
| | Strikes | 0 | 0 | 1 | 0 | 1 | |
| Total Pitches On Each Count | | 476 | 191 | 224 | 69 | 118 | 1078 |
| **Fast** | Balls | 21 | 24 | 21 | 32 | 18 | 22 |
| | Strikes | 30 | 46 | 41 | 67 | 69 | 42 |
| **Curve** | Balls | 7 | 2 | 4 | | | 4 |
| | Strikes | 10 | 4 | 9 | | 2 | 7 |
| **Slider** | Balls | 3 | 3 | 1 | | 2 | 2 |
| | Strikes | 3 | 2 | 3 | | 2 | 3 |
| **Knuckleball** | Balls | | | | | | |
| | Strikes | | | | | | |
| **Screwball** | Balls | 10 | 8 | 7 | | 3 | 8 |
| | Strikes | 14 | 10 | 12 | 1 | 4 | 11 |
| **Sinker** | Balls | | | | | | |
| | Strikes | | | | | | |
| **Change-Up** | Balls | 1 | | 1 | | | 1 |
| | Strikes | 1 | 1 | 1 | | 1 | 1 |

Notice that the report on the preceding page is only for pitches Valenzuela throws to right-handed batters. A similar Pitch Information Report is generated for pitches to left-handed batters.

In the chart, each vertical column of figures represents the pitches thrown on the particular count that is shown at the top of the column. In the 'Ahead In The Count' section of the chart, under 0 balls and 1 strike, the first row of figures shows that a total of 368 pitches were recorded when Valenzuela went to 0 and 1 against a right-handed batter. Similarly, 158 pitches were recorded when the count was 0-2 (0 balls and 2 strikes), 299 pitches were recorded when the count was 1-2, etc.

The figure '1112' at the end of the row is the total number of pitches recorded by the BARS System when Valenzuela was ahead in the count against right-handed batters. Similarly, Valenzuela threw 1578 total pitches when even in the count, and 1078 total pitches when behind in the count.

The figures beside the types of pitches do not represent the actual number of pitches in each category. They represent *percentages* of the total number of pitches. The figure '25' directly beneath the figure '368', indicates that 25 percent of the 368 pitches thrown when the count was 0-1 were fastballs that were called balls. The next figure, '24', indicates that 24 percent of the 368 pitches were fastballs called strikes. The total percentages in each column total 100 percent. Slight discrepancies can arise due to rounding off.

A brief analysis of Valenzuela's Pitch Information Report will help indicate trends that have developed in his pitching.

Notice from the Pitch Information Report above that when Valenzuela is ahead or even in the count, he throws fastballs slightly more than half the time in most count situations. These are divided about fifty-fifty between balls and strikes. Notice that when Valenzuela is behind in the count, he throws more fastballs in comparison to other types of pitches than when he is ahead or even in the count.

When the count is 3-0, he throws fastballs almost exclusively (as does nearly every pitcher). When the count is 3-0, 32 percent of Valenzuela's pitches are fastballs that are called balls and 67 percent are fastballs that are called strikes.

When the count is 3-2 (which would seem to be equally as crucial) he throws fastballs only 62 percent of the time (12 percent fastballs that are called balls, 50 percent fastballs that are called strikes).

On all pitches other than those thrown when the count is 3-0, Valenzuela throws a significantly high percentage of pitches other than fastballs. He has confidence in his curve and screwball. He throws screwballs over 25 percent of the time when ahead in the count, over 20 percent of the time when even, and slightly under 20 percent when behind. In many instances, he throws more screwballs than curves.

## Key Counts

One of the most crucial counts for a batter is when the count is 0-2 (no balls and two strikes). On this count Valenzuela wastes a pitch well over half the time: a full 41 percent of his pitches on the 0-2 count are fastballs that are called balls. As the count goes to 1-2, 2-2 and 3-2, progressively more pitches are thrown for strikes than for balls.

Throughout this chapter, emphasis will be given to trends found in key counts. Each of the pitchers discussed has his own patterns in crucial situations.

An interesting statistic from the chart shown above is that Valenzuela is ahead in the count more often than he is behind. This can be seen by comparing the total number of pitches in his 'Ahead In The Count' columns (1112) with the total in his 'Behind In The Count' columns (1078). Valenzuela's overall ahead/behind-in-the-count ratio against right-handed batters is 1112/1078.

This statistic must be interpreted differently for every pitcher. A control pitcher like Valenzuela would ordinarily not be as concerned about getting behind in the count as a pitcher who relies on a hard fastball, because Valenzuela has good control of his breaking pitches and is not forced to go exclusively to his fastball when behind. A pitcher who relies heavily on his fastball would ordinarily do best by keeping ahead of the hitters as much as possible, because hitters would know that the pitcher is going to throw a fastball when behind.

Dwight Gooden, for example, throws mostly fastballs and is ahead in the count much more often than he is behind. With runners in scoring position, Gooden is ahead in the count more than twice as often as he is behind. The BARS pitching charts for Dwight Gooden and other fine pitchers are shown in this chapter.

Shown on the next few pages is the remainder of Fernando Valenzuela's Pitch Information Report against right-handed batters. These include information for when no runners are on base, when a runner is on first and when a runner or runners are in scoring postion. The BARS System has determined that pitchers throw differently not only when the count changes, but when the runners-on-base situation changes.

The BARS System pitching reports contain so many items of importance that only a few can be mentioned. The interested reader is encouraged to examine the charts on his own. As the charts become familiar, trends can be found easily.

Note that the Pitch Information Report on the following page for Valenzuela shows his performance against right-handed batters. A similar Report is generated for his performance against left-handed batters, but for the sake of clarity and for consideration of space, it is not shown here.

**BASE SITUATION:** No One on Base

| Various Counts on Batter | Ahead In The Count | | | | | Even Count | | | |
|---|---|---|---|---|---|---|---|---|---|
| Balls / Strikes | 0 / 1 | 0 / 2 | 1 / 2 | 2 / 2 | | 0 / 0 | 1 / 1 | 3 / 2 | |
| **Total Pitches On Each Count** | 204 | 87 | 164 | 180 | 635 | 537 | 204 | 129 | 870 |
| **Fast** Balls | 25 | 45 | 27 | 18 | 26 | 27 | 22 | 13 | 24 |
| **Fast** Strikes | 26 | 23 | 27 | 34 | 28 | 24 | 32 | 54 | 30 |
| **Curve** Balls | 4 | 2 | 4 | 4 | 4 | 10 | 6 | 2 | 8 |
| **Curve** Strikes | 15 | | 9 | 11 | 10 | 15 | 13 | 6 | 13 |
| **Slider** Balls | 3 | 5 | 2 | 1 | 3 | 2 | 1 | 1 | 1 |
| **Slider** Strikes | 2 | 2 | 4 | 2 | 3 | 2 | 3 | 3 | 3 |
| **Knuckleball** Balls | | | | | | | | | |
| **Knuckleball** Strikes | | | | | | | | | |
| **Screwball** Balls | 13 | 14 | 13 | 9 | 12 | 8 | 7 | 5 | 7 |
| **Screwball** Strikes | 12 | 7 | 10 | 17 | 12 | 11 | 13 | 16 | 12 |
| **Sinker** Balls | | | | | | | | | |
| **Sinker** Strikes | | | | | | | | | |
| **Change-Up** Balls | | | | 1 | | 1 | | | 1 |
| **Change-Up** Strikes | | 2 | 2 | 2 | 2 | 1 | 2 | | 1 |

| Various Counts on Batter | Behind In The Count | | | | | |
|---|---|---|---|---|---|---|
| Balls / Strikes | 1 / 0 | 2 / 0 | 2 / 1 | 3 / 0 | 3 / 1 | |
| **Total Pitches On Each Count** | 252 | 113 | 131 | 39 | 62 | 597 |
| **Fast** Balls | 25 | 24 | 18 | 31 | 21 | 23 |
| **Fast** Strikes | 25 | 48 | 49 | 69 | 73 | 43 |
| **Curve** Balls | 6 | 2 | 2 | | | 3 |
| **Curve** Strikes | 13 | 3 | 8 | | 2 | 8 |
| **Slider** Balls | 4 | 4 | 1 | | | 2 |
| **Slider** Strikes | 4 | 4 | 4 | | 2 | 4 |
| **Knuckleball** Balls | | | | | | |
| **Knuckleball** Strikes | | | | | | |
| **Screwball** Balls | 10 | 5 | 6 | | 3 | 7 |
| **Screwball** Strikes | 12 | 10 | 11 | | | 9 |
| **Sinker** Balls | | | | | | |
| **Sinker** Strikes | | | | | | |
| **Change-Up** Balls | 1 | | 1 | | | 1 |
| **Change-Up** Strikes | | 2 | 2 | 2 | 2 | 1 |

**BASE SITUATION:** Runner on First

| *Various Counts on Batter* | | Ahead In The Count | | | | | Even Count | | | |
|---|---|---|---|---|---|---|---|---|---|---|
| | Balls | 0 | 0 | 1 | 2 | | 0 | 1 | 3 | |
| | Strikes | 1 | 2 | 2 | 2 | | 0 | 1 | 2 | |
| Total Pitches On Each Count | | 73 | 40 | 54 | 35 | 202 | 193 | 62 | 31 | 286 |
| Fast | Balls | 16 | 38 | 17 | 23 | 22 | 18 | 18 | 10 | 17 |
| | Strikes | 27 | 18 | 30 | 9 | 23 | 23 | 29 | 35 | 26 |
| Curve | Balls | 11 | 5 | 15 | 3 | 9 | 11 | 8 | | 9 |
| | Strikes | 14 | 13 | 9 | 14 | 12 | 10 | 5 | | 8 |
| Slider | Balls | 1 | 3 | | 3 | 1 | 4 | 5 | | 3 |
| | Strikes | 4 | 3 | | 9 | 3 | 4 | 5 | 10 | 5 |
| Knuckleball | Balls | | | | | | | | | |
| | Strikes | | | | | | | | | |
| Screwball | Balls | 5 | 13 | 13 | 6 | 9 | 13 | 10 | 3 | 11 |
| | Strikes | 18 | 10 | 15 | 34 | 18 | 16 | 16 | 39 | 19 |
| Sinker | Balls | | | | | | | | | |
| | Strikes | | | | | | | | | |
| Change-Up | Balls | | | 2 | | | 1 | 5 | | 2 |
| | Strikes | 3 | | | | 1 | | | 3 | |

| *Various Counts on Batter* | | Behind In The Count | | | | | |
|---|---|---|---|---|---|---|---|
| | Balls | 1 | 2 | 2 | 3 | 3 | |
| | Strikes | 0 | 0 | 1 | 0 | 1 | |
| Total Pitches On Each Count | | 84 | 29 | 38 | 12 | 23 | 186 |
| Fast | Balls | 24 | 34 | 24 | 42 | 9 | 25 |
| | Strikes | 35 | 55 | 29 | 58 | 83 | 44 |
| Curve | Balls | 6 | | 13 | | | 5 |
| | Strikes | 6 | | 5 | | | 4 |
| Slider | Balls | 4 | | 3 | | 4 | 3 |
| | Strikes | 5 | | 3 | | | 3 |
| Knuckleball | Balls | | | | | | |
| | Strikes | | | | | | |
| Screwball | Balls | 6 | 7 | 5 | | | 5 |
| | Strikes | 11 | 3 | 13 | | | 8 |
| Sinker | Balls | | | | | | |
| | Strikes | | | | | | |
| Change-Up | Balls | 1 | | 3 | | | 1 |
| | Strikes | 4 | | 3 | | 4 | 3 |

**BASE SITUATION:** Runner(s) in Scoring Position

| *Various Counts on Batter* | | *Ahead In The Count* | | | | | *Even Count* | | | |
|---|---|---|---|---|---|---|---|---|---|---|
| | Balls | 0 | 0 | 1 | 2 | | 0 | 1 | 3 | |
| | Strikes | 1 | 2 | 2 | 2 | | 0 | 1 | 2 | |
| Total Pitches On Each Count | | 91 | 31 | 81 | 72 | 275 | 251 | 115 | 56 | 422 |
| **Fast** | Balls | 33 | 32 | 23 | 15 | 25 | 27 | 17 | 11 | 22 |
| | Strikes | 16 | 23 | 21 | 36 | 24 | 22 | 31 | 46 | 28 |
| **Curve** | Balls | 3 | | 4 | 7 | 4 | 12 | 7 | 2 | 9 |
| | Strikes | 11 | 6 | 14 | 10 | 11 | 10 | 16 | 13 | 12 |
| **Slider** | Balls | 1 | 3 | 4 | 3 | 3 | 2 | 1 | 2 | 1 |
| | Strikes | 4 | 3 | 5 | 4 | 4 | 2 | 3 | 4 | 2 |
| **Knuckleball** | Balls | | | | | | | | | |
| | Strikes | | | | | | | | | |
| **Screwball** | Balls | 12 | 13 | 14 | 8 | 12 | 15 | 6 | 4 | 11 |
| | Strikes | 16 | 16 | 16 | 14 | 16 | 9 | 17 | 18 | 12 |
| **Sinker** | Balls | | | | | | | | | |
| | Strikes | | | | | | | | | |
| **Change-Up** | Balls | 2 | | | 1 | 1 | | 1 | 2 | 1 |
| | Strikes | | 3 | | 1 | 1 | 1 | 2 | | 1 |

| *Various Counts on Batter* | | *Behind In The Count* | | | | | |
|---|---|---|---|---|---|---|---|
| | Balls | 1 | 2 | 2 | 3 | 3 | |
| | Strikes | 0 | 0 | 1 | 0 | 1 | |
| Total Pitches On Each Count | | 140 | 49 | 55 | 18 | 33 | 295 |
| **Fast** | Balls | 12 | 18 | 24 | 28 | 18 | 17 |
| | Strikes | 35 | 37 | 31 | 67 | 52 | 38 |
| **Curve** | Balls | 9 | 4 | 5 | | | 6 |
| | Strikes | 7 | 8 | 16 | | 3 | 8 |
| **Slider** | Balls | 1 | 2 | | | 3 | 1 |
| | Strikes | 1 | | 2 | | 3 | 1 |
| **Knuckleball** | Balls | | | | | | |
| | Strikes | | | | | | |
| **Screwball** | Balls | 14 | 16 | 9 | | 6 | 12 |
| | Strikes | 19 | 14 | 13 | 6 | 15 | 16 |
| **Sinker** | Balls | | | | | | |
| | Strikes | | | | | | |
| **Change-Up** | Balls | 1 | | | | | 1 |
| | Strikes | 1 | | | | | |

## Fernando Valenzuela: The Pitch Location Report

The Pitch Location Report is based on a nine-location strike zone grid similar to the grid used in the Super Summary batting reports.

Two separate Pitch Location Reports are generated for each pitcher: one for pitches made when facing right-handed batters, one for when facing left-handed batters. Each Report is divided into four categories: when no runners are on base, when a runner is on first, when a runner or runners are in scoring position, and 'All Situations,' which is a composite of the three categories.

The report shown below is the 'All Situations' Pitch Location Report for Valenzuela when facing right-handed batters. Following the discussion on this part of the Report, the three remaining categories will be shown.

### Pitch Location Report
### Fernando Valenzuela    Left-Handed Pitcher
### Against All Right-Handed Batters All Teams

**Base Situation:** All Situations          Total Pitches: 3768

**Totals:** 2057              620                187                0

| | Fast | | | | Curve | | | | Slider | | | | Knuckle | | |
|---|---|---|---|---|---|---|---|---|---|---|---|---|---|---|---|---|
| | I | M | O | | I | M | O | | I | M | O | | I | M | O |
| H | 3 | 5 | 12 | H | 4 | 5 | 9 | H | 2 | 3 | | H | | | |
| M | 5 | 2 | 20 | M | 8 | 3 | 13 | M | 4 | 2 | 2 | M | | | |
| L | 9 | 13 | 27 | L | 23 | 15 | 16 | L | 41 | 26 | 16 | L | | | |

**Totals:**     838              0              66

| | Screwball | | | | Sinkerball | | | | Change-Up | | |
|---|---|---|---|---|---|---|---|---|---|---|---|
| | I | M | O | | I | M | O | | I | M | O |
| H | | | 10 | H | | | | H | | 7 | 10 |
| M | | | 22 | M | | | | M | 3 | 4 | 25 |
| L | 2 | 7 | 54 | L | | | | L | 9 | 15 | 24 |

Looking at Valenzuela's 'All Situations' category, it can be seen that 2,057 fastballs have been recorded. This means that 2,057 fastballs were thrown to right-handed batters in all games recorded by the BARS System when Valenzuela was pitching.

The numbers in the fastball grid below are *percentages* of this number. Thus, 27 percent of the fastballs Valenzuela threw to right-handed batters were in the low-outside location, 20 percent were in the medium-high outside location, 12 percent were in the high-outside location, etc.

Curve balls, sliders, screwballs and change-ups were recorded in a similar manner. No knuckleballs or sinkerballs were recorded for Valenzuela.

It should be noted here that the BARS System records split-fingered fastballs in the sinkerball category. Valenzuela does not throw a split-fingered fastball, but other pitchers examined in this chapter do.

A brief analysis of Valenzuela's Pitch Location Report highlights trends that have developed in his pitching.

From the chart above, it can be seen that Valenzuela keeps his fastballs outside when throwing to right-handed batters. A low percentage of his fastballs are thrown inside. A very low percentage (two percent) are thrown medium-over-the-middle. This shows that he has excellent control and keeps the ball away from the heart of the plate.

Valenzuela keeps his curveballs down in the strike zone, with low percentages in the higher areas. As with fastballs, a low percentage of curves (three percent) are thrown medium-over-the-middle.

Valenzuela also keeps his sliders down in the strike zone. Forty-one percent of his sliders to right-handed batters are low-inside, 26 percent are low-over-the-middle and 16 percent are low-outside.

Notice that Valenzuela throws more screwballs than curves (838 screwballs, 620 curves). He keeps his screwballs outside and low, with 54 percent to the low-outside location and 22 percent to the medium-high outside location..

Valenzuela throws few change-ups. When he does, he keeps them low and outside.

The following charts show Valenzuela's pitch selection when no runners are on base, when there is a runner on first, and when a runner or runners are in scoring position.

**Base Situation:** No One on Base          Total Pitches: 2102

*Totals:* 1208      336      102      0

| | *Fast* | | | | *Curve* | | | | *Slider* | | | | *Knuckle* | | |
|---|---|---|---|---|---|---|---|---|---|---|---|---|---|---|---|
| | **I** | **M** | **O** | | **I** | **M** | **O** | | **I** | **M** | **O** | | **I** | **M** | **O** |
| **H** | 3 | 4 | 13 | **H** | 3 | 5 | 7 | **H** | 2 | 4 | 1 | **H** | | | |
| **M** | 4 | 2 | 20 | **M** | 6 | 3 | 14 | **M** | 5 | 1 | 2 | **M** | | | |
| **L** | 9 | 13 | 27 | **L** | 24 | 17 | 18 | **L** | 37 | 28 | 16 | **L** | | | |

*Totals:* 421      0      35

| | *Screwball* | | | | *Sinkerball* | | | | *Change-Up* | | |
|---|---|---|---|---|---|---|---|---|---|---|---|
| | **I** | **M** | **O** | | **I** | **M** | **O** | | **I** | **M** | **O** |
| **H** | | | 9 | **H** | | | | **H** | | 8 | 8 |
| **M** | | 1 | 21 | **M** | | | | **M** | 2 | | 28 |
| **L** | 2 | 7 | 56 | **L** | | | | **L** | 14 | 11 | 25 |

**Base Situation:** Runner on First          Total Pitches: 674

*Totals:* 340      111      43      0

| | *Fast* | | | | *Curve* | | | | *Slider* | | | | *Knuckle* | | |
|---|---|---|---|---|---|---|---|---|---|---|---|---|---|---|---|
| | **I** | **M** | **O** | | **I** | **M** | **O** | | **I** | **M** | **O** | | **I** | **M** | **O** |
| **H** | 3 | 6 | 12 | **H** | 7 | 4 | 13 | **H** | 4 | 4 | | **H** | | | |
| **M** | 6 | 3 | 16 | **M** | 10 | | 18 | **M** | 2 | 4 | 2 | **M** | | | |
| **L** | 10 | 13 | 26 | **L** | 21 | 10 | 11 | **L** | 48 | 18 | 14 | **L** | | | |

*Totals:* 164      0      16

| | *Screwball* | | | | *Sinkerball* | | | | *Change-Up* | | |
|---|---|---|---|---|---|---|---|---|---|---|---|
| | **I** | **M** | **O** | | **I** | **M** | **O** | | **I** | **M** | **O** |
| **H** | 1 | 1 | 11 | **H** | | | | **H** | | | 18 |
| **M** | 1 | | 25 | **M** | | | | **M** | | 12 | 25 |
| **L** | 4 | 7 | 45 | **L** | | | | **L** | 6 | 12 | 25 |

| Base Situation: Runner(s) in Scoring Position | | | | | | | | | | | Total Pitches: 992 | | |
|---|---|---|---|---|---|---|---|---|---|---|---|---|---|---|
| **Totals:** *509* | | | | *173* | | | | *42* | | | | *0* | | |
| *Fast* | | | | *Curve* | | | | *Slider* | | | | *Knuckle* | | |
| | I | M | O | | I | M | O | | I | M | O | | I | M | O |
| H | 3 | 5 | 11 | H | 4 | 7 | 9 | H | | | | H | | | |
| M | 5 | 2 | 20 | M | 11 | 4 | 9 | M | 2 | 2 | 2 | M | | | |
| L | 11 | 14 | 25 | L | 22 | 14 | 17 | L | 42 | 31 | 19 | L | | | |

| **Totals:** *253* | | | | *0* | | | | *15* | | |
|---|---|---|---|---|---|---|---|---|---|---|
| *Screwball* | | | | *Sinkerball* | | | | *Change-Up* | | |
| | I | M | O | | I | M | O | | I | M | O |
| H | | | 12 | H | | | | H | | 13 | 6 |
| M | | | 22 | M | | | | M | 6 | 6 | 20 |
| L | 1 | 5 | 56 | L | | | | L | | 26 | 20 |

## Valenzuela Against Left-Handed Batters

When facing left-handed batters, the left-handed Valenzuela throws a higher percentage of inside fastballs than when facing right-handed batters, and a higher percentage of his pitches are curves.

A comparison with the Report against right-handed batters shows that Valenzuela throws a higher percentage of his curves to the outside locations when facing left-handed batters.

Only Valenzuela's 'All Situations' Pitch Location Report against left-handed batters is shown here.

**Pitch Location Report**
**Fernando Valenzuela     Left-Handed Pitcher**
**Against All Left-Handed Batters All Teams**

| *Base Situation:* All Situations | | | | | | | | Total Pitches: 689 | | |
|---|---|---|---|---|---|---|---|---|---|---|
| *Totals:* 354 | | | 220 | | | 58 | | | 0 | |
| *Fast* | | | *Curve* | | | *Slider* | | | *Knuckle* | | |
| O | M | I | O | M | I | O | M | I | O | M | I |
| H 3 | 6 | 9 | H 1 | 9 | 5 | H | 8 | 3 | H | | |
| M 15 | 2 | 18 | M 17 | 6 | 8 | M 24 | | 6 | M | | |
| L 17 | 11 | 15 | L 32 | 12 | 5 | L 32 | 19 | 5 | L | | |

| *Totals:* 50 | | | 0 | | | 7 | | |
|---|---|---|---|---|---|---|---|---|
| *Screwball* | | | *Sinkerball* | | | *Change-Up* | | |
| O | M | I | O | M | I | O | M | I |
| H 2 | 2 | 4 | H | | | H | | |
| M 12 | | 20 | M | | | M 28 | 14 | |
| L 10 | 18 | 32 | L | | | L 28 | 28 | |

## Dwight Gooden, New York Mets

In contrast to Fernando Valenzuela, who throws a high percentage of breaking pitches, right-handed Dwight Gooden of the New York Mets relies on his fastball. Gooden also has an excellent curve, using it to make his fastball more effective.

**Pitch Information Report**
**Dwight Gooden     Right-Handed Pitcher**
**Against All Right-Handed Batters All Teams**

(Shown on opposite page)

**BASE SITUATION:** All Situations

| *Various Counts on Batter* | | *Ahead In The Count* | | | | | *Even Count* | | | |
|---|---|---|---|---|---|---|---|---|---|---|
| | Balls | 0 | 0 | 1 | 2 | | 0 | 1 | 3 | |
| | Strikes | 1 | 2 | 2 | 2 | | 0 | 1 | 2 | |
| Total Pitches On Each Count | | 412 | 264 | 324 | 236 | 1236 | 864 | 321 | 125 | 1310 |
| **Fast** | Balls | 20 | 23 | 19 | 12 | 19 | 28 | 26 | 20 | 27 |
| | Strikes | 48 | 46 | 47 | 47 | 47 | 50 | 51 | 72 | 52 |
| **Curve** | Balls | 16 | 12 | 15 | 17 | 15 | 12 | 11 | 3 | 11 |
| | Strikes | 15 | 18 | 19 | 23 | 18 | 9 | 10 | 5 | 9 |
| **Slider** | Balls | | | | | | | | | |
| | Strikes | | | | | | | 1 | | |
| **Knuckleball** | Balls | | | | | | | | | |
| | Strikes | | | | | | | | | |
| **Screwball** | Balls | | | | | | | | | |
| | Strikes | | | | | | | | | |
| **Sinker** | Balls | | | | | | | | | |
| | Strikes | | | | | | | | | |
| **Change-Up** | Balls | | | | | 1 | | | | |
| | Strikes | | | 1 | | | | 1 | | |

| *Various Counts on Batter* | | *Behind In The Count* | | | | | |
|---|---|---|---|---|---|---|---|
| | Balls | 1 | 2 | 2 | 3 | 3 | |
| | Strikes | 0 | 0 | 1 | 0 | 1 | |
| Total Pitches On Each Count | | 352 | 110 | 170 | 41 | 59 | 732 |
| **Fast** | Balls | 27 | 35 | 18 | 46 | 29 | 27 |
| | Strikes | 65 | 61 | 72 | 54 | 68 | 66 |
| **Curve** | Balls | 4 | 2 | 5 | | 2 | 3 |
| | Strikes | 3 | 2 | 4 | | 2 | 3 |
| **Slider** | Balls | | | | | | |
| | Strikes | | | | | | |
| **Knuckleball** | Balls | | | | | | |
| | Strikes | | | | | | |
| **Screwball** | Balls | | | | | | |
| | Strikes | | | | | | |
| **Sinker** | Balls | | | | | | |
| | Strikes | | | | | | |
| **Change-Up** | Balls | | | | | | |
| | Strikes | 1 | | 1 | | | |

On the 0-0 count, 50 percent of Gooden's pitches are fastballs thrown for strikes. When ahead on the critical 0-2, 1-2 and 2-2 counts, Gooden throws higher percentages of curves than when even or behind in the count. When the count reaches 3-2, the percentage of curves falls sharply and the percentage of fastballs jumps sharply (72 percent fastball strikes, 20 percent fastball balls).

When behind in the count, Gooden throws fastballs almost exclusively. On the 2-1 pitch, Gooden throws a fastball 90 percent of the time (72 percent strikes, 18 percent balls).

On the 3-0 count, Gooden throws only fastballs, but a surprisingly high percentage are balls (46 percent).

Due to consideration of space, Gooden's Pitch Information Report for when no runners are on base, for when a runner is on first and for when a runner or runners are in scoring position are not shown. His pitching trends change somewhat as runners reach base and move into scoring position. The 3-2 count is especially interesting. When the count is 3-2 with no runners on base, Gooden throws fastball strikes 80 percent of the time. This falls to 61 percent when a runner is on first base and 58 percent when runners are in scoring position.

Gooden is slightly more careful against left-handed batters. The percentage of strikes in most categories is lower than against right-handed batters. Overall, the statistics covered on right-handed batters applies to left-handed batters, so Gooden's Pitch Information Reports against left-handed batters are not shown.

**Gooden's Pitch Location Report**

## Pitch Location Report
### Dwight Gooden    Right-Handed Pitcher
### Against All Right-Handed Batters All Teams

| | **Base Situation:** All Situations | | | | | | | Total Pitches: 3278 | | | |
|---|---|---|---|---|---|---|---|---|---|---|---|
| **Totals:** 2535 | | | 720 | | | 4 | | | 0 | | |
| *Fast* | | | *Curve* | | | *Slider* | | | *Knuckle* | | |
| **I** | **M** | **O** | **I** | **M** | **O** | **I** | **M** | **O** | **I** | **M** | **O** |
| **H** 11 | 16 | 10 | **H** 6 | 7 | 7 | **H** | | | **H** | | |
| **M** 10 | 5 | 14 | **M** 6 | 3 | 17 | **M** | | | **M** | | |
| **L** 6 | 11 | 12 | **L** 8 | 12 | 30 | **L** 25 | | 75 | **L** | | |

| **Totals:** | 0 | | | 0 | | | 19 | | |
|---|---|---|---|---|---|---|---|---|---|
| *Screwball* | | | *Sinkerball* | | | *Change-Up* | | | |
| **I** | **M** | **O** | **I** | **M** | **O** | **I** | **M** | **O** |
| **H** | | | **H** | | | **H** 5 | 5 | 10 |
| **M** | | | **M** | | | **M** 21 | 5 | 26 |
| **L** | | | **L** | | | **L** 5 | 10 | 10 |

Notice that Gooden has thrown 2535 fastballs, 720 curves, 4 sliders and 19 change-ups to right-handed batters in games scouted by the BARS System.

Against right-handed batters, Gooden throws almost as many inside as outside fastballs. He throws a surprisingly large percentage of fastballs to the high locations. Gooden often throws as hard as he can and has excellent control. He may belong to the Dizzy Dean school. Dizzy always said that he tried to throw the ball over the heart of the plate because he knew he wouldn't be able to do it often.

Gooden keeps his curves low and outside, with nearly a third (30 percent) of his curves in the low-outside location. He keeps a high percentage of his curves over the outside part of the plate.

## Pitch Location Report
## Dwight Gooden     Right-Handed Pitcher
## Against All Left-Handed Batters All Teams

| *Base Situation:* All Situations | | | | | | Total Pitches: 2239 | | |
|---|---|---|---|---|---|---|---|---|

| *Totals:* 1771 | | | 443 | | | 0 | | | 0 | | |
|---|---|---|---|---|---|---|---|---|---|---|---|
| **Fast** | | | **Curve** | | | **Slider** | | | **Knuckle** | | |
| O | M | I | O | M | I | O | M | I | O | M | I |
| H 15 | 18 | 13 | H 10 | 6 | 4 | H | | | H | | |
| M 10 | 5 | 13 | M 17 | 2 | 6 | M | | | M | | |
| L 4 | 8 | 11 | L 15 | 16 | 19 | L | | | L | | |

| *Totals:* 0 | | | 0 | | | 25 | | |
|---|---|---|---|---|---|---|---|---|
| **Screwball** | | | **Sinkerball** | | | **Change-Up** | | |
| O | M | I | O | M | I | O | M | I |
| H | | | H | | | H 12 | 4 | 4 |
| M | | | M | | | M 12 | 4 | 12 |
| L | | | L | | | L 12 | 16 | 24 |

Against left-handed batters, Gooden also throws fastballs and curves almost exclusively (1771 fastballs, 443 curves and 25 change-ups). He throws about the same blend of fastballs to left-handed batters as to right-handed, with a large percentage to the high locations. Gooden throws a higher percentage of inside curves to left-handed batters than to right-handed ones. Nineteen percent of his curves are to the low-inside location. Very few of his curves are thrown medium-over-the-middle (2 percent).

### Roger Clemens, Boston Red Sox

When facing Roger Clemens, Boston Red Sox right-hander, hitters can be sure they're going to get a fastball, a curve or (very seldom) a slider. Over 70 percent of Clemens' pitches (in all count and runners-on-base situations) are fastballs In many situations over 90 percent are fastballs.

There are counts and runners-on-base situations, however, in which Clemens shows definite trends in his pitching. Recognizing these trends can help hitters.

## Pitch Information Report
## Roger Clemens    Right-Handed Pitcher
## Against All Right-Handed Batters All Teams

*BASE SITUATION:* All Situations

| *Various Counts on Batter* | | *Ahead In The Count* | | | | | *Even Count* | | | |
|---|---|---|---|---|---|---|---|---|---|---|
| | Balls | 0 | 0 | 1 | 2 | | 0 | 1 | 3 | |
| | Strikes | 1 | 2 | 2 | 2 | | 0 | 1 | 2 | |
| Total Pitches On Each Count | | 280 | 205 | 243 | 173 | 901 | 554 | 180 | 69 | 803 |
| Fast | Balls | 16 | 28 | 16 | 10 | 18 | 26 | 23 | 16 | 24 |
| | Strikes | 58 | 34 | 44 | 61 | 49 | 45 | 51 | 68 | 48 |
| Curve | Balls | 7 | 16 | 12 | 6 | 10 | 8 | 6 | 3 | 7 |
| | Strikes | 14 | 12 | 20 | 17 | 16 | 14 | 11 | 12 | 13 |
| Slider | Balls | | 6 | 4 | 4 | 3 | 4 | 2 | | 3 |
| | Strikes | 3 | 4 | 3 | 2 | 3 | 3 | 6 | 1 | 4 |
| Knuckleball | Balls | | | | | | | | | |
| | Strikes | | | | | | | | | |
| Screwball | Balls | | | | | | | | | |
| | Strikes | | | | | | | | | |
| Sinker | Balls | | | | | | | | | |
| | Strikes | | | | | | | | | |
| Change-Up | Balls | 1 | | | | | | | | |
| | Strikes | | | 1 | | | | 1 | | |

| *Various Counts on Batter* | | Behind In The Count | | | | | |
|---|---|---|---|---|---|---|---|
| | Balls | 1 | 2 | 2 | 3 | 3 | |
| | Strikes | 0 | 0 | 1 | 0 | 1 | |
| Total Pitches On Each Count | | 205 | 55 | 89 | 14 | 30 | 393 |
| **Fast** | Balls | 17 | 22 | 15 | 21 | 23 | 18 |
| | Strikes | 54 | 56 | 67 | 71 | 70 | 59 |
| **Curve** | Balls | 10 | 2 | 2 | | | 6 |
| | Strikes | 14 | 15 | 9 | 7 | 7 | 12 |
| **Slider** | Balls | | 2 | 3 | | | 1 |
| | Strikes | 3 | 4 | 3 | | | 3 |
| **Knuckleball** | Balls | | | | | | |
| | Strikes | | | | | | |
| **Screwball** | Balls | | | | | | |
| | Strikes | | | | | | |
| **Sinker** | Balls | | | | | | |
| | Strikes | | | | | | |
| **Change-Up** | Balls | | | | | | |
| | Strikes | | | | | | |

On the 0-0 pitch, Clemens throws fastballs and curves almost exclusively. Seventy-one percent of his 0-0 pitches are fastballs (45 percent strikes, 26 percent balls). Twenty-two percent of his 0-0 pitches are curves and 7 percent are sliders. These breaking pitches keep batters off balance, and make Clemens' fastball (which is thrown very hard) much more effective.

On the 0-2 count, Clemens throws almost as many fastballs for balls as for strikes. As the count moves to 1-2 and 2-2, Clemens' percentage of fastball strikes increases. When the count progresses to 3-2, about 70 percent of Clemens' pitches are fastball strikes. On the 3-0 and 3-1 counts, over 90 percent of Clemens' pitches are fastballs.

Clemens is ahead in the count much more often than he is behind (901 pitches when ahead, 393 when behind). When he is behind, he relies heavily on fastballs, as would be expected.

## Clemens Against Left-Handed Hitters

The right-handed Clemens relies even more heavily on his fastball when facing left-handed batters.

## Pitch Information Report
### Roger Clemens    Right-Handed Pitcher
### Against All Left-Handed Batters All Teams

*BASE SITUATION:* All Situations

| Various Counts on Batter | | Ahead In The Count | | | | | Even Count | | | |
|---|---|---|---|---|---|---|---|---|---|---|
| | Balls | 0 | 0 | 1 | 2 | | 0 | 1 | 3 | |
| | Strikes | 1 | 2 | 2 | 2 | | 0 | 1 | 2 | |
| Total Pitches On Each Count | | 243 | 141 | 223 | 173 | 780 | 567 | 200 | 108 | 875 |
| **Fast** | Balls | 24 | 36 | 22 | 24 | 26 | 36 | 24 | 19 | 31 |
| | Strikes | 49 | 33 | 51 | 57 | 48 | 52 | 50 | 71 | 54 |
| **Curve** | Balls | 8 | 10 | 4 | 2 | 6 | 4 | 7 | 2 | 4 |
| | Strikes | 12 | 16 | 13 | 13 | 13 | 4 | 11 | 5 | 5 |
| **Slider** | Balls | | | | 1 | | 1 | 2 | | 1 |
| | Strikes | | | 4 | 3 | 2 | | 3 | 3 | 1 |
| **Knuckleball** | Balls | | | | | | | | | |
| | Strikes | | | | | | | | | |
| **Screwball** | Balls | | | | | | | | | |
| | Strikes | | | | | | | | | |
| **Sinker** | Balls | | | | | | | | | |
| | Strikes | | | | | | | | | |
| **Change-Up** | Balls | 2 | 2 | 1 | 1 | 2 | 2 | 1 | | 1 |
| | Strikes | 4 | 4 | 4 | 1 | 3 | 2 | 4 | | 2 |

| *Various Counts on Batter* | | **Behind In The Count** | | | | | |
|---|---|---|---|---|---|---|---|
| | Balls | 1 | 2 | 2 | 3 | 3 | |
| | Strikes | 0 | 0 | 1 | 0 | 1 | |
| Total Pitches On Each Count | | 240 | 82 | 107 | 25 | 46 | 500 |
| **Fast** | Balls | 30 | 27 | 17 | 24 | 24 | 26 |
| | Strikes | 55 | 63 | 65 | 72 | 65 | 60 |
| **Curve** | Balls | 4 | 2 | 6 | 4 | 4 | 4 |
| | Strikes | 7 | 2 | 7 | | 2 | 6 |
| **Slider** | Balls | | 1 | 1 | | | 1 |
| | Strikes | 1 | 1 | 1 | | 4 | 1 |
| **Knuckleball** | Balls | | | | | | |
| | Strikes | | | | | | |
| **Screwball** | Balls | | | | | | |
| | Strikes | | | | | | |
| **Sinker** | Balls | | | | | | |
| | Strikes | | | | | | |
| **Change-Up** | Balls | | | 1 | | | |
| | Strikes | 3 | 2 | 2 | | | 2 |

Notice that on the 0-0 pitch, approximately 90 percent of Clemens' pitches to left-handed batters are fastballs. A relatively high percentage of his 0-0 pitches are fastballs thrown for balls (36 percent).

Clemens throws a higher percentages of curves when he is ahead in the count. When the count reaches 0-2, 26 percent of his pitches are curves.

When behind in the count against left-handed batters, Clemens throws fastballs almost exclusively. As the count moves to 2-0, 3-0, and 3-1, the percentage of curves falls sharply.

## Roger Clemens' Pitch Location Reports

Against right-handed batters, Clemens keeps his pitches outside. Notice the very high percentage of curves and sliders that he throws to the outside locations.

His fastball tends to be up in the strike zone. Thirty percent of his fastballs are to the high locations (13 percent high-inside, 9 percent high-over-the-middle and 8 percent high-outside). Fifty percent are to the medium-high locations and only 16 percent to the low locations.

## Pitch Location Report
### Roger Clemens    Right-Handed Pitcher
### Against Right-Handed Batters All Teams

| **Base Situation:** All Situations | | | | | | | | | | | Total Pitches: 2097 | | |
|---|---|---|---|---|---|---|---|---|---|---|---|---|---|
| **Totals:** *1488* | | | *471* | | | *128* | | | | | *0* | | |
| *Fast* | | | *Curve* | | | *Slider* | | | | *Knuckle* | | | |
| **I** | **M** | **O** | **I** | **M** | **O** | **I** | **M** | **O** | | **I** | **M** | **O** | |
| H 13 | 9 | 8 | H 3 | 5 | 5 | H 6 | 10 | 7 | H | | | | |
| M 14 | 5 | 31 | M 3 | 4 | 32 | M 5 | | 34 | M | | | | |
| L 4 | 5 | 7 | L 4 | 6 | 34 | L 3 | 3 | 30 | L | | | | |

| **Totals:** | *0* | | | *0* | | | *76* | | |
|---|---|---|---|---|---|---|---|---|---|
| *Screwball* | | | *Sinkerball* | | | *Change-Up* | | | |
| **I** | **M** | **O** | **I** | **M** | **O** | **I** | **M** | **O** | |
| H | | | H | | | H 10 | 10 | | |
| M | | | M | | | M | 10 | 30 | |
| L | | | L | | | L 30 | 10 | | |

Against left-handed batters, Clemens keeps his fastball outside, but it tends to move up in the strike zone. As against right-handed batters, only 16 percent of his fastballs are to the low locations.

Clemens comes low and inside more strongly with his curve and slider against left-handed than against right-handed batters. A higher percentage of his pitches are change-ups against left-handed batters, with a good blend between inside and outside change-ups.

## Pitch Location Report
## Roger Clemens    Right-Handed Pitcher
## Against Left-Handed Batters All Teams

| | *Base Situation:* All Situations | | | | | | Total Pitches: 2155 | | |
|---|---|---|---|---|---|---|---|---|---|
| *Totals:* 1750 | | | 282 | | | 47 | | | 0 |
| *Fast* | | | *Curve* | | | *Slider* | | | *Knuckle* |
| O | M | I | O | M | I | O | M | I | O M I |
| H 18 | 11 | 8 | H 6 | 3 | 3 | H | 8 | 6 | H |
| M 26 | 5 | 12 | M 31 | 3 | 9 | M 10 | 4 | 27 | M |
| L 4 | 4 | 8 | L 5 | 13 | 23 | L 2 | 6 | 34 | L |

| *Totals:* 0 | | | 0 | | | 76 | | |
|---|---|---|---|---|---|---|---|---|
| *Screwball* | | | *Sinkerball* | | | *Change-Up* | | |
| O | M | I | O | M | I | O | M | I |
| H | | | H | | | H 13 | 6 | 1 |
| M | | | M | | | M 26 | 2 | 11 |
| L | | | L | | | L 7 | 11 | 18 |

## Mike Scott, Houston Astros

Right-handed pitcher Mike Scott has a fine strikeout-to-walk ratio that helps him to a good win-loss record and ERA year after year.

## Pitch Information Report
## Mike Scott    Right-Handed Pitcher
## Against All Right-Handed Batters All Teams

(Shown on opposite page)

**BASE SITUATION:** All Situations

| *Various Counts on Batter* | | *Ahead In The Count* | | | | | *Even Count* | | | |
|---|---|---|---|---|---|---|---|---|---|---|
| | Balls | 0 | 0 | 1 | 2 | | 0 | 1 | 3 | |
| | Strikes | 1 | 2 | 2 | 2 | | 0 | 1 | 2 | |
| Total Pitches On Each Count | | 354 | 168 | 266 | 199 | 987 | 837 | 297 | 102 | 1236 |
| **Fast** | Balls | 21 | 35 | 18 | 14 | 21 | 32 | 20 | 15 | 28 |
| | Strikes | 39 | 39 | 36 | 59 | 42 | 46 | 48 | 72 | 49 |
| **Curve** | Balls | 6 | 2 | 3 | 4 | 4 | 2 | 2 | 3 | 2 |
| | Strikes | 6 | 7 | 12 | 4 | 7 | 2 | 4 | 2 | 3 |
| **Slider** | Balls | 4 | 4 | 3 | | 3 | 4 | 4 | | 3 |
| | Strikes | 6 | 1 | 9 | 5 | 6 | 4 | 4 | | 4 |
| **Knuckleball** | Balls | | | | | | | | | |
| | Strikes | | | | | | | | | |
| **Screwball** | Balls | | | | | | | | | |
| | Strikes | | | | | | | | | |
| **Sinker** | Balls | 6 | 5 | 3 | 4 | 4 | 2 | 3 | 2 | 3 |
| | Strikes | 8 | 6 | 12 | 8 | 9 | 5 | 7 | 3 | 5 |
| **Change-Up** | Balls | 3 | 1 | 1 | 1 | 1 | 2 | 2 | | 1 |
| | Strikes | 3 | 2 | 3 | 3 | 3 | 1 | 5 | 4 | 2 |

| *Various Counts on Batter* | | *Behind In The Count* | | | | | |
|---|---|---|---|---|---|---|---|
| | Balls | 1 | 2 | 2 | 3 | 3 | |
| | Strikes | 0 | 0 | 1 | 0 | 1 | |
| Total Pitches On Each Count | | 350 | 130 | 148 | 42 | 58 | 728 |
| **Fast** | Balls | 31 | 29 | 16 | 31 | 16 | 26 |
| | Strikes | 52 | 63 | 67 | 67 | 78 | 60 |
| **Curve** | Balls | | 1 | 1 | | | |
| | Strikes | 1 | 2 | 3 | | 2 | 2 |
| **Slider** | Balls | 1 | | 1 | | 1 | |
| | Strikes | 2 | | 1 | | | 1 |
| **Knuckleball** | Balls | | | | | | |
| | Strikes | | | | | | |
| **Screwball** | Balls | | | | | | |
| | Strikes | | | | | | |
| **Sinker** | Balls | 3 | 2 | 1 | | 2 | 2 |
| | Strikes | 5 | 2 | 6 | 2 | 2 | 4 |
| **Change-Up** | Balls | 2 | | 3 | | 2 | 2 |
| | Strikes | 3 | 1 | 2 | | | 2 |

Notice that Scott has five types of pitches: fastball, curve, slider, split-fingered fastball and change-up. The BARS System records split-fingered fastballs in the sinkerball category. In many situations, Scott throws his split-fingered fastball more frequently than he throws his curve. His balance of pitches keeps batters off balance.

On the 0-0 pitch, Scott throws fastballs nearly 80 percent of the time (32 percent balls, 46 percent strikes). He throws sliders 8 percent of the time, split-fingered fastballs (in the sinkerball category) 7 percent of the time, curves 4 percent of the time and change-ups 3 percent of the time.

On the 0-2 pitch, he throws fastballs 74 percent of the time, with a nearly equal percentage of fastball strikes and fastball balls (35 and 39 percents respectively). On the 1-2 and 2-2 counts, his percentages of fastballs thrown for balls falls sharply.

On all counts when he is even or ahead in the count, Scott throws a fairly high percentage of split-fingered fastballs and curves. When he falls behind in the count, however, his percentages of curves and split-fingered fastballs fall and his percentages of fastballs rise. When behind 3-0 and 3-1, almost all of his pitches are fastballs.

Looking at Scott's performance when behind in the count, it is evident that his money pitch is his fastball: he throws little else in tight situations.

### Scott's Pitch Information Against Left-Handed Batters

Against left-handed batters, Scott throws about the same percentages of fastballs that he throws against right-handed batters. He throws more split-fingered fastballs and fewer curves against left-handed batters.

**Pitch Information Report**
**Mike Scott    Right-Handed Pitcher**
**Against All Left-Handed Batters All Teams**

**BASE SITUATION:** All Situations

| *Various Counts on Batter* | | *Ahead In The Count* | | | | | | *Even Count* | | |
|---|---|---|---|---|---|---|---|---|---|---|
| | Balls | 0 | 0 | 1 | 2 | | | 0 | 1 | 3 |
| | Strikes | 1 | 2 | 2 | 2 | | | 0 | 1 | 2 |
| Total Pitches On Each Count | | 194 | 76 | 153 | 102 | 525 | | 506 | 187 | 68 | 761 |
| **Fast** | Balls | 28 | 29 | 20 | 19 | 24 | | 34 | 18 | 22 | 29 |
| | Strikes | 34 | 34 | 50 | 59 | 44 | | 39 | 49 | 68 | 44 |
| **Curve** | Balls | 3 | 3 | 2 | 2 | 2 | | 1 | 2 | | 1 |
| | Strikes | 3 | 4 | 5 | 4 | 4 | | 1 | 4 | | 1 |
| **Slider** | Balls | 1 | | 3 | 2 | 2 | | 1 | 2 | | 1 |
| | Strikes | 2 | | 1 | 2 | 1 | | 1 | 2 | 1 | 1 |
| **Knuckleball** | Balls | | | | | | | | | | |
| | Strikes | | | | | | | | | | |
| **Screwball** | Balls | | | | | | | | | | |
| | Strikes | | | | | | | | | | |
| **Sinker** | Balls | 7 | 7 | 4 | 2 | 5 | | 8 | 5 | | 7 |
| | Strikes | 11 | 18 | 13 | 6 | 12 | | 9 | 12 | 6 | 9 |
| **Change-Up** | Balls | 4 | 3 | 1 | 3 | 3 | | 2 | 2 | 1 | 2 |
| | Strikes | 6 | 3 | 2 | 2 | 3 | | 5 | 6 | 1 | 5 |

| *Various Counts on Batter* | | *Behind In The Count* | | | | | |
|---|---|---|---|---|---|---|---|
| | Balls | 1 | 2 | 2 | 3 | 3 | |
| | Strikes | 0 | 0 | 1 | 0 | 1 | |
| Total Pitches On Each Count | | 230 | 73 | 86 | 23 | 30 | 442 |
| **Fast** | Balls | 22 | 33 | 17 | 43 | 13 | 24 |
| | Strikes | 57 | 59 | 62 | 52 | 77 | 59 |
| **Curve** | Balls | | | | | | |
| | Strikes | | | 2 | | | |
| **Slider** | Balls | | | | | | 1 |
| | Strikes | 1 | | 2 | 4 | | 1 |
| **Knuckleball** | Balls | | | | | | |
| | Strikes | | | | | | |
| **Screwball** | Balls | | | | | | |
| | Strikes | | | | | | |
| **Sinker** | Balls | 4 | | 3 | | 3 | 3 |
| | Strikes | 5 | 7 | 9 | | 7 | 6 |
| **Change-Up** | Balls | 3 | | | | 1 | |
| | Strikes | 6 | 1 | 3 | | 4 | |

## Mike Scott's Pitch Location Reports

Against right-handed batters, Scott keeps his pitches outside. His fastball, however, tends to come in high in the strike zone. Thirty-three percent of his fastballs are to the high locations.

He catches the low-outside corner with his curve and slider, and keeps both his split-fingered fastball (listed in the sinkerball category) and change-ups low.

### Pitch Location Report
### Mike Scott    Right-Handed Pitcher
### Against All Right-Handed Batters All Teams

**Base Situation:** All Situations          Total Pitches: 2951

**Totals:** *2195*          *186*          *189*          *0*

| | *Fast* | | | | *Curve* | | | | *Slider* | | | | *Knuckle* | | |
|---|---|---|---|---|---|---|---|---|---|---|---|---|---|---|---|
| | **I** | **M** | **O** | | **I** | **M** | **O** | | **I** | **M** | **O** | | **I** | **M** | **O** |
| **H** | 11 | 13 | 9 | **H** | 9 | 9 | 3 | **H** | 3 | 6 | 6 | **H** | | | |
| **M** | 9 | 6 | 17 | **M** | 4 | 4 | 17 | **M** | 5 | 4 | 24 | **M** | | | |
| **L** | 7 | 9 | 14 | **L** | 7 | 13 | 30 | **L** | 6 | 4 | 37 | **L** | | | |

**Totals:** *0*          *266*          *115*

| | *Screwball* | | | | *Sinkerball* | | | | *Change-Up* | | |
|---|---|---|---|---|---|---|---|---|---|---|---|
| | **I** | **M** | **O** | | **I** | **M** | **O** | | **I** | **M** | **O** |
| **H** | | | | **H** | | 1 | | **H** | 7 | 15 | 7 |
| **M** | | | | **M** | 7 | 5 | 5 | **M** | 13 | 4 | 3 |
| **L** | | | | **L** | 20 | 25 | 32 | **L** | 13 | 14 | 19 |

Against left-handed batters, Scott's fastball tends to come in very high in the strike zone. Forty percent of his fastballs are to the high locations.

Scott throws a much higher percentage of split-fingered fastballs and change-ups against left-handed batters than against right-handed ones.

## Pitch Location Report
## Mike Scott    Right-Handed Pitcher
## Against All Left-Handed Batters All Teams

**Base Situation:** All Situations          Total Pitches: 1728

**Totals:** *1276*                *54*                *43*                *0*

|   | Fast | | | Curve | | | Slider | | | Knuckle | | |
|---|---|---|---|---|---|---|---|---|---|---|---|---|
|   | O | M | I | O | M | I | O | M | I | O | M | I |
| H | 15 | 14 | 11 | 13 | 7 |  | 4 | 4 | 9 |  |  |  |
| M | 16 | 4 | 10 | 29 | 1 | 9 | 4 | 2 | 23 |  |  |  |
| L | 6 | 8 | 13 | 13 | 13 | 13 | 7 | 9 | 34 |  |  |  |

**Totals:**     *0*                *249*                *106*

|   | Screwball | | | Sinkerball | | | Change-Up | | |
|---|---|---|---|---|---|---|---|---|---|
|   | O | M | I | O | M | I | O | M | I |
| H |  |  |  |  |  |  | 15 | 10 | 3 |
| M |  |  |  | 8 | 2 | 3 | 16 | 4 | 5 |
| L |  |  |  | 33 | 22 | 27 | 19 | 17 | 7 |

### Dave Righetti, New York Yankees

Left-handed Yankee reliever Dave Righetti set a major-league record in 1986 with 46 saves. His ERA was 2.45 and his won-loss record was 8-8. In 1987 he had 31 saves with an 8-6 record and a 3.51 ERA.

Righetti essentially is a fastball pitcher with a good curve and slider. Only rarely does he throw a change-up.

## Pitch Information Report
## Dave Righetti    Left-Handed Pitcher
## Against All Left-Handed Batters All Teams

(Shown on following page)

**BASE SITUATION:** All Situations

| *Various Counts on Batter* | | *Ahead In The Count* | | | | | *Even Count* | | | |
|---|---|---|---|---|---|---|---|---|---|---|
| | Balls | 0 | 0 | 1 | 2 | | 0 | 1 | 3 | |
| | Strikes | 1 | 2 | 2 | 2 | | 0 | 1 | 2 | |
| Total Pitches On Each Count | | 287 | 140 | 239 | 215 | 881 | 592 | 237 | 89 | 918 |
| Fast | Balls | 30 | 42 | 28 | 19 | 28 | 27 | 23 | 19 | 25 |
| | Strikes | 41 | 29 | 35 | 53 | 40 | 45 | 44 | 72 | 47 |
| Curve | Balls | 9 | 4 | 6 | 2 | 6 | 4 | 3 | | 3 |
| | Strikes | 6 | 2 | 11 | 7 | 7 | 7 | 5 | 2 | 6 |
| Slider | Balls | 5 | 4 | 5 | 3 | 4 | 7 | 6 | 1 | 6 |
| | Strikes | 7 | 18 | 13 | 16 | 12 | 8 | 17 | 6 | 10 |
| Knuckleball | Balls | | | | | | | | | |
| | Strikes | | | | | | | | | |
| Screwball | Balls | | | | | | | | | |
| | Strikes | | | | | | | | | |
| Sinker | Balls | | | | | | | | | |
| | Strikes | | | | | | | | | |
| Change-Up | Balls | 2 | 1 | 1 | | 1 | 1 | 2 | | 1 |
| | Strikes | | 1 | 1 | | | 1 | 1 | | 1 |

| *Various Counts on Batter* | | *Behind In The Count* | | | | | |
|---|---|---|---|---|---|---|---|
| | Balls | 1 | 2 | 2 | 3 | 3 | |
| | Strikes | 0 | 0 | 1 | 0 | 1 | |
| Total Pitches On Each Count | | 229 | 86 | 118 | 21 | 40 | 494 |
| Fast | Balls | 26 | 28 | 17 | 43 | 30 | 25 |
| | Strikes | 47 | 65 | 57 | 52 | 55 | 53 |
| Curve | Balls | 2 | | 2 | | | 1 |
| | Strikes | 6 | 2 | 5 | 5 | 3 | 5 |
| Slider | Balls | 7 | 1 | 5 | | 3 | 5 |
| | Strikes | 11 | 3 | 13 | | 10 | 10 |
| Knuckleball | Balls | | | | | | |
| | Strikes | | | | | | |
| Screwball | Balls | | | | | | |
| | Strikes | | | | | | |
| Sinker | Balls | | | | | | |
| | Strikes | | | | | | |
| Change-Up | Balls | 1 | | 1 | | | 1 |
| | Strikes | | | 1 | | | |

Against right-handed batters, Righetti throws 45 percent fastball strikes on the 0-0 pitch. When the count is 0-2, Righetti is likely to waste a pitch. On that count he throws more fastballs for balls than for strikes (42 percent balls, 29 percent strikes), but comes in hard with slider strikes (18 percent slider strikes, 4 percent slider balls).

As the count moves to 1-2, 2-2 and 3-2, Righetti progressively throws a higher percentage of strikes, with an emphasis on fastball strikes. On the 3-2 count, 91 percent of Righetti's pitches are fastballs (72 percent strikes, 19 percent balls).

When behind in the count, Righetti throws mostly fastballs But on the 2-1 count, 18 percent of his pitches are sliders (13 percent strikes, 5 percent balls). Like many pitchers, Righetti throws a higher percentage of strikes on the 2-0 pitch than on the 3-1 pitch.

Although there are several differences, Righetti's Pitch Information Report against left-handed batters is similar to his report against right-handers, so it is not included here.

## Righetti's Pitch Location Report

Against right-handed batters, the left-handed Righetti keeps his fastball and curveball outside. His slider he keeps low and predominately inside.

Righetti does not keep his fastball particularly low in the strike zone. Seven percent of his fastballs are thrown directly over the heart of the plate. This is a high percentage. Since the large majority of Righetti's pitches are fastballs, this may eventually cause him trouble. His chart is shown on the next page.

## Pitch Location Report
## Dave Righetti    Left-Handed Pitcher
## Against All Right-Handed Batters All Teams

**Base Situation:** All Situations          Total Pitches: 2293

| *Totals:* 1665 | | | 229 | | | 366 | | | 0 | | |
|---|---|---|---|---|---|---|---|---|---|---|---|
| *Fast* | | | *Curve* | | | *Slider* | | | *Knuckle* | | |
| I | M | O | I | M | O | I | M | O | I | M | O |
| H | 6 | 10 | 13 | H | 1 | 3 | 7 | H | 3 | 4 | 3 | H |
| M | 10 | 7 | 20 | M | 10 | 6 | 19 | M | 16 | 3 | 12 | M |
| L | 9 | 12 | 10 | L | 12 | 21 | 18 | L | 25 | 20 | 11 | L |

| *Totals:* 0 | | | 0 | | | 33 | | |
|---|---|---|---|---|---|---|---|---|
| *Screwball* | | | *Sinkerball* | | | *Change-Up* | | |
| I | M | O | I | M | O | I | M | O |
| H | | | H | | | H | 9 | 15 |
| M | | | M | | | M | 9 | 9 | 21 |
| L | | | L | | | L | 9 | 9 | 18 |

Against left-handed batters, Righetti throws both his curveball and slider low and outside. He shows no definite pattern with his fastballs, although slightly more are to the outside locations.

### Pitch Location Report
### Dave Righetti    Left-Handed Pitcher
### Against All Left-Handed Batters All Teams

**Base Situation:** All Situations    Total Pitches: 648

| Totals: 490 | | | 47 | | | 108 | | | 0 | | |
|---|---|---|---|---|---|---|---|---|---|---|---|
| *Fast* | | | *Curve* | | | *Slider* | | | *Knuckle* | | |
| O | M | I | O | M | I | O | M | I | O | M | I |
| H 8 | 10 | 13 | H | 4 | 6 | H 2 | 5 | 4 | H | | |
| M 20 | 6 | 10 | M 23 | 4 | 2 | M 18 | | 6 | M | | |
| L 12 | 10 | 7 | L 38 | 17 | 4 | L 41 | 17 | 2 | L | | |

| Totals: | 0 | | | 0 | | | 3 | | |
|---|---|---|---|---|---|---|---|---|---|
| | *Screwball* | | | *Sinkerball* | | | *Change-Up* | | |
| | O | M | I | O | M | I | O | M | I |
| | H | | | H | | | H | | |
| | M | | | M | | | M | | 33 |
| | L | | | L | | | L | 33 | 33 |

## Joe Niekro, Minnesota Twins

Right-handed Joe Niekro throws three types of pitches: knuckleballs, fastballs and sliders. He throws an occasional curve and change-up, but he stays with his three central pitches more than 90 percent of the time. Niekro's primary pitch, of course, is a knuckleball.

Since control is the primary concern for a knuckleball pitcher, we first examine his Pitch Location Report.

## Pitch Location Report
### Joe Niekro    Right-Handed Pitcher
### Against All Right-Handed Batters All Teams

| *Base Situation:* All Situations | | | | | | | | | Total Pitches: 4529 | | |
|---|---|---|---|---|---|---|---|---|---|---|---|
| *Totals:* 979 | | | 108 | | | 385 | | | 3046 | | |
| *Fast* | | | *Curve* | | | *Slider* | | | *Knuckle* | | |
| I | M | O | I | M | O | I | M | O | I | M | O |
| H 5 | 8 | 8 | H 5 | 5 | 8 | H 1 | 3 | 1 | H 6 | 6 | 6 |
| M 11 | 6 | 17 | M 8 | 3 | 14 | M 6 | 2 | 21 | M 8 | 4 | 15 |
| L 10 | 13 | 18 | L 15 | 18 | 19 | L 11 | 10 | 41 | L 14 | 12 | 26 |

| *Totals:* 0 | | | 0 | | | 11 | | |
|---|---|---|---|---|---|---|---|---|
| *Screwball* | | | *Sinkerball* | | | *Change-Up* | | |
| I | M | O | I | M | O | I | M | O |
| H | | | H | | | H | 18 | |
| M | | | M | | | M | 9 | 27 |
| L | | | L | | | L | 36 | 9 |

Notice that against right-handed batters Niekro throws about three knuckleballs for every fastball (3,046 recorded knuckleballs, 979 recorded fastballs). This ratio rises to over four knuckleballs for every fastball when runners are in scoring position (see below).

Niekro keeps his knuckleballs low in the strike zone and predominately to the outside locations. One-quarter (26 percent) of his knucklers are to the low-outside location.

Most of Niekro's fastballs are to the low or medium-high locations, with a slightly greater percentage thrown to the outside locations.

Niekro is accurate with his slider, throwing a high percentage to the low-outside location (41 percent). Notice that a very low percentage of his sliders are medium-over-the-middle.

The following charts show that Niekro throws a higher percentage of knucklers when there are runners in scoring position than when there is a runner on first base. His control seems about the same in both runner-on-base situations.

## Pitch Location Report
### Joe Niekro    Right-Handed Pitcher
### Against All Right-Handed Batters All Teams

**Base Situation:** Runner on First          Total Pitches: 770

*Totals: 235*          *13*          *74*          *447*

| *Fast* | | | *Curve* | | | *Slider* | | | *Knuckle* | | |
|---|---|---|---|---|---|---|---|---|---|---|---|
| **I** | **M** | **O** | **I** | **M** | **O** | **I** | **M** | **O** | **I** | **M** | **O** |
| **H** 4 | 5 | 8 | **H** 7 | | 23 | **H** | 5 | 1 | **H** 6 | 4 | 5 |
| **M** 9 | 6 | 12 | **M** 7 | | 7 | **M** 5 | 2 | 20 | **M** 6 | 4 | 15 |
| **L** 11 | 14 | 26 | **L** 7 | 38 | 7 | **L** 8 | 9 | 47 | **L** 16 | 13 | 28 |

*Totals:*          0          0          1

| *Screwball* | | | *Sinkerball* | | | *Change-Up* | | |
|---|---|---|---|---|---|---|---|---|
| **I** | **M** | **O** | **I** | **M** | **O** | **I** | **M** | **O** |
| **H** | | | **H** | | | **H** | | |
| **M** | | | **M** | | | **M** | 100 | |
| **L** | | | **L** | | | **L** | | |

**Base Situation:** Runner(s) in Scoring Position          Total Pitches: 1133

*Totals: 191*          *23*          *84*          *832*

| *Fast* | | | *Curve* | | | *Slider* | | | *Knuckle* | | |
|---|---|---|---|---|---|---|---|---|---|---|---|
| **I** | **M** | **O** | **I** | **M** | **O** | **I** | **M** | **O** | **I** | **M** | **O** |
| **H** 4 | 7 | 11 | **H** 4 | 4 | 8 | **H** 2 | 3 | 4 | **H** 6 | 7 | 5 |
| **M** 15 | 2 | 18 | **M** 8 | 4 | 8 | **M** 6 | 3 | 25 | **M** 7 | 3 | 15 |
| **L** 9 | 14 | 16 | **L** 13 | 21 | 26 | **L** 13 | 6 | 35 | **L** 15 | 12 | 26 |

*Totals:*          0          0          3

| *Screwball* | | | *Sinkerball* | | | *Change-Up* | | |
|---|---|---|---|---|---|---|---|---|
| **I** | **M** | **O** | **I** | **M** | **O** | **I** | **M** | **O** |
| **H** | | | **H** | | | **H** | 33 | |
| **M** | | | **M** | | | **M** | | 33 |
| **L** | | | **L** | | | **L** | 33 | |

Against left-handed batters, Niekro keeps his fastball outside, his slider inside and his knuckleball low. He throws a lower percentage of knuckleballs to left-handed than right-handed batters.

## Pitch Location Report
## Joe Niekro    Right-Handed Pitcher
## Against All Left-Handed Batters All Teams

*Base Situation:* All Situations          Total Pitches: 764

| | Fast | | | Curve | | | Slider | | | Knuckle | | |
|---|---|---|---|---|---|---|---|---|---|---|---|---|
| *Totals:* 229 | | | | *6* | | | *23* | | | *502* | | |
| | O | M | I | O | M | I | O | M | I | O | M | I |
| H | 10 | 5 | 3 | 33 | | | | 8 | 4 | 9 | 2 | 3 |
| M | 28 | 3 | 8 | | | 16 | | 4 | 17 | 24 | 2 | 5 |
| L | 23 | 11 | 5 | 16 | 33 | | 8 | 13 | 43 | 17 | 16 | 18 |

| | Screwball | | | Sinkerball | | | Change-Up | | |
|---|---|---|---|---|---|---|---|---|---|
| *Totals:* | *0* | | | *0* | | | *4* | | |
| | O | M | I | O | M | I | O | M | I |
| H | | | | | | | | | |
| M | | | | | | | | | 25 |
| L | | | | | | | 50 | 25 | |

## Niekro's Pitch Information Reports

Niekro's Pitch Information Report shows his heavy reliance on knuckle-balls.

## Pitch Information Report
## Joe Niekro    Right-Handed Pitcher
## AgainstAll Right-Handed Batters All Teams

(Shown on opposite page)

***BASE SITUATION:*** All Situations

| *Various Counts on Batter* | | *Ahead In The Count* | | | | | *Even Count* | | | |
|---|---|---|---|---|---|---|---|---|---|---|
| | Balls | 0 | 0 | 1 | 2 | | 0 | 1 | 3 | |
| | Strikes | 1 | 2 | 2 | 2 | | 0 | 1 | 2 | |
| Total Pitches On Each Count | | 420 | 195 | 290 | 267 | 1172 | 1234 | 482 | 191 | 1907 |
| **Fast** | Balls | 3 | | 1 | 2 | 2 | 6 | 3 | 8 | 6 |
| | Strikes | 3 | 1 | 3 | 10 | 4 | 8 | 5 | 30 | 9 |
| **Curve** | Balls | | 2 | 1 | 2 | 1 | 1 | 1 | 2 | 1 |
| | Strikes | 1 | 1 | 1 | 6 | 2 | 1 | 1 | 2 | 1 |
| **Slider** | Balls | 2 | 5 | 1 | 2 | 2 | 2 | 2 | 5 | 3 |
| | Strikes | 2 | 4 | 4 | 6 | 4 | 3 | 2 | 18 | 4 |
| **Knuckleball** | Balls | 41 | 29 | 31 | 25 | 33 | 44 | 37 | 12 | 39 |
| | Strikes | 47 | 59 | 58 | 46 | 52 | 35 | 49 | 25 | 37 |
| **Screwball** | Balls | | | | | | | | | |
| | Strikes | | | | | | | | | |
| **Sinker** | Balls | | | | | | | | | |
| | Strikes | | | | | | | | | |
| **Change-Up** | Balls | 1 | | | | | | | | |
| | Strikes | | | 1 | | | | | | |

| *Various Counts on Batter* | | *Behind In The Count* | | | | | |
|---|---|---|---|---|---|---|---|
| | Balls | 1 | 2 | 2 | 3 | 3 | |
| | Strikes | 0 | 0 | 1 | 0 | 1 | |
| Total Pitches On Each Count | | 660 | 247 | 310 | 91 | 142 | 1450 |
| **Fast** | Balls | 8 | 24 | 11 | 27 | 23 | 14 |
| | Strikes | 23 | 38 | 24 | 55 | 38 | 29 |
| **Curve** | Balls | 1 | 1 | 1 | | 1 | 1 |
| | Strikes | 1 | 1 | 2 | 1 | 2 | 2 |
| **Slider** | Balls | 4 | 3 | 5 | 2 | 3 | 4 |
| | Strikes | 8 | 11 | 11 | 3 | 6 | 9 |
| **Knuckleball** | Balls | 25 | 9 | 11 | 7 | 9 | 16 |
| | Strikes | 30 | 13 | 35 | 4 | 19 | 25 |
| **Screwball** | Balls | | | | | | |
| | Strikes | | | | | | |
| **Sinker** | Balls | | | | | | |
| | Strikes | | | | | | |
| **Change-Up** | Balls | | | | | | |
| | Strikes | | | | | | |

On the 0-0 count, 79 percent of Niekro's pitches are knuckleballs. More are balls than strikes (44 percent balls, 35 percent strikes). On the 0-0 count, only 14 percent of his pitches are fastballs (6 percent balls, 8 percent strikes).

Niekro's control of the knuckleball is demonstrated when he is ahead and even in the count. He consistently throws more knuckleballs for strikes than for balls. On the 0-2 count, 59 percent of his pitches are knuckleballs thrown for strikes, 31 percent are knuckleballs thrown for balls. The 1-2 and 2-2 counts show similar percentages.

When he falls behind in the count, he turns more to his fastball, although a high percentage of his pitches are still knuckleballs. On the 2-0 count, 62 percent of his pitches are fastballs (24 percent balls, 38 percent strikes) and 22 percent are knuckleballs. On the 2-1 count, 35 percent are fastballs and 46 percent are knuckleballs. On the 3-0 count, 82 percent of his pitches are fastballs and only 11 percent are knuckleballs.

Notice that Niekro is behind in the count more often than he is ahead. The BARS System has recorded 1450 pitches for Niekro when behind, 1172 when ahead.

### Niekro's Pitch Information Report Against Left-Handed Batters

Against left-handed batters, Niekro's Pitch Information Report is varied and interesting.

**Pitch Information Report**
**Joe Niekro    Right-Handed Pitcher**
**Against All Left-Handed Batters All Teams**

(Shown on opposite page)

**BASE SITUATION:** All Situations

| *Various Counts on Batter* | | *Ahead In The Count* | | | | | *Even Count* | | | |
|---|---|---|---|---|---|---|---|---|---|---|
| | Balls | 0 | 0 | 1 | 2 | | 0 | 1 | 3 | |
| | Strikes | 1 | 2 | 2 | 2 | | 0 | 1 | 2 | |
| Total Pitches On Each Count | | 75 | 23 | 47 | 44 | 189 | 195 | 84 | 44 | 323 |
| **Fast** | Balls | 5 | 4 | 2 | 2 | 4 | 7 | 4 | 9 | 7 |
| | Strikes | 3 | 4 | 11 | 18 | 8 | 8 | 11 | 57 | 15 |
| **Curve** | Balls | | | | 2 | 1 | | | 2 | |
| | Strikes | | 4 | 2 | 5 | 2 | | | | |
| **Slider** | Balls | 4 | 4 | | | 2 | 1 | 1 | 2 | 1 |
| | Strikes | 1 | | | | 1 | 1 | 2 | 2 | 1 |
| **Knuckleball** | Balls | 53 | 43 | 34 | 30 | 42 | 43 | 46 | 11 | 39 |
| | Strikes | 32 | 39 | 49 | 43 | 40 | 40 | 36 | 16 | 36 |
| **Screwball** | Balls | | | | | | | | | |
| | Strikes | | | | | | | | | |
| **Sinker** | Balls | | | | | | | | | |
| | Strikes | | | | | | | | | |
| **Change-Up** | Balls | | | | | | | | | |
| | Strikes | 1 | | 2 | | 1 | 1 | | | |

| *Various Counts on Batter* | | *Behind In The Count* | | | | | |
|---|---|---|---|---|---|---|---|
| | Balls | 1 | 2 | 2 | 3 | 3 | |
| | Strikes | 0 | 0 | 1 | 0 | 1 | |
| Total Pitches On Each Count | | 100 | 42 | 64 | 16 | 30 | 252 |
| **Fast** | Balls | 16 | 24 | 13 | 44 | 13 | 18 |
| | Strikes | 26 | 31 | 41 | 50 | 57 | 36 |
| **Curve** | Balls | | | | | | |
| | Strikes | | | | | | |
| **Slider** | Balls | 1 | 2 | 6 | | 3 | 3 |
| | Strikes | | | 3 | | 3 | 1 |
| **Knuckleball** | Balls | 27 | 14 | 19 | | 7 | 19 |
| | Strikes | 30 | 29 | 19 | 6 | 13 | 23 |
| **Screwball** | Balls | | | | | | |
| | Strikes | | | | | | |
| **Sinker** | Balls | | | | | | |
| | Strikes | | | | | | |
| **Change-Up** | Balls | | | | | 3 | |
| | Strikes | | | | | | |

On the 0-0 pitch, Niekro's pitch-type percentages are nearly the same for left-handed batters as for right-handed. Eighty-three percent of his 0-0 pitches are knucklers (43 percent balls, 40 percent strikes).

When he is ahead in the count, he throws a very high percentage of knucklers. The farther he falls behind in the count, the fewer knucklers and the more fastballs he throws.

### Bret Saberhagen, Kansas City Royals

Right-handed Bret Saberhagen of the Kansas City Royals has three main pitches: fastballs, curves and change-ups. Occasionally he throws a slider, but it accounts for less than five percent of his pitches. Saberhagen's Pitch Information Report show definite trends, and can be of great value to hitters.

**Pitch Information Report**
**Bret Saberhagen    Right-Handed Pitcher**
**Against All Right-Handed Batters All Teams**


(Shown on opposite page)

*BASE SITUATION:* All Situations

| *Various Counts on Batter* | | *Ahead In The Count* | | | | | *Even Count* | | | |
|---|---|---|---|---|---|---|---|---|---|---|
| | Balls | 0 | 0 | 1 | 2 | | 0 | 1 | 3 | |
| | Strikes | 1 | 2 | 2 | 2 | | 0 | 1 | 2 | |
| Total Pitches On Each Count | | 366 | 152 | 269 | 202 | 989 | 745 | 301 | 92 | 1138 |
| Fast | Balls | 24 | 39 | 18 | 16 | 23 | 22 | 14 | 14 | 19 |
| | Strikes | 39 | 28 | 42 | 50 | 40 | 41 | 48 | 75 | 46 |
| Curve | Balls | 12 | 10 | 13 | 7 | 11 | 13 | 10 | 3 | 11 |
| | Strikes | 13 | 14 | 17 | 15 | 15 | 16 | 14 | 4 | 14 |
| Slider | Balls | 2 | 5 | 3 | 1 | 3 | 2 | 2 | | 2 |
| | Strikes | 2 | 2 | 3 | 2 | 3 | 2 | 2 | 2 | 2 |
| Knuckleball | Balls | | | | | | | | | |
| | Strikes | | | | | | | | | |
| Screwball | Balls | | | | | | | | | |
| | Strikes | | | | | | | | | |
| Sinker | Balls | | | | | | | | | |
| | Strikes | | | | | | | | | |
| Change-Up | Balls | 3 | 1 | | 3 | 2 | 1 | 5 | | 2 |
| | Strikes | 4 | | 3 | 5 | 4 | 2 | 5 | 1 | 3 |

| *Various Counts on Batter* | | *Behind In The Count* | | | | | |
|---|---|---|---|---|---|---|---|
| | Balls | 1 | 2 | 2 | 3 | 3 | |
| | Strikes | 0 | 0 | 1 | 0 | 1 | |
| Total Pitches On Each Count | | 288 | 73 | 124 | 15 | 42 | 542 |
| Fast | Balls | 18 | 19 | 15 | 13 | 24 | 18 |
| | Strikes | 57 | 70 | 62 | 87 | 67 | 61 |
| Curve | Balls | 4 | | 2 | | | 3 |
| | Strikes | 10 | 10 | 6 | | | 8 |
| Slider | Balls | 1 | 1 | 2 | | | 1 |
| | Strikes | 2 | | 2 | | 5 | 2 |
| Knuckleball | Balls | | | | | | |
| | Strikes | | | | | | |
| Screwball | Balls | | | | | | |
| | Strikes | | | | | | |
| Sinker | Balls | | | | | | |
| | Strikes | | | | | | |
| Change-Up | Balls | 2 | | 3 | | 2 | 2 |
| | Strikes | 6 | | 6 | | 2 | 5 |

On the 0-0 count, 63 percent of Saberhagen's pitches are fastballs (41 percent strikes, 22 percent balls). Twenty-nine percent of his 0-0 pitches are curves (16 percent strikes, 13 percent balls).

These percentages vary little when Saberhagen is ahead in the count. The only marked difference is on the 0-2 count, when 39 percent of Saberhagen's pitches are fastballs thrown for balls, 28 percent for strikes. On the 2-2 pitch, 50 percent of his pitches are fastball strikes.

When behind in the count, Saberhagen relies heavily on his fastball. On the 2-0 count, 89 percent of his pitches are fastballs (70 percent strikes, 19 percent balls). On the 3-1 count, 91 percent of his pitches are fastballs (67 percent strikes, 24 percent balls). And on the 3-0 pitch, only fastballs have been recorded.

## Saberhagen Against Left-Handed Batters

Very clear patterns can be seen in Saberhagen's reports against left-handed batters.

**Pitch Information Report**
**Bret Saberhagen    Right-Handed Pitcher**
**Against All Left-Handed Batters All Teams**


(Shown on opposite page)

**BASE SITUATION:** All Situations

| *Various Counts on Batter* | | *Ahead In The Count* | | | | | *Even Count* | | | |
|---|---|---|---|---|---|---|---|---|---|---|
| | Balls | 0 | 0 | 1 | 2 | | 0 | 1 | 3 | |
| | Strikes | 1 | 2 | 2 | 2 | | 0 | 1 | 2 | |
| Total Pitches On Each Count | | 336 | 154 | 268 | 241 | 999 | 776 | 304 | 125 | 1205 |
| Fast | Balls | 29 | 44 | 24 | 16 | 27 | 25 | 22 | 14 | 23 |
| | Strikes | 39 | 39 | 42 | 51 | 43 | 47 | 45 | 75 | 49 |
| Curve | Balls | 9 | 6 | 10 | 6 | 8 | 11 | 6 | | 9 |
| | Strikes | 8 | 3 | 13 | 11 | 9 | 8 | 11 | 2 | 8 |
| Slider | Balls | 1 | | 1 | 2 | 1 | 1 | | 1 | 1 |
| | Strikes | | 1 | 1 | | 1 | 1 | | | 1 |
| Knuckleball | Balls | | | | | | | | | |
| | Strikes | | | | | | | | | |
| Screwball | Balls | | | | | | | | | |
| | Strikes | | | | | | | | | |
| Sinker | Balls | | 1 | | | | | | | |
| | Strikes | | | | | | | | | |
| Change-Up | Balls | 7 | 2 | 3 | 3 | 4 | 2 | 2 | 2 | 2 |
| | Strikes | 8 | 4 | 8 | 11 | 8 | 5 | 13 | 6 | 7 |

| *Various Counts on Batter* | | *Behind In The Count* | | | | | |
|---|---|---|---|---|---|---|---|
| | Balls | 1 | 2 | 2 | 3 | 3 | |
| | Strikes | 0 | 0 | 1 | 0 | 1 | |
| Total Pitches On Each Count | | 302 | 86 | 137 | 20 | 45 | 590 |
| Fast | Balls | 18 | 21 | 18 | 35 | 13 | 18 |
| | Strikes | 53 | 69 | 60 | 65 | 80 | 59 |
| Curve | Balls | 4 | 1 | 2 | | | 3 |
| | Strikes | 7 | 1 | 1 | | 2 | 4 |
| Slider | Balls | 1 | | | | | 1 |
| | Strikes | 1 | 1 | 1 | | | 1 |
| Knuckleball | Balls | | | | | | |
| | Strikes | | | | | | |
| Screwball | Balls | | | | | | |
| | Strikes | | | | | | |
| Sinker | Balls | | | | | | |
| | Strikes | | | | | | |
| Change-Up | Balls | 6 | 2 | 4 | | | 4 |
| | Strikes | 11 | 5 | 14 | | 4 | 10 |

On the 0-0 count against left-handed batters, Saberhagen throws 72 percent fastballs (47 percent strikes, 25 percent balls).  Fastball strikes predominate in most counts when he is ahead.  The exception is on the 0-2 pitch, when more of his fastball are thrown for balls than for strikes (44 percent balls, 39 percent strikes).

When behind in the count against left-handers, almost all of Saberhagen's pitches are fastballs.  On the 2-0, the 2-1 and the 3-0 pitches, he comes in with 69, 60 and 65 percent fastball strikes respectively.  On the 3-1 count, 80 percent of his pitches are fastball strikes.

It is interesting that on the 2-1 count against left-handed batters, 18 percent of his pitches are change-ups (14 percent strikes, 4 percent balls).

Saberhagen generally has good control and can throw a strike when he needs to.  Therefore when the fastball strike percentage is high in a certain category, a left-handed hitter can get an advantage by preparing for a fastball in the strike zone.

### Saberhagen's Pitch Location Reports

Against right-handed batters, Saberhagen shows good control with his curve and slider, but many of his fastballs slip into easier-to-hit locations..

### Pitch Location Report
### Bret Saberhagen    Right-Handed Pitcher
### Against All Right-Handed Batters All Teams

**Base Situation:** All Situations          Total Pitches: 2669

| **Totals:** 1800 | | | 601 | | | 113 | | | 0 | | |
|---|---|---|---|---|---|---|---|---|---|---|---|
| *Fast* | | | *Curve* | | | *Slider* | | | *Knuckle* | | |
| **I** | **M** | **O** | **I** | **M** | **O** | **I** | **M** | **O** | **I** | **M** | **O** |
| H 6 | 8 | 4 | H 8 | 6 | 2 | H 8 | 2 | 1 | H | | |
| M 13 | 9 | 21 | M 15 | 7 | 16 | M 7 | 3 | 10 | M | | |
| L 5 | 11 | 17 | L 5 | 12 | 26 | L 5 | 8 | 53 | L | | |

| **Totals:** 1 | | | 1 | | | 153 | | |
|---|---|---|---|---|---|---|---|---|
| *Screwball* | | | *Sinkerball* | | | *Change-Up* | | |
| **I** | **M** | **O** | **I** | **M** | **O** | **I** | **M** | **O** |
| H | | | H | | | H 6 | 9 | 7 |
| M | | | M | | | M 16 | 5 | 13 |
| L | 100 | | L | | 100 | L 9 | 14 | 17 |

Notice that Saberhagen keeps his fastballs outside overall, but a high percentage slip into the medium-over-the-middle location (9 percent). When runners are in scoring position, 15 percent of his fastballs are to the medium-over-the-middle location (see below). This indicates that Saberhagen throws his fastballs hard with little concern for precise control.

He has good control of his curve and slider. He keeps his curves low, with 26 percent in the low-outside location. He throws 53 percent of his sliders to the low-outside location.

Saberhagen throws more change-ups than sliders. No definite change-up patterns emerge, although he does throw slightly more to the outside locations and is able to keep his change-ups down in the strike zone.

As mentioned above, Saberhagen throws a surprisingly high percentage of his fastballs to the medium-over-the-middle location when runners are in scoring position. Notice also that he throws few sliders and change-ups when runners are in scoring position.

### Pitch Location Report
### Bret Saberhagen    Right-Handed Pitcher
### Against All Right-Handed Batters All Teams

| **Base Situation:** Runner(s) in Scoring Position | | | | | | | | | | Total Pitches: 486 | | |
|---|---|---|---|---|---|---|---|---|---|---|---|---|
| *Totals: 336* | | | 105 | | | 1*º* | | | 0 | | | |
| | *Fast* | | | | *Curve* | | | *Slider* | | | *Knuckle* | |
| | I | M | O | I | M | O | I | M | O | I | M | O |
| H | 6 | 7 | 5 | H 7 | 7 | 1 | H 15 | | 5 | H | | |
| M | 8 | 15 | 19 | M 19 | 6 | 18 | M 5 | | 5 | M | | |
| L | 7 | 11 | 18 | L 4 | 13 | 21 | L 5 | | 63 | L | | |

| | Totals: | 0 | | | 0 | | | 26 | | |
|---|---|---|---|---|---|---|---|---|---|---|---|
| | | *Screwball* | | | *Sinkerball* | | | *Change-Up* | | |
| | | I | M | O | I | M | O | I | M | O |
| | H | | | | H | | | H | 7 | 7 | 15 |
| | M | | | | M | | | M | 15 | 3 | 15 |
| | L | | | | L | | | L | 3 | 11 | 19 |

Saberhagen's Pitch Location Report against left-handed batters shows many similar trends. It is not shown here.

## Personal Comments

The next chapter talks about the BARS System Batting Order Report, which highlights nine offensive categories that can help a manager determine the best batting order for his team against left- and right-handed pitchers.

A lot of times managers don't change their batting orders when their teams are facing left-handers and right-handers. I think eventually computers will show that they should use different batting orders, not only against lefties and righties, but against specific pitchers.

The new score-forecasting program we're working on now will be able to set up a batting order that will score the most runs against right- and left-handed pitchers. The forecasting program shows that a different number of runs are scored every time a team's batting order is changed, even if just two batters are transposed in the order. We don't know how many additional runs the perfect batting order could produce, but it might be as much as one or two a game. Over an entire season, that would make a tremendous difference.

Dick Howser was very interested in the Batting Order Report. He wanted to know how batters advance runners by hitting away, versus how they advance runners by bunting. He and Earl Weaver both liked to play for a big inning; they were reluctant to give up the out that would result by bunting.

The following chapter shows that hitters advance runners almost as well by hitting away as by bunting. Hitters advance runners about 55 to 60 percent of the time when hitting away and about 65 to 70 percent of the time when bunting. It is questionable whether the five or ten percentage points gained by bunting are worth the almost sure out resulting from the batter being thrown out at first base. With the widespread use of artificial surfaces, fielders can almost always get to the ball in time to throw the runner out at first. And it isn't unusual these days to see a sacrifice bunt result in the advanced runner being thrown out — or even in a double play.

# Chapter Fourteen

# Projected Batting-Order Report

This report gives information for each player on nine specific offensive categories. The report does not designate which position in the batting order a player should be; the report merely gives detailed information about the nine categories, so that managers can have complete information when determining their batting orders. The Projected Batting-Order Report also gives information that is useful for selecting pinch hitters.

The nine categories are:

1. Batting Average
2. Ability To Get On Base
3. Runs Batted In
4. Runs Scored
5. Total Bases Gained On Base Hits
6. Strike Outs
7. Stolen Bases
8. Advancing A Runner By Hitting
9. Advancing A Runner By Bunting

This information is defined as:

**Batting Average** — Base hits divided by times-at-bat. Times-at-bat is defined as total plate appearances less walks, sacrifices, and times hit by pitches.

**Ability To Get On Base** — Total plate appearances divided by times reaching base (base hits, walks, and times hit by pitches).

**Runs Batted In** — Total hit balls (base hits, outs, sacrifices, errors) divided by total RBIs (runs batted in plus runs walked in).

**Runs Scored** — Total plate appearances divided by runs scored.

**Total Bases Gained On Base Hits** — Total plate appearances divided by total bases gained.

**Strike Outs** — Total plate appearances divided by strike outs.

**Stolen Bases** — Attempted stolen bases divided by stolen bases.

**Advancing A Runner By Hitting** — Times at the plate with men on base divided by number of times runner or runners advanced.

**Advancing A Runner By Bunting** — Bunt attempts with men on base divided by times runners were advanced by bunting.

Two Projected Batting-Order Reports are printed for each team, one against right-handed pitchers and one against left-handed pitchers faced. Normally, information is not printed out for a particular hitter against a particular pitcher because there would be too few instances to get meaningful records.

In the appendix of this book, Projected Batting-Order Reports are shown for the New York Yankees, New York Mets, Atlanta Braves, Los Angeles Dodgers, Kansas City Royals, Detroit Tigers, Chicago Cubs and Baltimore Orioles.

**Example:  Dave Winfield, New York Yankees**

The following Projected Batting-Order Report for Dave Winfield of the New York Yankees is used as an example. This report is for Winfield when facing right-handed pitchers. A separate report would be made for Winfield facing left-handers. Note that the statistics are only for games scouted by the BARS System.

### Dave Winfield
### Projected Batting-Order Report
### Against All Right-Handed Pitchers All Teams

| Batting Average | Ability To Get On Base | RBI | Runs Scored | Total Bases Gained |
|---|---|---|---|---|
| .270 717/194 | 783/266 | 584/123 | 783/72 | 783/388 |

| Strike Outs | Stolen Bases | Advancing A Runner By Hitting | Advancing A Runner By Bunting |
|---|---|---|---|
| 783/117 | 12/9 | 214/147 | 6/1 |

Following along with the chart, the first column, Batting Average, shows that Winfield batted .270. He had 717 at-bats and got 194 hits. The 717 at-bats represents a composite for the total at-bats Winfield had in Yankee games scouted by the BARS System. It includes 42 games in 1983, 59 in 1984, 81 in 1985, 85 in 1986 and 85 in 1987.

The second column, Ability To Get On Base, shows that in 783 total plate appearances, he reached base 266 times. Note that Winfield's total plate appearances is a larger number than his total at bats as recorded in the first column of the report. This is because total plate appearances includes instances omitted from times at bat, as explained above in the definition of each category.

The third column, RBI, shows that he had 123 RBIs in his 584 total times at bat with a runner or runners on base.

The fourth column, Runs Scored, shows that in his 783 total plate appearances he scored 72 runs.

The fifth column, Total Bases Gained On Base Hits, shows that he gained 388 bases by hits in his 783 total plate appearances.

The sixth column, Strike Outs, shows that he struck out 117 times in 783 plate appearances.

The seventh column, Stolen Bases, shows that in 12 attempts to steal a base, Winfield was successful nine times.

The eighth column, Advancing A Runner By Hitting, shows that in 214 at-bats with runners on base he advanced a runner 147 times.

The ninth column, Advancing A Runner By Bunting, shows that in six bunt attempts with runners on base he advanced a runner once.

## Use Of The Projected Batting-Order Report

The Projected Batting-Order Report allows a manager to evaluate the performance of his hitters. Usually a manager knows how to set up his batting order, but many teams experiment with batting orders during the season.

Each position in the batting order emphasizes certain of the categories more than other positions. The lead off batter's job is to get on base. Among the Yankees, Don Mattingly is second in on-base percentage (.383 on 296 times reaching base in 772 plate appearances), but Mattingly's great power and clutch hitting make him more effective at the number 3 or 4 spot in the lineup. Rickey Henderson leads the Yankees at getting on base (.388 on 257 in 663), making him the ideal Yankee lead off man. Some teams may not have as obvious a player for lead off, and an overall evaluation of the BARS system Projected Batting-Order Report could help determine the best for that batting position.

## Hitting Vs. Bunting: Which Is Best To Advance A Runner?

One category that invariably attracts attention among managers is the information in column eight: Advancing A Runner By Hitting. It is surprising how high the percentage is for this statistic. It varies slightly when teams face right- and left-handed pitchers, but overall the average for both leagues is close to 60%.

There are different types of outs that a hitter can make. Strikeouts are "dead outs." Nothing happens on a strikeout. Runners do not advance and there is no chance for fielders to make errors or mistakes. Even a weakly-hit ground ball allows the chance for something to happen.

Nothing is more demoralizing for a team than to continually leave runners stranded. When the leadoff hitter in an inning gets on base, it is crucial to advance him to scoring position. The team that can consistently advance runners in key situations will win more games than teams that cannot.

Most teams have a slightly higher percentage of advancing a runner by bunting than by hitting, but the difference is less than would be expected. The New York Yankees, for example, have advanced runners 61 percent of the time by hitting over the last five years when facing right-handed pitchers, and 66 percent of the time when bunting. Against left-handed pitchers, the Yankees have advanced runners 58 percent of the time when hitting and 60 percent when bunting.

The Atlanta Braves have advanced runners 58 percent of the time by hitting when facing right-handed pitchers and 73 percent by bunting. When facing left-handers, the Braves have advanced runners 59 percent of the time by hitting and 66 percent by bunting.

These percentages by the Yankees and the Braves are typical for major league teams. These figures are for games scouted by the BARS System.

Considering that a sacrifice bunt almost always results in the batter being thrown out at first base, these figures make a person wonder whether there is an advantage in sacrificing. By allowing batters to hit away when there are men to advance, there is at least a chance that the batter will be safe while advancing the runner.

The sacrifice bunt may have been the superior method of advancing runners in the past, but with the use of artificial surfaces that offer little resistance to the ball and allow fielders to reach bunts easily, the sacrifice bunt may have to re-examined. It is not unusual today to see sacrifice bunts result in double plays.

## Pitchers As Bunters

In the National League, pitchers are often as good or better than regular hitters at advancing runners by bunting. For the Houston Astros, Nolan Ryan is 5-for-6, Bob Knepper is 8-for-12, and Mike Scott is 10-for-10 in games scouted by the BARS System. For the Mets, Ron Darling is 10-for-11 and Dwight Gooden is 9-for-9.

Pitchers probably practice bunting more than hitters and, being good natural athletes in most cases anyway, are just as proficient at advancing runners by bunting in key situations. In some cases, managers might want to consider using a pitcher as a pinch hitter when a good bunt is needed.

## Special Items of Information Can Be Requested

As with all the BARS system charts, many additional items of information can be printed if specially requested. For instance, it might be valuable to know how specific hitters do in advancing runners in late innings, or how their RBI proficiency is in late innings. Special charts can be printed on these and many other particular items of information when requested.

## *Personal Comments*

The Field Chart shown in the following chapter is no longer used in the BARS System. As I explained earlier, we gather so much information that it's impossible to position fielders using this chart. There are too many recorded hit balls, and the field is a big jumble of fastballs hit to a certain spot when the batter was ahead or behind in the count, and curves hit to a certain spot when the batter was ahead or behind, etc. It's just too complicated for a human being to figure out.

That's why we let the computer take all the information and automatically position the fielders. The Field Chart shown in this chapter is the basis for the BARS fielding strategy, but it's no longer used for that.

I've noticed that some teams have charts like the Field Chart, and that they use them to position their fielders for certain batters on opposing teams. But their charts only show how an opposing hitter has done against their team or against a specific pitcher. These charts are not very accurate, because there isn't much information. In fact, a small amount of information can be worse than none at all.

Managers tell me that they want information about how a specific hitter does against a specific pitcher. But it's not possible to get enough information to be accurate. Hitters just don't face specific pitchers that often. If the BARS System made up batting charts for hitters against specific pitchers, in most cases we couldn't fill up even the fastball charts. And there would be mostly zeros in the other charts.

That's why we break a hitter's performance into two categories: against right-handed pitchers and against left-handed pitchers. Using these two categories we can get a large amount of information, and the 90 percent accuracy we consistently get with the BARS fielding strategy shows that using these two categories is the correct way to approach the problem.

This accuracy should improve as we get more information, but even 90 percent isn't too bad. I know a lot of people who would love to go to Las Vegas knowing that something has happened a certain way 9 out of 10 times in the past.

# Chapter Fifteen

# The Field Chart

The Field Chart is a graphic representation of a baseball field, divided into fielding positions.

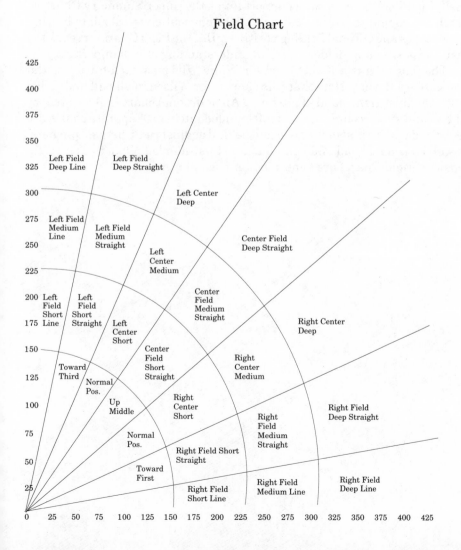

Field Chart

The Scouting Report records the angle of each hit ball, the initial and final distances a ball is hit, the pitch location and the type of pitch thrown for each hit ball. The Field Chart combines these pieces of information to graphically illustrate:

(1) Where each hit ball landed or was fielded on the playing field
(2) What type of pitch was hit (fastball, curve, slider, etc.)
(3) Where each pitch was located in or around the strike zone (high inside, high middle, etc.)

The purpose of the Field Chart is to graphically illustrate where hitters tend to hit certain types of pitches that are thrown in certain locations. In itself, the Field Chart is not as important as the Super Summary Chart, in which the computer uses all hit and pitch information to calculate batting percentages and optimal fielding positions. But the Field Chart serves as the basis for positioning fielders, and an understanding of it is important.

The following is a Field Chart for Willie Wilson, switch-hitter for the Kansas City Royals. Note that this chart is for Wilson in all ball and strike counts against right-handed pitchers. An additional chart is generated for all ball and strike counts against left-handed pitchers. Separate charts are generated when a player is ahead and behind against right-handed pitchers, as well as when ahead and behind against left-handed pitchers. Thus, six separate Field Charts are generated for each player.

## Field Chart
### Willie Wilson    Switch-Hitter
### Against All Right-Handed Pitchers All Teams
### Total Number of Hits Recorded: 1,017

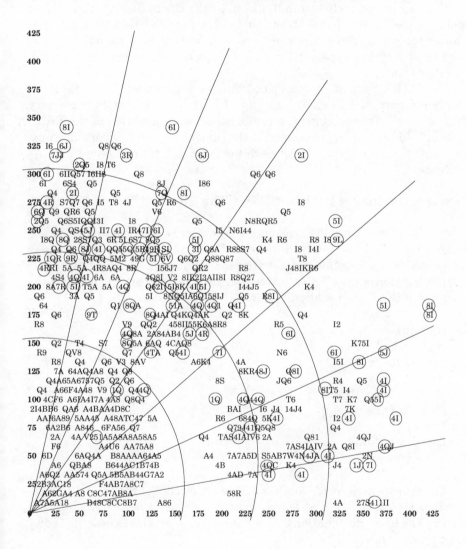

Note that the Field Chart shown on the preceding page illustrates only a small percentage of the 1,017 hits for Wilson against right-handed pitchers. There is not enough room on the chart for all the hit balls to be recorded, so the computer displays only a percentage of the hit balls.

Without the powerful computer used by the BARS System, it would be nearly impossible to calculate trends in the direction and distance of hits that a hitter has made, especially when considering that each hit ball must be linked with a certain type and location of pitch, as well as with a certain ball and strike count.

The BARS System computer coordinates information from the Pitch Location Chart, the Pitch Information Chart, and the Super Summary batting chart. This combined information allows calculation of the BARS System fielding strategy contained in the Super Summary Report, in which the optimal fielding position for each fielder is determined on a pitch-by-pitch basis.

### How Information Is Designated For The Chart

On the Field Chart the type and location of the pitch that was hit are designated by a letter and a number. The actual location of the hit is designated by the position of the letter and number on the chart.

The location of the pitch is designated by numerals corresponding to the locations of the Pitch Location Report:

| | |
|---|---|
| High Inside | 1 |
| High Over Middle | 2 |
| High Outside | 3 |
| Medium Inside | 4 |
| Medium Over Middle | 5 |
| Medium Outside | 6 |
| Low Inside | 7 |
| Low Over Middle | 8 |
| Low Outside | 9 |

The type of pitch corresponds to the seven pitches of the Pitch Information Report: fastball, curve, slider, knuckleball, screwball, change-up and sinker. The letter designation of these seven types of pitches determined by three types of hits:

| Ground Balls | Balls Hit Hard | Other |
|---|---|---|
| A Fast | I Fast | Q Fast |
| B Curve | J Curve | R Curve |
| C Slider | K Slider | S Slider |
| D Knuckle | L Knuckle | T Knuckle |
| E Screwball | M Screwball | U Screwball |
| F Change-Up | N Change-Up | V Change-Up |
| G Sinkerball | O Sinkerball | W Sinkerball |

Thus, a hit designated 'I3' would be a high-outside fastball hit as a line drive. 'J1' would be a high-inside curve ball hit as a line drive. 'V7' would be a low-inside change-up hit as a fly ball. The location of each letter-number combination graphically shows where the ball landed (in the case of a line drive or fly ball) or was fielded (in the case of a ground ball). Any ball hit less than five feet high is considered a ground ball.

To further simplify the chart, each line drive or fly ball that results in any type of base hit is circled with a color. Hits that are highlighted in green are ground ball base hits. Hits highlighted in blue are not base hits but were hit hard. Green is designated for ground ball base hits because of the green grass. Blue is used because of the blue sky. All letters and numbers that are not circled with a color or highlighted in green are not base hits. The Field Chart records all hit balls, whether base hits or outs, but the chart does not record whether base hits are singles, doubles, triples or home runs.

Six separate Field Charts are generated for each player: three for performance against right-handed pitchers, three for performance against left-handed pitchers. Against both right- and left-handed pitchers there is a Field Chart for hits made when the batter was ahead in the count, behind in the count and a composite for all count situations.

## *Personal Comments*

The single most crucial factor of the BARS System is that the initial information gathered by the BARS scouts be entirely accurate. A saying about computers is "garbage in, garbage out," meaning that if the initial information isn't accurate, the resulting statistics won't be reliable. That's why in the BARS System we put so much emphasis on making sure that our scouts get accurate information. The proof that the scouts are getting correct information is the 90 percent accuracy we regularly get in the Super Summary fielding strategy. If the scouts weren't doing things right, there's no way we could have this high percentage of accuracy in a statistic that coordinates so many variables.

When we first started travelling and scouting with the Kansas City Royals, a BARS scout sat with the Royals' pitcher who would be starting the following day. The pitcher's job was to call the type and location of pitches, while the BARS scout recorded the direction and distance of hits, how the runners advanced, and all the other information we record. This was not an extra duty for the pitcher, since most major league teams ask the pitcher who will be starting the next day to chart pitches.

We soon found out that the pitchers were doing such a poor job that their information was useless. I had to stop using them. They didn't care about accuracy; they didn't take it seriously. And I guarantee you that even today most pitchers who chart pitches for their team couldn't care less about keeping accurate records. If pitchers do the same kind of job they did then, their information couldn't be used as the basis of any scouting system.

At that point I designed the Scouting Report, which is described in the following chapter, so all the information could be taken by one knowledgeable person who would get paid for his work, enjoy it and take responsibility for it. Since then our information has been as accurate as we can make it. We have a system of checks and double checks to eliminate even the smallest error. The results have been as good or better than I could have hoped for.

# Chapter Sixteen

---

# The Scouting Report

---

The Scouting Report is the most important document in the BARS System. For reliability of all analyses and trends, information must be recorded with complete accuracy on a pitch-by-pitch basis. Several major league managers and scouts have commented that accuracy in the Scouting Report is one of their primary concerns, and because of that, great effort has been taken to insure that every pitch, swing or miss, hit or out, and all the ensuing activities of fielding and base running are recorded with exactness.

In order to accumulate the information, it is necessary for a BARS System scout to watch each game and record items of information on a specially prepared Scouting Form. This form has been designed for ease, completeness and accuracy of reporting. It gives the scout a clearly designated and repeatable system to record each game on a pitch-by-pitch basis with complete accuracy.

### Explanation of the Scouting Report

The chart shown on the following page is a facsimile of the first page of the Scouting Report:

## Scouting Report
### *Game Information*

**Date** (MMDDYY) _____

**Stadium Number** _____

**Field Condition**

| | | |
|---|---|---|
| Astroturf | 1 | _____ |
| Fast | 2 | _____ |
| Average | 3 | _____ |
| Slow | 4 | _____ |

**Weather**

| | | |
|---|---|---|
| Indoor | 1 | _____ |
| Sunny | 2 | _____ |
| Overcast | 3 | _____ |
| Light Precipitation | 4 | _____ |
| Night | 5 | _____ |

**Wind Direction**

| | | |
|---|---|---|
| No Wind | 0 | _____ |
| In | 1 | _____ |
| Out | 2 | _____ |
| Across, 3rd to 1st | 3 | _____ |
| Across, 1st to 3rd | 4 | _____ |

**Wind Speed** (MPH) _____

**Temperature** (Degrees F) _____

**Time of Day** (Not Daylight
Savings Time) _____

**Double Header**

| | | |
|---|---|---|
| No | 0 | _____ |
| Yes | 1 | _____ |

**Double Header Game #** _____

**Opposing Team #** _____

**Attendance** _____

**Final Score**

Home _____

_____  _____

## Batter Lineup
### *Number*        *Name*

1. _____
2. _____
3. _____
4. _____
5. _____
6. _____
7. _____
8. _____
9. _____

1. _____
2. _____
3. _____
4. _____
5. _____
6. _____
7. _____
8. _____
9. _____

The information on the left side of this form is self-explanatory. The date of the game, the designated stadium number, the field condition at playing time, the weather, the wind direction and speed, the temperature at game time, and the time of day are factors that conceivably could affect a player's performance. A manager may want this information to analyze how well or poorly a particular player performs in certain situations. Double-headers, opposing team, attendance and the final score are also recorded.

The right side of the first page of the Scouting Report gives space for the batting order of each team to be recorded. The correct batting order is important because the BARS system has the capacity for determining how each hitter does in accordance with his position in the batting order.

Each player's uniform number is used to store the player's information in the BARS System computer. In addition to the uniform number, each player has a unique number that remains the same even when the player is traded. By using specific numbers to designate each player, it is possible to know what each hitter does on every pitch and to break down the information according to the count on the batter, pitch location, and who and where the base runners are.

## Recording Information on a Pitch-by-Pitch Basis

The second and ensuing pages of the Scouting Report allow the recording of specific information on a pitch-by-pitch basis.

### Baseball Input

Date _____          Inning No. _____

Pitcher No. _____          Page No. _____

Catcher No. _____          Batter No. _____

| Pitch Number | 1 | 2 | 3 | 4 | 5 | 6 | 7 | 8 | 9 | 10 | 11 | 12 | 13 | 14 | 15 |
|---|---|---|---|---|---|---|---|---|---|---|---|---|---|---|---|
| 47 Designated/Pinch Hitter | | | | | | | | | | | | | | | |
| 48 Number of Outs | | | | | | | | | | | | | | | |
| 49 Base Situation | | | | | | | | | | | | | | | |
| 50-51 Count                Ball | | | | | | | | | | | | | | | |
| Strike | | | | | | | | | | | | | | | |
| 52 Type of Pitch | | | | | | | | | | | | | | | |
| 53 Location | | | | | | | | | | | | | | | |
| 54 Call                Hit 1 | | | | | | | | | | | | | | | |
| Foul 2 | | | | | | | | | | | | | | | |
| Strike Swing 3 | | | | | | | | | | | | | | | |
| Strike No Swing 4 | | | | | | | | | | | | | | | |
| Ball 5 | | | | | | | | | | | | | | | |
| Pitchout 6 | | | | | | | | | | | | | | | |
| Walk 7 | | | | | | | | | | | | | | | |
| Balk 8 | | | | | | | | | | | | | | | |
| Bunt 9 | | | | | | | | | | | | | | | |
| Bunt Attempt 0 | | | | | | | | | | | | | | | |
| Hit By Pitch A | | | | | | | | | | | | | | | |
| Interference B | | | | | | | | | | | | | | | |
| Wild Pitch C | | | | | | | | | | | | | | | |
| Pitch Off To First Base D | | | | | | | | | | | | | | | |
| 55-56 Angle | | | | | | | | | | | | | | | |
| 57-59 Initial Distance | | | | | | | | | | | | | | | |
| 60-62 Final Distance | | | | | | | | | | | | | | | |
| 63 Fielder of Ball (Position #) | | | | | | | | | | | | | | | |
| 64 Type of Hit | | | | | | | | | | | | | | | |
| 65 Base Gained (Base Hit) | | | | | | | | | | | | | | | |
| 66 Sacrifice Bunt/Sacrifice Fly | | | | | | | | | | | | | | | |
| 67-74 Runner Scored        First | | | | | | | | | | | | | | | |
| Second | | | | | | | | | | | | | | | |
| Third | | | | | | | | | | | | | | | |
| Fourth | | | | | | | | | | | | | | | |
| 75 Error (Position #) | | | | | | | | | | | | | | | |
| 76 Ball Thrown to Base Number | | | | | | | | | | | | | | | |
| 77 Accuracy of Throw/Good Play | | | | | | | | | | | | | | | |
| 78-79 Stolen Base (Player #) | | | | | | | | | | | | | | | |
| 80 Covering Second | | | | | | | | | | | | | | | |

A new page is started each time the next hitter in the lineup comes to bat. At the top of the page, the date of the game, the pitcher number, the catcher number, the inning number, and the batter number are recorded. The inning number would have T1 recorded for the top of the first inning, B1 for the bottom of the first inning, etc. The page number of the Scouting Report is recorded to assure the continuity of the entire game report.

The next item is the pitch number. There is a column for each pitch thrown, from the first pitch to the fifteenth.

In the columns below each pitch, results are recorded according to designated codes. The first item of concern (line 47) is whether the batter is a designated hitter, pinch hitter or regular hitter in the lineup. If the batter was a regular hitter in the batting order, a 0 would be put in the first column of line 47. For a designated hitter, a 1 would be put in the space, and for a pinch hitter, a 2.

The next two rows, 'Number of Outs' (line 48) and 'Base Situation' (line 49) may change with each pitch. For instance, when the first pitch is delivered, there could be no outs and a runner on first base. On that pitch, the runner could be thrown out while attempting to steal second. In such a situation, at the delivery of the second pitch there would be one out and no one on base.

The number of outs, 0, 1 or 2, is recorded in the space in the first column. This doesn't need to be changed until another out is made. For the base situation, the following codes are used to record the exact runners-on-base situation for each pitch:

Base Situation

| No one on base | 0 |
| 1st | 1 |
| 2nd | 2 |
| 3rd | 3 |
| 1st and 2nd | 4 |
| 2nd and 3rd | 5 |
| 1st and 3rd | 6 |
| 1st, 2nd and 3rd | 7 |

The next two lines (50-51) are used to record the count. Before the delivery of the first pitch, there is always a count of 0 balls and 0 strikes. If the first pitch was a ball, a 1 would be put in column two along the line designated for ball, and a 0 would be put in column two along the line designated for strikes. The opposite would be the case if the first pitch was a strike. This proceeds along pitch by pitch.

The type of pitch is recorded in the columns along the next row (line 52). The code for each pitch is:

Type of Pitch

| | |
|---|---|
| Fast | 1 |
| Curve | 2 |
| Slider | 3 |
| Knuckle | 4 |
| Screwball | 5 |
| Sinker/split-fingered fastball | 6 |
| Change-up/curve | 7 |
| Change-up/fast | 8 |

The location of each pitch over the plate is recorded on line 53. The strike zone and the area around the strike zone is divided into a a nine-location grid, so that the location of each pitch can be recorded exactly.

Location

| | |
|---|---|
| High Inside | 1 |
| High Over Middle | 2 |
| High Outside | 3 |
| Medium-High Inside | 4 |
| Medium-High Over Middle | 5 |
| Medium-High Outside | 6 |
| Low Inside | 7 |
| Low Over Middle | 8 |
| Low Outside | 9 |

Every pitch will have a result. The specific result, listed as 'Call' (line 54), is recorded for each pitch in one of the following categories:

| | |
|---|---|
| Hit | Balk |
| Foul | Bunt |
| Strike Swing | Bunt Attempt |
| Strike No Swing | Hit By Pitch |
| Ball | Interference |
| Pitchout | Wild Pitch |
| Walk | Pitch Off To First Base |

For greater speed and accuracy, the 'Call' categories are recorded differently than the preceding categories. Instead of using a numerical code system, all the possibilities are listed and the scout checks the proper column adjacent to the proper 'Call' category. Thus, a check next to 'Foul' in the column under pitch number one means that the batter fouled off the first pitch. A check next to 'Ball' under pitch number two means that the batter took the second pitch for a ball. The count then would be 1 ball and 1 strike going into the third pitch.

All the terms listed under the 'Call' category are baseball terms that are easily understood, but to achieve consistency the following explanations are given:

**Hit** – A ball hit into fair territory, whether the batter gets on base or not. This should not be confused with a base hit (single, double, triple or home run), because a base hit is only one type of a hit ball.

**Foul** – A ball hit into foul territory.

**Strike Swing** – A swing and miss on a pitch thrown in the strike zone. This category is distinct from 'Ball Swing', in which a batter swings and misses a pitch thrown outside of the strike zone.

**Strike No Swing** – A pitch that is called a strike when the batter does not swing. This information is included to determine if there is a pattern to the pitches that a batter takes for called strikes.

**Ball** – A pitch that is called a ball when the batter does not swing.

**Pitchout** – A pitch purposefully thrown out of the strike zone in anticipation of a base runner attempting to steal.

**Walk** – This column is marked on ball 4 instead of putting a check adjacent to 'Ball,' as would have been done on the three previous balls.

**Balk** – This is marked when a pitcher commits a balk.

**Bunt** – This is checked only when the pitch is bunted into fair territory.

**Interference** – This is marked when there is an interference play.

**Wild Pitch** – A poorly thrown pitch that the catcher cannot handle and which allows a base runner to advance. For a passed ball, the scout would designate that the catcher (position #1) made an error.

**Pitch Off To First Base** – This is checked when the pitcher throws to first base to hold a base runner closer to the first base bag.

## Pitch-by-Pitch Example

The chart below is a facsimile of a page from an actual Scouting Report.

---

### Baseball Input

Date _____          Inning No. ____1T____

Pitcher No. _____          Page No. _____

Catcher No. _____          Batter No. _____

| Pitch Number | 1 | 2 | 3 | 4 | 5 | 6 | 7 | 8 | 9 | 10 | 11 | 12 | 13 | 14 | 15 |
|---|---|---|---|---|---|---|---|---|---|---|---|---|---|---|---|
| 47 Designated/Pinch Hitter | 0 | | | | | | | | | | | | | | |
| 48 Number of Outs | 1 | | | | | | | | | | | | | | |
| 49 Base Situation | 2 | | | | | | | | | | | | | | |
| 50-51 Count          Ball | 0 | 0 | 1 | 1 | | | | | | | | | | | |
| Strike | 0 | 1 | 1 | 2 | | | | | | | | | | | |
| 52 Type of Pitch | 1 | 2 | 2 | 1 | | | | | | | | | | | |
| 53 Location | 6 | 9 | 7 | 2 | | | | | | | | | | | |
| 54 Call          Hit 1 | | | | √ | | | | | | | | | | | |
| Foul 2 | √ | | | | | | | | | | | | | | |
| Strike Swing 3 | | | √ | | | | | | | | | | | | |
| Strike No Swing 4 | | | | | | | | | | | | | | | |
| Ball 5 | √ | | | | | | | | | | | | | | |
| Pitchout 6 | | | | | | | | | | | | | | | |
| Walk 7 | | | | | | | | | | | | | | | |
| Balk 8 | | | | | | | | | | | | | | | |
| Bunt 9 | | | | | | | | | | | | | | | |
| Bunt Attempt 0 | | | | | | | | | | | | | | | |
| Hit By Pitch A | | | | | | | | | | | | | | | |
| Interference B | | | | | | | | | | | | | | | |
| Wild Pitch C | | | | | | | | | | | | | | | |
| Pitch Off to First Base D | | | | | | | | | | | | | | | |
| 55-56 Angle | | | | 72 | | | | | | | | | | | |
| 57-59 Initial Distance | | | | 307 | | | | | | | | | | | |
| 60-62 Final Distance | | | | 307 | | | | | | | | | | | |
| 63 Fielder of Ball (Position #) | | | | 7 | | | | | | | | | | | |
| 64 Type of Hit | | | | 3 | | | | | | | | | | | |
| 65 Base Gained (Base Hit) | | | | 0 | | | | | | | | | | | |
| 66 Sacrifice Bunt/Sacrifice Fly | | | | | | | | | | | | | | | |
| 67-74 Runner Scored          First | | | | | | | | | | | | | | | |
| Second | | | | | | | | | | | | | | | |
| Third | | | | | | | | | | | | | | | |
| Fourth | | | | | | | | | | | | | | | |
| 75 Error (Position #) | | | | | | | | | | | | | | | |
| 76 Ball Thrown to Base Number | | | | | | | | | | | | | | | |
| 77 Accuracy of Throw/Good Play | | | | | | | | | | | | | | | |
| 78-79 Stolen Base (Player #) | | | | | | | | | | | | | | | |
| 80 Covering Second | | | | | | | | | | | | | | | |

Following along with the chart on the opposite page, notice that the batter came to bat in the top of the first inning (1T in the upper right hand corner of the page). He was a regular hitter in the batting order (0 recorded on line 47). There was one out when he came to the plate (line 48). There was a runner on second base (line 49), and the count naturally was 0 balls and 0 strikes at the time of the first pitch.

The first pitch was a fastball (indicated by the 1 in the first column of row 52, 'Type of Pitch'). The fastball was medium high on the outside part of the plate (indicated by the 6 in the first column of row 53, 'Location').

The batter fouled off the first pitch (indicated by the check mark beside 'Foul' underneath the 0-0 count pitch). This made the count 0 balls and 1 strike for the second pitch (line 50-51).

The second pitch, a curveball low and outside, was a ball, bringing the count even at 1 ball and 1 strike. The third pitch was also a curve, low over the inside part of the plate, at which the batter swung and missed, bringing the count to 1 ball and 2 strikes. The fourth pitch was a fastball high over the middle of the plate, which the batter hit.

### Recording Hit Information On The Scouting Report

When a ball is hit into fair territory, a variety of information is recorded regarding the location and result of the hit. Recording the angle of the hit (line 55-56) and the distance the ball travels (line 60-62) are important, because this information is used in two of the reports generated by the BARS system, the Hit Location Report and the Super Summary Report. The angle is recorded to the nearest degree possible.

The angles are assigned as: 0 degrees to the first base line, 45 degrees to second base (straightaway center field), and 90 degrees to the third base line. Referring to the Scouting Report shown on the opposite page, a hit recorded at 72 degrees (indicated in column 4 of row 55-56, 'Angle') would be roughly in the direction between the third baseman and the shortstop.

The 'Initial Distance' (line 57-59) refers to the point where the ball first touches the ground or a player. The 'Final Distance' (line 60-62) designates the point where the ball comes to a stop. In the Scouting Report on the opposite page, the batter hit a fly ball to left field which was caught (indicated by 307 feet in rows 57-59, 'Initial Distance,' and rows 60-62, 'Final Distance'). The left fielder caught the ball (indicated by the 7 in row 53, 'Fielder of Ball').

The point of reception was both the 'Initial Distance' and the 'Final Distance' since the left fielder caught the ball on the fly. If the ball had been lined over the shortstop's head for a base hit, the point where the ball first touched the ground would be the 'Initial Distance' and the point where the left fielder first touched the ball would be the 'Final Distance.'

Each time a ball is hit in fair territory, the position number of the player who fielded the ball is recorded (line 63). The identification system used in baseball is: 1 for pitcher, 2 for catcher, 3 for first baseman, 4 for second baseman, 5 for third baseman, 6 for shortstop, 7 for left fielder, 8 for center fielder and 9 for right fielder.

Three categories are used for recording the type of hit (line 64): 1 for ground ball, 2 for line drive and 3 for fly ball.

'Base Gained' (line 65) indicates whether a hitter had a single (1), double (2), triple (3) or home run (4). If a hitter gets on base due to an error, this space is left blank, and an error is recorded below (line 75).

'Sacrifice Bunt' (line 66) is registered only when the batter successfully advances a runner by bunting the ball into fair territory. The code that is inserted into this category is based on which fielder charges the bunt attempt. The code numbers are: (1) First baseman charges; (2) Second baseman charges; (3) Third baseman charges; (4) First and Third basemen charge; (5) Second and Third basemen charge. A sacrifice fly is designated by a '6.'

The base runner's uniform number is recorded in the proper column along the 'Runner Scored' lines (67-74) when the runner scores. The base which the runner occupied when the pitch was thrown is designated by First, Second, Third and Fourth. For example, if there were base runners on second and third and a base hit scored both, the number of the runner who scored from third would be recorded in the column of the last pitch after 'First.' The number of the runner who scored from second would be listed after 'Second.' If the bases were loaded and the batter hit a home run, all the columns would be recorded, with the hitter's uniform number recorded after 'Fourth.'

When a fielder commits an error, his player position number is recorded on line 75. For example, if the shortstop commits an error, a 6 is recorded in line 75.

'Ball Thrown to Base Number' (line 76) and 'Accuracy of Throw' (line 77) record the accuracy of throws from the catcher to second or third base on steals and throws from infielders and outfielders to first, second, third or home plate. First base is designated '1', second '2' and third '3'. In line 77, a '1' designates a throw that is on target and a '2' designates a throw that is off target. An exceptionally good play is designated by a '3'.

When a player steals a base, his uniform number is recorded in line 78-79. When second base is stolen, a '1' is recorded on line 80 if the second baseman covers second, and a '2' is recorded if the shortstop covers.

## Comprehensive Information Available

It can readily be seen that by recording such information on a pitch-by-pitch basis, extremely exact, complete records can be kept. The BARS System information and computer analysis allows uniuqe and comprehensive statistics to be generated.

The comprehensive information about each pitch and the ensuing results allows tremendous flexibility in the recording of statistics. Individual managers and players may require unique information in attempts to spot specific trends. The BARS system allows widely diverse information about hitters and pitchers to be studied.

The following charts show the number of games that the BARS System has recorded. Note that the totals at the bottom of each column must be divided by two to determine the actual number of games scouted, since each game involves two teams.

For example, the 1987 total for the American League was 964. Since there were two teams involved in each game, 482 actual games were recorded.

### *American League*

| Name | 1983 | 1984 | 1985 | 1986 | 1987 | TOTAL |
|------|------|------|------|------|------|-------|
| BALTIMORE ORIOLES | 46 | 50 | 78 | 87 | 93 | 354 |
| BOSTON RED SOX | 32 | 56 | 83 | 95 | 90 | 356 |
| CALIFORNIA ANGELS | 30 | 28 | 47 | 61 | 50 | 216 |
| CHICAGO WHITE SOX | 34 | 58 | 86 | 74 | 79 | 331 |
| CLEVELAND INDIANS | 14 | 34 | 39 | 50 | 45 | 182 |
| DETROIT TIGERS | 25 | 60 | 67 | 83 | 78 | 313 |
| KANSAS CITY ROYALS | 97 | 100 | 116 | 111 | 113 | 537 |
| MILWAUKEE BREWERS | 25 | 50 | 46 | 41 | 47 | 209 |
| MINNESOTA TWINS | 28 | 29 | 42 | 52 | 52 | 203 |
| NEW YORK YANKEES | 42 | 59 | 81 | 85 | 88 | 355 |
| OAKLAND ATHLETICS | 27 | 34 | 47 | 39 | 46 | 193 |
| SEATTLE MARINERS | 26 | 35 | 46 | 41 | 55 | 203 |
| TEXAS RANGERS | 34 | 75 | 71 | 73 | 73 | 326 |
| TORONTO BLUE JAYS | 20 | 35 | 65 | 54 | 55 | 229 |
| | 480 | 704 | 914 | 946 | 964 | 4,008 |

## National League

| Name | 1983 | 1984 | 1985 | 1986 | 1987 | TOTAL |
|---|---|---|---|---|---|---|
| ATLANTA BRAVES | 90 | 103 | 116 | 97 | 88 | 494 |
| CHICAGO CUBS | 82 | 128 | 147 | 139 | 137 | 633 |
| CINCINNATI REDS | 18 | 37 | 45 | 52 | 35 | 187 |
| HOUSTON ASTROS | 31 | 61 | 91 | 101 | 66 | 350 |
| LOS ANGELES DODGERS | 42 | 34 | 57 | 64 | 45 | 242 |
| MONTREAL EXPOS | 18 | 40 | 59 | 59 | 38 | 214 |
| NEW YORK METS | 15 | 67 | 75 | 60 | 55 | 272 |
| PHILADELPHIA PHILLIES | 36 | 37 | 50 | 43 | 43 | 209 |
| PITTSBURGH PIRATES | 23 | 38 | 41 | 41 | 53 | 196 |
| ST. LOUIS CARDINALS | 27 | 55 | 58 | 52 | 58 | 250 |
| SAN DIEGO PADRES | 22 | 40 | 47 | 52 | 49 | 210 |
| SAN FRANCISCO GIANTS | 26 | 36 | 50 | 44 | 55 | 211 |
| | 430 | 676 | 836 | 804 | 7 22 | 3,468 |

## Magnitude Of The BARS Scouting

In the 3,783 games that the BARS System has scouted during the past five baseball seasons (1983-1987), an enormous amount of data has been collected. This data is the foundation for the accuracy of the hitting, fielding and pitching charts. A glimpse at a few of the statistical totals shows the magnitude of the BARS scouting effort.

During the past five seasons, over 15 million different items of information have been collected, filed in the BARS computer and used for generating the BARS reports.

Included in this total are 980,595 pitches to batters — 332,216 of which were strikes and 340,964 of which were balls. Overall, the BARS System has recorded 22,685 walks, 43,053 singles, 10,781 doubles, 1556 triples and 6,286 home runs

One thousand two hundred and thirty batters were hit by pitches; 2,434 pitch-outs were made; 302 balks were committed (that total will go up considerably after the 1988 season); and 996 wild pitches were made.

Once batters reached base, 21,609 throws were made to first base to keep the runner close. Runners stole second or third 8,019 times.

An interesting statistic kept by the BARS System is the inning in which pitchers are relieved. In each of the last five seasons, the BARS scouts have recorded the most pitching changes in the eighth inning. With the large number of games that have been scouted, the BARS figures for pitching changes are likely to be proportionately correct inning by inning for all games played during the last five years in the major leagues.

The following list shows the total number of pitching changes recorded by the BARS System.

| Inning | Number of Pitching Changes |
|:---:|:---:|
| 1 | 204 |
| 2 | 307 |
| 3 | 424 |
| 4 | 592 |
| 5 | 1019 |
| 6 | 1704 |
| 7 | 2700 |
| 8 | 3413 |
| 9 | 2054 |
| 10 | 283 |
| 11 | 111 |
| 12 | 67 |
| 13 | 29 |
| After 13 | 33 |

The large number of recorded strikes, balls, singles, doubles, etc. are representative of the totals in many different categories of information collected by the BARS System. Much of the information is directly used in the BARS reports, but some will not be used until the upcoming BARS Forecasting Report is finished.

The BARS Forecasting Report will utilize almost every item of information gathered over the years. The purpose of this report will be to forecast the final scores of games, using the vast amount of data the BARS System has gathered.

More will be written about the Forecasting Program in future BARS publications.

## *Personal Comments*

I'd like to thank all the hard-working employees who have been so dedicated to the BARS System over the years. I've been fortunate to work with individuals who have been committed to quality in every detail of their work. The BARS scouts, the computer operators, the secretaries and the programmers have done an excellent job.

My primary concern has always been to have the most accurate and reliable system possible. It's taken some expense and effort, but the results that we're having now — 90 percent accuracy in the fielding strategy and 65 to 75 percent accuracy in the pitching reports — make everything worthwhile. I could never have done everything alone. It's been a group effort, and I thank everyone for it.

The next chapter describes the process of recording information into the computer. We've developed specific, systematic procedures that assure accuracy. These procedures are described here so you can feel confident that the BARS System information is accurate from the time it is scouted to the time it is entered into the computer and generated into the hitting, fielding and pitching reports. We've gathered a lot of information over the past five years; we're looking forward to gathering a similar or even greater amount over the next five.

# Chapter Seventeen

# Recording The BARS System Information Into The Computer

As seen in the preceding chapter, which described the Scouting Report, a large amount of information is gathered for every game scouted by the BARS System. In fact, a large amount of information is gathered for every pitch of a scouted game.

It is crucial for this information to be entered accurately into the central BARS System computer, because it is the basis for all charts and analyses generated by the BARS System. To insure complete accuracy, guidelines have been established for the checking and re-checking of information, and for the systematic entering of information into the computer.

### Initial Checking of the Scouting Reports

When Scouting Reports are sent to the BARS System Computer Center, the games are first divided into two categories: American League games and National League games. Each team has a unique identifying number, and an ongoing total of Scouting Reports is kept for each team.

Attached to the Scouting Report is a batting lineup for each of the two teams that played. Every player in the lineup is checked to make sure that he is recorded correctly according to the BARS System Master Player File. The Master Player File lists all players in each league alpabetically, designating each player with a specific number that remains the same even when the player is traded to another team. Also checked is the actual number the player wears, whether he hits right-handed, left-handed or is a switch hitter; and whether he is a left-handed or right-handed pitcher.

After checking all players in the batting lineup against the Master Player File for the league, the Scouting Report is checked to make sure that the innings are in correct sequence and that there is a top and bottom for each inning. If the pages of the Scouting Report have not been numbered by the BARS System scout, they are numbered by the person checking the report.

This initial inspection, which takes approximately 20 minutes for each game, takes place before the Scouting Report is given to the computer operator who enters the data into the computer. The thoroughness of this checking process is the first step in assuring accuracy for every BARS System detail.

### Entry of the Information: A 60 Minute Procedure for Each Game

The Scouting Report, along with any changes or additions to The Master Player File, is then given to the BARS System data entry personnel. The information for each game scouted is entered on diskette, with six games per diskette.

Depending on the length of the game, it takes approximately 30 minutes to enter the pitch-by-pitch information. After one data entry operator has entered the information for a game, a second operator repeats the process, entering all information without reference to the work of the first operator. This second process takes another 30 minutes.

The two reports are then compared by computer. In the comparison, the smallest discrepancy or omission will be noted. If there is a variance of even a single numeral or letter, the computer will note it. The operators check and correct any errors before making a final record of the game. This attention to detail assures the accuracy required by the BARS System.

The first part of the record for each game is called The Header, which consists of the following: the date of the game, the stadium number (which is the same as the number for the home team), the field condition, the weather, the wind direction, the wind speed (miles per hour), the temperature, the time the game started, whether or not the game was a double-header, the opposing team's number, the attendance and the final score.

After The Header has been completed for a game, information is entered on a pitch-by-pitch basis starting with the top of the first inning. Entered for each pitch is a 'T' or a 'B' for top or bottom of an inning, the inning number, page number of the Scouting Report, the batter's actual number, the pitcher's actual number, whether the batter is a designated or pinch hitter, number of outs, runners-on-base situation, ball-and-strike count, type of pitch, location of pitch and whether the pitch was called a ball or a strike.

When a ball is hit, the following information is entered: the angle of the hit, the initial distance the ball travelled before striking the ground, the total distance the ball travelled before it was fielded, the position number of the fielder of the ball, the outcome of the hit (single, double, triple or home run), whether the hit was a sacrifice fly or sacrifice bunt, runners scored (using the runner's actual number), whether the hit resulted in an error (designating the position number of the fielder committing the error), the base to which the ball was thrown and the accuracy of the throw.

If a base is stolen on a pitch, the runner's actual number is recorded, along with the position (shortstop or second baseman) of the player covering second base.

## The Master File for Quick and Easy Access To Information

When the six games on each diskette are entered into the Master File, each game becomes a part of the permanent record of the BARS System. A separate Master File is kept for each baseball season. Records for players or teams can be drawn out of the computer for individual years or for the summation of all years.

## *Personal Comments*

I know that managers will say they don't care how a batter hits against all right-handed or left-handed pitchers. Managers will say they want to know how a batter hits against one particular pitcher — usually the pitcher he's facing that night.

The BARS Super Summary is right 90 percent of the time. I doubt that any information a manager has on how a batter hits against a certain pitcher will be accurate that often. We could have started charting individual hitters against individual pitchers, but we have had such success charting hitters against right- and left-handed pitchers that we will continue using that system until we get enough information to start charting hitters against individual pitchers.

At most, a batter faces a pitcher only four times in a game. Even that's unlikely, but for argument's sake, say it is four times in a game. And maybe the pitcher will start against the team four or five times in a year. That makes 16 to 20 times a hitter will face a particular pitcher in one year.

Taking that over five years of gathering records, at most a hitter will face a pitcher 80 or 100 times. That won't be enough to gather complete and reliable records. There will be a shortage or complete lack of information for certain types and locations of pitches. For instance, a batter might not have hit a low-outside fastball or low-outside slider in those at-bats.

That's why we're better off using information about how a hitter does against all right- or left-handed pitchers. For some hitters we have 50, a 100, even 200 recorded instances in which they hit a certain type and location of pitch. That ensures very high accuracy in the batting averages and fielding strategy. Our BARS fielding strategy is running at 90 percent accuracy now, and as we gather more information, we should be able to get even higher percentages of accuracy.

# Chapter Eighteen

# The Hitters, Continued

This chapter is a continuation of Chapter Two, in which the BARS System Super Summaries for many of the top hitters in the game were examined. In this chapter, the batting charts of other top hitters are discussed.

The slider and change-up charts are shown only when specific mention is made to them. In many instances, there is less information in the slider and change-up charts, and only the fastball and curve charts are shown.

## Super Summary For Tony Gwynn

Tony Gwynn, left-handed hitter for the San Diego Padres, hits extremely well against both left- and right-handed pitchers.

First, against right-handers:

**Tony Gwynn    Left-Handed Hitter**
**Against All Right-Handed Pitchers All Teams**
**Overall Batting Average Is .360**

Fastball Average .388                    Curve Average .393

| | Outside | Middle | Inside | Outside | Middle | Inside |
|---|---|---|---|---|---|---|
| High | 19/ 578 / 11 | 39/ 538 / 21 | 24/ 291 / 7 | 1/ 1000/ 1 | 4/ 500 / 2 | 3/ 666 / 2 |
| Med | 58/ 327 / 19 | 23/ 478 / 11 | 48/ 270 / 13 | 11/ 181 / 2 | 4/ 500 / 2 | 11/ 363 / 4 |
| Low | 13/ 384 / 5 | 35/ 457 / 16 | 42/ 333 / 14 | 5/ 200 / 1 | 14/ 428 / 6 | 8/ 500 / 4 |

Slide Average .390

| | Outside | Middle | Inside |
|---|---|---|---|
| High | 1 / 0 / 0 | 3 / 666 / 2 | 5 / 400 / 2 |
| Med | 0 / 0 / 0 | 1 / 0 / 0 | 9 / 222 / 2 |
| Low | 1 / 1000 / 1 | 7 / 571 / 4 | 14 / 357 / 5 |

Change-Up Average .354

| | Outside | Middle | Inside |
|---|---|---|---|
| High | 1 / 1000 / 1 | 5 / 600 / 3 | 1 / 0 / 0 |
| Med | 3 / 333 / 1 | 2 / 1000 / 2 | 2 / 500 / 1 |
| Low | 4 / 250 / 1 | 8 / 0 / 0 | 5 / 400 / 2 |

Against right-handed pitchers Gwynn does not have a weak fastball location. The only location that comes close to being weak is medium-high inside (.270). He hits medium-high outside fastballs very much like Boggs and Brett.

MEDIUM-HIGH OUTSIDE FASTBALLS

BATTING AVERAGE .327
> PLAY

| | |
|---|---|
| LEFTFIELDER | Deep and shifted toward the left field line |
| CENTERFIELDER | Medium-deep in straightaway center field |
| RIGHTFIELDER | Medium-deep in straightaway right field |
| SHORTSTOP | Up middle (shifted toward second base) |
| SECOND | Shifted toward first base |

Gwynn has several weak curve locations (medium-high outside and low-outside), but the other curve locations are solid. He hits both low and high curves extremely well. He tends to pull curveballs slightly more than he does fastballs.

LOW-OVER-THE-MIDDLE CURVEBALLS

BATTING AVERAGE .428
> PLAY

| | |
|---|---|
| LEFTFIELDER | Medium-deep in straightaway left field |
| CENTERFIELDER | Deep and shifted toward right field |
| RIGHTFIELDER | Deep in straightaway right field |
| SHORTSTOP | Up middle (shifted toward second base) |
| SECOND | Shifted toward first base |

Gwynn hits sliders and change-ups very well overall, although he has weak locations in both charts.

Against right-handed pitchers, Gwynn hits considerably better when he is ahead in the count.

**Tony Gwynn   Left-Handed Hitter**
**Against Right-Handed Pitchers When Ahead In The Count**
**Batting Average Is .398**

Fastball Average .412

|  | Outside | Middle | Inside |
|---|---|---|---|
| High | 10 / 700 / 7 | 21 / 619 / 13 | 8 / 250 / 2 |
| Med | 28 / 285 / 8 | 12 / 416 / 5 | 24 / 333 / 8 |
| Low | 9 / 444 / 4 | 18 / 500 / 9 | 18 / 277 / 5 |

Curve Average .437

|  | Outside | Middle | Inside |
|---|---|---|---|
| High | 0 / 0 / 0 | 1 / 1000 / 1 | 0 / 0 / 0 |
| Med | 2 / 0 / 0 | 1 / 0 / 0 | 3 / 333 / 1 |
| Low | 1 / 0 / 0 | 5 / 600 / 3 | 3 / 666 / 2 |

**Tony Gwynn   Left-Handed Hitter**
**Against Right-Handed Pitchers When Behind In The Count**
**Batting Average Is .273**

Fastball Average .288

|  | Outside | Middle | Inside |
|---|---|---|---|
| High | 5 / 600 / 3 | 3 / 0 / 0 | 10 / 300 / 3 |
| Med | 9 / 444 / 4 | 2 / 0 / 0 | 7 / 0 / 0 |
| Low | 0 / 0 / 0 | 11 / 454 / 5 | 5 / 0 / 0 |

Curve Average .363

|  | Outside | Middle | Inside |
|---|---|---|---|
| High | 1 / 1000 / 1 | 1 / 0 / 0 | 1 / 1000 / 1 |
| Med | 3 / 0 / 0 | 2 / 500 / 1 | 2 / 500 / 1 |
| Low | 2 / 0 / 0 | 8 / 375 / 3 | 2 / 500 / 1 |

Gwynn's fastball average jumps when he is ahead in the count. His .412 overall fastball average consists of solid averages in every fastball location. His high-outside and high-over-the-middle fastball locations are exceptional. These averages (.700 and .619) will undoubtedly fall as more instances are recorded.

Gwynn slaps high-over-the-middle fastballs down the left field line and pulls them to deep right center when he is ahead in the count.

HIGH-OVER-THE-MIDDLE FASTBALLS
(THROWN TO GWYNN WHEN HE IS AHEAD IN THE COUNT)

BATTING AVERAGE .619
  *PLAY*
LEFTFIELDER        Medium-deep and shifted toward center field
CENTERFIELDER      Deep and shifted toward right field
RIGHTFIELDER       Deep in straightaway right field
SHORTSTOP          Up middle (shifted toward second base)
SECOND             Normal position

Gwynn hits medium-high inside fastballs to all fields.

MEDIUM-HIGH INSIDE FASTBALLS
(THROWN TO GWYNN WHEN HE IS AHEAD IN THE COUNT)

BATTING AVERAGE .333
  *PLAY*
LEFTFIELDER        Medium-deep and shifted toward center field
CENTERFIELDER      Deep and shifted toward left field
RIGHTFIELDER       Deep and shifted toward the right field line
SHORTSTOP          Up middle (shifted toward second base)
SECOND             Normal position

When he is behind in the count, Gwynn hits medium-high inside fastballs much differently.

MEDIUM-HIGH INSIDE FASTBALLS
(THROWN TO GWYNN WHEN HE IS BEHIND IN THE COUNT)

BATTING AVERAGE .000
  *PLAY*
LEFTFIELDER        Deep and shifted toward the left field line
CENTERFIELDER      Medium-deep in straightaway center field
RIGHTFIELDER       No instances recorded
SHORTSTOP          Normal position
SECOND             Normal position

## Gwynn Against Left-Handed Pitchers

Gwynn's fastball averages are also high against left-handed pitchers, but his curve averages are low.

### Tony Gwynn    Left-Handed Hitter
### Against All Left-Handed Pitchers All Teams
### Overall Batting Average Is .326

Fastball Average .367                    Curve Average .166

| | Outside | Middle | Inside | Outside | Middle | Inside |
|---|---|---|---|---|---|---|
| High | 1/ 0 / 0 | 9/ 444 / 4 | 12/ 416 / 5 | 0/ 0 / 0 | 0/ 0 / 0 | 0/ 0 / 0 |
| Med | 15/ 400 / 6 | 2/ 500 / 1 | 20/ 250 / 5 | 0/ 0 / 0 | 3/ 333 / 1 | 1/ 0 / 0 |
| Low | 7/ 285 / 2 | 19/ 315 / 6 | 13/ 538 / 7 | 5/ 0 / 0 | 8/ 250 / 2 | 1/ 0 / 0 |

Against lefties, Gwynn tends to hit outside fastballs on the ground to the right side of the infield.

MEDIUM-HIGH OUTSIDE FASTBALLS
(THROWN TO GWYNN BY LEFT-HANDED PITCHERS)

BATTING AVERAGE .400
*PLAY*
LEFTFIELDER          No instances recorded
CENTERFIELDER        Medium-deep in straightaway center field
RIGHTFIELDER         No instances recorded
SHORTSTOP            Up middle (shifted toward second base)
SECOND               Shifted toward first base

He tends to hit high-inside fastballs thrown by left-handers deep and to the opposite field.

HIGH-INSIDE FASTBALLS
(THROWN TO GWYNN BY LEFT-HANDED PITCHERS)

BATTING AVERAGE .416
*PLAY*
LEFTFIELDER          Medium-deep in straightaway left field
CENTERFIELDER        Deep and shifted toward left field
RIGHTFIELDER         Deep and shifted toward center field
SHORTSTOP            Shifted toward third base
SECOND               Normal position

Gwynn hits about equally well when ahead and when behind-in-the-count against left-handed pitchers. His ahead and behind in the count charts are not shown.

## Super Summary For Jack Clark

Jack Clark, right-handed hitter for the New York Yankees, hits considerably better overall against left-handed pitchers. He is a pull hitter who tends to hit very few types and locations of pitches to the opposite field.

First, against right-handed pitchers:

### Jack Clark    Right-Handed Hitter
### Against All Right-Handed Pitchers All Teams
### Overall Batting Average Is .277

Fastball Average .312

| | Inside | Middle | Outside |
|---|---|---|---|
| High | 16/ 125 / 2 | 29/ 275 / 8 | 15/ 333 / 5 |
| Med | 17/ 411 / 7 | 16/ 625 / 10 | 49/ 367 / 18 |
| Low | 6/ 0 / 0 | 36/ 333 / 12 | 21/ 95 / 2 |

Curve Average .200

| | Inside | Middle | Outside |
|---|---|---|---|
| High | 1/ 0 / 0 | 2/ 0 / 0 | 1/ 0 / 0 |
| Med | 4/ 500 / 2 | 4/ 0 / 0 | 11/ 272 / 3 |
| Low | 2/ 0 / 0 | 8/ 250 / 2 | 17/ 176 / 3 |

Slider Average .358

| | Inside | Middle | Outside |
|---|---|---|---|
| High | 0/ 0 / 0 | 2/ 0 / 0 | 3/ 666 / 2 |
| Med | 1/ 0 / 0 | 1/ 1000 / 1 | 15/ 400 / 6 |
| Low | 0/ 0 / 0 | 4/ 250 / 1 | 13/ 307 / 4 |

Change-Up Average .235

| | Inide | Middle | Outside |
|---|---|---|---|
| High | 0/ 0 / 0 | 0/ 0 / 0 | 0/ 0 / 0 |
| Med | 2/ 0 / 0 | 0/ 0 / 0 | 2/ 500 / 1 |
| Low | 0/ 0 / 0 | 4/ 0 / 0 | 9/ 333 / 3 |

Notice Clark's weaknesses against low-inside and low-outside fastballs. These weaknesses extend into the same curveball locations.

Clark hits waist-high fastballs extremely well. He has difficulty with high-inside fastballs.

Clark's overall curve grid indicates that right-handed pitchers could find an edge by throwing him outside curveballs. But the opposite is true with outside sliders: he hits them very well. Notice that Clark also has trouble with low curves.

As would be expected of a hitter who looks for fastballs, Clark hits much better when ahead in the count. When ahead against right-handed pitchers his average is over 100 points higher than when behind.

### Jack Clark    Right-Handed Hitter
### Against All Right-Handed Pitchers When Ahead In The Count
### Batting Average Is .421

Fastball Average .506          Curve Average .266

| | Inside | Middle | Outside | Inside | Middle | Outside |
|---|---|---|---|---|---|---|
| High | 2/ 500 / 1 | 8/ 500 / 4 | 3/ 333 / 1 | 0/ 0 / 0 | 1/ 0 / 0 | 0/ 0 / 0 |
| Med | 8/ 750 / 6 | 9/ 555 / 5 | 19/ 578 / 11 | 1/ 1000 / 1 | 2/ 0 / 0 | 3/ 333 / 1 |
| Low | 3/ 0 / 0 | 15/ 466 / 7 | 6/ 333 / 2 | 0/ 0 / 0 | 3/ 333 / 1 | 5/ 200 / 1 |

### Jack Clark    Right-Handed Hitter
### Against All Right-Handed Pitchers When Behind In The Count
### Batting Average Is .285

Fastball Average .268          Curve Average .363

| | Inside | Middle | Outside | Inside | Middle | Outside |
|---|---|---|---|---|---|---|
| High | 3/ 0 / 0 | 8/ 125 / 1 | 5/ 600 / 3 | 0/ 0 / 0 | 0/ 0 / 0 | 0/ 0 / 0 |
| Med | 1/ 0 / 0 | 3/ 1000 / 3 | 13/ 230 / 3 | 1/ 1000 / 1 | 1/ 0 / 0 | 5/ 400 / 2 |
| Low | 0/ 0 / 0 | 4/ 250 / 1 | 4/ 0 / 0 | 0/ 0 / 0 | 0/ 0 / 0 | 4/ 250 / 1 |

Notice that his fastball average rockets when he is ahead (when he can wait for the fastball), and that his curve average is much higher when he is behind.

When ahead in the count, Clark hits every fastball location well. A pitcher's best chance would be to keep fastballs low-inside, low-outside or high-outside.

When ahead, he hits the ball harder and pulls it more, as indicated by the suggested fielding positions for his medium-high outside locations.

MEDIUM-HIGH OUTSIDE FASTBALLS
(THROWN TO CLARK WHEN HE IS AHEAD IN THE COUNT)

BATTING AVERAGE .578
 *PLAY*
LEFTFIELDER   Deep in straightaway left field
CENTERFIELDER  Deep and shifted toward left field
RIGHTFIELDER   Deep and shifted toward center field
SHORTSTOP    Normal position
SECOND     No instances recorded

MEDIUM-HIGH OUTSIDE FASTBALLS
(THROWN TO CLARK WHEN HE IS BEHIND IN THE COUNT)

BATTING AVERAGE .230
 *PLAY*
LEFTFIELDER   Medium-deep in straightaway left field
CENTERFIELDER  Medium-deep in straightaway center field
RIGHTFIELDER   Deep in straightaway right field
SHORTSTOP    Normal position
SECOND     No instances recorded

**Clark Against Left-Handed Pitchers**

Against left-handed pitchers, Clark's overall average is .321. Against left-handers he hits fastballs and curves better than against right-handers.

**Jack Clark    Right-Handed Hitter**
**Against All Left-Handed Pitchers All Teams**
**Overall Batting Average Is .321**

Fastball Average .394                Curve Average .347

| | Inside | Middle | Outside | | Inside | Middle | Outside |
|---|---|---|---|---|---|---|---|
| High | 2/ 0 / 0 | 7/ 285 / 2 | 11/ 181 / 2 | | 0/ 0 / 0 | 2/ 500 / 1 | 4/ 250 / 1 |
| Med | 3/ 333 / 1 | 7/ 571 / 4 | 18/ 333 / 6 | | 1/ 1000 / 1 | 2/ 500 / 1 | 4/ 250 / 1 |
| Low | 1/ 0 / 0 | 15/ 533 / 8 | 12/ 583 / 7 | | 2/ 0 / 0 | 3/ 666 / 2 | 5/ 200 / 1 |

Notice how strongly he hits low pitches against left-handers. He has trouble with high-outside fastballs, but his other fastball locations are solid. Notice, in particular, his excellent .583 average against low-outside fastballs.

His curve percentages are strong throughout the locations, with the exception of low-outside and the few instance in the low-inside location.

Against left-handers, Clark pulls fastballs to all fields.

MEDIUM-HIGH OUTSIDE FASTBALLS
(THROWN BY LEFT-HANDED PITCHERS)

BATTING AVERAGE .333
　　PLAY
LEFTFIELDER　　　　Deep and shifted toward the left field line
CENTERFIELDER　　　Deep and shifted toward left field
RIGHTFIELDER　　　　Deep and shifted toward center field
SHORTSTOP　　　　　Shifted toward third base
SECOND　　　　　　　No instances recorded

Clark hits well both when ahead and behind in the count against left-handers. His fastball percentages when ahead are strong throughout.

### Jack Clark     Right-Handed Hitter
### Against Left-Handed Pitchers When Behind In The Count
### Batting Average Is .444

Fastball Average .666

|      | Inside | Middle | Outside |
|------|--------|--------|---------|
| High | 0 / 0 / 0 | 1 / 0 / 0 | 1 / 0 / 0 |
| Med  | 1 / 1000 / 1 | 1 / 1000 / 1 | 2 / 500 / 1 |
| Low  | 0 / 0 / 0 | 1 / 1000 / 1 | 2 / 1000 / 2 |

Curve Average .500

|      | Inside | Middle | Outside |
|------|--------|--------|---------|
| High | 0 / 0 / 0 | 0 / 0 / 0 | 0 / 0 / 0 |
| Med  | 1 / 1000 / 1 | 0 / 0 / 0 | 0 / 0 / 0 |
| Low  | 0 / 0 / 0 | 0 / 0 / 0 | 1 / 0 / 0 |

### Jack Clark     Right-Handed Hitter
### Against Left-Handed Pitchers When Ahead In The Count
### Batting Average Is .416

Fastball Average .548

|      | Inside | Middle | Outside |
|------|--------|--------|---------|
| High | 0 / 0 / 0 | 4 / 500 / 2 | 5 / 400 / 2 |
| Med  | 0 / 0 / 0 | 4 / 500 / 2 | 8 / 375 / 3 |
| Low  | 0 / 0 / 0 | 7 / 714 / 5 | 3 / 1000 / 3 |

Curve Average .250

|      | Inside | Middle | Outside |
|------|--------|--------|---------|
| High | 0 / 0 / 0 | 0 / 0 / 0 | 0 / 0 / 0 |
| Med  | 0 / 0 / 0 | 0 / 0 / 0 | 1 / 0 / 0 |
| Low  | 0 / 0 / 0 | 1 / 1000 / 1 | 2 / 0 / 0 |

Left-handed pitchers would do well to throw Clark at least an occasional inside fastball, because he is feasting on outside fastballs.

## Super Summary For Dale Murphy

Overall, Dale Murphy, right-handed hitting outfielder for the Atlanta Braves, hits just about as well against right-handed pitchers (.273) as against left-handed pitchers (.272).

### Dale Murphy    Right-Handed Hitter
### Against All Right-Handed Pitchers All Teams
### Overall Batting Average Is .273

Fastball Average .319

|      | Inside | Middle | Outside |
|------|--------|--------|---------|
| High | 16 / 62 / 1 | 47 / 340 / 16 | 31 / 258 / 8 |
| Med  | 76 / 302 / 23 | 60 / 366 / 22 | 118 / 347 / 41 |
| Low  | 35 / 257 / 9 | 126 / 365 / 46 | 67 / 268 / 18 |

Curve Average .228

|      | Inside | Middle | Outside |
|------|--------|--------|---------|
| High | 0 / 0 / 0 | 12 / 500 / 6 | 5 / 400 / 2 |
| Med  | 7 / 428 / 3 | 17 / 352 / 6 | 41 / 195 / 8 |
| Low  | 10 / 200 / 2 | 42 / 142 / 6 | 76 / 197 / 15 |

Slider Average .294

|      | Inside | Middle | Outside |
|------|--------|--------|---------|
| High | 1 / 0 / 0 | 8 / 375 / 3 | 2 / 1000 / 2 |
| Med  | 6 / 0 / 0 | 6 / 666 / 4 | 33 / 333 / 11 |
| Low  | 5 / 200 / 1 | 28 / 464 / 13 | 50 / 140 / 7 |

Change-Up Average .176

|      | Inside | Middle | Outside |
|------|--------|--------|---------|
| High | 1 / 0 / 0 | 2 / 500 / 1 | 0 / 0 / 0 |
| Med  | 2 / 0 / 0 | 2 / 500 / 1 | 8 / 250 / 2 |
| Low  | 0 / 0 / 0 | 10 / 0 / 0 | 9 / 222 / 2 |

### Dale Murphy    Right-Handed Hitter
### Against All Left-Handed Pitchers All Teams
### Overall Batting Average Is .272

Fastball Average .309

|      | Inside | Middle | Outside |
|------|--------|--------|---------|
| High | 4 / 0 / 0 | 20 / 300 / 6 | 20 / 200 / 4 |
| Med  | 21 / 190 / 4 | 18 / 388 / 7 | 52 / 480 / 25 |
| Low  | 15 / 200 / 3 | 36 / 277 / 10 | 40 / 275 / 11 |

Curve Average .206

|      | Inside | Middle | Outside |
|------|--------|--------|---------|
| High | 0 / 0 / 0 | 4 / 500 / 2 | 3 / 0 / 0 |
| Med  | 9 / 0 / 0 | 2 / 0 / 0 | 11 / 363 / 4 |
| Low  | 8 / 125 / 1 | 11 / 272 / 3 | 10 / 200 / 2 |

|  | Slider Average .319 | | | Change-Up Average .210 | | |
|---|---|---|---|---|---|---|
|  | Inside | Middle | Outside | Inside | Middle | Outside |
| High | 1/ **0**/0 | 2/ **0**/0 | 1/ **0**/0 | 0/ **0**/0 | 2/ **0**/0 | 3/ **333**/1 |
| Med | 9/ **333**/3 | 0/ **0**/0 | 6/ **666**/4 | 1/ **1000**/1 | 0/ **0**/0 | 12/ **416**/5 |
| Low | 9/ **111**/1 | 9/ **333**/3 | 10/ **400**/4 | 2/ **0**/0 | 5/ **200**/1 | 13/ **0**/0 |

Notice that Murphy is a fastball hitter. His total average against fastballs is much higher than against other types of pitches, but he does have trouble with high-inside fastballs against both right-handers and left-handers. Pitchers may be afraid to throw high-inside fastballs to the hard-hitting Murphy, but statistics show that they should challenge him high-inside.

Murphy has trouble with inside fastballs thrown by left-handed pitchers. He hits low-outside fastballs adequately and medium-high outside very strongly. His .480 against medium-high outside fastballs thrown by left-handers is very strong, considering the high number of recorded instances (52).

Murphy hits medium-high outside fastballs to center field against both left- and right-handers.

MEDIUM-HIGH OUTSIDE FASTBALLS
(THROWN TO MURPHY BY RIGHT-HANDED PITCHERS)

BATTING AVERAGE .347
    PLAY
LEFTFIELDER      Deep and shifted toward center field
CENTERFIELDER      Deep in straightaway center field
RIGHTFIELDER      Deep and shifted toward center field
SHORTSTOP      Normal position
SECOND      Normal position

MEDIUM-HIGH OUTSIDE FASTBALLS
(THROWN TO MURPHY BY LEFT-HANDED PITCHERS)

BATTING AVERAGE .480
*PLAY*
LEFTFIELDER       Medium-deep in straightaway left field
CENTERFIELDER     Deep in straightaway center field
RIGHTFIELDER      Deep and shifted toward center field
SHORTSTOP         Shifted toward third base
SECOND            Normal position

Murphy hits medium-high inside fastballs well against right-handers (.302) but has difficulty with this location against left-handers (.190). He tends to pull these pitches more against right-handers.

MEDIUM-HIGH INSIDE FASTBALLS
(THROWN TO MURPHY BY RIGHT-HANDED PITCHERS)

BATTING AVERAGE .302
*PLAY*
LEFTFIELDER       Deep and shifted toward the left field line
CENTERFIELDER     Medium-deep and shifted toward left field
RIGHTFIELDER      Medium-deep and shifted toward center field
SHORTSTOP         Normal position
SECOND            Shifted toward first base

MEDIUM-HIGH INSIDE FASTBALLS
(THROWN TO MURPHY BY LEFT-HANDED PITCHERS)

BATTING AVERAGE .190
*PLAY*
LEFTFIELDER       Medium-deep in straightaway left field
CENTERFIELDER     Deep in straightaway center field
RIGHTFIELDER      Deep and shifted toward the right field line
SHORTSTOP         Shifted toward third base
SECOND            Normal position

Murphy hits curves for low averages against both right- and left-handers. In general he has trouble with low curves. His difficulty against low curves thrown by right-handers is apparent. In addition, the .195 average in Murphy's medium-high outside curve location is a weakness.

Murphy hits sliders well. He has an overall slider average of .294 against right-handed pitchers in spite of a very low .140 in the low-outside slider location. He pulls low-outside sliders deep to all fields. Fielders obviously play Murphy to pull the ball, because these hits are mostly fly-ball outs.

Murphy has trouble with change-ups in general and low change-ups in particular. He strikes out often on change-ups. When he hits them, he mostly pops up to medium-deep right center and right field toward the line.

Against right-handed pitchers, Murphy hits better when ahead in the count.

### Dale Murphy    Right-Handed Hitter
### Against Right-Handed Pitchers When Ahead In The Count
### Batting Average Is .350

**Fastball Average .400**

|       | Inside | Middle | Outside |
|-------|--------|--------|---------|
| High  | 3 / 0 / 0 | 17 / 647 / 11 | 10 / 500 / 5 |
| Med   | 32 / 406 / 13 | 28 / 392 / 11 | 56 / 392 / 22 |
| Low   | 16 / 312 / 5 | 63 / 365 / 23 | 22 / 409 / 9 |

**Curve Average .352**

|       | Inside | Middle | Outside |
|-------|--------|--------|---------|
| High  | 0 / 0 / 0 | 6 / 500 / 3 | 4 / 250 / 1 |
| Med   | 2 / 1000 / 2 | 6 / 333 / 2 | 9 / 333 / 3 |
| Low   | 2 / 500 / 1 | 5 / 0 / 0 | 17 / 352 / 6 |

**Slider Average .312**

|       | Inside | Middle | Outside |
|-------|--------|--------|---------|
| High  | 0 / 0 / 0 | 1 / 0 / 0 | 1 / 1000 / 1 |
| Med   | 3 / 0 / 0 | 2 / 0 / 0 | 12 / 333 / 4 |
| Low   | 1 / 0 / 0 | 16 / 500 / 8 | 12 / 166 / 2 |

**Change-Up Average .000**

|       | Inside | Middle | Outside |
|-------|--------|--------|---------|
| High  | 0 / 0 / 0 | 1 / 0 / 0 | 0 / 0 / 0 |
| Med   | 0 / 0 / 0 | 1 / 0 / 0 | 0 / 0 / 0 |
| Low   | 0 / 0 / 0 | 3 / 0 / 0 | 2 / 0 / 0 |

## Dale Murphy    Right-Handed Hitter
## Against Right-Handed Pitchers When Behind In The Count
## Batting Average Is .317

### Fastball Average .345

|       | Inside | Middle | Outside |
|-------|--------|--------|---------|
| High  | 1 / 1000 / 1 | 12 / 250 / 3 | 6 / 166 / 1 |
| Med   | 18 / 333 / 6 | 13 / 384 / 5 | 23 / 347 / 8 |
| Low   | 4 / 0 / 0 | 17 / 529 / 9 | 13 / 307 / 4 |

### Curve Average .294

|       | Inside | Middle | Outside |
|-------|--------|--------|---------|
| High  | 0 / 0 / 0 | 2 / 0 / 0 | 0 / 0 / 0 |
| Med   | 0 / 0 / 0 | 7 / 571 / 4 | 15 / 266 / 4 |
| Low   | 2 / 0 / 0 | 8 / 375 / 3 | 17 / 235 / 4 |

### Slider Average .434

|       | Inside | Middle | Outside |
|-------|--------|--------|---------|
| High  | 0 / 0 / 0 | 2 / 1000 / 2 | 0 / 0 / 0 |
| Med   | 0 / 0 / 0 | 2 / 1000 / 2 | 5 / 600 / 3 |
| Low   | 1 / 1000 / 1 | 5 / 400 / 2 | 8 / 0 / 0 |

### Change-Up Average .400

|       | Inside | Middle | Outside |
|-------|--------|--------|---------|
| High  | 0 / 0 / 0 | 0 / 0 / 0 | 0 / 0 / 0 |
| Med   | 1 / 0 / 0 | 0 / 0 / 0 | 3 / 666 / 2 |
| Low   | 0 / 0 / 0 | 1 / 0 / 0 | 0 / 0 / 0 |

Murphy hits fastballs extremely well when ahead in the count. With the exception of the high-inside location, which has few recorded instances, he has no weak locations. His .647 average in the high-over-the-middle fastball location when ahead is superb. His averages are exceptional in the medium-high fastball locations when ahead in the count.

The ahead and behind in the count charts shown above are interesting from another standpoint. They show that Murphy, who is a excellent fastball hitter, is thrown many more fastballs than any other type of pitch, even when he is behind in the count.

The total of the recorded number of instances in the charts shows that when behind in the count, Murphy ended 97 at-bats by fastballs, 51 by curves, 23 by sliders and five by change-ups. When ahead, he ended 247 by fastballs, 51 by curves, 48 by sliders and seven by change-ups.

Murphy's ahead and behind in the count charts against left-handed pitchers are similar overall and are not shown.

## Super Summary For Kent Hrbek

Kent Hrbek, left-handed hitter for the Minnesota Twins, hits better against right-handed pitchers.

### Kent Hrbek     Left-Handed Hitter
### Against All Right-Handed Pitchers All Teams
### Overall Batting Average Is .273

Fastball Average .297

| | Outside | Middle | Inside |
|---|---|---|---|
| High | 19 / 263 / 5 | 28 / 392 / 11 | 3 / 0 / 0 |
| Med | 71 / 380 / 27 | 22 / 500 / 11 | 33 / 212 / 7 |
| Low | 19 / 210 / 4 | 36 / 166 / 6 | 14 / 142 / 2 |

Curve Average .255

| | Outside | Middle | Inside |
|---|---|---|---|
| High | 3 / 0 / 0 | 5 / 600 / 3 | 0 / 0 / 0 |
| Med | 9 / 222 / 2 | 6 / 833 / 5 | 5 / 200 / 1 |
| Low | 5 / 0 / 0 | 6 / 166 / 1 | 8 / 0 / 0 |

Slider Average .210

| | Outside | Middle | Inside |
|---|---|---|---|
| High | 0 / 0 / 0 | 1 / 0 / 0 | 1 / 0 / 0 |
| Med | 4 / 500 / 2 | 0 / 0 / 0 | 2 / 500 / 1 |
| Low | 2 / 0 / 0 | 3 / 0 / 0 | 6 / 166 / 1 |

Change-Up Average .233

| | Outside | Middle | Inside |
|---|---|---|---|
| High | 3 / 0 / 0 | 5 / 0 / 0 | 0 / 0 / 0 |
| Med | 7 / 428 / 3 | 0 / 0 / 0 | 2 / 500 / 1 |
| Low | 6 / 166 / 1 | 4 / 250 / 1 | 3 / 333 / 1 |

Hrbek has fine averages in many locations. His .380 in the medium-high outside fastball location and his .500 in medium-over-the-middle are very strong. He has weaknesses against low fastballs and inside fastballs.

Hrbek, for all his power, is not a pull hitter.

MEDIUM-HIGH OUTSIDE FASTBALLS

BATTING AVERAGE .380
   *PLAY*
| | |
|---|---|
| LEFTFIELDER | Deep in straightaway left field |
| CENTERFIELDER | Deep in straightaway center field |
| RIGHTFIELDER | Deep in straightaway right field |
| SHORTSTOP | Up middle (shifted toward second base) |
| SECOND | Normal position |

In the high-over-the-middle location, in which he hits .392, he tends to hit straightaway to left and center, and to pull the ball deep down the right field line.

HIGH-OVER-THE-MIDDLE FASTBALLS

BATTING AVERAGE .392
   *PLAY*
| | |
|---|---|
| LEFTFIELDER | Deep in straightaway left field |
| CENTERFIELDER | Medium-deep in straightaway center field |
| RIGHTFIELDER | Deep and shifted toward the right field line |
| SHORTSTOP | Up middle (shifted toward second base) |
| SECOND | Shifted toward first base |

Hrbek has trouble with all low curves and sliders. He tends to pop them up to center field and right field or to ground out to the right side of the infield. Hrbek hits better against right-handers when he is ahead in the count.

**Kent Hrbek    Left-Handed Hitter**
**Against Right-Handed Pitchers When Behind In The Count**
**Batting Average Is .256**

Fastball Average .186          Curve Average .466

| | Outside | Middle | Inside | Outside | Middle | Inside |
|---|---|---|---|---|---|---|
| High | 9 / **0** / 0 | 9 / **111** / 1 | 1 / **0** / 0 | 1 / **0** / 0 | 2 / **1000** / 2 | 0 / **0** / 0 |
| Med | 13 / **538** / 7 | 0 / **0** / 0 | 4 / **0** / 0 | 5 / **200** / 1 | 3 / **1000** / 3 | 2 / **0** / 0 |
| Low | 1 / **0** / 0 | 3 / **0** / 0 | 3 / **0** / 0 | 0 / **0** / 0 | 2 / **500** / 1 | 0 / **0** / 0 |

## Kent Hrbek    Left-Handed Hitter
### Against Right-Handed Pitchers When Ahead In The Count
### Batting Average Is .333

**Fastball Average .363**

|  | Outside | Middle | Inside |
|------|---------|--------|--------|
| High | 4 / 500 / 2 | 11 / 727 / 8 | 1 / 0 / 0 |
| Med | 35 / 428 / 15 | 14 / 500 / 7 | 16 / 312 / 5 |
| Low | 12 / 250 / 3 | 23 / 130 / 3 | 5 / 200 / 1 |

**Curve Average .000**

|  | Outside | Middle | Inside |
|------|---------|--------|--------|
| High | 0 / 0 / 0 | 1 / 0 / 0 | 0 / 0 / 0 |
| Med | 2 / 0 / 0 | 0 / 0 / 0 | 1 / 0 / 0 |
| Low | 1 / 0 / 0 | 3 / 0 / 0 | 2 / 0 / 0 |

When pitchers keep their fastballs to Hrbek low, they get him out. Notice how well he hits high and medium-high fastballs when ahead in the count. But even when ahead in the count he has trouble with low fastballs.

Hrbek's ahead in the count chart is even more interesting than Murphy's in regard to the large percentage of fastballs thrown. The totaled recorded instances show that Hrbek finished at-bats on 121 fastballs and only 10 curves.

## Hrbek Against Left-Handed Pitchers

Against left-handed pitchers, Hrbek hits fastballs well but has great difficulty with breaking pitches.

**Kent Hrbek    Left-Handed Hitter**
**Against All Left-Handed Pitchers All Teams**
**Overall Batting Average Is .230**

Fastball Average .324          Curve Average .093

| | Outside | Middle | Inside | Outside | Middle | Inside |
|---|---|---|---|---|---|---|
| High | 4/ 250 /1 | 11/ 272 /3 | 3/ 333 /1 | 1/ 0 /0 | 3/ 333 /1 | 2/ 0 /0 |
| Med | 18/ 388 /7 | 7/ 714 /5 | 19/ 315 /6 | 8/ 250 /2 | 1/ 0 /0 | 9/ 111 /1 |
| Low | 12/ 83 /1 | 17/ 294 /5 | 17/ 352 /6 | 14/ 0 /0 | 3/ 0 /0 | 2/ 0 /0 |

The .083 average in his low-outside fastball location represents the only weakness Hrbek has against fastballs thrown by left-handers.  He hits solidly across the medium-high locations and adequately in the high locations.

Hrbek's curve chart against left-handed pitchers is almost a complete wash-out. He does not have a recorded hit in any low location, and his Super Summary fielding strategy shows that he seldom gets these pitches out of the infield.

When ahead in the count against lefties, he hits fastballs very well, even in the low locations.

**Kent Hrbek    Left-Handed Hitter**
**Against Left-Handed Pitchers When Ahead In The Count**
**Batting Average Is .320**

Fastball Average .384          Curve Average .142

| | Outside | Middle | Inside | Outside | Middle | Inside |
|---|---|---|---|---|---|---|
| High | 2/ 500 /1 | 4/ 250 /1 | 1/ 0 /0 | 0/ 0 /0 | 2/ 500 /1 | 0/ 0 /0 |
| Med | 6/ 500 /3 | 5/ 600 /3 | 10/ 400 /4 | 3/ 333 /1 | 0/ 0 /0 | 3/ 0 /0 |
| Low | 4/ 250 /1 | 12/ 333 /4 | 8/ 375 /3 | 3/ 0 /0 | 2/ 0 /0 | 1/ 0 /0 |

### Kent Hrbek    Left-Handed Hitter
### Against Left-Handed Pitchers When Behind In The Count
### Batting Average Is .176

Fastball Average .315

| | Outside | Middle | Inside |
|---|---|---|---|
| High | 0 / 0 / 0 | 3 / 0 / 0 | 1 / 0 / 0 |
| Med | 7 / 428 / 3 | 1 / 1000 / 1 | 2 / 500 / 1 |
| Low | 2 / 0 / 0 | 2 / 500 / 1 | 1 / 0 / 0 |

Curve Average .000

| | Outside | Middle | Inside |
|---|---|---|---|
| High | 1 / 0 / 0 | 1 / 0 / 0 | 0 / 0 / 0 |
| Med | 1 / 0 / 0 | 0 / 0 / 0 | 2 / 0 / 0 |
| Low | 6 / 0 / 0 | 0 / 0 / 0 | 0 / 0 / 0 |

## Super Summary for Pete Rose

Pete Rose, switch-hitter for the Cincinnati Reds, has not played much during the last few years. Therefore, there is less BARS System information available on him than many other players scouted by the BARS System over the last five seasons.

Nonetheless, Rose has had such a dramatic and long-reaching effect on the game that his Super Summary reports are included here. He is a sure Hall-of-Famer and deserves a place in any book on baseball.

Batting left-handed against right-handed pitchers, Rose's overall average of .245 reflects the averages of his last few years, which were considerably lower than the consistent .300 averages of his prime.

### Pete Rose    Batting Left-Handed
### Against All Right-Handed Pitchers All Teams
### Overall Batting Average Is .245

Fastball Average .250

| | Outside | Middle | Inside |
|---|---|---|---|
| High | 12 / 166 / 2 | 33 / 303 / 10 | 7 / 285 / 2 |
| Med | 33 / 242 / 8 | 21 / 190 / 4 | 44 / 227 / 10 |
| Low | 9 / 111 / 1 | 41 / 243 / 10 | 24 / 375 / 9 |

Curve Average .212

| | Outside | Middle | Inside |
|---|---|---|---|
| High | 0 / 0 / 0 | 4 / 250 / 1 | 2 / 0 / 0 |
| Med | 7 / 285 / 2 | 0 / 0 / 0 | 5 / 0 / 0 |
| Low | 5 / 0 / 0 | 9 / 444 / 4 | 1 / 0 / 0 |

Notice Rose's low average against low-outside fastballs. In general, he had trouble his last years with outside pitches. His low-inside fastball average, however, was very strong. Rose went to left field with outside fastballs.

MEDIUM-HIGH OUTSIDE FASTBALLS

BATTING AVERAGE .242
*PLAY*

| | |
|---|---|
| LEFTFIELDER | Deep in straightaway left field |
| CENTERFIELDER | Deep and shifted toward left field |
| RIGHTFIELDER | No instances recorded |
| SHORTSTOP | Up middle (shifted toward second base) |
| SECOND | Normal position |

He hit medium-high inside fastballs straightaway.

MEDIUM-HIGH INSIDE FASTBALLS

BATTING AVERAGE .227
*PLAY*

| | |
|---|---|
| LEFTFIELDER | Medium-deep in straightaway left field |
| CENTERFIELDER | Medium-deep in straightaway center field |
| RIGHTFIELDER | Deep and shifted toward center field |
| SHORTSTOP | Up middle (shifted toward second base) |
| SECOND | Shifted toward first base |

Rose's low medium-over-the-middle fastball average (.190) indicates the struggles of the last few years of his career.

The batting charts on the next page show that Rose hit better when behind in the count.

## Pete Rose     Batting Left-Handed
### Against Right-Handed Pitchers When Ahead In The Count
### Batting Average Is .262

Fastball Average .236

|  | Outside | Middle | Inside |
|---|---|---|---|
| **High** | 6 / 166 / 1 | 20 / 200 / 4 | 5 / 400 / 2 |
| **Med** | 18 / 333 / 6 | 12 / 83 / 1 | 28 / 178 / 5 |
| **Low** | 2 / 500 / 1 | 19 / 157 / 3 | 17 / 411 / 7 |

Curve Average .333

|  | Outside | Middle | Inside |
|---|---|---|---|
| **High** | 0 / 0 / 0 | 0 / 0 / 0 | 0 / 0 / 0 |
| **Med** | 1 / 1000 / 1 | 0 / 0 / 0 | 1 / 0 / 0 |
| **Low** | 0 / 0 / 0 | 1 / 0 / 0 | 0 / 0 / 0 |

## Pete Rose     Batting Left-Handed
### Against Right-Handed Pitchers When Behind In The Count
### Batting Average Is .311

Fastball Average .464

|  | Outside | Middle | Inside |
|---|---|---|---|
| **High** | 0 / 0 / 0 | 5 / 200 / 1 | 0 / 0 / 0 |
| **Med** | 4 / 250 / 1 | 4 / 500 / 2 | 5 / 600 / 3 |
| **Low** | 1 / 0 / 0 | 7 / 714 / 5 | 2 / 500 / 1 |

Curve Average .222

|  | Outside | Middle | Inside |
|---|---|---|---|
| **High** | 0 / 0 / 0 | 2 / 0 / 0 | 2 / 0 / 0 |
| **Med** | 5 / 200 / 1 | 0 / 0 / 0 | 2 / 0 / 0 |
| **Low** | 2 / 0 / 0 | 5 / 600 / 3 | 0 / 0 / 0 |

Against left-handers, Rose (batting right-handed) hit for a first-rate overall average of .355.

## Pete Rose    Batting Right-Handed
### Against All Left-Handed Pitchers All Teams
### Overall Batting Average Is .355

Fastball Average .424                    Curve Average .200

| | Inside | Middle | Outside | Inside | Middle | Outside |
|---|---|---|---|---|---|---|
| High | 1000 / 1<br>1 | 333 / 3<br>1 | 1000 / 1<br>1 | 0 / 0<br>0 | 0 / 1<br>0 | 0 / 0<br>0 |
| Med | 500 / 4<br>2 | 333 / 3<br>1 | 500 / 8<br>4 | 0 / 1<br>0 | 0 / 0<br>0 | 0 / 0<br>0 |
| Low | 333 / 3<br>1 | 333 / 6<br>2 | 250 / 4<br>1 | 0 / 1<br>0 | 1000 / 1<br>1 | 0 / 1<br>0 |

Rose hit fastballs solidly in all locations. It would have been fascinating to study Rose's Super Summary for his prime years, when he was playing every day and more information could have been recorded.

## Super Summary For Reggie Jackson

Like Pete Rose, Reggie Jackson's career slowed down for several years before his retirement, and the BARS System, which has actively gathered information for five years, does not have a great deal of information about him. But like Rose, Jackson is a sure Hall-of-Famer and a great personality in the game. For that reason his BARS System Super Summary Charts are reported.

Jackson is a left-handed hitter who had a slightly higher average against left-handed pitchers.

The following page shows Jackson's batting charts against right-handed pitchers:

**Reggie Jackson    Left-Handed Hitter**
**Against All Right-Handed Pitchers All Teams**
**Overall Batting Average Is .198**

Fastball Average .245

|  | Outside | Middle | Inside |
|---|---|---|---|
| High | 12/<br>166 / 2 | 23/<br>86 / 2 | 7/<br>142 / 1 |
| Med | 76/<br>197 / 15 | 19/<br>315 / 6 | 34/<br>235 / 8 |
| Low | 16/<br>0 / 0 | 38/<br>421 / 16 | 23/<br>478 / 11 |

Curve Average .121

|  | Outside | Middle | Inside |
|---|---|---|---|
| High | 1/<br>0 / 0 | 1/<br>0 / 0 | 1/<br>0 / 0 |
| Med | 5/<br>200 / 1 | 4/<br>500 / 2 | 3/<br>333 / 1 |
| Low | 2/<br>0 / 0 | 11/<br>0 / 0 | 5/<br>0 / 0 |

Slider Average .047

|  | Outside | Middle | Inside |
|---|---|---|---|
| High | 0/<br>0 / 0 | 2/<br>0 / 0 | 0/<br>0 / 0 |
| Med | 2/<br>0 / 0 | 0/<br>0 / 0 | 7/<br>0 / 0 |
| Low | 2/<br>500 / 1 | 3/<br>0 / 0 | 5/<br>0 / 0 |

Change-Up Average .166

|  | Outside | Middle | Inside |
|---|---|---|---|
| High | 2/<br>0 / 0 | 4/<br>500 / 2 | 2/<br>0 / 0 |
| Med | 1/<br>1000 / 1 | 2/<br>0 / 0 | 0/<br>0 / 0 |
| Low | 4/<br>0 / 0 | 3/<br>0 / 0 | 0/<br>0 / 0 |

Jackson had difficulty in many fastball locations, including the highly pitched medium-high outside location. Notice how well he hit low-over-the-middle and low-inside fastballs. The averages in these two locations were very high, considering the number of instances recorded in each.

Jackson hit fastballs in both of these locations deep to the outfield.

## LOW-OVER-THE-MIDDLE FASTBALLS

BATTING AVERAGE .421
*PLAY*

| | |
|---|---|
| LEFTFIELDER | Deep in straightaway left field |
| CENTERFIELDER | Deep in straightaway center field |
| RIGHTFIELDER | Deep in straightaway right field |
| SHORTSTOP | Up middle (shifted toward second base) |
| SECOND | Normal position |

## LOW-INSIDE FASTBALLS

BATTING AVERAGE .478
*PLAY*

| | |
|---|---|
| LEFTFIELDER | Deep and shifted toward the left field line |
| CENTERFIELDER | Deep in straightaway center field |
| RIGHTFIELDER | Deep and shifted toward center field |
| SHORTSTOP | Up middle (shifted toward second base) |
| SECOND | Normal position |

Right-handers threw Jackson few curves, sliders and change-ups, which seems to have been a mistake considering the low averages he recorded against these types of pitches.

Jackson hit better against right-handers when behind in the count.

### Reggie Jackson    Left-Handed Hitter
### Against Right-Handed Pitchers When Behind In The Count
### Batting Average Is .270

Fastball Average .345

| | Outside | Middle | Inside |
|---|---|---|---|
| High | 1 / 1000 / 1 | 1 / 0 / 0 | 3 / 333 / 1 |
| Med | 24 / 291 / 7 | 4 / 500 / 2 | 6 / 0 / 0 |
| Low | 2 / 0 / 0 | 7 / 714 / 5 | 7 / 428 / 3 |

Curve Average .142

| | Outside | Middle | Inside |
|---|---|---|---|
| High | 0 / 0 / 0 | 0 / 0 / 0 | 1 / 0 / 0 |
| Med | 0 / 0 / 0 | 1 / 1000 / 1 | 0 / 0 / 0 |
| Low | 0 / 0 / 0 | 3 / 0 / 0 | 2 / 0 / 0 |

## Reggie Jackson    Left-Handed Hitter
### Against Right-Handed Pitchers When Ahead In The Count
### Batting Average Is .230

| Fastball Average .272 | | | Curve Average .200 | | |
| --- | --- | --- | --- | --- | --- |
| Outside | Middle | Inside | Outside | Middle | Inside |
| **High** 2/500/1 | 13/76/1 | 0/0/0 | 0/0/0 | 0/0/0 | 0/0/0 |
| **Med** 24/250/6 | 7/428/3 | 16/187/3 | 2/0/0 | 0/0/0 | 3/333/1 |
| **Low** 3/0/0 | 15/266/4 | 8/750/6 | 0/0/0 | 0/0/0 | 0/0/0 |

Since so few breaking and off-speed pitches were thrown to Jackson, his fastball averages are of primary importance in the above charts. His .345 fastball average when behind was very good, and his .272 when ahead was respectable considering Jackson's hard-swinging batting style.

The batting percentages for all counts in his low-inside fastball locations show that he must have worked hard to hit that particular pitch.

## Jackson Against Left-Handed Pitchers

Jackson's fastball average against left-handers was good.

## Reggie Jackson    Left-Handed Hitter
### Against All Left-Handed Pitchers All Teams
### Overall Batting Average Is .247

| Fastball Average .285 | | | Curve Average .250 | | |
| --- | --- | --- | --- | --- | --- |
| Outside | Middle | Inside | Outside | Middle | Inside |
| **High** 2/0/0 | 6/333/2 | 5/200/1 | 0/0/0 | 1/1000/1 | 0/0/0 |
| **Med** 18/277/5 | 3/0/0 | 14/428/6 | 8/375/3 | 2/0/0 | 1/1000/1 |
| **Low** 5/200/1 | 9/333/3 | 8/250/2 | 7/0/0 | 0/0/0 | 1/0/0 |

His .277 and .428 in the medium-high outside and medium-high inside fastball locations were solid. He sent medium-high inside fastballs thrown by left-handers deep to left field.

MEDIUM-HIGH INSIDE FASTBALLS

BATTING AVERAGE .428
PLAY
LEFTFIELDER        Deep and shifted toward the left field line
CENTERFIELDER      Medium-deep in straightaway center field
RIGHTFIELDER       Deep in straightaway right field
SHORTSTOP          Up middle (shifted toward second base)
SECOND             Shifted toward first base

Against left-handers, Jackson had difficulty with low curves. He did not get a hit in these locations in games scouted by the BARS System.

Jackson hit better when behind-in-the-count against left-handers. Little information is available for his ahead and behind in the count charts against left-handers, so those charts are not shown here.

**Super Summary For Keith Hernandez**

Left-handed Keith Hernandez of the New York Mets is a fastball hitter who has problems with curves and off-speed pitches. He hits fastballs about as well against right-handed and left-handed pitchers.

First, against right-handers:

### Keith Hernandez   Left-Handed Hitter
### Against All Right-Handed Pitchers All Teams
### Overall Batting Average Is .280

Fastball Average .336                     Curve Average .250

|      | Outside | Middle | Inside | Outside | Middle | Inside |
|------|---------|--------|--------|---------|--------|--------|
| High | 13 / 230 / 3 | 48 / 333 / 16 | 24 / 291 / 7 | 2 / 0 / 0 | 11 / 0 / 0 | 2 / 0 / 0 |
| Med  | 65 / 338 / 22 | 32 / 281 / 9 | 51 / 372 / 19 | 11 / 363 / 4 | 3 / 0 / 0 | 2 / 1000 / 2 |
| Low  | 20 / 300 / 6 | 71 / 394 / 28 | 44 / 318 / 14 | 6 / 166 / 1 | 12 / 416 / 5 | 7 / 285 / 2 |

### Slider Average .166

| | Outside | Middle | Inside |
|---|---|---|---|
| **High** | 0 / 0 / 0 | 3 / 0 / 0 | 2 / 0 / 0 |
| **Med** | 2 / 1000 / 2 | 3 / 0 / 0 | 8 / 125 / 1 |
| **Low** | 3 / 0 / 0 | 6 / 333 / 2 | 15 / 133 / 2 |

### Change-Up Average .135

| | Outside | Middle | Inside |
|---|---|---|---|
| **High** | 4 / 0 / 0 | 2 / 0 / 0 | 1 / 0 / 0 |
| **Med** | 5 / 400 / 2 | 1 / 0 / 0 | 2 / 500 / 1 |
| **Low** | 8 / 0 / 0 | 9 / 222 / 2 | 5 / 0 / 0 |

Hernandez hits fastballs well against right-handed pitchers. The high-outside location (.230) is his only fastball weakness. His medium-high inside and low-over-the-middle averages are especially good.

Hernandez hits medium-high inside, medium-high outside and low-over-the-middle fastballs fairly straightaway to all fields. He punches high-inside fastballs down the left field line.

HIGH-INSIDE FASTBALLS

BATTING AVERAGE .291
> PLAY

LEFTFIELDER — Medium-deep and shifted toward the left field line
CENTERFIELDER — Medium-deep in straightaway center field
RIGHTFIELDER — Deep and shifted toward center field
SHORTSTOP — Up middle (shifted toward second base)
SECOND — Normal position

In almost every pitching location, one or two fielders are required to shift to cover Hernandez's hits to the opposite field, but overall Hernandez hits fastballs straightaway.

Hernandez has difficulty with curveballs. He has not yet had a base hit recorded in the high curve locations. He hits high-over-the-middle curves straightaway and medium deep, but he hits low-over-the-middle curves (.416) deep to the opposite field.

LOW-OVER-THE-MIDDLE CURVEBALLS

BATTING AVERAGE .416
 *PLAY*
LEFTFIELDER        Deep and shifted toward the left field line
CENTERFIELDER      Deep and shifted toward left field
RIGHTFIELDER       Deep and shifted toward center field
SHORTSTOP          Normal position
SECOND             Normal position

He hits medium-high outside curves to all fields.

MEDIUM-HIGH OUTSIDE CURVES

BATTING AVERAGE .363
 *PLAY*
LEFTFIELDER        Deep and shifted toward the left field line
CENTERFIELDER      Deep and shifted toward right field
RIGHTFIELDER       Deep in straightaway right field
SHORTSTOP          Normal position
SECOND             Normal position

Hernandez hits for a very low overall percentage against sliders and change-ups. He has pronounced weaknesses against inside sliders, low change-ups and high change-ups.

Hernandez hits better when ahead in the count against right-handers.

**Keith Hernandez   Left-Handed Hitter**
**Against Right-Handed Pitchers When Ahead In The Count**
**Batting Average Is .365**

Fastball Average .409          Curve Average .250

| | Outside | Middle | Inside | | Outside | Middle | Inside |
|---|---|---|---|---|---|---|---|
| High | 5 / 0 / 0 | 24 / 458 / 11 | 8 / 625 / 5 | | 0 / 0 / 0 | 3 / 0 / 0 | 0 / 0 / 0 |
| Med | 30 / 433 / 13 | 17 / 294 / 5 | 23 / 565 / 13 | | 0 / 0 / 0 | 0 / 0 / 0 | 0 / 0 / 0 |
| Low | 7 / 285 / 2 | 46 / 391 / 18 | 23 / 347 / 8 | | 1 / 1000 / 1 | 3 / 333 / 1 | 1 / 0 / 0 |

**Keith Hernandez   Left-Handed Hitter**
**Against Right-Handed Pitchers When Behind In The Count**
**Batting Average Is .245**

Fastball Average .245              Curve Average .411

| | Outside | Middle | Inside | | Outside | Middle | Inside |
|---|---|---|---|---|---|---|---|
| High | 2/ 500 / 1 | 6/ 166 / 1 | 10/ 200 / 2 | | 0/ 0 / 0 | 3/ 0 / 0 | 0/ 0 / 0 |
| Med | 13/ 384 / 5 | 6/ 166 / 1 | 8/ 0 / 0 | | 4/ 500 / 2 | 2/ 0 / 0 | 2/ 1000/ 2 |
| Low | 3/ 666 / 2 | 8/ 250 / 2 | 5/ 200 / 1 | | 2/ 0 / 0 | 3/ 666 / 2 | 1/ 1000/ 1 |

Hernandez's fastball average soars when he is ahead in the count. When ahead, his only weak location is high-outside. Every other location is strong, and some are outstanding.

When behind, Hernandez hits medium-high inside fastballs medium-deep and fairly straightaway to all fields, but when ahead he pulls these pitches.

MEDIUM-HIGH INSIDE FASTBALLS
(THROWN TO HERNANDEZ WHEN HE IS AHEAD IN THE COUNT)

BATTING AVERAGE .565
   *PLAY*
LEFTFIELDER        Deep and shifted toward center field
CENTERFIELDER    Deep in straightaway center field
RIGHTFIELDER     Deep and shifted toward the right field line
SHORTSTOP         Up middle (shifted toward second base)
SECOND              Shifted toward first base

When behind, he hits low-over-the-middle fastballs medium-deep and straightaway. When ahead, he hits deep to the opposite field.

LOW-OVER-THE-MIDDLE FASTBALLS
(THROWN TO HERNANDEZ WHEN HE IS AHEAD IN THE COUNT)

BATTING AVERAGE .391
  *PLAY*
LEFTFIELDER       Deep and shifted toward the left field line
CENTERFIELDER     Deep in straightaway center field
RIGHTFIELDER      Deep and shifted toward center field
SHORTSTOP         Up middle (shifted toward second base)
SECOND            Normal position

## Hernandez Against Left-Handed Pitchers

Hernandez hits fastballs well against left-handers. He has trouble with breaking pitches.

### Keith Hernandez   Left-Handed Hitter
### Against All Left-Handed Pitchers All Teams
### Overall Batting Average Is .294

Fastball Average .352

| | Outside | Middle | Inside |
|---|---|---|---|
| High | 3 / 0 / 0 | 22 / 318 / 7 | 9 / 444 / 4 |
| Med | 22 / 272 / 6 | 7 / 714 / 5 | 43 / 465 / 20 |
| Low | 7 / 428 / 3 | 27 / 444 / 12 | 33 / 121 / 4 |

Curve Average .229

| | Outside | Middle | Inside |
|---|---|---|---|
| High | 0 / 0 / 0 | 4 / 250 / 1 | 2 / 0 / 0 |
| Med | 8 / 250 / 2 | 3 / 666 / 2 | 7 / 285 / 2 |
| Low | 11 / 181 / 2 | 12 / 83 / 1 | 1 / 1000 / 1 |

Many left-handed pitchers come inside against Hernandez with fastballs, but he hits these pitches extremely well. His .465 against medium-high inside fastballs is excellent.

MEDIUM-HIGH INSIDE FASTBALLS
(THROWN TO HERNANDEZ BY LEFT-HANDED PITCHERS)

BATTING AVERAGE .465
*PLAY*

| | |
|---|---|
| LEFTFIELDER | Medium-deep and shifted toward center field |
| CENTERFIELDER | Short in straightaway center field |
| RIGHTFIELDER | Deep and shifted toward the right field line |
| SHORTSTOP | Up middle (shifted toward second base) |
| SECOND | Normal position |

Hernandez hits low-over-the-middle fastballs well in almost every situation. His low-over-the-middle average against right-handed pitchers is .394 (with 71 recorded instances). Against left-handed pitchers his low-over-the-middle average is .444 (with 27 recorded instances). Against left-handers, he scatters these pitches to all fields.

LOW-OVER-THE-MIDDLE FASTBALLS
(THROWN TO HERNANDEZ BY LEFT-HANDED PITCHERS)

BATTING AVERAGE .444
*PLAY*

| | |
|---|---|
| LEFTFIELDER | Deep and shifted toward the left field line |
| CENTERFIELDER | Deep and shifted toward right field |
| RIGHTFIELDER | Deep and shifted toward the right field line |
| SHORTSTOP | Up middle (shifted toward second base) |
| SECOND | Normal position |

Hernandez has difficulty with low curves thrown by lefties. This difficulty with low breaking pitches extends into the low slider locations.

Hernandez hits better when ahead in the count against left-handers.

### Keith Hernandez   Left-Handed Hitter
### Against Left-Handed Pitchers When Ahead In The Count
### Batting Average Is .373

Fastball Average .432     Curve Average .200

| | Outside | Middle | Inside |
|---|---|---|---|
| High | 1/ — 0 / 0 | 10/ — 300 / 3 | 2/ — 1000/ 2 |
| Med | 8/ — 250 / 2 | 4/ — 750 / 3 | 19/ — 578 / 11 |
| Low | 3/ — 333 / 1 | 16/ — 562 / 9 | 11/ — 90 / 1 |

| | Outside | Middle | Inside |
|---|---|---|---|
| High | 0/ — 0 / 0 | 0/ — 0 / 0 | 0/ — 0 / 0 |
| Med | 2/ — 0 / 0 | 0/ — 0 / 0 | 3/ — 333 / 1 |
| Low | 0/ — 0 / 0 | 0/ — 0 / 0 | 0/ — 0 / 0 |

### Keith Hernandez    Left-Handed Hitter
### Against Left-Handed Pitchers When Behind In The Count
### Batting Average Is .317

Fastball Average .342     Curve Average .142

| | Outside | Middle | Inside |
|---|---|---|---|
| High | 0/ — 0 / 0 | 5/ — 400 / 2 | 4/ — 250 / 1 |
| Med | 7/ — 428 / 3 | 1/ — 1000/ 1 | 8/ — 500 / 4 |
| Low | 0/ — 0 / 0 | 5/ — 0 / 0 | 5/ — 200 / 1 |

| | Outside | Middle | Inside |
|---|---|---|---|
| High | 0/ — 0 / 0 | 1/ — 0 / 0 | 2/ — 0 / 0 |
| Med | 3/ — 333 / 1 | 0/ — 0 / 0 | 1/ — 0 / 0 |
| Low | 1/ — 1000/ 1 | 6/ — 0 / 0 | 0/ — 0 / 0 |

When ahead against left-handers, Hernandez's only weak fastball location is low-inside (.090). For a medium-high inside fastball, all fielders should play him to pull the ball:

MEDIUM-HIGH INSIDE FASTBALLS
(WHEN AHEAD IN THE COUNT AGAINST LEFT-HANDED PITCHERS)

BATTING AVERAGE .578
  *PLAY*
LEFTFIELDER     Medium-deep and shifted toward center field
CENTERFIELDER   Deep and shifted toward right field
RIGHTFIELDER    Deep and shifted toward the right field line
SHORTSTOP       Shifted toward third base
SECOND          Shifted toward first base

## Super Summary For Mike Schmidt

Mike Schmidt, right-handed hitter for the Philadelphia Phillies, hits with great power against both right- and left-handed pitchers.

### Mike Schmidt    Right-Handed Hitter
### Against All Right-Handed Pitchers All Teams
### Overall Batting Average Is .221

Fastball Average .231

| | Inside | Middle | Outside |
|---|---|---|---|
| High | 14 / 0 / 0 | 14 / 500 / 7 | 16 / 125 / 2 |
| Med | 32 / 250 / 8 | 21 / 380 / 8 | 64 / 203 / 13 |
| Low | 15 / 266 / 4 | 57 / 263 / 15 | 44 / 159 / 7 |

Curve Average .258

| | Inside | Middle | Outside |
|---|---|---|---|
| High | 1 / 1000 / 1 | 4 / 500 / 2 | 4 / 0 / 0 |
| Med | 2 / 0 / 0 | 5 / 600 / 3 | 11 / 272 / 3 |
| Low | 4 / 250 / 1 | 9 / 444 / 4 | 18 / 55 / 1 |

Slider Average .222

| | Inside | Middle | Outside |
|---|---|---|---|
| High | 1 / 0 / 0 | 3 / 333 / 1 | 2 / 0 / 0 |
| Med | 1 / 0 / 0 | 1 / 1000 / 1 | 17 / 235 / 4 |
| Low | 5 / 600 / 3 | 12 / 166 / 2 | 30 / 166 / 5 |

Change-Up Average .333

| | Inside | Middle | Outside |
|---|---|---|---|
| High | 0 / 0 / 0 | 1 / 1000 / 1 | 0 / 0 / 0 |
| Med | 2 / 0 / 0 | 0 / 0 / 0 | 5 / 400 / 2 |
| Low | 0 / 0 / 0 | 2 / 0 / 0 | 2 / 500 / 1 |

Schmidt has difficulty with many fastball locations. His averages are very low in the high-outside and low-outside fastball locations.

In the high-inside location his 0-for-14 performance presents a definite weakness for pitchers to attack.

Schmidt does not have a pronounced tendency to pull the ball. Most of his locations require the fielders to position themselves fairly straightaway.

## MEDIUM-HIGH OUTSIDE FASTBALLS

BATTING AVERAGE .203
*PLAY*

| | |
|---|---|
| LEFTFIELDER | Deep in straightaway left field |
| CENTERFIELDER | Deep and shifted toward left field |
| RIGHTFIELDER | Deep in straightaway right field |
| SHORTSTOP | Normal position |
| SECOND | Normal position |

## MEDIUM-HIGH INSIDE FASTBALLS

BATTING AVERAGE .250
*PLAY*

| | |
|---|---|
| LEFTFIELDER | Deep in straightaway left field |
| CENTERFIELDER | Deep and shifted toward left field |
| RIGHTFIELDER | Deep in straightaway right field |
| SHORTSTOP | Normal position |
| SECOND | Shifted toward first base |

Schmidt does pull medium-over-the-middle fastballs deep to left.

## MEDIUM-OVER-THE-MIDDLE FASTBALLS

BATTING AVERAGE .380
*PLAY*

| | |
|---|---|
| LEFTFIELDER | Deep and shifted toward the left field line |
| CENTERFIELDER | Deep and shifted toward left field |
| RIGHTFIELDER | Deep in straightaway right field |
| SHORTSTOP | No instances recorded |
| SECOND | No instances recorded |

Schmidt hits curves well, but has trouble with pitches to several locations. The low-outside curve location is a glaring weakness (1 for 18), and his high-outside is a possible weakness.

LOW-OUTSIDE CURVEBALLS

BATTING AVERAGE .055
  *PLAY*
LEFTFIELDER       No instances recorded
CENTERFIELDER     Medium-deep in straightaway center field
RIGHTFIELDER      No instances recorded
SHORTSTOP         Up middle (shifted toward second base)
SECOND            Shifted toward first base

Pitchers throw Schmidt quite a few sliders. He has trouble with low-over-the-middle and low-outside sliders.

Schmidt hits better against right-handed pitchers when ahead in the count.

### Mike Schmidt    Right-Handed Hitter
### Against Right-Handed Pitchers When Ahead In The Count
### Batting Average Is .321

Fastball Average .313

|      | Inside | Middle | Outside |
|------|--------|--------|---------|
| High | 1/ 0 / 0 | 7/ 428 / 3 | 5/ 400 / 2 |
| Med  | 15/ 200 / 3 | 10/ 500 / 5 | 30/ 300 / 9 |
| Low  | 4/ 500 / 2 | 30/ 266 / 8 | 16/ 312 / 5 |

Curve Average .500

|      | Inside | Middle | Outside |
|------|--------|--------|---------|
| High | 0/ 0 / 0 | 3/ 666 / 2 | 1/ 0 / 0 |
| Med  | 0/ 0 / 0 | 2/ 500 / 1 | 2/ 500 / 1 |
| Low  | 0/ 0 / 0 | 1/ 1000/ 1 | 1/ 0 / 0 |

Slider Average .400

|      | Inside | Middle | Outside |
|------|--------|--------|---------|
| High | 0/ 0 / 0 | 0/ 0 / 0 | 0/ 0 / 0 |
| Med  | 0/ 0 / 0 | 0/ 0 / 0 | 7/ 428 / 3 |
| Low  | 4/ 500 / 2 | 6/ 166 / 1 | 8/ 500 / 4 |

Change-Up Average .500

|      | Inside | Middle | Outside |
|------|--------|--------|---------|
| High | 0/ 0 / 0 | 0/ 0 / 0 | 0/ 0 / 0 |
| Med  | 0/ 0 / 0 | 0/ 0 / 0 | 1/ 1000/ 1 |
| Low  | 0/ 0 / 0 | 1/ 0 / 0 | 0/ 0 / 0 |

## Mike Schmidt    Right-Handed Hitter
## Against Right-Handed Pitchers When Behind In The Count
## Batting Average Is .268

### Fastball Average .244

| | Inside | Middle | Outside |
|---|---|---|---|
| High | 2 / 0 / 0 | 5 / 400 / 2 | 1 / 0 / 0 |
| Med | 6 / 166 / 1 | 4 / 500 / 2 | 9 / 0 / 0 |
| Low | 0 / 0 / 0 | 10 / 400 / 4 | 8 / 250 / 2 |

### Curve Average .416

| | Inside | Middle | Outside |
|---|---|---|---|
| High | 0 / 0 / 0 | 0 / 0 / 0 | 2 / 0 / 0 |
| Med | 1 / 0 / 0 | 2 / 1000 / 2 | 3 / 666 / 2 |
| Low | 1 / 0 / 0 | 2 / 0 / 0 | 1 / 1000 / 1 |

### Slider Average .250

| | Inside | Middle | Outside |
|---|---|---|---|
| High | 0 / 0 / 0 | 1 / 1000 / 1 | 0 / 0 / 0 |
| Med | 0 / 0 / 0 | 0 / 0 / 0 | 3 / 333 / 1 |
| Low | 0 / 0 / 0 | 0 / 0 / 0 | 8 / 125 / 1 |

### Change-Up Average 1.000

| | Inside | Middle | Outside |
|---|---|---|---|
| High | 0 / 0 / 0 | 0 / 0 / 0 | 0 / 0 / 0 |
| Med | 0 / 0 / 0 | 0 / 0 / 0 | 1 / 1000 / 1 |
| Low | 0 / 0 / 0 | 0 / 0 / 0 | 1 / 1000 / 1 |

When ahead in the count, his only weak fastball location is medium-high inside (.200).

Notice how much better Schmidt hits medium-high outside fastballs when he is ahead in the count. When ahead, he pulls the ball and hits it deep to all fields. When behind, he hits these pitches weakly.

MEDIUM-HIGH OUTSIDE FASTBALLS
(THROWN TO SCHMIDT WHEN HE IS AHEAD IN THE COUNT)

BATTING AVERAGE .300
    *PLAY*

| | |
|---|---|
| LEFTFIELDER | Deep and shifted toward the left field line |
| CENTERFIELDER | Deep and shifted toward left field |
| RIGHTFIELDER | Deep in straightaway right field |
| SHORTSTOP | Normal position |
| SECOND | Normal position |

MEDIUM-HIGH OUTSIDE FASTBALLS
(THROWN TO SCHMIDT WHEN HE IS BEHIND IN THE COUNT)

BATTING AVERAGE .000
   *PLAY*
| | |
|---|---|
| LEFTFIELDER | No instances recorded |
| CENTERFIELDER | Short and shifted toward right field |
| RIGHTFIELDER | Deep in straightaway right field |
| SHORTSTOP | Up middle (shifted toward second base) |
| SECOND | Shifted toward first base |

Notice Schmidt's excellent record against sliders when ahead in the count. He hits low-outside sliders extremely well when ahead (.500), but has difficulty with them when behind (.125).

## Schmidt Against Left-Handed Pitchers

Schmidt hits for a higher average against left-handers than against right-handers.

**Mike Schmidt    Right-Handed Hitter**
**Against All Left-Handed Pitchers All Teams**
**Overall Batting Average Is .372**

Fastball Average .380           Curve Average .444

| | Inside | Middle | Outside | | Inside | Middle | Outside |
|---|---|---|---|---|---|---|---|
| High | 4 / 500 / 2 | 5 / 400 / 2 | 4 / 250 / 1 | | 0 / 0 / 0 | 1 / 0 / 0 | 0 / 0 / 0 |
| Med | 3 / 0 / 0 | 4 / 500 / 2 | 19 / 210 / 4 | | 1 / 0 / 0 | 2 / 1000 / 2 | 1 / 0 / 0 |
| Low | 10 / 400 / 4 | 14 / 571 / 8 | 8 / 500 / 4 | | 2 / 1000 / 2 | 4 / 250 / 1 | 7 / 428 / 3 |

Notice how well he hits low fastballs thrown by lefties. He goes to all fields with low-over-the-middle fastballs.

LOW-OVER-THE-MIDDLE FASTBALLS
(THROWN TO SCHMIDT BY LEFT-HANDED PITCHERS)

BATTING AVERAGE .571
   *PLAY*
LEFTFIELDER       Deep in straightaway left field
CENTERFIELDER    Medium-deep in straightaway center field
RIGHTFIELDER     Deep and shifted toward the right field line
SHORTSTOP        Normal position
SECOND           No instances recorded

He pulls medium-high outside fastballs and hits them deeply.

MEDIUM-HIGH OUTSIDE FASTBALLS
(THROWN TO SCHMIDT BY LEFT-HANDED PITCHERS)

BATTING AVERAGE .210
   *PLAY*
LEFTFIELDER       Deep and shifted toward the left field line
CENTERFIELDER    Deep in straightaway center field
RIGHTFIELDER     Deep and shifted toward center field
SHORTSTOP        Shifted toward third base
SECOND           No instances recorded

Schmidt's strength against low pitches thrown by left-handers continues into curveballs and sliders. He hits low-outside curves to center field.

LOW-OUTSIDE CURVEBALLS
(THROWN TO SCHMIDT BY LEFT-HANDED PITCHERS)

BATTING AVERAGE .428
   *PLAY*
LEFTFIELDER       Medium-deep and shifted toward center field
CENTERFIELDER    Deep in straightaway center field
RIGHTFIELDER     No instances recorded
SHORTSTOP        Normal position
SECOND           Normal position

The charts on the following page show that Schmidt hits much better against left-handers when ahead in the count.

### Mike Schmidt    Right-Handed Hitter
### Against Left-Handed Pitchers When Ahead In The Count
### Batting Average Is .462

**Fastball Average .485**

|      | Inside | Middle | Outside |
|------|--------|--------|---------|
| High | 1 / 0 / 0 | 1 / 1000 / 1 | 1 / 1000 / 1 |
| Med  | 3 / 0 / 0 | 3 / 666 / 2 | 12 / 250 / 3 |
| Low  | 3 / 666 / 2 | 10 / 700 / 7 | 1 / 1000 / 1 |

**Curve Average .666**

|      | Inside | Middle | Outside |
|------|--------|--------|---------|
| High | 0 / 0 / 0 | 0 / 0 / 0 | 0 / 0 / 0 |
| Med  | 0 / 0 / 0 | 0 / 0 / 0 | 0 / 0 / 0 |
| Low  | 0 / 0 / 0 | 2 / 500 / 1 | 1 / 1000 / 1 |

### Mike Schmidt    Right-Handed Hitter
### Against Left-Handed Pitchers When Behind In The Count
### Batting Average Is .230

**Fastball Average .230**

|      | Inside | Middle | Outside |
|------|--------|--------|---------|
| High | 1 / 1000 / 1 | 2 / 500 / 1 | 0 / 0 / 0 |
| Med  | 0 / 0 / 0 | 1 / 0 / 0 | 2 / 0 / 0 |
| Low  | 3 / 0 / 0 | 1 / 0 / 0 | 3 / 333 / 1 |

**Curve Average .000**

|      | Inside | Middle | Outside |
|------|--------|--------|---------|
| High | 0 / 0 / 0 | 1 / 0 / 0 | 0 / 0 / 0 |
| Med  | 1 / 0 / 0 | 0 / 0 / 0 | 0 / 0 / 0 |
| Low  | 0 / 0 / 0 | 2 / 0 / 0 | 1 / 0 / 0 |

When ahead in the count, he hits low-over-the-middle fastballs (.700) to right field and pulls medium-high outside fastballs (.250) to left field.

## Super Summary For Alan Trammell

Right-handed Alan Trammell of the Detroit Tigers hits fastballs very well against both left- and right-handed pitchers, but he hits better overall against left-handers.

First, his record against right-handers:

## Alan Trammell   Right-Handed Hitter
### Against All Right-Handed Pitchers All Teams
### Overall Batting Average Is .265

Fastball Average .313

|  | Inside | Middle | Outside |
|---|---|---|---|
| High | 26/269 / 7 | 36/222 / 8 | 13/384 / 5 |
| Med | 61/409 / 25 | 46/500 / 23 | 105/285 / 30 |
| Low | 20/150 / 3 | 69/289 / 20 | 32/218 / 7 |

Curve Average .164

|  | Inside | Middle | Outside |
|---|---|---|---|
| High | 0/0 / 0 | 5/0 / 0 | 0/0 / 0 |
| Med | 9/111 / 1 | 5/0 / 0 | 21/190 / 4 |
| Low | 2/500 / 1 | 8/250 / 2 | 23/173 / 4 |

Slider Average .160

|  | Inside | Middle | Outside |
|---|---|---|---|
| High | 1/0 / 0 | 2/0 / 0 | 0/0 / 0 |
| Med | 5/200 / 1 | 4/250 / 1 | 15/200 / 3 |
| Low | 1/0 / 0 | 7/285 / 2 | 21/95 / 2 |

Change-Up Average .333

|  | Inside | Middle | Outside |
|---|---|---|---|
| High | 0/0 / 0 | 5/600 / 3 | 3/666 / 2 |
| Med | 1/0 / 0 | 0/0 / 0 | 1/0 / 0 |
| Low | 0/0 / 0 | 6/333 / 2 | 5/0 / 0 |

Against right-handed pitchers, Trammell has both strong and weak fastball locations. His .409 average against medium-high inside fastballs is excellent, especially considering the high number of instances recorded in that location (61). His .500 against medium-over-the-middle is also strong, and his medium-high outside (.285) and low-over-the-middle (.289) are solid enough.

But his low-inside (.150), low-outside (.218) and high-over-the-middle (.222) fastball locations offer targets for pitchers. Trammell hits both medium-high inside and medium-high outside fastballs fairly straightaway, as the charts on the following pages show.

## MEDIUM-HIGH OUTSIDE FASTBALLS

BATTING AVERAGE .285
 *PLAY*
LEFTFIELDER          Deep in straightaway left field
CENTERFIELDER        Deep in straightaway center field
RIGHTFIELDER         Deep in straightaway right field
SHORTSTOP            Normal position
SECOND               Shifted toward first base

## MEDIUM-HIGH INSIDE FASTBALLS

BATTING AVERAGE .409
 *PLAY*
LEFTFIELDER          Deep and shifted toward the left field line
CENTERFIELDER        Medium-deep and shifted toward right field
RIGHTFIELDER         Medium-deep in straightaway right field
SHORTSTOP            Normal position
SECOND               Shifted toward first base

Trammell tends to hit low-outside fastballs medium deep to the outfield and to the right side of the infield.

## LOW-OUTSIDE FASTBALLS

BATTING AVERAGE .218
 *PLAY*
LEFTFIELDER          Medium-deep and shifted toward the left field line
CENTERFIELDER        Medium-deep in straightaway center field
RIGHTFIELDER         Medium-deep and shifted toward center field
SHORTSTOP            Up middle (shifted toward second base)
SECOND               Shifted toward first base

He has many weak locations against curveballs, and his overall curve average of .164 is low. He hits low-outside curves much differently than he hits medium-high outside curves. It is interesting that such a small change of the location in the strike zone could result in such a difference in direction and distance of hit balls.

MEDIUM-HIGH OUTSIDE CURVEBALLS

BATTING AVERAGE .190
*PLAY*
LEFTFIELDER          Medium-deep in straightaway left field
CENTERFIELDER        Deep and shifted toward left field
RIGHTFIELDER         Deep in straightaway right field
SHORTSTOP            Shifted toward third base
SECOND               Shifted toward first base


LOW-OUTSIDE CURVEBALLS

BATTING AVERAGE .173
*PLAY*
LEFTFIELDER          Medium-deep and shifted toward center field
CENTERFIELDER        Medium-deep in straightaway center field
RIGHTFIELDER         Medium-deep and shifted toward center field
SHORTSTOP            Normal position
SECOND               Normal position

Trammell's slider averages are also weak, with the exception of the low-over-the-middle location (.285). It is interesting that every slider that Trammell hit in the low-over-the-middle location was into the hole between the shortstop and third baseman.

Trammell hits high change-ups well, but has difficulty with low change-ups. He struck out on all five recorded low-outside change-ups.


**Trammell Ahead And Behind In The Count**

Trammell hits nearly as well when behind in the count against right-handers as when ahead, but he hits fastballs better when ahead. Please see his charts on the following page.

### Alan Trammell    Right-Handed Hitter
### Against Right-Handed Pitchers When Ahead In The Count
### Batting Average Is .295

Fastball Average .329

| | Inside | Middle | Outside |
|---|---|---|---|
| High | 8/ 250 /2 | 19/ 263 /5 | 4/ 500 /2 |
| Med | 27/ 444 /12 | 22/ 500 /11 | 49/ 346 /17 |
| Low | 11/ 90 /1 | 33/ 242 /8 | 9/ 222 /2 |

Curve Average .285

| | Inside | Middle | Outside |
|---|---|---|---|
| High | 0/ 0 /0 | 0/ 0 /0 | 0/ 0 /0 |
| Med | 2/ 0 /0 | 0/ 0 /0 | 4/ 250 /1 |
| Low | 0/ 0 /0 | 1/ 1000 /1 | 0/ 0 /0 |

### Alan Trammell    Right-Handed Hitter
### Against Right-Handed Pitchers When Behind In The Count
### Batting Average Is .260

Fastball Average .267

| | Inside | Middle | Outside |
|---|---|---|---|
| High | 5/ 600 /3 | 8/ 125 /1 | 3/ 333 /1 |
| Med | 12/ 250 /3 | 11/ 454 /5 | 21/ 95 /2 |
| Low | 4/ 250 /1 | 13/ 461 /6 | 9/ 111 /1 |

Curve Average .272

| | Inside | Middle | Outside |
|---|---|---|---|
| High | 0/ 0 /0 | 2/ 0 /0 | 0/ 0 /0 |
| Med | 5/ 200 /1 | 2/ 0 /0 | 6/ 333 /2 |
| Low | 1/ 1000 /1 | 0/ 0 /0 | 6/ 333 /2 |

So many more fastballs are thrown to Trammell than other types of pitches that these charts are essentially records of his fastball performance. Trammell's slider and change-up charts were not included because almost no pitches of these types were thrown to him.

Notice his weakness against low-outside and medium-high outside fastballs when behind in the count. His medium-high outside location is strong when he is ahead in the count. When ahead, he pulls the ball more and hits it deeper.

MEDIUM-HIGH INSIDE FASTBALLS
(THROWN TO TRAMMELL WHEN HE IS AHEAD IN THE COUNT)

BATTING AVERAGE .444
*PLAY*

| | |
|---|---|
| LEFTFIELDER | Deep and shifted toward the left field line |
| CENTERFIELDER | Medium-deep and shifted toward left field |
| RIGHTFIELDER | Deep and shifted toward center field |
| SHORTSTOP | Normal position |
| SECOND | No recorded instances |


MEDIUM-HIGH INSIDE FASTBALLS
(THROWN TO TRAMMELL WHEN HE IS BEHIND IN THE COUNT)

BATTING AVERAGE .250
*PLAY*

| | |
|---|---|
| LEFTFIELDER | Medium-deep in straightaway left field |
| CENTERFIELDER | Deep and shifted toward right field |
| RIGHTFIELDER | Medium-deep in straightaway right field |
| SHORTSTOP | Normal position |
| SECOND | No instances recorded |

Trammell also pulls low-over-the-middle fastballs more when he is ahead in the count, although his average is higher in that location when he is behind.

LOW-OVER-THE-MIDDLE FASTBALLS
(THROWN TO TRAMMELL WHEN HE IS AHEAD IN THE COUNT)

BATTING AVERAGE .242
*PLAY*

| | |
|---|---|
| LEFTFIELDER | Medium-deep in straightaway left field |
| CENTERFIELDER | Deep and shifted toward left field |
| RIGHTFIELDER | Deep and shifted toward center field |
| SHORTSTOP | Normal position |
| SECOND | No instances recorded |

LOW-OVER-THE-MIDDLE FASTBALLS
(THROWN TO TRAMMELL WHEN HE IS BEHIND IN THE COUNT)

BATTING AVERAGE .461
   PLAY

| | |
|---|---|
| LEFTFIELDER | No instances recorded |
| CENTERFIELDER | Deep and shifted toward right field |
| RIGHTFIELDER | Deep in straightaway right field |
| SHORTSTOP | Up middle (shifted toward second base) |
| SECOND | Shifted toward first base |

### Trammell Against Left-Handed Pitchers

Trammell's overall fastball average against left-handers is strong.

### Alan Trammell    Right-Handed Hitter
### Against All Left-Handed Pitchers All Teams
### Overall Batting Average Is .318

Fastball Average .356

| | Inside | Middle | Outside |
|---|---|---|---|
| High | 5 / 0 / 0 | 12 / 416 / 5 | 16 / 187 / 3 |
| Med | 27 / 481 / 13 | 18 / 555 / 10 | 56 / 267 / 15 |
| Low | 7 / 285 / 2 | 25 / 360 / 9 | 22 / 454 / 10 |

Curve Average .279

| | Inside | Middle | Outside |
|---|---|---|---|
| High | 0 / 0 / 0 | 3 / 333 / 1 | 3 / 333 / 1 |
| Med | 3 / 333 / 1 | 3 / 333 / 1 | 11 / 363 / 4 |
| Low | 5 / 0 / 0 | 8 / 250 / 2 | 7 / 285 / 2 |

Slider Average .347

| | Inside | Middle | Outside |
|---|---|---|---|
| High | 0 / 0 / 0 | 1 / 1000 / 1 | 1 / 1000 / 1 |
| Med | 1 / 1000 / 1 | 3 / 333 / 1 | 3 / 333 / 1 |
| Low | 7 / 0 / 0 | 5 / 600 / 3 | 2 / 0 / 0 |

Change-Up Average .125

| | Inside | Middle | Outside |
|---|---|---|---|
| High | 0 / 0 / 0 | 1 / 0 / 0 | 0 / 0 / 0 |
| Med | 0 / 0 / 0 | 0 / 0 / 0 | 2 / 500 / 1 |
| Low | 2 / 0 / 0 | 0 / 0 / 0 | 3 / 0 / 0 |

Except for the high-inside and high-outside fastball locations, Trammell has no weak locations against fastballs thrown by left-handed pitchers. He has some extremely high percentages. Note in particular his .454 against low-outside fastballs, a fine average in a location that is difficult for many hitters.

He pulls these low-outside fastballs and hits them deep.

LOW-OUTSIDE FASTBALLS
(THROWN TO TRAMMELL BY LEFT-HANDED PITCHERS)

BATTING AVERAGE .454
*PLAY*

| | |
|---|---|
| LEFTFIELDER | Deep and shifted toward the left field line |
| CENTERFIELDER | Deep and shifted toward left field |
| RIGHTFIELDER | Medium-deep in straightaway right field |
| SHORTSTOP | Normal position |
| SECOND | No recorded instances |

His curve averages are also strong, with one weakness in the low-inside location. He tends to hit low-inside curves to medium-deep left and center fields.

He scatters medium-high outside curves thrown by lefties.

MEDIUM-HIGH OUTSIDE CURVEBALLS
(THROWN TO TRAMMELL BY LEFT-HANDED PITCHERS)

BATTING AVERAGE .363
*PLAY*

| | |
|---|---|
| LEFTFIELDER | Deep in straightaway left field |
| CENTERFIELDER | Deep and shifted toward left field |
| RIGHTFIELDER | Deep and shifted toward the right field line |
| SHORTSTOP | Up middle (shifted toward second base) |
| SECOND | Shifted toward first base |

Trammell hits sliders thrown by left-handers well, although he has a weakness in the low-inside location. He tends to pull low-over-the-middle sliders (.600) to all fields medium-deep.

Trammell hits well both when ahead and when behind in the count against left-handers.

### Alan Trammell     Right-Handed Hitter
### Against Left-Handed Pitchers When Behind In The Count
### Batting Average Is .358

Fastball Average .432                    Curve Average .312

| | Inside | Middle | Outside |
|---|---|---|---|
| **High** | 2 / 0 / 0 | 4 / 750 / 3 | 5 / 0 / 0 |
| **Med** | 3 / 1000 / 3 | 2 / 500 / 1 | 14 / 357 / 5 |
| **Low** | 2 / 0 / 0 | 1 / 1000 / 1 | 4 / 750 / 3 |

| | Inside | Middle | Outside |
|---|---|---|---|
| **High** | 0 / 0 / 0 | 2 / 500 / 1 | 1 / 0 / 0 |
| **Med** | 0 / 0 / 0 | 1 / 0 / 0 | 4 / 250 / 1 |
| **Low** | 0 / 0 / 0 | 5 / 400 / 2 | 3 / 333 / 1 |

### Alan Trammell     Right-Handed Hitter
### Against Left-Handed Pitchers When Ahead In The Count
### Batting Average Is .382

Fastball Average .402                    Curve Average .250

| | Inside | Middle | Outside |
|---|---|---|---|
| **High** | 0 / 0 / 0 | 2 / 500 / 1 | 6 / 166 / 1 |
| **Med** | 14 / 428 / 6 | 9 / 555 / 5 | 29 / 310 / 9 |
| **Low** | 2 / 1000 / 2 | 11 / 363 / 4 | 9 / 555 / 5 |

| | Inside | Middle | Outside |
|---|---|---|---|
| **High** | 0 / 0 / 0 | 1 / 0 / 0 | 1 / 0 / 0 |
| **Med** | 1 / 1000 / 1 | 0 / 0 / 0 | 2 / 500 / 1 |
| **Low** | 1 / 0 / 0 | 0 / 0 / 0 | 2 / 0 / 0 |

## Super Summary For Andre Dawson

Right-handed hitter Andre Dawson of the Chicago Cubs hits curveballs better than fastballs against right-handed pitchers. Against left-handers, the reverse is true.

### Andre Dawson    Right-Handed Hitter
### Against All Right-Handed Pitchers All Teams
### Overall Batting Average Is .266

**Fastball Average .274**

|      | Inside | Middle | Outside |
|------|--------|--------|---------|
| High | 22 / 90 / 2 | 50 / 300 / 15 | 16 / 62 / 1 |
| Med  | 32 / 312 / 10 | 10 / 400 / 4 | 70 / 271 / 19 |
| Low  | 15 / 200 / 3 | 43 / 511 / 22 | 44 / 159 / 7 |

**Curve Average .299**

|      | Inside | Middle | Outside |
|------|--------|--------|---------|
| High | 1 / 0 / 0 | 12 / 250 / 3 | 6 / 333 / 2 |
| Med  | 3 / 666 / 2 | 8 / 375 / 3 | 30 / 466 / 14 |
| Low  | 1 / 0 / 0 | 12 / 250 / 3 | 34 / 147 / 5 |

**Slider Average .286**

|      | Inside | Middle | Outside |
|------|--------|--------|---------|
| High | 3 / 333 / 1 | 10 / 300 / 3 | 6 / 333 / 2 |
| Med  | 1 / 1000 / 1 | 3 / 333 / 1 | 44 / 363 / 16 |
| Low  | 1 / 0 / 0 | 11 / 545 / 6 | 57 / 157 / 9 |

**Change-Up Average .173**

|      | Inside | Middle | Outside |
|------|--------|--------|---------|
| High | 0 / 0 / 0 | 3 / 666 / 2 | 0 / 0 / 0 |
| Med  | 0 / 0 / 0 | 1 / 0 / 0 | 3 / 0 / 0 |
| Low  | 3 / 0 / 0 | 1 / 1000 / 1 | 12 / 83 / 1 |

Dawson has several strong fastball locations. His .511 in the low-over-the-middle fastball location is extremely high, especially considering the large number of recorded instances (43). But he has weaknesses on all four corners of his fastball chart. The .090 in his high-inside fastball location and the .062 in his high-outside location leave him especially vulnerable to sharp pitching. The .159 in his low-outside location (with a high number of recorded instances) increases his vulnerability.

Dawson hits medium-high outside fastballs to the opposite field (right field). In the medium-high inside location he scatters his hits.

MEDIUM-HIGH OUTSIDE FASTBALLS

BATTING AVERAGE .271
   *PLAY*

| | |
|---|---|
| LEFTFIELDER | Deep and shifted toward center field |
| CENTERFIELDER | Deep in straightaway center field |
| RIGHTFIELDER | Deep and shifted toward the right field line |
| SHORTSTOP | Up middle (shifted toward second base) |
| SECOND | Shifted toward first base |

MEDIUM-HIGH INSIDE FASTBALLS

BATTING AVERAGE .312
   *PLAY*

| | |
|---|---|
| LEFTFIELDER | Deep and shifted toward the left field line |
| CENTERFIELDER | Deep and shifted toward left field |
| RIGHTFIELDER | Deep and shifted toward the right field line |
| SHORTSTOP | Normal position |
| SECOND | Shifted toward first base |

Dawson hits for a respectable .299 overall against curves thrown by right-handers. His .466 in the medium-high outside curve location is excellent, but he has difficulty with low curves.

MEDIUM-HIGH OUTSIDE CURVEBALLS

BATTING AVERAGE .466
   *PLAY*

| | |
|---|---|
| LEFTFIELDER | Deep and shifted toward center field |
| CENTERFIELDER | Medium-deep in straightaway center field |
| RIGHTFIELDER | Deep in straightaway right field |
| SHORTSTOP | Up middle (shifted toward second base) |
| SECOND | Normal position |

Dawson also hits sliders well overall, with a solid .363 against medium-high outside sliders. The .157 he hits against low-outside sliders is comparable to the .159 he hits against low-outside fastballs and the .147 against low-outside curves. In this location he hits these pitches almost identically with respect to depth and distance.

LOW-OUTSIDE FASTBALLS, CURVEBALLS AND SLIDERS

BATTING AVERAGES .159, .147 AND .157
    *PLAY*
LEFTFIELDER      Deep and shifted toward the left field line
CENTERFIELDER   Deep and shifted toward right field
RIGHTFIELDER    Medium-deep in straightaway right field
SHORTSTOP       Normal position
SECOND          Normal position

The fact that he hits these three types of pitches for low averages indicates that, in general, fielders are positioning themselves correctly for pitches in these locations and that he is hitting pop flies that are easily caught.

Dawson hits only slightly better against right-handed pitchers when ahead in the count.

**Andre Dawson    Right-Handed Hitter**
**Against Right-Handed Pitchers When Ahead In The Count**
**Batting Average Is .326**

Fastball Average .309

| | Inside | Middle | Outside |
|---|---|---|---|
| High | 8/ 250 / 2 | 11/ 272 / 3 | 5/ 0 / 0 |
| Med | 14/ 142 / 2 | 6/ 500 / 3 | 30/ 333 /10 |
| Low | 3/ 0 / 0 | 19/ 684 /13 | 14/ 71 / 1 |

Curve Average .390

| | Inside | Middle | Outside |
|---|---|---|---|
| High | 0/ 0 / 0 | 7/ 142 / 1 | 3/ 333 / 1 |
| Med | 2/ 500 / 1 | 5/ 400 / 2 | 16/ 437 / 7 |
| Low | 0/ 0 / 0 | 3/ 666 / 2 | 5/ 400 / 2 |

Slider Average .428

| | Inside | Middle | Outside |
|---|---|---|---|
| High | 1/ 1000/ 1 | 3/ 0 / 0 | 2/ 500 / 1 |
| Med | 0/ 0 /. 0 | 0/ 0 / 0 | 13/ 538 / 7 |
| Low | 0/ 0 / 0 | 7/ 571 / 4 | 9/ 222 / 2 |

Change-Up Average .200

| | Inside | Middle | Outside |
|---|---|---|---|
| High | 0/ 0 / 0 | 1/ 1000/ 1 | 0/ 0 / 0 |
| Med | 0/ 0 / 0 | 0/ 0 / 0 | 0/ 0 / 0 |
| Low | 0/ 0 / 0 | 0/ 0 / 0 | 4/ 0 / 0 |

**Andre Dawson    Right-Handed Hitter**
**Against Right-Handed Pitchers When Behind In The Count**
**Batting Average Is .287**

Fastball Average .324                Curve Average .333

|  | Inside | Middle | Outside |
|---|---|---|---|
| High | 4/ 0 / 0 | 18/ 333 / 6 | 7/ 142 / 1 |
| Med | 6/ 666 / 4 | 1/ 0 / 0 | 14/ 285 / 4 |
| Low | 5/ 200 / 1 | 9/ 333 / 3 | 10/ 500 / 5 |

|  | Inside | Middle | Outside |
|---|---|---|---|
| High | 1/ 0 / 0 | 3/ 333 / 1 | 2/ 0 / 0 |
| Med | 1/ 1000/ 1 | 2/ 500 / 1 | 3/ 666 / 2 |
| Low | 0/ 0 / 0 | 2/ 500 / 1 | 10/ 200 / 2 |

Slider Average .263                Change-Up Average .200

|  | Inside | Middle | Outside |
|---|---|---|---|
| High | 2/ 0 / 0 | 2/ 0 / 0 | 0/ 0 / 0 |
| Med | 1/ 1000/ 1 | 1/ 1000/ 1 | 13/ 307 / 4 |
| Low | 0/ 0 / 0 | 1/ 0 / 0 | 18/ 222 / 4 |

|  | Inside | Middle | Outside |
|---|---|---|---|
| High | 0/ 0 / 0 | 1/ 0 / 0 | 0/ 0 / 0 |
| Med | 0/ 0 / 0 | 0/ 0 / 0 | 2/ 0 / 0 |
| Low | 0/ 0 / 0 | 0/ 0 / 0 | 2/ 500 / 1 |

Dawson's total fastball average is about the same when ahead and when behind, but his curve and slider averages are considerably higher. Notice Dawson's strength against waist-high curves and waist-high sliders when ahead.

**Dawson Against Left-Handed Pitchers**

Dawson's fastball average is higher against left-handed pitchers than against right-handers, but his curve average is much lower.

## Andre Dawson    Right-Handed Hitter
## Against All Left-Handed Pitchers All Teams
## Overall Batting Average Is .269

### Fastball Average .351

|      | Inside | Middle | Outside |
|------|--------|--------|---------|
| High | 5/ 200/1 | 9/ 333/3 | 13/ 384/5 |
| Med  | 8/ 375/3 | 2/ 500/1 | 23/ 434/10 |
| Low  | 5/ 200/1 | 14/ 214/3 | 29/ 379/11 |

### Curve Average .222

|      | Inside | Middle | Outside |
|------|--------|--------|---------|
| High | 0/ 0/0 | 1/ 0/0 | 0/ 0/0 |
| Med  | 4/ 250/1 | 1/ 1000/1 | 5/ 400/2 |
| Low  | 4/ 0/0 | 9/ 111/1 | 3/ 333/1 |

### Slider Average .235

|      | Inside | Middle | Outside |
|------|--------|--------|---------|
| High | 0/ 0/0 | 1/ 0/0 | 0/ 0/0 |
| Med  | 1/ 0/0 | 1/ 1000/1 | 0/ 0/0 |
| Low  | 8/ 0/0 | 6/ 500/3 | 0/ 0/0 |

### Change-Up Average .181

|      | Inside | Middle | Outside |
|------|--------|--------|---------|
| High | 0/ 0/0 | 0/ 0/0 | 3/ 0/0 |
| Med  | 0/ 0/0 | 1/ 0/0 | 6/ 333/2 |
| Low  | 0/ 0/0 | 4/ 250/1 | 8/ 125/1 |

Dawson scatters medium-high outside fastballs against left-handers.

MEDIUM-HIGH OUTSIDE FASTBALLS
(THROWN TO DAWSON BY LEFT-HANDED PITCHERS)

BATTING AVERAGE .434
   *PLAY*
LEFTFIELDER        Deep and shifted toward the left field line
CENTERFIELDER     Deep and shifted toward left field
RIGHTFIELDER      Deep and shifted toward the right field line
SHORTSTOP          Shifted toward third base
SECOND              Normal position

Dawson is strong in the low-outside fastball location against left-handed pitchers. Certainly he is much stronger than against right-handers in this location.

## LOW-OUTSIDE FASTBALLS
## (THROWN TO DAWSON BY LEFT-HANDED PITCHERS)

BATTING AVERAGE .379
*PLAY*

| | |
|---|---|
| LEFTFIELDER | Deep in straightaway left field |
| CENTERFIELDER | Deep and shifted toward left field |
| RIGHTFIELDER | Deep and shifted toward the right field line |
| SHORTSTOP | Up middle (shifted toward second base) |
| SECOND | Normal position |

Dawson has as much trouble with low curves against left-handed pitchers as he does against right-handers. He pulls low-over-the-middle curves, but the fielders are playing him correctly and his fly balls are just long outs.

## LOW-OVER-THE-MIDDLE CURVEBALLS
## (THROWN TO DAWSON BY LEFT-HANDED PITCHERS)

BATTING AVERAGE .111
*PLAY*

| | |
|---|---|
| LEFTFIELDER | Deep and shifted toward the left field line |
| CENTERFIELDER | Deep in straightaway center field |
| RIGHTFIELDER | No instances recorded |
| SHORTSTOP | Shifted toward third base |
| SECOND | No instances recorded |

Against left-handed pitchers, Dawson hits better when he is ahead in the count. Relatively few instances have been recorded for Dawson when he is behind in the count against left-handers, but an adequate number have been recorded when he is ahead.

### Andre Dawson    Right-Handed Hitter
### Against Left-Handed Pitchers When Ahead In The Count
### Batting Average Is .333

Fastball Average .388                    Curve Average .375

| | Inside | Middle | Outside | | Inside | Middle | Outside |
|---|---|---|---|---|---|---|---|
| High | 1/ 0 / 0 | 5/ 400 / 2 | 5/ 600 / 3 | | 0/ 0 / 0 | 0/ 0 / 0 | 0/ 0 / 0 |
| Med | 3/ 0 / 0 | 2/ 500 / 1 | 12/ 416 / 5 | | 2/ 0 / 0 | 0/ 0 / 0 | 4/ 500 / 2 |
| Low | 2/ 500 / 1 | 8/ 250 / 2 | 16/ 437 / 7 | | 0/ 0 / 0 | 1/ 0 / 0 | 1/ 1000 / 1 |

### Andre Dawson    Right-Handed Hitter
### Against Left-Handed Pitchers When Behind In The Count
### Batting Average Is .230

Fastball Average .238                    Curve Average .333

| | Inside | Middle | Outside | | Inside | Middle | Outside |
|---|---|---|---|---|---|---|---|
| High | 2/ 0 / 0 | 4/ 250 / 1 | 5/ 0 / 0 | | 0/ 0 / 0 | 1/ 0 / 0 | 0/ 0 / 0 |
| Med | 0/ 0 / 0 | 0/ 0 / 0 | 3/ 333 / 1 | | 1/ 1000 / 1 | 0/ 0 / 0 | 0/ 0 / 0 |
| Low | 0/ 0 / 0 | 4/ 250 / 1 | 3/ 666 / 2 | | 0/ 0 / 0 | 3/ 333 / 1 | 1/ 0 / 0 |

## *Personal Comments*

The next chapter shows additional examples of hits that could have been prevented by using the BARS System fielding strategy. Nine games are examined, with a discussion about every hit that could have been prevented. Also discussed are instances in which runners could have been held to fewer bases on extra-base hits. Preventing these extra bases is every bit as important as preventing base hits.

A few of the games in the next chapter were high-scoring, and they had a higher-than-average number of hits that could have been prevented. When teams combine for a large number of hits, there will almost always be many hits that could have been prevented by positioning fielders according to the BARS System fielding strategy.

Also included in the chapter are several low-scoring games in which there were a lower-than-average number of hits. The number of hits that could have been prevented in these games is usually less than in high-scoring games. The selection of low-scoring games shows how important preventing even one or two key hits can be.

Over the course of a season, some games will be high-scoring, some will be low-scoring. The important thing for a team is to position fielders as correctly as possible on every pitch. This will assure that the maximum number of hits, extra-base hits and runs are prevented. Over a 162-game season, preventing an average of two to three hits per game would make a tremendous difference in a team's final standing.

# Chapter Nineteen

## Preventable Hits: Additional Games

In this chapter, additional games are examined to show numerous examples of hits and runs that could have been prevented by using the BARS System fielding strategy.

### San Francisco at Cincinnati, August 12, 1986
### San Francisco 2, Cincinnati 1

In this low-scoring game San Francisco had three hits that could have been prevented, including two that led to the run that tied the score 1-1 in the top of the sixth.

Cincinnati had two hits that could have been prevented.

1. In the top of the second inning, San Francisco batter Bob Melvin (batting RH) came up to face Cincinnati right-hander Bill Gullickson. There were two outs and no runners on base. The count went full (3-2), and Melvin lined a medium-high outside fastball into right field for a long single.

Cincinnati right fielder Dave Parker could have caught the ball if he had been playing medium-deep in straightaway right field.

### Bob Melvin     Right-Handed Hitter
### Against All Right-Handed Pitchers All Teams

Fastball Average .223

|  | Inside | Middle | Outside |
|---|---|---|---|
| High | 8/ 125 / 1 | 8/ 375 / 3 | 7/ 142 / 1 |
| Med | 11/ 363 / 4 | 2/ 500 / 1 | 10/ 200 / 2 |
| Low | 4/ 250 / 1 | 8/ 125 / 1 | 9/ 111 / 1 |

The following chart shows the suggested positions fielders should have taken against Melvin when a medium-high outside fastball by a right-handed pitcher was thrown with the count even.

MEDIUM-HIGH OUTSIDE FASTBALLS
(THROWN TO MELVIN WITH THE COUNT EVEN)

BATTING AVERAGE .200

*PLAY*

| | |
|---|---|
| LEFTFIELDER | No recorded instances |
| CENTERFIELDER | Deep and shifted toward right field |
| **RIGHTFIELDER** | **Medium-deep in straightaway right field** |
| SHORTSTOP | Up middle |
| SECOND | Normal position |

Note the suggested fielding position for the right fielder. If Dave Parker, the Cincinnati right fielder, had been positioned as suggested by the BARS fielding strategy on this particular pitch to Melvin (medium-high outside fastball thrown by a right-handed pitchers with the count even), he would have been positioned correctly to catch the ball.

2. In the bottom of the fifth, Cincinnati batter Kurt Stillwell (batting RH) came up against San Francisco left-hander Vida Blue. There were no outs and no runners on base. On the 1-0 pitch, a low-over-the-middle fastball, Stillwell lined a single to left field that could have been caught if the Giants' left fielder, Candy Maldonado, had been playing medium-deep in left. As it was, Maldonado was playing deep and could not reach the ball.

**BARS: LEFTFIELDER Medium-deep in straightaway left field**

The ball could have been caught if the left fielder had been positioned as suggested for this type and location of pitch to Stillwell.

**Kurt Stillwell    Right-Handed Hitter**
**Against All Left-Handed Pitchers All Teams**

Fastball Average .242

| | Inside | Middle | Outside |
|---|---|---|---|
| High | 2/ 0 / 0 | 2/ 0 / 0 | 4/ 500 / 2 |
| Med | 4/ 250 / 1 | 0/ 0 / 0 | 12/ 166 / 2 |
| Low | 2/ 500 / 1 | 3/ 333 / 1 | 4/ 250 / 1 |

For the remainder of this chapter, the BARS System Super Summary fielding strategy will be shown for only the fielder or fielders that could have prevented the hit.

3. The next Cincinnati batter, Buddy Bell (RH), hit the first pitch, a medium-high inside fastball, into left field for a single, advancing Stillwell to second.

If the San Francisco left fielder had been playing medium-deep and straightaway, or deep and straightaway, he could have caught the ball for the out.

### BARS: LEFTFIELDER  Deep in straightaway left field

This long single could have been caught if the left fielder had been positioned as suggested by the BARS System fielding strategy.

**Buddy Bell      Right-Handed Hitter**
**Against All Left-Handed Pitchers All Teams**

Fastball Average .267

| | Inside | Middle | Outside |
|---|---|---|---|
| High | 333 $3/1$ | 384 $13/5$ | 125 $8/1$ |
| Med | 250 $8/2$ | 400 $20/8$ | 228 $35/8$ |
| Low | 125 $8/1$ | 263 $19/5$ | 235 $17/4$ |

4. In the top of the sixth, San Francisco batter Bob Melvin (RH) came up against Gullickson (RH) with two outs and a runner on first (Bob Brenly). Melvin fell behind in the count 1-2, then blooped a high-inside fastball down the line into left field for a single, advancing Brenly to second.

If the Cincinnati left fielder, Nick Esasky, had been playing short or medium-deep along the line, he could have caught the ball for the out.

### BARS: LEFTFIELDER  Medium-deep and shifted
### toward the left field line

The Cincinnati left fielder would have been perfectly positioned to catch the ball if he had been positioned according to the BARS System fielding strategy.

## Bob Melvin    Right-Handed Hitter
## Against All Right-Handed Pitchers All Teams

Fastball Average .223

|  | Inside | Middle | Outside |
|---|---|---|---|
| High | 125 $^8/_1$ | 375 $^8/_3$ | 142 $^7/_1$ |
| Med | 363 $^{11}/_4$ | 500 $^2/_1$ | 200 $^{10}/_2$ |
| Low | 250 $^4/_1$ | 125 $^8/_1$ | 111 $^9/_1$ |

5. Still with two outs in the top of the sixth, left-handed pinch hitter Mike Aldrete came up for San Francisco. He fell behind in the count 0-2, then hit a high-inside fastball into the gap in right center for a double, driving in Brenly from second to tie the score 1-1.

If Dave Parker, the Cincinnati right fielder, had been positioned deep and shifted toward center field, he could have caught the ball to end the inning.

## BARS: RIGHTFIELDER  Deep and shifted toward center field

Parker could have caught the ball to end the inning if he had been shifted toward center field, as suggested by the BARS System fielding strategy for this particular pitch to Aldrete.

## Mike Aldrete    Left-Handed Hitter
## Against All Right-Handed Pitchers All Teams

Fastball Average .272

|  | Outside | Middle | Inside |
|---|---|---|---|
| High | 0 $^1/_0$ | 600 $^5/_3$ | 400 $^5/_2$ |
| Med | 300 $^{20}/_6$ | 500 $^2/_1$ | 250 $^4/_1$ |
| Low | 0 $^6/_0$ | 333 $^6/_2$ | 0 $^6/_0$ |

**Game Summary:**

San Francisco had three hits that could have been prevented by Cincinnati, including the hits that led to the tying run.

Cincinnati had two hits that could have been prevented by San Francisco.

**Toronto at New York, September 30, 1986**
**New York 5, Toronto 2**

In this game, New York had three runs in the first inning, including the game-winning run, that resulted directly from hits that could have been prevented if Toronto had positioned its fielders according to the BARS System fielding strategy.

In the game, New York had four hits that could have been prevented. Toronto had two.

1. In the top of the first inning, with Toronto at bat and one out, Rance Mulliniks (LH) came up to hit against Yankee pitcher Scott Nielsen (RH). The first pitch was a low-over-the-middle fastball that Mulliniks hit on the ground about 10 feet to the shortstop-side of second base. The ball skipped through for a single.

The Yankee shortstop was playing in his normal straightaway position. He could have gotten to the ball and thrown Mulliniks out if he had been playing more up the middle (shifted toward second base).

**BARS: SHORTSTOP  Up middle (shifted toward second base)**

If the Yankee infield had been positioned according to the BARS System fielding strategy, the shortstop would have been perfectly positioned to field the ball and throw Mulliniks out.

### Rance Mulliniks    Left-Handed Hitter
### Against All Right-Handed Pitchers All Teams

Fastball Average .307

|  | Outside | Middle | Inside |
|---|---|---|---|
| High | 222 $\diagup$ 2 $^{9}$ | 260 $\diagup$ 6 $^{23}$ | 100 $\diagup$ 1 $^{10}$ |
| Med | 281 $\diagup$ 18 $^{64}$ | 666 $\diagup$ 12 $^{18}$ | 238 $\diagup$ 5 $^{21}$ |
| Low | 250 $\diagup$ 4 $^{16}$ | 392 $\diagup$ 11 $^{28}$ | 250 $\diagup$ 4 $^{16}$ |

2. With two outs in the top of the first, Toronto batter George Bell (RH) came up against Nielsen. With the count 1-2, Nielsen threw a medium-high outside slider that Bell lined to short right center for a single.

The Yankee center fielder was playing deep in center shaded toward left. He couldn't reach the ball.

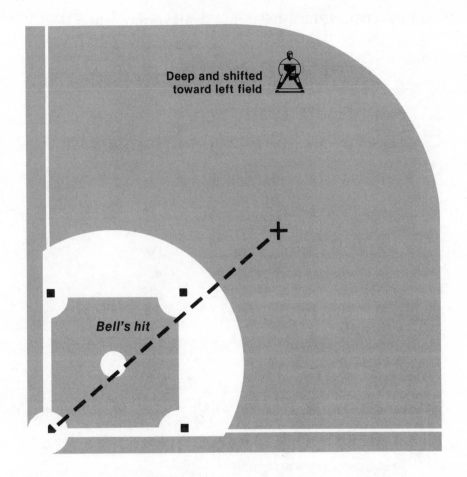

**Deep and shifted toward left field**

**Bell's hit**

If the Yankee center fielder had been playing medium-deep or short straightaway, he could have caught the ball.

**BARS: CENTERFIELDER** Short in straightaway center field

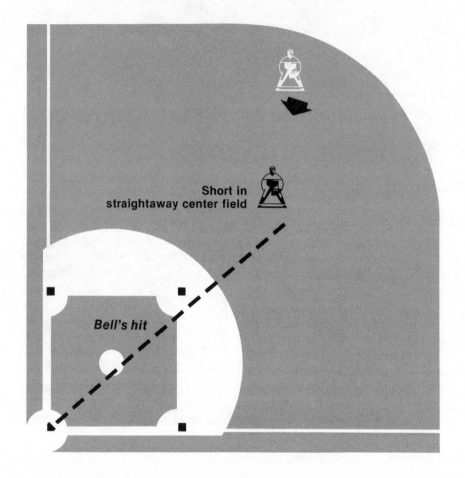

The center fielder could have caught this ball if he had been positioned as suggested.

One point to mention is that the fielding strategy called for by the BARS System will occasionally contrast greatly with generally accepted fielding strategy. A center fielder may feel it unwise to play shallow against a hitter of Bell's power, even though the BARS System long-term computer trends show that the center fielder is best positioned in short straightaway center.

In such a situation the center fielder could play in his normal deep or medium-deep position while anticipating that Bell might hit the ball to shallow center. This would allow the center fielder to get a jump on the ball if it were hit as the BARS System trends indicate.

By following such strategy, fielders could position themselves as they normally would, while using the BARS System fielding strategy to anticipate where the ball might be hit.

The following chart shows the suggested fielding positions from the BARS System Super Summary.

MEDIUM-HIGH OUTSIDE SLIDERS
(THROWN TO BELL BY RIGHT-HANDED PITCHERS)

BATTING AVERAGE .200
   *PLAY*
LEFTFIELDER         Deep in straightaway left field
**CENTERFIELDER**   **Short in straightaway center field**
RIGHTFIELDER      Deep in straightaway right field
SHORTSTOP         Shifted toward third base
SECOND             Shifted toward first base

**George Bell     Right-Handed Hitter**
**Against All Right-Handed Pitchers All Teams**

Slider Average .348

|  | Inside | Middle | Outside |
|------|--------|--------|---------|
| High | 1 / <br>**0** / 0 | 2 / <br>**0** / 0 | 3 / <br>**333** / 1 |
| Med | 3 / <br>**666** / 2 | 3 / <br>**333** / 1 | 10 / <br>**200** / 2 |
| Low | 1 / <br>**0** / 0 | 9 / <br>**444** / 4 | 11 / <br>**454** / 5 |

3. In the bottom of the first, New York batter Don Mattingly (LH) came up against Toronto pitcher Dave Stieb (RH). With no outs and a runner on first, the count went to 3-1 and Mattingly grounded a medium-high inside fastball between the first and second basemen for a single.

The second baseman was playing in his normal straightaway position. He could have fielded the ball if he had been playing shifted toward first.

**BARS: SECOND Shifted toward first base**

It is interesting to note that if Mattingly had been behind in the count instead of ahead, the BARS fielding strategy would have suggested that the second baseman play at his normal position instead of shifted toward first base.

## Don Mattingly    Left-Handed Hitter
## Against All Right-Handed Pitchers All Teams

Fastball Average .361

|  | Outside | Middle | Inside |
|---|---|---|---|
| High | 42/<br>**428**/18 | 34/<br>**323**/11 | 14/<br>**571**/8 |
| Med | 124/<br>**290**/36 | 39/<br>**435**/17 | 33/<br>**272**/9 |
| Low | 35/<br>**457**/16 | 73/<br>**383**/28 | 24/<br>**333**/8 |

4. Two batters later in the bottom of the first, with one out and runners on first and third, Dave Winfield (RH) came to bat against Stieb. The 1-1 pitch was a low-outside slider that Winfield hit between the shortstop and the third baseman, scoring the runner from third.

The shortstop was playing at his normal straightaway position and couldn't reach the ball. If he had been playing shifted toward third, he could have fielded it, preventing the hit and the run.

**BARS: SHORTSTOP Shifted toward third base**

The BARS System fielding strategy would have positioned the shortstop more toward third base on this particular location and type of pitch to Winfield. Shifted toward third, the shortstop could have fielded the ball.

**Dave Winfield     Right-Handed Hitter**
**Against All Right-Handed Pitchers All Teams**

Slider Average .231

|  | Inside | Middle | Outside |
|---|---|---|---|
| High | $^1/_0$  **0** | $^9/_3$  **333** | $^1/_1$  **1000** |
| Med | $^4/_2$  **500** | $^7/_4$  **571** | $^{32}/_7$  **218** |
| Low | $^4/_0$  **0** | $^{11}/_1$  **90** | $^{26}/_4$  **153** |

The above batting chart shows that a low-outside slider is a good pitch to throw Winfield. He hits only .153 in that location. But if the fielders are not positioned correctly, even the best pitch can result in a hit.

5. Still in the bottom of the first, with one out and runners on first and third, Dan Pasqua (LH) came to the plate for the Yankees. The first pitch was a low-over-the-middle fastball that Pasqua hit to very deep left center field, scoring both runners (the second being the game-winning RBI).

The Toronto center fielder was playing medium-deep in right center. He could have caught the ball if he had been playing deeper or more straightaway.

## BARS: CENTERFIELDER  Deep in straightaway center field

The center fielder would have caught the ball if he had been positioned according to the BARS System fielding strategy. The runner on third would have scored on the sacrifice, but the hit and the second run (the game-winning RBI) could have been prevented.

### Dan Pasqua    Left-Handed Hitter
### Against All Right-Handed Pitchers All Teams

Fastball Average .255

|  | Outside | Middle | Inside |
|---|---|---|---|
| High | 11/<br>272 / 3 | 6/<br>166 / 1 | 1/<br>0 / 0 |
| Med | 49/<br>265 / 13 | 14/<br>428 / 6 | 12/<br>166 / 2 |
| Low | 9/<br>222 / 2 | 19/<br>263 / 5 | 8/<br>125 / 1 |

6. Rounding out the Yankees' bottom of the first, Mike Pagliarulo (LH) came up to hit against Stieb. With one out and a runner (Pasqua) on second, Pagliarulo hit the 1-1 pitch, a low-inside slider, into shallow left field down the line.

The left fielder was playing medium-deep in straightaway left and couldn't quite get to the ball. He could have caught it if he had been playing shifted more toward the left field line.

**BARS: LEFTFIELDER  Medium-deep and shifted toward left field line**

### Mike Pagliarulo    Left-Handed Hitter
### Against All Right-Handed Pitchers All Teams

Slider Average .244

|  | Outside | Middle | Inside |
|---|---|---|---|
| High | 0/<br>0 / 0 | 0/<br>0 / 0 | 3/<br>0 / 0 |
| Med | 4/<br>500 / 2 | 5/<br>0 / 0 | 6/<br>333 / 2 |
| Low | 5/<br>0 / 0 | 9/<br>222 / 2 | 17/<br>352 / 6 |

**Game Summary:**

Toronto had two hits that New York could have prevented.

New York had four hits that Toronto could have prevented, including the hit that drove in the game's winning run.

**Atlanta at New York, April 12, 1987**
**Atlanta 12, New York 4**

In this game the Mets had six hits that could have been prevented. Atlanta had three.

1. In the bottom of the second, Len Dykstra (LH) came to bat against Atlanta right-hander Randy O'Neal with two outs and a runner on first. On the 2-2 pitch, Dykstra hit a high-inside fastball down the left field line.

The Braves' left fielder, Gary Roenicke, was playing deep in straight-away left and couldn't reach the ball. If he had been playing medium-deep and shifted toward the line, he could have caught the ball for the out.

**BARS: LEFTFIELDER  Medium-deep and shifted**
**toward the left field line**

If Roenicke had been positioned as suggested by the BARS System Super Summary, he could have easily caught this bloop single.

**Len Dykstra      Left-Handed Hitter**
**Against All Right-Handed Pitchers All Teams**

Fastball Average .288

|      | Outside | Middle | Inside |
|------|---------|--------|--------|
| High | 15 / 266 / 4 | 21 / 428 / 9 | 19 / 263 / 5 |
| Med  | 27 / 185 / 5 | 8 / 500 / 4 | 33 / 272 / 9 |
| Low  | 10 / 100 / 1 | 34 / 294 / 10 | 17 / 352 / 6 |

2. In the bottom of the fourth with one out, Dykstra came up to face O'Neal a second time. The 1-1 pitch was a low-over-the-middle fastball that Dykstra lined into left field past Atlanta's shortstop Andres Thomas, who was playing shifted toward second base.

Thomas could have caught the ball for the out if he had been playing in his normal straightaway position.

## BARS: SHORTSTOP  Normal position

Thomas was playing shifted slightly toward second base. He could have caught the ball if he had been playing as suggested by the BARS System fielding strategy.

### Len Dykstra    Left-Handed Hitter
### Against All Right-Handed Pitchers All Teams

Fastball Average .288

|  | Outside | Middle | Inside |
|---|---|---|---|
| High | 15/<br>266 / 4 | 21/<br>428 / 9 | 19/<br>263 / 5 |
| Med | 27/<br>185 / 5 | 8/<br>500 / 4 | 33/<br>272 / 9 |
| Low | 10/<br>100 / 1 | 34/<br>294 /10 | 17/<br>352 / 6 |

3. In the top of the seventh with no outs and the bases loaded, Atlanta's Ken Griffey (LH) came to bat against Doug Sisk (RH). On the 2-1 pitch, Sisk threw a high-over-the-middle fastball. Griffey grounded it up the middle into center field for a single, driving in Randy O'Neal from third and Dion James from second.

The grounder was hit to the shortstop-side of second base. The Mets' shortstop, Rafael Santana, was playing at the normal shortstop position and couldn't reach the ball. Had he been playing shifted toward second, he could have fielded the ball, starting a double play and preventing the hit. The runner on third probably would have scored in any case on this ground ball up the middle, but the second run could have been prevented.

## BARS: SHORTSTOP  Up middle (shifted toward second base)

Following the suggested fielding strategy could have prevented the hit and the second run.

**Ken Griffey     Left-Handed Hitter**
**Against All Right-Handed Pitchers All Teams**

Fastball Average .340

|  | Outside | Middle | Inside |
|------|---------|--------|--------|
| High | 24/333 / 8 | 27/296 / 8 | 6/333 / 2 |
| Med | 97/391 /38 | 33/303 /10 | 29/310 / 9 |
| Low | 23/347 / 8 | 48/312 /15 | 36/333 /12 |

4. In the top of the seventh, still with no outs, Andres Thomas (RH) came to bat for the Braves against Sisk. The first pitch was a high-inside fastball that Thomas hit into medium-deep left field toward the line for a single.

New York left fielder Kevin McReynolds was playing deep in straight-away left and couldn't reach the ball. If he had been playing medium-deep in left and more toward the line, he could have caught it.

**BARS:  LEFTFIELDER  Medium-deep and shifted**
**toward the left field line**

McReynolds would have been perfectly positioned to catch the ball if he had been positioned according to the BARS System fielding strategy.

**Andres Thomas     Right-Handed Hitter**
**Against All Right-Handed Pitchers All Teams**

Fastball Average .192

|  | Inside | Middle | Outside |
|------|--------|--------|---------|
| High | 15/133 / 2 | 16/312 / 5 | 8/0 / 0 |
| Med | 16/62 / 1 | 4/0 / 0 | 30/166 / 5 |
| Low | 6/333 / 2 | 11/454 / 5 | 8/250 / 2 |

5. In the bottom of the seventh, New York's Wally Backman (batting LH) came up to hit against O'Neal. The 1-0 pitch was a low fastball over the middle part of the plate that Backman lined to deep left field for a double.

The Braves' left fielder, Ken Griffey, was playing medium-deep in straightaway left. If he had been playing deeper he could have caught the ball.

## BARS: LEFTFIELDER  Deep in straightaway left field

Griffey would have had no problem catching the ball if he had been positioned deeper in left.

### Wally Backman    Left-Handed Hitter
### Against All Right-Handed Pitchers All Teams

Fastball Average .317

|  | Outside | Middle | Inside |
|---|---|---|---|
| High | 17/<br>117 / 2 | 47/<br>468 /22 | 28/<br>285 / 8 |
| Med | 49/<br>224 /11 | 37/<br>351 /13 | 78/<br>333 /26 |
| Low | 8/<br>125 / 1 | 56/<br>357 /20 | 36/<br>277 /10 |

6. In the top of the eighth, with one out and a runner on first base, Ken Griffey (LH) came up to bat against Sisk. The 0-1 pitch to Griffey was a medium-high fastball over the outside part of the plate. Griffey hit it on a line to medium-deep left center for a double.

The New York center fielder, Len Dykstra, was playing deep and straightaway in center and couldn't quite reach the ball. If he had been playing medium-deep he could have made the catch.

## BARS: CENTERFIELDER  Medium-deep in straightaway
## center field

The New York center fielder could have caught the line drive if he had been positioned medium-deep in straightaway center field as suggested.

### Ken Griffey    Left-Handed Hitter
### Against All Right-Handed Pitchers All Teams

Fastball Average .340

| | Outside | Middle | Inside |
|---|---|---|---|
| High | 24/333 /8 | 27/296 /8 | 6/333 /2 |
| Med | 97/391 /38 | 33/303 /10 | 29/310 /9 |
| Low | 23/347 /8 | 48/312 /15 | 36/333 /12 |

7. In the bottom of the eighth with one out and no runners on base, right-handed Mets batter Rafael Santana came up to hit against against Charlie Puleo (RH). Santana blooped the first pitch, a medium-high inside fastball, into left center field.

The Atlanta center fielder, Dion James, was playing medium-deep and shifted toward right field. He couldn't quite reach the ball. If he had been medium-deep and shifted toward left field, he could have made the catch.

### BARS: CENTERFIELDER  Medium-deep and shifted toward left field

James would have had no trouble reaching the ball if he had been positioned as suggested by the BARS System fielding strategy.

### Rafael Santana    Right-Handed Hitter
### Against All Right-Handed Pitchers All Teams

Fastball Average .282

| | Inside | Middle | Outside |
|---|---|---|---|
| High | 17/117 /2 | 28/178 /5 | 8/250 /2 |
| Med | 34/294 /10 | 8/625 /5 | 41/268 /11 |
| Low | 9/555 /5 | 30/300 /9 | 16/312 /5 |

8. In the bottom of the ninth, Tim Teufel (RH) came to bat against Atlanta left-hander Ed Olwine. The first pitch was a waist-high fastball over the outside part of the plate. Teufel hit it to deep center field for a double.

Atlanta center fielder Dion James was playing shallow and shifted toward right field. He couldn't get to the ball.

If James had been deep in center he could have made the catch.

**BARS: CENTERFIELDER  Deep in straightaway center field**

The ball would have been hit almost directly to James if he had been playing deep and straightaway, as suggested.

### Tim Teufel    Right-Handed Hitter
### Against All Left-Handed Pitchers All Teams

Fastball Average .227

| | Inside | Middle | Outside |
|---|---|---|---|
| High | 5/<br>200 / 1 | 10/<br>300 / 3 | 10/<br>300 / 3 |
| Med | 10/<br>100 / 1 | 11/<br>272 / 3 | 25/<br>160 / 4 |
| Low | 7/<br>0 / 0 | 16/<br>437 / 7 | 7/<br>142 / 1 |

9. In the bottom of the ninth with two outs and Teufel on third, Darryl Strawberry (LH) came to bat for the Mets against Olwine. Strawberry fell behind in the count 1-2, then grounded a medium-high outside curveball into center field for a single. The ground ball was hit through the second baseman's normal position.

The Atlanta second baseman, Glenn Hubbard, was playing shifted toward first against the left-handed Strawberry and couldn't get to the ball.

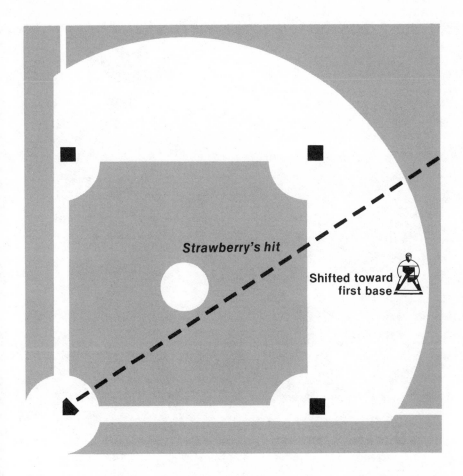

If he had been in his normal position, he could have fielded the ball and thrown Strawberry out at first base to end the game.

**BARS: SECOND  Normal position**

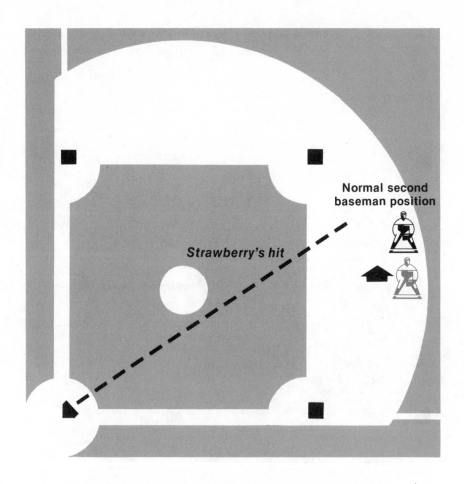

The Atlanta second baseman, Glenn Hubbard, would have had no trouble reaching the ball if he had been playing as suggested.

### Darryl Strawberry    Left-Handed Hitter
### Against All Left-Handed Pitchers All Teams

Curve Average .200

|  | Outside | Middle | Inside |
|---|---|---|---|
| High | 1000⁄1 | 0⁄0 | 0⁄0 |
| Med | 200⁄1 | 333⁄2 | 250⁄1 |
| Low | 0⁄0 | 333⁄1 | 0⁄0 |

**Game Summary:**

New York had six hits that could have been prevented by Atlanta.

Atlanta had three hits that could have been prevented by New York.

## Chicago at Atlanta, May 30, 1987
## Chicago 11, Atlanta 6

This game is noteworthy in that Chicago had a total of seven hits that could have been prevented by use of the BARS System Super Summary, plus one instance in which a runner could have been held to fewer bases. In all, eight of Chicago's 11 runs resulted directly from hits that could have been prevented.

Atlanta had three hits that could have been prevented. From these, two runs resulted.

1. In the bottom of the first inning, Atlanta's Ken Oberkfell (LH) came to the plate against Greg Maddux (RH) with one out and no runners on base. Oberkfell worked the count to 3-1, then lined a medium-high inside fastball 300 feet into right center field.

The Cubs' right fielder, Andre Dawson, was playing straightaway and medium-deep in right. If he had been playing deep and shifted toward center field, he could have caught the ball for the out.

### BARS: RIGHTFIELDER Deep and shifted toward center field

The Cubs' right fielder would have been perfectly positioned to catch the ball if he had been playing deep and shifted toward center field, as suggested by the BARS System fielding strategy.

### Ken Oberkfell Left-Handed Hitter
### Against All Right-Handed Pitchers All Teams

Fastball Average .304

| | Outside | Middle | Inside |
|------|---------|--------|--------|
| High | 16/ 312 / 5 | 53/ 264 /14 | 19/ 263 / 5 |
| Med | 77/ 337 /26 | 31/ 419 /13 | 66/ 348 /23 |
| Low | 34/ 235 / 8 | 90/ 277 /25 | 48/ 270 /13 |

2. Shawon Dunston (RH) led off for Chicago in the top of the third, facing left-hander Zane Smith. On the 2-1 pitch, Dunston hit a low-over-the-middle fastball through the shortstop's normal position into center field for a single.

The Braves' shortstop; Andres Thomas, was playing shifted toward third and couldn't reach the ball. If he had been playing in his normal straightaway shortstop position, he could have fielded the ball and thrown Dunston out at first.

### BARS: SHORTSTOP Normal position

### Shawon Dunston Right-Handed Hitter
### Against All Left-Handed Pitchers All Teams

Fastball Average .165

| | Inside | Middle | Outside |
|------|--------|--------|---------|
| High | 5/ 0 / 0 | 8/ 125 / 1 | 10/ 100 / 1 |
| Med | 5/ 0 / 0 | 1/ 1000/ 1 | 28/ 250 / 7 |
| Low | 5/ 200 / 1 | 24/ 208 / 5 | 17/ 58 / 1 |

3. With one out in the top of the third and Dunston on second base, Chicago batter Ryne Sandberg (RH) came up to face Smith. On the 2-1 pitch, Sandberg hit a medium-high outside fastball between the shortstop and third baseman into left field for a single, driving in Dunston from second base.

The Atlanta shortstop, Andres Thomas, was playing shifted toward second and couldn't reach Sandberg's grounder. If he had been playing shifted toward third, he could have fielded the ball, throwing Sandberg out and holding Dunston at second.

### BARS: SHORTSTOP  Shifted toward third base

Thomas could have prevented the hit and the run if he had been playing as suggested by the BARS System fielding strategy. The Braves' shortstop was incorrectly positioned twice in the same inning, allowing two key hits that could have been prevented.

**Ryne Sandberg    Right-Handed Hitter**
**Against All Left-Handed Pitchers All Teams**

Fastball Average .292

|  | Inside | Middle | Outside |
|---|---|---|---|
| High | 6/<br>166 / 1 | 17/<br>176 / 3 | 18/<br>222 / 4 |
| Med | 27/<br>222 / 6 | 10/<br>300 / 3 | 63/<br>253 / 16 |
| Low | 9/<br>222 / 2 | 50/<br>440 / 22 | 50/<br>320 / 16 |

4. In the top of the sixth with two outs and no runners on base, Chicago's Leon Durham (LH) came up to face Smith. The 2-1 pitch was a medium-high outside fastball that Durham hit on the ground into center field for a single.

The Braves' second baseman, Glenn Hubbard, was playing shifted toward first base and couldn't reach the ball. If he had been playing at his normal position, he could have fielded the ball and thrown Durham out. Durham scored later in the inning.

### BARS: SECOND  Normal position

This hit could have been prevented if the second baseman has been positioned according to the suggested BARS System fielding strategy.

**Leon Durham     Left-Handed Hitter**
**Against All Left-Handed Pitchers All Teams**

Fastball Average .255

|  | Outside | Middle | Inside |
|------|---------|--------|--------|
| High | 7/<br>142 / 1 | 15/<br>133 / 2 | 13/<br>153 / 2 |
| Med | 28/<br>250 / 7 | 4/<br>250 / 1 | 41/<br>365 / 15 |
| Low | 12/<br>83 / 1 | 33/<br>242 / 8 | 15/<br>400 / 6 |

5. In the top of the sixth with two outs and runners on first and second, Shawon Dunston came to the plate against Atlanta right-hander Jim Acker. Dunston hit the 1-0 pitch, a low-outside slider, over the second baseman's head into short right center field.

Dale Murphy was playing medium-deep in straightaway right. The ball would have been a hit in any case, but if Murphy had been playing short in right and shifted toward center, he possibly could have fielded the ball in time to  prevent the runner on second from scoring.

**BARS:  RIGHTFIELDER  Short and shifted toward center field**

Positioned in short right field and shifted toward center, Murphy could have charged the ball and fielded it on the hop. He then would have possibly been able to prevent the run.

**Shawon Dunston     Right-Handed Hitter**
**Against All Right-Handed Pitchers All Teams**

Slider Average .300

|  | Inside | Middle | Outside |
|------|--------|--------|---------|
| High | 1/<br>1000/ 1 | 1/<br>0 / 0 | 5/<br>200 / 1 |
| Med | 2/<br>500 / 1 | 2/<br>500 / 1 | 33/<br>303 / 10 |
| Low | 1/<br>1000/ 1 | 10/<br>700 / 7 | 45/<br>177 / 8 |

Notice in the above chart that the pitch was to Dunston's weakest slider location (.177 in low-outside). The fielders were not properly positioned, and a good pitch went to waste.

6. Still with two outs in the top of the sixth, Bob Dernier (RH) came up to hit against Acker. There were runners on first (Dunston) and third (Gary Mathews). On the 1-0 pitch, Dernier hit a low-over-the-middle fastball between the shortstop and third baseman into left field for a single, driving in Mathews and moving Dunston to second.

The Braves' shortstop, Andres Thomas, was playing in his normal position. If he had been shifted toward third base, he could have prevented the hit and the run.

### BARS: SHORTSTOP  Shifted toward third base

The ball would have been hit almost directly at Thomas, who could have thrown Dernier out at first, ending the inning and preventing the run.

### Bob Dernier    Right-Handed Hitter
### Against All Right-Handed Pitchers All Teams

Fastball Average .244

|  | Inside | Middle | Outside |
|---|---|---|---|
| High | 30/100 / 3 | 83/228 / 19 | 30/100 / 3 |
| Med | 41/219 / 9 | 23/347 / 8 | 144/298 / 43 |
| Low | 28/142 / 4 | 103/300 / 31 | 63/206 / 13 |

7. In the top of the seventh, Keith Moreland (RH) came to bat for Chicago against Acker. There were two outs and a runner was on first base. The first pitch was a medium-high outside fastball that Moreland lined between the shortstop and the third baseman for a single.

Atlanta shortstop Thomas was playing in his normal position. If he had been playing shifted toward third, the ball would have been lined right at him, and he could have caught it for the out.

### BARS: SHORTSTOP  Shifted toward third base

The Atlanta shortstop would have been perfectly positioned to catch this line drive if he had been playing according to the BARS System fielding strategy.

### Keith Moreland    Right-Handed Hitter
### Against All Right-Handed Pitchers All Teams

Fastball Average .309

|  | Inside | Middle | Outside |
|---|---|---|---|
| High | 39/<br>179 / 7 | 94/<br>265 /25 | 43/<br>302 /13 |
| Med | 100/<br>430 /43 | 37/<br>324 /12 | 182/<br>329 /60 |
| Low | 35/<br>314 /11 | 198/<br>338 /67 | 99/<br>181 /18 |

8. Still with two outs in the top of the seventh, Shawon Dunston came up against Acker with Moreland on first base and Dayett on second. The first pitch was a low-over-the-middle fastball that Dunston lined to deep left field.

Atlanta left fielder Ken Griffey was playing straightaway at normal depth. The ball went over his head for a double, scoring both runners.

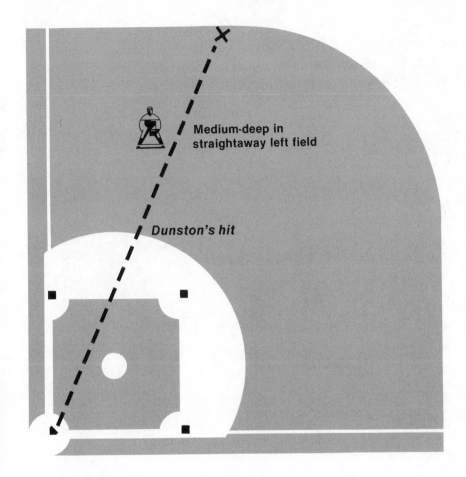

If Griffey had been playing straightaway and deep in left field, he could have caught the ball.

**BARS: LEFTFIELDER  Deep in straightaway left field**

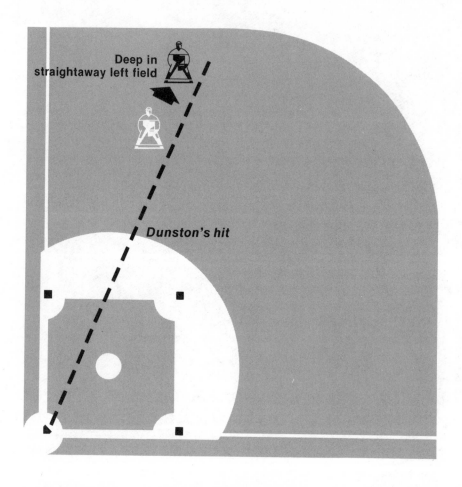

Griffey was not playing deep enough for this type and location of pitch to Dunston. If Griffey had been playing as suggested, he could have caught the ball, ending the inning and preventing two runs.

**Shawon Dunston    Right-Handed Hitter**
**Against All Right-Handed Pitchers All Teams**

Fastball Average .304

|  | Inside | Middle | Outside |
|---|---|---|---|
| High | 32/<br>**156** / 5 | 31/<br>**258** / 8 | 23/<br>**86** / 2 |
| Med | 27/<br>**333** / 9 | 2/<br>**0** / 0 | 42/<br>**333** /14 |
| Low | 25/<br>**400** /10 | 56/<br>**428** /24 | 35/<br>**314** /11 |

9. In the top of the eighth with two outs and no runners on, Chicago batter Manny Trillo (RH) came to the plate facing Atlanta right-hander Randy O'Neal. The first pitch was a medium-high outside fastball that Trillo hit between the shortstop and the third baseman into left field for a single.

Atlanta shortstop Thomas was playing at his normal position. If he had been playing shifted toward third, he could have prevented the hit.

**BARS: SHORTSTOP Shifted toward third base**

**Manny Trillo    Batting Right-Handed**
**Against All Right-Handed Pitchers All Teams**

Fastball Average .293

|  | Inside | Middle | Outside |
|---|---|---|---|
| High | 10/<br>**200** / 2 | 12/<br>**0** / 0 | 9/<br>**222** / 2 |
| Med | 18/<br>**277** / 5 | 6/<br>**666** / 4 | 39/<br>**333** /13 |
| Low | 7/<br>**428** / 3 | 26/<br>**384** /10 | 16/<br>**187** / 3 |

10. In the bottom of the ninth, Atlanta batter Ted Simmons (batting LH) came to bat against Chicago right-hander Dickie Noles with two outs and a

runner (Graig Nettles) on third. The 1-1 pitch was a medium-high inside fastball that Simmons grounded into center field, scoring Nettles.

Chicago shortstop Shawon Dunston was playing at his normal straightaway position. If he had been playing shifted toward second, he could have fielded the ball, preventing the hit and the run.

## BARS: SHORTSTOP Up middle (shifted toward second base)

Dunston could have fielded the ball to end the game if he had been positioned as suggested by the BARS System fielding strategy.

### Ted Simmons    Left-Handed Hitter
### Against All Right-Handed Pitchers All Teams

Fastball Average .305

|  | Outside | Middle | Inside |
|---|---|---|---|
| High | 17/294 / 5 | 24/250 / 6 | 7/428 / 3 |
| Med | 54/351 / 19 | 29/448 / 13 | 19/368 / 7 |
| Low | 14/142 / 2 | 21/95 / 2 | 5/200 / 1 |

11. Several batters later in the Braves' bottom of the ninth, Dale Murphy (RH) came to the plate with two outs. There were runners on first (Gerald Perry) and second (Ted Simmons). The first pitch was a medium-high outside fastball that Murphy grounded into right field between the second and first basemen. Simmons scored and Perry went to second.

Chicago second baseman Ryne Sandberg was playing shifted toward second. If he had been playing in his normal position, he could have fielded the ball and ended the game.

## BARS: SECOND Normal position

The BARS System fielding strategy would have positioned Sandberg closer to first base. As it was, he just missed the ball. If he had been playing in his normal straightaway position, he could have fielded it, preventing the hit and the run.

### Dale Murphy    Right-Handed Hitter
### Against All Right-Handed Pitchers All Teams

Fastball Average .317

|  | Inside | Middle | Outside |
|---|---|---|---|
| High | 17/<br>58 / 1 | 47/<br>340 / 16 | 32/<br>250 / 8 |
| Med | 77/<br>311 /24 | 61/<br>360 /22 | 123/<br>349 /43 |
| Low | 36/<br>250 / 9 | 127/<br>362 /46 | 69/<br>260 /18 |

**Game Summary:**

Chicago had seven hits that could have been prevented by Atlanta, plus one instance (Dunston's blooper in the sixth that drove in a run) in which a runner could have been held to fewer bases.

Atlanta had three hits that could have been prevented by Chicago.

**California at Detroit, May 13, 1987**
**Detroit 10, California 7**

This game is an excellent example of how early RBIs could have been avoided by preventing key hits. In the bottom of the first inning Detroit had three hits and three RBIs (including the game-winning RBI) that could have been prevented by California positioning its fielders as suggested by the BARS System fielding strategy.

1. In the bottom of the first, with the Tigers at bat, Mike Heath (RH) came up to hit against John Candelaria (LH). There was one out and no runners were on base. On the 2-2 pitch, Heath hit a low-inside fastball on the ground between the shortstop and the third baseman into left field for a single.
California shortstop Dick Schofield was playing at the normal straight-away shortstop position. If he had been playing shifted toward third base, he could have fielded the ball and thrown Heath out at first.

**BARS: SHORTSTOP Shifted toward third base**

Heath scored the game-winning run later in the inning. If the California shortstop had been shifted toward third base, as suggested, he could have fielded the ball and thrown Heath out.

### Mike Heath    Right-Handed Hitter
### Against All Left-Handed Pitchers All Teams

Fastball Average .286

|  | Inside | Middle | Outside |
|---|---|---|---|
| High | 1/ 0 / 0 | 8/ 375 / 3 | 11/ 90 / 1 |
| Med | 13/ 307 / 4 | 4/ 500 / 2 | 47/ 340 /16 |
| Low | 11/ 272 / 3 | 15/ 266 / 4 | 12/ 166 / 2 |

2. Several batters later, with two outs in the bottom of the first, Larry Herndon (RH) came up to face Candelaria. There were runners on first and second. Herndon fell behind in the count 1-2, then hit a medium-high outside fastball to deep left center between the center fielder and left fielder. On the hit, Heath scored from second with the game-winning RBI.

California center fielder Gary Pettis was playing medium-deep in straightaway center and couldn't get to the ball. If he had been playing deep and shifted toward left, he could have caught it, preventing the hit and the run.

**BARS: CENTERFIELDER Deep and shifted toward left field**

The California center fielder could have prevented this key hit if he had been positioned as suggested.

**Larry Herndon      Right-Handed Hitter**
**Against All Left-Handed Pitchers All Teams**

Fastball Average .258

|  | Inside | Middle | Outside |
|---|---|---|---|
| High | 125 $\overset{8}{/}$ 1 | 571 $\overset{7}{/}$ 4 | 333 $\overset{12}{/}$ 4 |
| Med | 153 $\overset{13}{/}$ 2 | 461 $\overset{13}{/}$ 6 | 108 $\overset{37}{/}$ 4 |
| Low | 333 $\overset{12}{/}$ 4 | 318 $\overset{22}{/}$ 7 | 266 $\overset{15}{/}$ 4 |

Notice Herndon's very low average in the medium-high outside location. The pitch was good; the fielders were not positioned correctly.

3. Detroit's next batter, Terry Harper (RH), fell behind in the count 2-2 against Candelaria. He then lined a medium-high outside fastball to right center for a double, driving in the runners from first and second.

California right fielder Devon White was playing straightaway in right field. If he had been shifted toward center field he could have caught the ball.

**BARS:  RIGHTFIELDER  Medium-deep and shifted**
**toward center field**

With this hit, the second and third Detroit runs were driven in. If the California right fielder had been positioned as suggested, the hit and the runs could have been prevented.

Note that Detroit's first three runs resulted directly from hits that could have been prevented.

**Terry Harper     Right-Handed Hitter**
**Against All Left-Handed Pitchers All Teams**

Fastball Average .210

|  | Inside | Middle | Outside |
|---|---|---|---|
| High | 9/<br>0 / 0 | 15/<br>133 / 2 | 3/<br>0 / 0 |
| Med | 14/<br>285 / 4 | 5/<br>200 / 1 | 36/<br>277 /10 |
| Low | 9/<br>333 / 3 | 40/<br>250 /10 | 26/<br>115 /3 |

4. In the bottom of the third, Alan Trammell (RH) faced Candelaria with no outs and a runner on first. The 1-1 pitch was a high-outside fastball that Trammell hit on the ground past the shortstop into center field.

The Angels' shortstop Dick Schofield was playing shifted toward third. If he had been playing in his normal position, he could have fielded the ball and possibly started a double play. At least he could have forced out one of the runners.

## BARS: SHORTSTOP Normal Position

If California's shortstop had been positioned as suggested by the BARS System fielding strategy, he could have fielded the ball and possibly started a double play.

**Alan Trammell     Batting Right-Handed**
**Against All Left-Handed Pitchers All Teams**

Fastball Average .349

|  | Inside | Middle | Outside |
|---|---|---|---|
| High | 5/<br>0 / 0 | 12/<br>416 / 5 | 14/<br>71 / 1 |
| Med | 24/<br>458 /11 | 16/<br>562 / 9 | 47/<br>255 /12 |
| Low | 7/<br>285 / 2 | 24/<br>375 / 9 | 20/<br>500 /10 |

For this high outside fastball (.071), the Angel's shortstop was playing Trammell to pull the ball. The pitch was to a good location, but the fielders were not in correct position.

5. Doug DeCinces (RH) led off the top of the ninth, facing Detroit right-hander Nate Snell. On the 1-1 pitch, DeCinces lined a single into left field between the shortstop and the third baseman.

Detroit shortstop Alan Trammell was playing at his normal position. If he had been playing shifted toward third, he could have caught the ball.

**BARS: SHORTSTOP  Shifted toward third base**

If Trammel had been shifted toward third, he could have caught this line drive. DeCinces scored later in the inning.

### Doug DeCinces    Right-Handed Hitter
### Against All Right-Handed Pitchers All Teams

Fastball Average .271

|  | Inside | Middle | Outside |
|---|---|---|---|
| High | 5 / 400 / 2 | 14 / 357 / 5 | 5 / 0 / 0 |
| Med | 13 / 230 / 3 | 24 / 500 / 12 | 50 / 200 / 10 |
| Low | 7 / 428 / 3 | 25 / 280 / 7 | 19 / 105 / 2 |

**Game Summary:**

Detroit had four hits that California could have prevented.

California had one hit that Detroit could have prevented.

**San Francisco at St. Louis, May 4, 1987**
**San Francisco 10, St. Louis 7**

In this game, five of San Francisco's first eight runs resulted directly from hits that could have been prevented. This included the game-winning run in the top of the eighth inning that made the score 8-7 San Francisco.
In all, San Francisco had seven hits that St. Louis could have prevented.

1. In the top of the first inning, with no outs and Mike Aldrete on first base, San Francisco's Chili Davis (batting LH) came up to hit against Danny Cox (RH). The 1-2 pitch was a low-over-the-middle fastball. Davis hit a low pop fly down the left field line that fell in for a double. Aldrete scored on the hit.

St. Louis left fielder Vince Coleman was playing deep in straightaway left and couldn't reach the ball. If Coleman had been playing medium-deep and shifted toward the left field line, he could have caught this soft pop fly.

### BARS: LEFTFIELDER  Medium-deep and shifted toward the left field line

Coleman would have been perfectly positioned to make the catch, preventing the double and holding Aldrete on first base.

### Chili Davis    Left-Handed Hitter
### Against All Right-Handed Pitchers All Teams

#### Fastball Average .274

| | Outside | Middle | Inside |
|---|---|---|---|
| High | 9/ 111 / 1 | 17/ 352 / 6 | 11/ 90 / 1 |
| Med | 25/ 120 / 3 | 14/ 357 / 5 | 34/ 323 / 11 |
| Low | 13/ 230 / 3 | 59/ 355 / 21 | 26/ 230 / 6 |

2. In the top of the third inning, Candy Maldonado (RH) came up to hit against Cox with two outs and a runner on first. The 2-2 pitch was a high-outside fastball that Maldonado hit down the left field line. The ball landed about 280 feet from home plate.

St. Louis right fielder Jim Lindeman was playing deep in right and shifted toward center. He just missed getting to the softly hit fly ball. If he had been playing medium-deep and straightaway, he could have caught it for the out, ending the inning.

### BARS: RIGHTFIELDER  Medium-deep in straightaway right field

Lindeman could have caught this ball if he had been positioned as suggested, preventing the hit and the RBI. As it was, the runner on first was running with two outs and scored easily.

**Candy Maldonado    Right-Handed Hitter**
**Against All Right-Handed Pitchers All Teams**

Fastball Average .329

|  | Inside | Middle | Outside |
|---|---|---|---|
| High | 11/<br>181 / 2 | 9/<br>444 / 4 | 7/<br>428 / 3 |
| Med | 6/<br>333 / 2 | 5/<br>400 / 2 | 20/<br>350 / 7 |
| Low | 6/<br>0 / 0 | 14/<br>357 / 5 | 13/<br>384 / 5 |

3. In the top of the fourth inning, Matt Williams (RH) came to the plate against Cox. There were no outs and a runner was on first base. The 2-0 pitch was a medium-high outside fastball that Williams hit on the ground through the normal shortstop position into left field.

The St. Louis shortstop, Ozzie Smith, was playing shifted toward second base and couldn't reach the ball. If he had been playing in his normal straightaway position, he could have fielded the ball, possibly starting a double play.

**BARS: SHORTSTOP  Normal position**

Ozzie Smith could have fielded this ball if he had been positioned as suggested by the BARS System fielding strategy.

**Matt Williams    Right-Handed Hitter**
**Against All Right-Handed Pitchers All Teams**

Fastball Average .250

|  | Inside | Middle | Outside |
|---|---|---|---|
| High | 1/<br>0 / 0 | 4/<br>500 / 2 | 2/<br>0 / 0 |
| Med | 3/<br>0 / 0 | 1/<br>1000 / 1 | 9/<br>111 / 1 |
| Low | 2/<br>1000 / 2 | 1/<br>1000 / 1 | 5/<br>0 / 0 |

4. Chris Speier (RH) came up to hit against Cox in San Francisco's top of the sixth. There were no outs and no runners on base. The 1-1 pitch was a low-over-the-middle fastball that Speier lined into left center field for a single.

The ball was hit about 300 feet. Willie McGee, the St. Louis center fielder, was playing medium-deep and straightaway in center. If he had been playing medium-deep and shifted toward left field, he could have caught the ball.

**BARS: CENTERFIELDER  Medium-deep and shifted
toward left field**

The ball would have been lined almost directly at McGee if he had been positioned as suggested by the BARS System fielding strategy.

### Chris Speier      Right-Handed Hitter
### Against All Right-Handed Pitchers All Teams

Fastball Average .263

|  | Inside | Middle | Outside |
|---|---|---|---|
| High | 9/ 333 /3 | 27/ 259 /7 | 6/ 166 /1 |
| Med | 16/ 187 /3 | 11/ 363 /4 | 56/ 214 /12 |
| Low | 5/ 400 /2 | 35/ 371 /13 | 21/ 190 /4 |

5. Later in the top of the sixth, Mike Aldrete (LH) came to the plate against Cox with two outs and Matt Williams on second base. The 0-1 pitch was a high-inside fastball that Aldrete hit into medium-deep left center field.

St. Louis' center fielder Willie McGee was playing deep in straightaway center and couldn't reach the ball. If he had been playing medium-deep he could have caught it. As it was, the ball dropped in for a single, scoring Williams from second.

**BARS: LEFTFIELDER  Medium-deep in straightaway left field**

McGee could have caught this ball if he had been positioned as suggested, preventing the hit and the run.

### Mike Aldrete    Left-Handed Hitter
### Against All Right-Handed Pitchers All Teams

Fastball Average .272

|  | Outside | Middle | Inside |
|---|---|---|---|
| High | 1/ <br> 0 / 0 | 5/ <br> 600 / 3 | 5/ <br> 400 / 2 |
| Med | 20/ <br> 300 / 6 | 2/ <br> 500 / 1 | 4/ <br> 250 / 1 |
| Low | 6/ <br> 0 / 0 | 6/ <br> 333 / 2 | 6/ <br> 0 / 0 |

6. In the top of the eighth, with one out and a runner on first base, Aldrete (LH) came up to hit against Pat Perry (LH). The 1-1 pitch was a high-inside fastball that Aldrete grounded into right field between the first and second basemen for a single.

Rod Booker, the St. Louis second baseman, was playing shifted toward second base and couldn't reach the ball. If he had been playing shifted toward first base, he could have fielded the ball and started an inning-ending double play.

**BARS: SECOND  Shifted toward first base**

If Booker had been positioned at second base as suggested by the BARS System fielding strategy, he would have been perfectly positioned to field the ball and start a double play to end the inning. At least he could have thrown Aldrete out at first base. Aldrete scored later in the inning.

7. Still with one out in the top of the eighth, Jose Uribe (batting RH) came to bat against Ricky Horton (LH). There were runners on first and second. The first pitch was a high-over-the-middle fastball that Uribe lined into left field for a single, driving in the runner from second base (Candy Maldonado) for the game-winning RBI.

St. Louis left fielder Vince Coleman was playing deep in straightaway left. If he had been playing medium-deep he could have caught the ball, preventing the hit and the game-winning run.

**BARS: LEFTFIELDER  Medium-deep in straightaway left field**

Coleman could have caught this line drive if he had been playing medium-deep instead of deep. This is another important example of a line drive single that could have been prevented with proper fielding strategy.

### Jose Uribe    Right-Handed Hitter
### Against All Left-Handed Pitchers All Teams

Fastball Average .341

|  | Inside | Middle | Outside |
|------|--------|--------|---------|
| High | 1 / 0 | 6 / 500 / 31 | 2 / 0 / 0 |
| Med | 3 / 0 | 2 / 1000 / 2 | 7 / 428 / 3 |
| Low | 4 / 500 / 2 | 11 / 272 / 3 | 5 / 200 / 1 |

**Game Summary:**

San Francisco had seven hits that could have been prevented.

**San Diego at Atlanta, June 6, 1987**
**San Diego 5, Atlanta 3**

In this game, Atlanta and San Diego each had two hits that could have been prevented by using the BARS System fielding strategy. Atlanta also had two instances in which runners could have been held to fewer bases.

The key difference in the game was that one of San Diego's preventable hits produced the game-winning RBI.

1. In the bottom of the first, with no outs and no runners on base, Atlanta left-handed batter Albert Hall faced San Diego right-hander Ed Whitson. The first pitch was a high-over-the-middle fastball that Hall hit hard between the first baseman and the first base bag. The ball rolled to the right field corner for a double.

Tony Gwynn was playing medium-deep in straightaway right field and couldn't get to the ball in time to prevent Hall from going to second.

No harm was done because the relay throw caught Hall at third trying to stretch the double into a triple. Nonetheless, Gwynn would have been perfectly positioned to hold Hall to a single if he had been medium-deep or deep along the right-field line.

**BARS: RIGHTFIELDER**  Deep and shifted
toward the right-field line

Gwynn could have held Hall to a single if he had been properly positioned.

### Albert Hall     Left-Handed Hitter
### Against All Right-Handed Pitchers All Teams

Fastball Average .316

|  | Outside | Middle | Inside |
|---|---|---|---|
| High | 9/111 / 1 | 4/250 / 1 | 9/222 / 2 |
| Med | 22/454 /10 | 7/142 / 1 | 15/333 / 5 |
| Low | 6/166 / 1 | 19/421 / 8 | 7/285 / 2 |

2. With one out in the bottom of the first, Ken Oberkfell (LH) came to bat. The 1-1 pitch was a high-outside fastball that Oberkfell hit hard down the left field line for a double.

Kevin Mitchell, the San Diego left fielder, was playing deep and shifted toward center. He couldn't get to the ball in time to prevent Oberkfell from going to second.

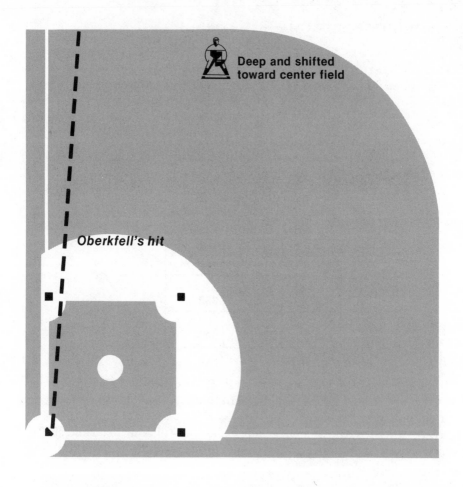

Deep and shifted toward center field

Oberkfell's hit

Although Mitchell probably couldn't have caught the ball, he could possibly have held Oberkfell to a single if he had been playing shifted toward the left field line.

**BARS: LEFTFIELDER Deep and shifted toward the left field line**

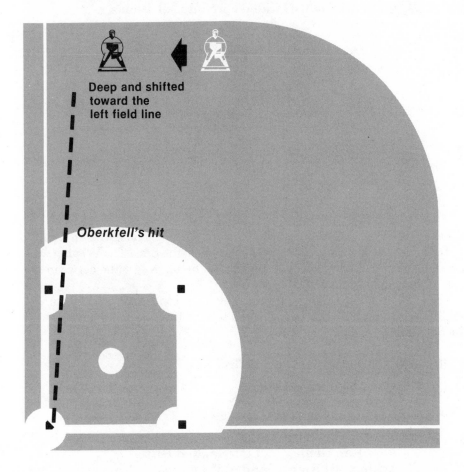

The left fielder possibly could have held Oberkfell to a single if he had been positioned according to the BARS System fielding strategy.

**Ken Oberkfell    Left-Handed Hitter
Against All Right-Handed Pitchers All Teams**

Fastball Average .304

|        | Outside   | Middle    | Inside    |
|--------|-----------|-----------|-----------|
| High   | 16/<br>312 / 5 | 53/<br>264 /14 | 19/<br>263 / 5 |
| Med    | 77/<br>337 /26 | 31/<br>419 /13 | 66/<br>348 /23 |
| Low    | 34/<br>235 / 8 | 90/<br>277 /25 | 48/<br>270 /13 |

3. After the bases had been cleared by Dale Murphy's homer, Ken Griffey (LH) came up, still with two outs in the bottom of the first. The 1-0 pitch was a medium-high outside curveball that Griffey hit on the ground between the first and second basemen.

San Diego's Tim Flannery was playing second base at his normal fielding position. If he had been shifted toward first, he could have fielded the ball and thrown Griffey out.

**BARS:  SECOND  Shifted toward first base**

This hit could have been prevented if the second baseman had been positioned according to the BARS System fielding strategy.

**Ken Griffey    Left-Handed Hitter
Against All Right-Handed Pitchers All Teams**

Curve Average .333

|        | Outside   | Middle    | Inside    |
|--------|-----------|-----------|-----------|
| High   | 5/<br>600 / 3 | 2/<br>500 / 1 | 0/<br>0 / 0 |
| Med    | 13/<br>230 / 3 | 7/<br>571 / 4 | 7/<br>571 / 4 |
| Low    | 6/<br>0 / 0 | 12/<br>333 / 4 | 5/<br>0 / 0 |

4. With two outs in the top of the third, Kevin Mitchell (RH) came to bat for San Diego, facing Atlanta left-hander Larry McWilliams. There was a runner on  first base. On the 2-1 pitch, Mitchell hit a medium-high outside curve into medium-deep right center field for a single.

   Albert Hall, the Atlanta center fielder, was playing deep in straightaway center. He ran in and dived headlong for the ball but couldn't quite make the catch. If he had been playing medium-deep instead of deep, he could have caught this fly ball.

## BARS:  CENTERFIELDER  Medium-deep in straightaway center field

By playing medium-deep instead of deep, Albert Hall could have made the catch.

### Kevin Mitchell    Batting Right-Handed
### Against All Left-Handed Pitchers All Teams

Curve Average .222

|      | Inside | Middle | Outside |
|------|--------|--------|---------|
| High | 1/ 0 0 | 2/ 0 0 | 1/ 1000 1 |
| Med  | 5/ 200 1 | 0/ 0 0 | 3/ 333 1 |
| Low  | 1/ 0 0 | 4/ 250 1 | 1/ 0 0 |

5. In the top of the fourth, with one out and runners on first and third, Randy Ready (RH) came to bat for San Diego, facing Atlanta right-hander Charlie Puleo. Ready hit the 1-1 pitch, a low-over-the-middle fastball, on the ground between the third baseman and the shortstop.

   The Atlanta shortstop, Andres Thomas, was playing shifted toward second and couldn't reach the ball. If he had been playing shifted toward third base, he could have fielded the ball and possibly started an inning-ending double play, preventing the runner on third from scoring the game-winning run.

## BARS: SHORTSTOP Shifted toward third base

If the shortstop had been shifted toward third, he would have been perfectly positioned to prevent the runner on third from scoring. As it was, the ball went through the infield into left field, and the game-winning RBI was scored.

### Randy Ready     Right-Handed Hitter
### Against All Right-Handed Pitchers All Teams

Fastball Average .420

|  | Inside | Middle | Outside |
|------|--------|--------|---------|
| High | 666 $3/2$ | 333 $3/1$ | 0 $1/0$ |
| Med | 571 $7/4$ | 500 $6/3$ | 300 $10/3$ |
| Low | 200 $5/1$ | 400 $10/4$ | 600 $5/3$ |

6. Glenn Hubbard (RH) led off the bottom of the fifth for Atlanta. Whitson was still pitching for San Diego. Hubbard blooped the 2-1 pitch, a low-inside curve, into short center field.

Shane Mack, the San Diego center fielder, was playing deep in straightaway center and couldn't reach the ball. If he had been playing shorter he would have had plenty of time to catch this high blooper.

## BARS: CENTERFIELDER Short in straightaway center field

Mack would have been able to catch this ball easily if he had been positioned according to the BARS System fielding strategy. Even if he had not wanted to play Hubbard short in center, Mack could have been aware that Hubbard has a tendency to hit to short center field. In this way, Mack could have played medium-deep to guard against long hits, while anticipating a hit to short center.

**Glenn Hubbard     Right-Handed Hitter**
**Against All Right-Handed Pitchers All Teams**

Curve Average .277

|  | Inside | Middle | Outside |
|---|---|---|---|
| High | 1 / 0 / 0 | 14 / 285 / 4 | 3 / 333 / 1 |
| Med | 17 / 411 / 7 | 11 / 272 / 3 | 35 / 228 / 8 |
| Low | 5 / 0 / 0 | 30 / 433 / 13 | 46 / 195 / 9 |

## Game Summary:

Atlanta had two hits that could have been prevented by San Diego, plus two instances in which runners could have been held to fewer bases.

San Diego had two hits that could have been prevented  by Atlanta, including the hit that produced the game-winning RBI.

## Minnesota at Oakland, April 8, 1986
## Minnesota 3, Oakland 2

In this game, two of Minnesota's three runs and both of Oakland's runs resulted from hits that could have been prevented by using the BARS System fielding strategy. Each team had three hits that could have been prevented.

1. In the top of the first inning, with no outs and no runners on base, Minnesota's Kirby Puckett (RH) came up to hit against Chris Codiroli (RH). The 1-0 pitch was a low-outside fastball that Puckett lined between the shortstop and third baseman into left field for a single.
 If the Oakland shortstop, Alfredo Griffin, had been shifted toward third base, he could have caught this line drive for the out.

**BARS: SHORTSTOP  Shifted toward third base**

Griffin was playing at his normal straightaway position. If he had been playing shifted toward third, as suggested, he could have caught this line drive. Puckett scored later in the inning.

**Kirby Puckett     Right-Handed Hitter**
**Against All Right-Handed Pitchers All Teams**

Fastball Average .311

|  | Inside | Middle | Outside |
|---|---|---|---|
| High | 125 $\diagup$ 1 <sup>8</sup> | 222 $\diagup$ 4 <sup>18</sup> | 666 $\diagup$ 2 <sup>3</sup> |
| Med | 423 $\diagup$ 11 <sup>26</sup> | 409 $\diagup$ 9 <sup>22</sup> | 274 $\diagup$ 14 <sup>51</sup> |
| Low | 200 $\diagup$ 2 <sup>10</sup> | 291 $\diagup$ 7 <sup>24</sup> | 333 $\diagup$ 6 <sup>18</sup> |

2. In the top of the second, with no outs and no runners on, Roy Smalley (batting LH) came to the plate against Codiroli. The 0-1 pitch was a low-outside fastball that Smalley lined into right field for a single.

The ball was hit about 250 feet. The Oakland right fielder, Mike Davis, was playing deep in right. He could have caught the ball if he had been playing medium-deep and straightaway.

**BARS: RIGHTFIELDER  Medium-deep in straightaway right field**

**Roy Smalley     Left-Handed Hitter**
**Against All Right-Handed Pitchers All Teams**

Fastball Average .225

|  | Outside | Middle | Inside |
|---|---|---|---|
| High | 9/ 0 / 0 | 13/ 461 / 6 | 2/ 0 / 0 |
| Med | 57/ 122 / 7 | 17/ 352 / 6 | 15/ 66 / 1 |
| Low | 13/ 230 / 3 | 30/ 300 / 9 | 17/ 411 / 7 |

3. In the bottom of the second, Oakland's Mike Davis (LH) came up to face Frank Viola (LH). There were no outs and no runners on base. The 1-1 pitch was a medium-high inside fastball that Davis blooped into left center field for a single.

If Kirby Puckett, Minnesota's center fielder, had been medium-deep and shifted toward left field, he could have caught this ball. As it was, the ball dropped in for a base hit. Davis scored later in the inning.

**BARS: CENTERFIELDER  Medium-deep and shifted**
**toward left field**

**Mike Davis     Left-Handed Hitter**
**Against All Left-Handed Pitchers All Teams**

Fastball Average .242

|  | Outside | Middle | Inside |
|---|---|---|---|
| High | 3/ 0 / 0 | 5/ 0 / 0 | 3/ 0 / 0 |
| Med | 10/ 400 / 4 | 4/ 500 / 2 | 18/ 333 / 6 |
| Low | 5/ 200 / 1 | 12/ 250 / 3 | 10/ 100 / 1 |

4. With two outs in the top of the fifth, Minnesota's Kent Hrbek (LH) came up to hit against Codiroli. There was a runner on first base. Hrbek hit the 0-1 pitch, a low-over-the-middle fastball, on the ground between the first and second basemen into right field.

If Oakland's second baseman, Tony Phillips, had been playing shifted toward first base, he could have fielded the ball and thrown Hrbek out.

**BARS: SECOND   Shifted toward first base**

### Kent Hrbek   Left-Handed Hitter
### Against All Right-Handed Pitchers All Teams

Fastball Average .297

|  | Outside | Middle | Inside |
|---|---|---|---|
| High | 19/<br>263 / 5 | 28/<br>392 / 11 | 3/<br>0 / 0 |
| Med | 71/<br>380 / 27 | 22/<br>500 / 11 | 33/<br>212 / 7 |
| Low | 19/<br>210 / 4 | 36/<br>166 / 6 | 14/<br>142 / 2 |

5. In Oakland's bottom of the seventh, with two outs and a runner (Tony Phillips) on second, Dwayne Murphy (LH) fell behind in the count against Viola 2-2, then hit a low-over-the-middle curveball into right field for a single, driving in the run.

The ball was hit about 250 feet. If Minnesota's right fielder Tom Brunansky had been playing medium-deep instead of deep, he could have caught the ball for the out.

**BARS: RIGHTFIELDER   Medium-deep and straightaway**
**in right field**

Brunansky would have had to run in on this ball, but if he had been positioned as suggested, he could have made the catch, preventing the hit and the run.

### Dwayne Murphy    Left-Handed Hitter
### Against All Left-Handed Pitchers All Teams

Curve Average .161

|      | Outside | Middle | Inside |
|------|---------|--------|--------|
| High | 1 / 0 <br> **0** | 3 / 0 <br> **0** | 2 / 1 <br> **500** |
| Med  | 5 / 0 <br> **0** | 3 / 0 <br> **0** | 6 / 2 <br> **333** |
| Low  | 6 / 1 <br> **166** | 4 / 1 <br> **250** | 1 / 0 <br> **0** |

6. With one out in the bottom of the ninth, Tony Phillips (batting LH) came to the plate for Oakland, facing Roy Smith (RH). There was a runner on first base. Phillips fell behind in the count 0-2, then lined a double into deep right field that Tom Brunansky couldn't quite reach.

   The ball was hit nearly 370 feet. If Brunansky been positioned deep in straightaway right, he could have caught the ball, preventing the hit.

## BARS: RIGHTFIELDER  Deep in straightaway right field

### Tony Phillips    Left-Handed Hitter
### Against All Right-Handed Pitchers All Teams

Fastball Average .240

|      | Outside | Middle | Inside |
|------|---------|--------|--------|
| High | 6 / 1 <br> **166** | 26 / 4 <br> **153** | 5 / 1 <br> **200** |
| Med  | 36 / 13 <br> **361** | 16 / 6 <br> **375** | 26 / 7 <br> **269** |
| Low  | 10 / 3 <br> **300** | 25 / 2 <br> **80** | 12 / 2 <br> **166** |

**Game Summary:**

Minnesota had three hits that could have been prevented.

Oakland had three hits that could have been prevented.

# *Conclusion*

This book is a milestone of sorts for me, because over the last six or seven years we've gathered a tremendous amount of information and I've wanted to share it with fans. Even with all the examples we've included in the book, there are thousands that we didn't have room for. Future books and BARS newspapers will have updated examples of everything included here, and more.

In a lot of ways, it almost feels like the Good Lord has been trying to take care of me on all this. When I first started with the BARS System, back in the late '60s and early '70s, I was fortunate that Mr. Kaufmann of the Royals showed an interest and a desire to help. But things didn't develop quite as quickly as he and I had hoped, and baseball people didn't show much interest. As a result, I got away from it for awhile. Then the satellite dishes came along, and I realized that I could scout games all over the country. This spurred me on again and I hired full-time scouts to watch as many games as they could during the season. They even began taping games so they could scout them during the winter.

Over the next few years I compiled information from thousands of games. I went back to the baseball people but they still weren't really interested. Even so, I kept gathering information.

Then, fortunately, we changed computers at the bank because our business had grown. We bought an IBM 4331, and it turned out to be big enough to handle the Super Summary with the batting charts and the fielding strategy. Probably one of the reasons it took me so long to get the Super Summary was because the old computer couldn't handle it.

Then I had the problem of finding someone to program it. We had an enormous amount of information and the program was too complicated for anyone at the bank to work out. Fortunately, Larry Birch came along and turned out to be a tremendous programmer. It took him about four months to have the Super Summary program working perfectly. Once that was done, we had everything we need to supply all the information anyone could want, and to present it in a simple, easy-to-understand way.

At that point I decided to write a book, and again I was fortunate. It turned out that if I had started the book two or three years earlier, it wouldn't have been nearly as good because typesetting had advanced so much during that time. The charts and diagrams would have been much more difficult and time consuming to design if I'd started the book any earlier.

We're also publishing two new BARS books that give a complete report on every regular hitter for every team. These books are the *Baseball Analysis And Reporting System American League Report* and the *National League Report*. They're designed so baseball fans can take the information with them to the ballpark or follow along as they watch games on TV. The reports on hitters in these two books are similar to the reports in this book. The difference is that almost every hitter will be covered on a team-by-team basis.

We know that the real interest is going to be among fans, the dyed-in-the-wool baseball fans. Any fan who buys a BARS American League or National League Report will know more about their favorite players than the players and managers themselves. As a matter of fact, I guarantee you that the players will buy the books and read them. The managers probably will too. I can see a manager going to the pitcher's mound carrying a BARS System book and showing the pitcher how to pitch.

We're moving in other directions. They're coming out now with small computers that can do more than large ones used to. The bank is thinking of buying a small computer to replace the large, expensive one that we have now. Computers are going to keep getting more and more powerful, and within a few years a lot of people are going to have computers right in their home that will be able to handle all the BARS System information.

With these good small computers coming along, I plan to sell the BARS information on disks so fans can have the actual information on their own computers. I also plan to develop a computer baseball game that would let fans play games using the BARS System information. The game would be much more realistic and exciting than anything on the market now, because the user could plan his strategy based on all the information we've taken from real games.

The computer is bound to become more widely used in baseball. If football didn't make use of computers for the special plays and special players and for chalkboards on TV, the game wouldn't be as exciting as it is today. If football was played the way it was when they just handed the ball to the fullback and he ran up the middle, professional and college football wouldn't be what it is today, with all its TV revenue.

I have never been in a hurry developing the BARS System. I just feel as though someone's leading me by the hand. Things have worked out step by step, and I'm thankful. I'll tell you one thing, working out this system has gotten in my blood. It's almost like I've become addicted to it. I just hope the diehard baseball fan will also like it. I love to talk about it, because for me, talking about it is just like going on vacation.

# Appendix

The Batting-Order Reports in this section were selected to show complete records for four American and four National League teams. For in-depth information about the Projected Batting-Order Report, please refer to Chapter Fourteen starting on page 333.

**Batting-Order Report**
**Detroit Tigers Against All Right-Handed Pitchers**

| No. | Name | Batting Average | Ability to get on Base | RBI | Runs Scored | Total Bases Gained | Strike Outs | Stolen Bases | Advancing a Runner by Hitting | Advancing a Runner by Bunting |
|---|---|---|---|---|---|---|---|---|---|---|
| 01 | Lou Whitaker | 301 | 676/204 | 767/298 | 595/69 | 767/100 | 767/432 | 767/65 | 5/4 | 149/87 | 18/6 |
| 23 | Kirk Gibson | 253 | 575/146 | 666/240 | 440/110 | 666/79 | 666/378 | 666/118 | 35/25 | 155/126 | 13/5 |
| 31 | Larry Herndon | 251 | 330/83 | 361/115 | 263/33 | 361/29 | 361/167 | 361/62 | 1/1 | 93/50 | 1/0 |
| 34 | Chet Lemon | 239 | 514/123 | 572/185 | 427/68 | 572/48 | 572/279 | 572/74 | 1/1 | 153/79 | 5/2 |
| 20 | German Rivera | 189 | 37/7 | 44/14 | 31/4 | 44/1 | 44/19 | 44/6 | 1/1 | 13/7 | 1/0 |
| 15 | Pat Sheridan | 249 | 737/184 | 806/260 | 595/61 | 806/36 | 806/342 | 806/131 | 29/25 | 203/110 | 16/10 |
| 08 | Mike Heath | 196 | 260/51 | 282/73 | 199/27 | 282/6 | 282/96 | 282/50 | 4/4 | 60/35 | 7/3 |
| 03 | Alan Trammell | 266 | 627/167 | 686/230 | 534/17 | 686/27 | 686/316 | 686/74 | 20/13 | 195/115 | 17/10 |
| 16 | Tom Brookens | 208 | 374/78 | 398/103 | 303/32 | 398/33 | 398/141 | 398/58 | 14/12 | 116/58 | 12/7 |
| 07 | Bill Madlock | 271 | 331/90 | 362/122 | 292/40 | 362/16 | 362/177 | 362/28 | 5/3 | 107/70 | 5/3 |
| 41 | Darrell Evans | 241 | 575/139 | 695/260 | 463/98 | 695/81 | 695/398 | 695/91 | 2/1 | 138/83 | 3/2 |
| 37 | Bruce Fields | 307 | 13/4 | 13/4 | 11/3 | 13/1 | 13/4 | 13/2 | 0/0 | 3/2 | 0/0 |
| 33 | Matt Nokes | 351 | 111/39 | 116/45 | 97/20 | 116/17 | 116/78 | 116/41 | 1/0 | 34/23 | 0/0 |
| 30 | John Grubb | 261 | 279/73 | 323/118 | 233/55 | 323/30 | 323/178 | 323/41 | 0/0 | 82/59 | 1/1 |
| 14 | Dave Bergman | 239 | 234/56 | 283/105 | 198/31 | 283/30 | 283/146 | 283/31 | 1/0 | 65/43 | 1/0 |
| 38 | Tim Tolman | 285 | 14/4 | 15/5 | 13/3 | 15/2 | 15/9 | 15/1 | 0/0 | 7/2 | 1/0 |
| 32 | Jim Walewander | 285 | 7/2 | 7/2 | 7/0 | 7/2 | 7/3 | 7/0 | 0/0 | 4/1 | 1/1 |
| 12 | Dwight Lowry | 246 | 69/17 | 75/23 | 58/7 | 75/9 | 75/31 | 75/11 | 0/0 | 18/13 | 3/3 |
| 19 | Darnell Coles | 228 | 223/51 | 243/71 | 178/34 | 243/22 | 243/109 | 243/41 | 0/0 | 70/34 | 5/5 |
| 04 | Billy Beane | 205 | 39/8 | 44/13 | 29/4 | 44/3 | 44/14 | 44/0 | 0/0 | 8/7 | 5/5 |
| 09 | Doug Baker | 156 | 51/8 | 55/12 | 38/5 | 55/5 | 55/13 | 55/0 | 0/0 | 13/7 | 2/1 |
| 40 | Mark Thurmond | 142 | 35/5 | 36/6 | 32/0 | 36/0 | 36/7 | 36/3 | 0/0 | 8/3 | 5/5 |
| 35 | Walt Terrell | 90 | 22/2 | 23/2 | 12/0 | 23/1 | 23/3 | 23/10 | 0/0 | 4/0 | 0/0 |

Batting-Order Report
Detroit Tigers Against All Left-Handed Pitchers

| No. | Name | Batting Average | Ability to get on Base | RBI | | Runs Scored | Total Bases Gained | Strike Outs | Stolen Bases | Advancing a Runner by Hitting | Advancing a Runner by Bunting |
|---|---|---|---|---|---|---|---|---|---|---|---|
| 09 | Doug Baker | 181 | 11/ 2 | 12/ 3 | 11/ 2 | 12/ 0 | 12/ 4 | 12/ 0 | 1/ 1 | 4/ 3 | 0/ 0 |
| 19 | Darnel Coles | 248 | 129/ 32 | 141/ 44 | 141/ 20 | 141/ 7 | 141/ 55 | 141/ 19 | 2/ 2 | 36/ 21 | 2/ 2 |
| 16 | Tom Brookens | 315 | 228/ 72 | 250/ 96 | 194/ 19 | 250/ 30 | 250/ 128 | 250/ 29 | 8/ 6 | 63/ 35 | 4/ 3 |
| 07 | Bill Madlock | 229 | 131/ 30 | 143/ 43 | 116/ 17 | 143/ 7 | 143/ 59 | 143/ 10 | 2/ 2 | 41/ 20 | 1/ 1 |
| 23 | Kirk Gibson | 241 | 228/ 55 | 270/ 100 | 166/ 33 | 270/ 33 | 270/ 140 | 270/ 57 | 9/ 6 | 51/ 33 | 8/ 2 |
| 08 | Mike Heath | 253 | 217/ 55 | 233/ 72 | 182/ 28 | 233/ 12 | 233/ 107 | 233/ 32 | 5/ 3 | 43/ 32 | 2/ 2 |
| 14 | Dave Bergman | 347 | 23/ 8 | 28/ 13 | 19/ 1 | 28/ 7 | 28/ 19 | 28/ 2 | 0/ 0 | 4/ 4 | 1/ 0 |
| 03 | Alan Trammell | 319 | 291/ 93 | 320/ 123 | 259/ 41 | 320/ 37 | 320/ 186 | 320/ 26 | 4/ 1 | 70/ 52 | 6/ 5 |
| 34 | Chet Lemon | 255 | 239/ 61 | 267/ 92 | 203/ 39 | 267/ 30 | 267/ 148 | 267/ 30 | 2/ 1 | 68/ 39 | 4/ 3 |
| 01 | Lou Whitaker | 214 | 271/ 58 | 301/ 89 | 223/ 32 | 301/ 35 | 301/ 116 | 301/ 43 | 4/ 2 | 70/ 41 | 11/ 4 |
| 40 | Mark Thurmond | 500 | 2/ 1 | 2/ 1 | 2/ 0 | 2/ 0 | 2/ 1 | 2/ 0 | 0/ 0 | 0/ 0 | 0/ 0 |
| 12 | Dwight Lowry | 269 | 26/ 7 | 29/ 10 | 21/ 2 | 29/ 3 | 29/ 10 | 29/ 3 | 0/ 0 | 7/ 4 | 3/ 3 |
| 31 | Larry Herndon | 259 | 277/ 72 | 300/ 95 | 232/ 42 | 300/ 20 | 300/ 139 | 300/ 37 | 1/ 0 | 85/ 52 | 1/ 0 |
| 41 | Darrell Evans | 233 | 197/ 46 | 224/ 73 | 148/ 29 | 224/ 19 | 224/ 104 | 224/ 37 | 1/ 0 | 54/ 32 | 2/ 2 |
| 30 | John Grubb | 200 | 15/ 3 | 17/ 5 | 11/ 3 | 17/ 1 | 17/ 6 | 17/ 4 | 0/ 0 | 4/ 3 | 0/ 0 |
| 38 | Tim Tolman | 166 | 30/ 5 | 38/ 13 | 24/ 5 | 38/ 3 | 38/ 20 | 38/ 6 | 0/ 0 | 10/ 2 | 0/ 0 |
| 15 | Pat Sheridan | 173 | 98/ 17 | 104/ 24 | 66/ 7 | 104/ 6 | 104/ 35 | 104/ 31 | 0/ 0 | 26/ 14 | 3/ 2 |
| 33 | Matt Nokes | 111 | 18/ 2 | 19/ 3 | 14/ 2 | 19/ 2 | 19/ 6 | 19/ 4 | 0/ 0 | 7/ 2 | 0/ 0 |
| 04 | Billy Beane | 115 | 26/ 3 | 28/ 6 | 23/ 0 | 28/ 0 | 28/ 7 | 28/ 1 | 0/ 0 | 8/ 1 | 0/ 0 |
| 20 | German Rivera | 151 | 33/ 5 | 34/ 6 | 24/ 1 | 34/ 0 | 34/ 10 | 34/ 7 | 0/ 0 | 8/ 1 | 1/ 0 |

Batting-Order Report
New York Yankees Against All Right-Handed Pitchers

| No. | Name | Batting Average | Ability to get on Base | RBI | Runs Scored | Total Bases Gained | Strike Outs | Stolen Bases | Advancing a Runner by Hitting | Advancing a Runner by Bunting |
|---|---|---|---|---|---|---|---|---|---|---|
| 21 | Dan Pasqua | 252 | 269/ 68 | 316/ 117 | 194/ 47 | 316/ 39 | 316/ 186 | 316/ 72 | 3/ 3 | 63/ 46 | 1/ 1 |
| 33 | Ron Kittle | 239 | 397/ 95 | 430/ 128 | 283/ 65 | 430/ 34 | 430/ 228 | 430/101 | 1/ 1 | 93/ 66 | 0/ 0 |
| 17 | Mike Easler | 274 | 653/ 179 | 724/ 251 | 542/ 96 | 724/ 43 | 724/ 363 | 724/106 | 1/ 1 | 177/116 | 3/ 3 |
| 31 | Dave Winfield | 270 | 717/ 194 | 783/ 266 | 584/123 | 783/ 72 | 783/ 388 | 783/117 | 6/ 1 | 214/147 | 6/ 1 |
| 24 | Rickey Henderson | 291 | 579/169 | 663/ 257 | 502/ 73 | 663/ 88 | 663/ 367 | 663/ 68 | 67/ 53 | 135/ 78 | 4/ 2 |
| 06 | Rick Cerone | 216 | 273/ 59 | 311/ 98 | 243/ 23 | 311/ 9 | 311/ 120 | 311/ 23 | 2/ 2 | 93/ 56 | 3/ 2 |
| 30 | Willie Randolph | 246 | 621/153 | 723/ 256 | 554/ 62 | 723/ 72 | 723/ 292 | 723/ 57 | 14/ 12 | 172/ 90 | 17/ 12 |
| 20 | Bobby Meacham | 240 | 329/ 79 | 355/ 107 | 261/ 26 | 355/ 34 | 355/ 127 | 355/ 61 | 8/ 7 | 88/ 48 | 31/ 20 |
| 18 | C. Washington | 280 | 860/241 | 950/ 334 | 705/103 | 950/ 45 | 950/ 490 | 950/145 | 37/ 30 | 192/115 | 6/ 1 |
| 27 | Mark Salas | 228 | 197/ 45 | 209/ 57 | 163/ 23 | 209/ 5 | 209/ 78 | 209/ 23 | 1/ 1 | 60/ 32 | 1/ 1 |
| 11 | Lenn Sakata | 197 | 76/ 15 | 85/ 24 | 63/ 1 | 85/ 0 | 85/ 27 | 85/ 11 | 2/ 2 | 26/ 8 | 1/ 1 |
| 22 | Gary Ward | 258 | 689/178 | 741/ 235 | 544/ 72 | 741/ 26 | 741/ 308 | 741/132 | 16/ 11 | 182/119 | 2/ 1 |
| 02 | Wayne Tolleson | 271 | 527/143 | 572/ 192 | 455/ 28 | 572/ 29 | 572/ 220 | 572/ 65 | 24/ 16 | 137/ 65 | 21/ 17 |
| 28 | Henry Cotto | 305 | 108/ 33 | 114/ 41 | 92/ 10 | 114/ 11 | 114/ 53 | 114/ 16 | 2/ 1 | 33/ 18 | 7/ 4 |
| 58 | Juan Espino | 200 | 15/ 3 | 15/ 3 | 9/ 2 | 15/ 0 | 15/ 7 | 15/ 6 | 0/ 0 | 1/ 2 | 0/ 0 |
| 23 | Don Mattingly | 325 | 709/231 | 772/ 296 | 661/104 | 772/ 76 | 772/ 425 | 772/ 39 | 0/ 0 | 225/160 | 3/ 2 |
| 46 | Rich Bordi | 83 | 12/ 1 | 13/ 2 | 8/ 0 | 13/ 1 | 13/ 2 | 13/ 4 | 0/ 0 | 3/ 0 | 1/ 0 |
| 13 | Mike Pagliarulo | 246 | 531/131 | 588/ 191 | 428/ 85 | 588/ 64 | 588/ 314 | 588/ 94 | 1/ 1 | 128/ 98 | 2/ 2 |
| 26 | Rick Rhoden | 283 | 67/ 19 | 69/ 21 | 62/ 7 | 69/ 0 | 69/ 25 | 69/ 3 | 0/ 0 | 22/ 15 | 3/ 2 |
| 47 | Juan Bonilla | 251 | 151/ 38 | 166/ 53 | 141/ 9 | 166/ 2 | 166/ 61 | 166/ 9 | 0/ 0 | 44/ 22 | 5/ 5 |
| 12 | Joel Skinner | 219 | 173/ 38 | 185/ 50 | 130/ 27 | 185/ 11 | 185/ 80 | 185/ 38 | 0/ 0 | 38/ 25 | 4/ 3 |
| 39 | Joe Niekro | 190 | 63/ 12 | 64/ 13 | 53/ 5 | 64/ 0 | 64/ 13 | 64/ 10 | 0/ 0 | 13/ 8 | 11/ 8 |
| 41 | Charles Hudson | 218 | 32/ 7 | 33/ 8 | 20/ 2 | 33/ 0 | 33/ 11 | 33/ 10 | 0/ 0 | 8/ 4 | 2/ 1 |
| 29 | Paul Zuvella | 183 | 98/ 18 | 104/ 24 | 86/ 2 | 104/ 0 | 104/ 29 | 104/ 11 | 0/ 0 | 34/ 9 | 0/ 0 |

## Batting-Order Report
### New York Yankees Against All Left-Handed Pitchers

| No. | Name | Batting Average | Ability to get on Base | RBI | Runs Scored | Total Bases Gained | Strike Outs | Stolen Bases | Advancing a Runner by Hitting | Advancing a Runner by Bunting |
|---|---|---|---|---|---|---|---|---|---|---|
| 36 | Al Holland | 1000  1/ 1 | 1/ 1 | 1/ 0 | 1/ 0 | 1/ 1 | 1/ 0 | 0/ 0 | 0/ 0 | 0/ 0 |
| 22 | Gary Ward | 348  270/ 94 | 291/115 | 232/ 55 | 291/ 16 | 291/166 | 291/ 32 | 6/ 6 | 78/ 57 | 1/ 0 |
| 31 | Dave Winfield | 265  380/101 | 439/161 | 323/ 72 | 439/ 40 | 439/266 | 439/ 49 | 2/ 2 | 109/ 72 | 2/ 1 |
| 26 | Rick Rhoden | 222  18/ 4 | 18/ 4 | 18/ 3 | 18/ 0 | 18/ 5 | 18/ 0 | 1/ 1 | 6/ 5 | 0/ 0 |
| 24 | Rickey Henderson | 285  280/ 80 | 338/139 | 241/ 27 | 338/ 57 | 338/203 | 338/ 35 | 26/ 20 | 67/ 34 | 1/ 1 |
| 02 | Wayne Tolleson | 266  218/ 58 | 238/ 79 | 172/ 19 | 238/ 14 | 238/101 | 238/ 43 | 6/ 0 | 43/ 24 | 11/ 3 |
| 17 | Mike Easler | 250  252/ 63 | 268/ 80 | 178/ 21 | 268/ 7 | 268/103 | 268/ 71 | 1/ 1 | 74/ 42 | 1/ 1 |
| 21 | Dan Pasqua | 187  48/ 9 | 54/ 15 | 29/ 7 | 54/ 7 | 54/ 27 | 54/ 18 | 1/ 1 | 11/ 6 | 0/ 0 |
| 20 | Bobby Meacham | 250  176/ 44 | 196/ 64 | 146/ 10 | 196/ 12 | 196/ 74 | 196/ 29 | 5/ 4 | 50/ 21 | 19/ 11 |
| 30 | Willie Randolph | 297  329/ 98 | 378/150 | 300/ 18 | 378/ 51 | 378/180 | 378/ 22 | 7/ 4 | 103/ 50 | 6/ 5 |
| 18 | C. Washington | 235  187/ 44 | 209/ 66 | 136/ 17 | 209/ 7 | 209/ 81 | 209/ 48 | 9/ 7 | 38/ 24 | 1/ 0 |
| 06 | Rick Cerone | 200  175/ 35 | 188/ 49 | 152/ 15 | 188/ 3 | 188/ 63 | 188/ 19 | 1/ 1 | 63/ 25 | 3/ 3 |
| 27 | Mark Salas | 375  16/ 6 | 17/ 8 | 13/ 3 | 17/ 0 | 17/ 8 | 17/ 3 | 0/ 0 | 7/ 6 | 1/ 1 |
| 23 | Don Mattingly | 320  399/128 | 429/159 | 369/ 87 | 429/ 38 | 429/242 | 429/ 27 | 0/ 0 | 145/107 | 3/ 2 |
| 33 | Ron Kittle | 250  256/ 64 | 287/ 98 | 184/ 31 | 287/ 13 | 287/145 | 287/ 63 | 0/ 0 | 55/ 38 | 1/ 1 |
| 47 | Juan Bonilla | 214  84/ 18 | 92/ 28 | 77/ 5 | 92/ 0 | 92/ 29 | 92/ 5 | 0/ 0 | 28/ 16 | 1/ 1 |
| 11 | Lenn Sakata | 291  48/ 14 | 51/ 17 | 41/ 4 | 51/ 5 | 51/ 27 | 51/ 6 | 0/ 0 | 15/ 5 | 0/ 0 |
| 13 | Mike Pagliarulo | 210  147/ 31 | 160/ 44 | 91/ 16 | 160/ 15 | 160/ 67 | 160/ 52 | 0/ 0 | 37/ 24 | 2/ 2 |
| 28 | Henry Cotto | 256  82/ 21 | 85/ 24 | 65/ 5 | 85/ 6 | 85/ 30 | 85/ 16 | 1/ 0 | 28/ 11 | 5/ 1 |
| 29 | Paul Zuvella | 194  72/ 14 | 78/ 20 | 61/ 0 | 78/ 1 | 78/ 22 | 78/ 7 | 1/ 0 | 23/ 8 | 1/ 1 |
| 12 | Joel Skinner | 197  91/ 18 | 94/ 21 | 66/ 12 | 94/ 3 | 94/ 28 | 94/ 25 | 0/ 0 | 23/ 8 | 0/ 0 |
| 58 | Juan Espino | 222  9/ 2 | 9/ 2 | 8/ 0 | 9/ 0 | 9/ 2 | 9/ 1 | 0/ 0 | 1/ 0 | 0/ 0 |
| 39 | Joe Niekro | 148  27/ 4 | 27/ 5 | 24/ 0 | 27/ 0 | 27/ 5 | 27/ 3 | 0/ 0 | 12/ 4 | 3/ 3 |

Batting-Order Report
Los Angeles Dodgers Against All Right-Handed Pitchers

| No. | Name | Batting Average | Ability to get on Base | RBI | Runs Scored | Total Bases Gained | Strike Outs | Stolen Bases | Advancing a Runner by Hitting | Advancing a Runner by Bunting |
|---|---|---|---|---|---|---|---|---|---|---|
| 14 | Mike Scioscia | 272 | 352/ 96 | 421/ 165 | 324/ 36 | 421/ 18 | 421/ 196 | 421/ 20 | 5/ 5 | 113/ 72 | 8/ 4 |
| 44 | Ken Landreaux | 263 | 475/ 125 | 501/ 155 | 424/ 49 | 501/ 43 | 501/ 231 | 501/ 33 | 9/ 9 | 155/ 84 | 4/ 3 |
| 60 | Mike Sharperson | 214 | 28/ 6 | 32/ 11 | 23/ 4 | 32/ 0 | 32/ 13 | 32/ 5 | 15/ 12 | 8/ 7 | 0/ 0 |
| 29 | Alex Trevino | 247 | 234/ 58 | 252/ 76 | 197/ 33 | 252/ 6 | 252/ 104 | 252/ 31 | 2/ 2 | 81/ 46 | 6/ 4 |
| 22 | Franklin Stubbs | 221 | 235/ 52 | 261/ 78 | 158/ 25 | 261/ 24 | 261/ 119 | 261/ 67 | 3/ 3 | 48/ 28 | 2/ 0 |
| 03 | Steve Sax | 306 | 578/ 177 | 633/ 237 | 503/ 29 | 633/ 49 | 633/ 277 | 633/ 63 | 39/ 33 | 136/ 69 | 17/ 6 |
| 28 | Pedro Guerrero | 278 | 381/ 106 | 429/ 155 | 300/ 63 | 429/ 48 | 429/ 253 | 429/ 62 | 9/ 6 | 105/ 67 | 0/ 0 |
| 37 | Glenn Hoffman | 220 | 186/ 41 | 206/ 62 | 159/ 15 | 206/ 1 | 206/ 77 | 206/ 23 | 2/ 2 | 54/ 25 | 7/ 4 |
| 18 | Bill Russell | 287 | 212/ 61 | 225/ 74 | 193/ 13 | 225/ 11 | 225/ 82 | 225/ 13 | 6/ 5 | 48/ 29 | 13/ 10 |
| 10 | Dave Anderson | 209 | 210/ 44 | 239/ 76 | 179/ 8 | 239/ 16 | 239/ 91 | 239/ 26 | 9/ 9 | 65/ 20 | 10/ 4 |
| 20 | Phil Garner | 233 | 385/ 90 | 423/ 132 | 320/ 46 | 423/ 9 | 423/ 179 | 423/ 58 | 7/ 5 | 116/ 65 | 4/ 3 |
| 12 | Danny Heep | 251 | 282/ 71 | 309/ 99 | 250/ 25 | 309/ 5 | 309/ 134 | 309/ 28 | 3/ 2 | 94/ 47 | 1/ 1 |
| 56 | Brad Wellman | 235 | 106/ 25 | 114/ 34 | 78/ 10 | 114/ 1 | 114/ 41 | 114/ 23 | 5/ 4 | 33/ 16 | 5/ 2 |
| 26 | Alejandro Pena | 93 | 32/ 3 | 33/ 4 | 24/ 4 | 33/ 1 | 33/ 4 | 33/ 6 | 1/ 1 | 5/ 3 | 5/ 2 |
| 05 | Mike Marshall | 265 | 433/ 115 | 472/ 155 | 328/ 57 | 472/ 43 | 472/ 233 | 472/ 97 | 2/ 1 | 127/ 73 | 0/ 0 |
| 31 | John Shelby | 190 | 352/ 67 | 368/ 85 | 276/ 31 | 368/ 6 | 368/ 117 | 368/ 71 | 15/ 12 | 85/ 36 | 24/ 13 |
| 25 | Mariano Duncan | 193 | 264/ 51 | 277/ 64 | 200/ 18 | 277/ 24 | 277/ 89 | 277/ 52 | 18/ 12 | 54/ 27 | 22/ 12 |
| 40 | Rick Honeycutt | 54 | 37/ 2 | 42/ 7 | 26/ 1 | 42/ 1 | 42/ 7 | 42/ 11 | 2/ 2 | 3/ 2 | 4/ 3 |
| 07 | Tracy Woodson | 173 | 23/ 4 | 25/ 6 | 16/ 5 | 25/ 1 | 25/ 11 | 25/ 6 | 0/ 0 | 3/ 5 | 0/ 0 |
| 17 | Len Matuszek | 258 | 201/ 52 | 227/ 80 | 165/ 31 | 227/ 14 | 227/ 121 | 227/ 36 | 0/ 0 | 55/ 32 | 0/ 0 |
| 46 | Ralph Bryant | 230 | 26/ 6 | 27/ 7 | 15/ 5 | 27/ 3 | 27/ 16 | 27/ 11 | 0/ 0 | 5/ 5 | 0/ 0 |
| 27 | Tito Landrum | 237 | 59/ 14 | 64/ 19 | 46/ 7 | 64/ 0 | 64/ 19 | 64/ 12 | 1/ 0 | 18/ 12 | 0/ 0 |
| 09 | Mickey Hatcher | 257 | 249/ 64 | 257/ 74 | 231/ 22 | 257/ 1 | 257/ 87 | 257/ 10 | 1/ 0 | 80/ 45 | 2/ 2 |
| 21 | Reggie Williams | 203 | 64/ 13 | 70/ 19 | 48/ 3 | 70/ 5 | 70/ 21 | 70/ 10 | 1/ 1 | 9/ 7 | 3/ 3 |
| 38 | Craig Shipley | 333 | 3/ 1 | 3/ 1 | 2/ 1 | 3/ 0 | 3/ 2 | 3/ 1 | 0/ 0 | 1/ 1 | 0/ 0 |
| 33 | Jeff Hamilton | 195 | 46/ 9 | 47/ 10 | 29/ 5 | 47/ 7 | 47/ 21 | 47/ 17 | 0/ 0 | 23/ 13 | 0/ 0 |
| 34 | F. Valenzuela | 159 | 88/ 14 | 89/ 15 | 81/ 12 | 89/ 2 | 89/ 21 | 89/ 7 | 0/ 0 | 9/ 8 | 9/ 8 |
| 55 | Orel Hershiser | 171 | 70/ 12 | 72/ 15 | 49/ 3 | 72/ 3 | 72/ 17 | 72/ 17 | 0/ 0 | 12/ 6 | 11/ 3 |
| 35 | Bob Welch | 123 | 65/ 8 | 66/ 9 | 44/ 4 | 66/ 2 | 66/ 12 | 66/ 20 | 0/ 0 | 6/ 4 | 11/ 6 |
| 23 | Tim Leary | 200 | 5/ 1 | 5/ 1 | 4/ 0 | 5/ 0 | 5/ 1 | 5/ 1 | 0/ 0 | 0/ 0 | 1/ 1 |
| 47 | Jose Gonzalez | 62 | 16/ 1 | 18/ 3 | 8/ 0 | 18/ 2 | 18/ 5 | 18/ 7 | 0/ 0 | 1/ 0 | 0/ 0 |

Batting-Order Report
Los Angeles Dodgers Against All Left-Handed Pitchers

| No. | Name | Batting Average | Ability to get on Base | RBI | Runs Scored | Total Bases Gained | Strike Outs | Stolen Bases | Advancing a Runner by Hitting | Advancing a Runner by Bunting |
|---|---|---|---|---|---|---|---|---|---|---|
| 21 | Reggie Williams | 328 | 64/ 21 | 71/ 30 | 50/ 8 | 71/ 8 | 71/ 39 | 71/ 13 | 1/ 1 | 17/ 12 | 7/ 2 |
| 28 | Pedro Guerrero | 308 | 123/ 38 | 143/ 58 | 99/ 18 | 143/ 12 | 143/ 76 | 143/ 23 | 4/ 3 | 33/ 24 | 0/ 0 |
| 44 | Ken Landreaux | 285 | 70/ 20 | 79/ 29 | 55/ 6 | 79/ 4 | 79/ 37 | 79/ 13 | 3/ 3 | 14/ 9 | 0/ 0 |
| 03 | Steve Sax | 323 | 201/ 65 | 218/ 82 | 182/ 16 | 218/ 19 | 218/ 103 | 218/ 15 | 12/ 12 | 43/ 21 | 7/ 4 |
| 27 | Tito Landrum | 227 | 145/ 33 | 165/ 53 | 119/ 21 | 165/ 8 | 165/ 69 | 165/ 22 | 2/ 2 | 47/ 30 | 1/ 0 |
| 29 | Alex Trevino | 206 | 97/ 20 | 116/ 40 | 78/ 7 | 116/ 5 | 116/ 44 | 116/ 15 | 2/ 2 | 30/ 15 | 1/ 1 |
| 20 | Phil Garner | 272 | 327/ 89 | 366/ 130 | 272/ 45 | 366/ 5 | 366/ 173 | 366/ 46 | 7/ 6 | 100/ 60 | 0/ 0 |
| 33 | Jeff Hamilton | 409 | 22/ 9 | 22/ 9 | 20/ 7 | 22/ 4 | 22/ 13 | 22/ 2 | 0/ 0 | 6/ 5 | 0/ 0 |
| 18 | Bill Russell | 283 | 120/ 34 | 134/ 48 | 109/ 4 | 134/ 9 | 134/ 51 | 134/ 9 | 1/ 1 | 44/ 18 | 1/ 1 |
| 25 | Mariano Duncan | 173 | 138/ 24 | 142/ 30 | 114/ 7 | 142/ 4 | 142/ 34 | 142/ 20 | 3/ 2 | 40/ 15 | 10/ 3 |
| 09 | Mickey Hatcher | 374 | 147/ 55 | 155/ 65 | 138/ 18 | 155/ 4 | 155/ 85 | 155/ 7 | 0/ 0 | 50/ 31 | 1/ 1 |
| 12 | Danny Heep | 275 | 29/ 8 | 34/ 13 | 25/ 8 | 34/ 0 | 34/ 17 | 34/ 4 | 0/ 0 | 7/ 7 | 0/ 0 |
| 60 | Mike Sharperson | 200 | 15/ 3 | 15/ 3 | 13/ 1 | 15/ 0 | 15/ 3 | 15/ 2 | 6/ 4 | 5/ 1 | 1/ 1 |
| 31 | John Shelby | 197 | 192/ 38 | 205/ 51 | 152/ 16 | 205/ 6 | 205/ 79 | 205/ 36 | 4/ 2 | 37/ 15 | 15/ 5 |
| 05 | Mike Marshall | 253 | 158/ 40 | 181/ 64 | 112/ 21 | 181/ 11 | 181/ 88 | 181/ 42 | 0/ 0 | 43/ 29 | 1/ 1 |
| 10 | Dave Anderson | 216 | 60/ 13 | 71/ 25 | 50/ 6 | 71/ 5 | 71/ 30 | 71/ 6 | 0/ 0 | 22/ 12 | 6/ 4 |
| 55 | Orel Hershiser | 227 | 22/ 5 | 25/ 8 | 19/ 1 | 25/ 5 | 25/ 8 | 25/ 3 | 0/ 0 | 3/ 2 | 3/ 3 |
| 14 | Mike Scioscia | 187 | 80/ 15 | 96/ 32 | 71/ 10 | 96/ 5 | 96/ 34 | 96/ 6 | 0/ 0 | 25/ 15 | 4/ 3 |
| 22 | Franklin Stubbs | 246 | 65/ 16 | 67/ 18 | 52/ 7 | 67/ 5 | 67/ 24 | 67/ 8 | 0/ 0 | 19/ 7 | 4/ 3 |
| 47 | Jose Gonzaelz | 210 | 19/ 4 | 20/ 5 | 15/ 0 | 20/ 3 | 20/ 6 | 20/ 4 | 0/ 0 | 9/ 5 | 1/ 1 |
| 56 | Brad Wellman | 147 | 34/ 5 | 38/ 9 | 28/ 3 | 38/ 0 | 38/ 11 | 38/ 5 | 0/ 0 | 5/ 3 | 1/ 1 |
| 38 | Craig Shipley | 200 | 10/ 2 | 10/ 2 | 9/ 1 | 10/ 1 | 10/ 2 | 10/ 0 | 0/ 0 | 6/ 2 | 0/ 0 |
| 35 | Bob Welch | 131 | 38/ 5 | 40/ 8 | 27/ 4 | 40/ 1 | 40/ 8 | 40/ 10 | 0/ 0 | 7/ 4 | 10/ 7 |
| 37 | Glenn Hoffman | 150 | 80/ 12 | 86/ 18 | 65/ 5 | 86/ 1 | 86/ 22 | 86/ 12 | 0/ 0 | 25/ 8 | 4/ 1 |
| 17 | Len Matuszek | 187 | 16/ 3 | 17/ 4 | 12/ 2 | 17/ 1 | 17/ 7 | 17/ 4 | 0/ 0 | 4/ 1 | 0/ 0 |
| 34 | F. Valenzuela | 146 | 41/ 6 | 41/ 6 | 37/ 2 | 41/ 1 | 41/ 8 | 41/ 3 | 0/ 0 | 15/ 3 | 3/ 3 |
| 40 | Rick Honeycutt | 111 | 9/ 1 | 11/ 3 | 6/ 0 | 11/ 0 | 11/ 3 | 11/ 2 | 0/ 0 | 1/ 0 | 1/ 0 |
| 07 | Tracy Woodson | 111 | 9/ 1 | 9/ 1 | 7/ 0 | 9/ 0 | 9/ 1 | 9/ 2 | 0/ 0 | 3/ 0 | 0/ 0 |

## Batting-Order Report
## New York Mets Against All Right-Handed Pitchers

| No. | Name | Batting Average | Ability to get on Base | RBI | Runs Scored | Total Bases Gained | Strike Outs | Stolen Bases | Advancing a Runner by Hitting | Advancing a Runner by Bunting |
|---|---|---|---|---|---|---|---|---|---|---|
| 18 | Darryl Strawberry | 284 | 488/139 | 584/237 | 368/108 | 584/63 | 584/373 | 584/114 | 30/27 | 109/90 | 4/0 |
| 08 | Gary Carter | 258 | 533/138 | 587/195 | 432/93 | 587/41 | 587/295 | 587/78 | 1/1 | 168/91 | 1/0 |
| 20 | Howard Johnson | 250 | 419/105 | 462/150 | 321/57 | 462/53 | 462/221 | 462/86 | 6/6 | 111/74 | 11/0 |
| 22 | Kevin McReynolds | 242 | 449/109 | 447/138 | 371/79 | 477/26 | 477/218 | 477/72 | 5/5 | 124/93 | 6/4 |
| 04 | Lenny Dykstra | 277 | 346/96 | 384/135 | 297/39 | 384/54 | 384/182 | 384/43 | 25/23 | 76/50 | 18/1 |
| 02 | Bill Almon | 231 | 138/32 | 149/43 | 109/21 | 149/2 | 149/56 | 149/29 | 2/2 | 30/28 | 5/4 |
| 01 | Mookie Wilson | 266 | 394/105 | 426/141 | 330/46 | 426/48 | 426/206 | 426/54 | 22/20 | 111/66 | 3/1 |
| 06 | Wally Backman | 286 | 604/173 | 655/227 | 518/35 | 655/84 | 655/261 | 655/83 | 37/32 | 156/81 | 50/29 |
| 03 | Rafael Santana | 246 | 386/95 | 403/112 | 338/28 | 403/27 | 403/133 | 403/41 | 2/2 | 114/53 | 7/4 |
| 13 | Lee Mazzilli | 231 | 177/41 | 210/74 | 151/15 | 210/8 | 210/90 | 210/24 | 8/6 | 47/28 | 2/1 |
| 12 | Ron Darling | 170 | 88/15 | 92/19 | 67/2 | 92/9 | 92/21 | 92/19 | 1/1 | 19/6 | 11/10 |
| 25 | Keith Miller | 500 | 4/2 | 6/4 | 4/0 | 6/1 | 6/5 | 6/0 | 0/0 | 2/0 | 0/0 |
| 10 | Rusty Staub | 225 | 62/14 | 71/24 | 55/10 | 71/7 | 71/28 | 71/5 | 0/0 | 27/13 | 0/0 |
| 31 | Gene Walter | 333 | 3/1 | 4/2 | 2/0 | 4/0 | 4/3 | 4/1 | 0/0 | 1/1 | 0/0 |
| 17 | Keith Hernandez | 276 | 565/156 | 665/260 | 488/99 | 665/71 | 665/353 | 665/70 | 1/0 | 171/127 | 0/0 |
| 29 | Dave Magadan | 290 | 31/9 | 32/11 | 28/4 | 32/3 | 32/13 | 32/3 | 0/0 | 8/6 | 1/1 |
| 07 | Clint Hurdle | 223 | 76/17 | 88/29 | 61/14 | 88/5 | 88/50 | 88/15 | 0/0 | 17/10 | 0/0 |
| 11 | Tim Teufel | 285 | 175/50 | 200/76 | 145/26 | 200/8 | 200/108 | 200/29 | 1/0 | 59/36 | 0/0 |
| 15 | Rick Aguilara | 181 | 22/4 | 24/7 | 19/2 | 24/1 | 24/7 | 24/3 | 0/0 | 4/2 | 5/4 |
| 35 | John Gibbons | 111 | 18/2 | 21/5 | 10/1 | 21/2 | 21/6 | 21/7 | 0/0 | 3/3 | 0/0 |
| 42 | Roger McDowell | 250 | 20/5 | 20/5 | 16/1 | 20/2 | 20/7 | 20/4 | 1/0 | 3/3 | 3/3 |
| 16 | Dwight Gooden | 127 | 94/12 | 97/15 | 77/6 | 97/10 | 97/15 | 97/14 | 1/0 | 20/15 | 9/9 |
| 33 | Barry Lyons | 166 | 24/4 | 26/6 | 19/1 | 26/1 | 26/7 | 26/4 | 0/0 | 11/2 | 0/0 |
| 50 | Sid Fernandez | 187 | 48/9 | 49/10 | 28/3 | 49/4 | 49/14 | 49/20 | 0/0 | 9/4 | 7/7 |
| 47 | Jesse Orosco | 200 | 5/1 | 6/1 | 2/1 | 6/0 | 6/2 | 6/3 | 0/0 | 1/1 | 7/7 |
| 21 | Kevin Elster | 200 | 5/1 | 6/1 | 4/0 | 6/0 | 6/2 | 6/1 | 0/0 | 1/0 | 0/0 |
| 39 | Doug Sisk | 100 | 10/1 | 11/1 | 11/0 | 11/0 | 11/4 | 11/4 | 0/0 | 3/1 | 0/0 |
| 19 | Bob Ojeda | 83 | 12/1 | 13/1 | 8/0 | 13/2 | 13/2 | 13/2 | 0/0 | 2/0 | 3/2 |
| 26 | Terry Leach | 166 | 12/2 | 13/2 | 6/0 | 13/0 | 13/4 | 13/6 | 0/0 | 1/0 | 1/1 |

## Batting-Order Report
### New York Mets Against All Left-Handed Pitchers

| No. | Name | Batting Average | Ability to get on Base | RBI | Runs Scored | Total Bases Gained | Strike Outs | Stolen Bases | Advancing a Runner by Hitting | Advancing a Runner by Bunting |
|---|---|---|---|---|---|---|---|---|---|---|
| 17 | Keith Hernandez | 289 | 283/ 82 | 326/ 126 | 241/ 28 | 326/ 34 | 326/ 161 | 326/ 39 | 1/ 1 | 79/ 50 | 0/ 0 |
| 20 | Howard Johnson | 266 | 120/ 32 | 134/ 46 | 93/ 23 | 134/ 10 | 134/ 68 | 134/ 20 | 5/ 5 | 30/ 25 | 3/ 2 |
| 18 | Darryl Strawberry | 229 | 205/ 47 | 230/ 74 | 145/ 34 | 230/ 18 | 230/ 110 | 230/ 60 | 4/ 4 | 53/ 40 | 2/ 1 |
| 01 | Mookie Wilson | 268 | 257/ 69 | 273/ 87 | 204/ 23 | 273/ 18 | 273/ 124 | 273/ 49 | 14/ 14 | 53/ 38 | 0/ 0 |
| 04 | Lenny Dykstra | 202 | 79/ 16 | 88/ 26 | 64/ 9 | 88/ 11 | 88/ 34 | 88/ 15 | 4/ 3 | 24/ 17 | 1/ 0 |
| 06 | Wally Backman | 150 | 80/ 12 | 89/ 21 | 63/ 8 | 89/ 6 | 89/ 22 | 89/ 17 | 1/ 1 | 12/ 9 | 5/ 4 |
| 25 | Keith Miller | 500 | 2/ 1 | 2/ 1 | 2/ 0 | 2/ 0 | 2/ 1 | 2/ 0 | 1/ 0 | 2/ 2 | 0/ 0 |
| 11 | Tim Teufel | 238 | 172/ 41 | 198/ 68 | 151/ 8 | 198/ 11 | 198/ 82 | 198/ 17 | 2/ 1 | 55/ 25 | 3/ 3 |
| 47 | Jesse Orosco | 500 | 3/ 1 | 4/ 3 | 2/ 0 | 3/ 0 | 4/ 3 | 3/ 0 | 0/ 0 | 1/ 0 | 0/ 0 |
| 42 | Roger McDowell | 333 | 3/ 1 | 4/ 2 | 2/ 0 | 4/ 1 | 4/ 1 | 4/ 1 | 0/ 0 | 0/ 0 | 0/ 0 |
| 03 | Rafael Santana | 290 | 193/ 56 | 212/ 76 | 166/ 24 | 212/ 14 | 212/ 84 | 212/ 20 | 0/ 0 | 52/ 36 | 2/ 1 |
| 08 | Gary Carter | 285 | 217/ 62 | 250/ 95 | 191/ 26 | 250/ 20 | 250/ 132 | 250/ 19 | 2/ 0 | 62/ 36 | 0/ 0 |
| 22 | Kevin McReynolds | 216 | 171/ 37 | 194/ 60 | 143/ 26 | 194/ 15 | 194/ 89 | 194/ 24 | 2/ 0 | 41/ 30 | 0/ 0 |
| 29 | Dave Magadan | 263 | 19/ 5 | 21/ 7 | 17/ 1 | 21/ 3 | 21/ 10 | 21/ 2 | 0/ 0 | 5/ 1 | 0/ 0 |
| 33 | Barry Lyons | 166 | 12/ 2 | 13/ 3 | 9/ 2 | 13/ 2 | 13/ 6 | 13/ 3 | 0/ 0 | 4/ 3 | 0/ 0 |
| 02 | Bill Almon | 288 | 90/ 26 | 104/ 41 | 76/ 6 | 104/ 3 | 104/ 57 | 104/ 14 | 0/ 0 | 21/ 7 | 0/ 0 |
| 43 | John Mitchell | 200 | 5/ 1 | 5/ 1 | 4/ 1 | 5/ 0 | 5/ 2 | 5/ 1 | 0/ 0 | 1/ 1 | 1/ 1 |
| 07 | Clint Hurdle | 333 | 3/ 1 | 3/ 1 | 2/ 1 | 3/ 0 | 3/ 2 | 3/ 1 | 0/ 0 | 0/ 1 | 0/ 0 |
| 16 | Dwight Gooden | 153 | 52/ 8 | 53/ 11 | 42/ 5 | 53/ 1 | 53/ 11 | 53/ 8 | 0/ 0 | 12/ 10 | 0/ 0 |
| 15 | Rick Aguilara | 153 | 13/ 2 | 14/ 3 | 9/ 1 | 14/ 1 | 14/ 3 | 14/ 4 | 0/ 0 | 9/ 9 | 1/ 1 |
| 10 | Rusty Staub | 200 | 5/ 1 | 5/ 1 | 3/ 0 | 5/ 1 | 5/ 1 | 5/ 2 | 0/ 0 | 1/ 1 | 0/ 0 |
| 13 | Lee Mazzilli | 210 | 38/ 8 | 44/ 14 | 33/ 2 | 44/ 3 | 44/ 17 | 44/ 5 | 0/ 0 | 13/ 2 | 1/ 0 |
| 12 | Ron Darling | 170 | 41/ 7 | 43/ 10 | 29/ 1 | 43/ 5 | 43/ 15 | 43/ 9 | 0/ 0 | 6/ 1 | 14/ 11 |
| 26 | Terry Leach | 111 | 9/ 1 | 9/ 1 | 5/ 0 | 9/ 1 | 9/ 1 | 9/ 4 | 0/ 0 | 3/ 1 | 1/ 1 |

**Batting-Order Report**
**Kansas City Royals Against All Right-Handed Pitchers**

| No. | Name | Batting Average | Ability to get on Base | RBI | Runs Scored | Total Bases Gained | Strike Outs | Stolen Bases | Advancing a Runner by Hitting | Advancing a Runner by Bunting |
|---|---|---|---|---|---|---|---|---|---|---|
| 33 | Kevin Seitzer | 336 232/ 78 | 259/ 106 | 196/ 33 | 259/ 37 | 259/ 134 | 259/ 33 | 3/ 3 | 60/ 49 | 4/ 1 |
| 16 | Bo Jackson | 273 190/ 52 | 204/ 66 | 115/ 33 | 204/ 22 | 204/ 107 | 207/ 71 | 5/ 5 | 35/ 30 | 2/ 0 |
| 04 | Danny Tartabull | 297 299/ 89 | 327/ 117 | 232/ 48 | 327/ 27 | 327/ 164 | 327/ 60 | 2/ 2 | 93/ 63 | 0/ 0 |
| 27 | Thad Bosley | 291 426/ 124 | 470/ 168 | 342/ 54 | 470/ 15 | 470/ 227 | 470/ 77 | 14/ 13 | 101/ 73 | 0/ 0 |
| 11 | Hal McRae | 266 592/ 158 | 641/ 211 | 507/ 90 | 641/ 25 | 641/ 277 | 641/ 74 | 1/ 1 | 202/ 123 | 3/ 2 |
| 05 | George Brett | 340 863/ 294 | 1039/ 470 | 786/ 163 | 1039/ 127 | 1039/ 700 | 1039/ 65 | 6/ 4 | 259/ 174 | 0/ 0 |
| 21 | Lonnie Smith | 266 601/ 160 | 682/ 244 | 501/ 54 | 682/ 58 | 682/ 304 | 682/ 92 | 42/ 35 | 137/ 74 | 17/ 5 |
| 06 | Willie Wilson | 271 1250/ 339 | 1337/ 435 | 1059/ 74 | 1337/ 129 | 1337/ 569 | 1337/ 163 | 88/ 70 | 303/ 161 | 22/ 13 |
| 20 | Frank White | 234 1167/ 274 | 1239/ 350 | 964/ 154 | 1239/ 85 | 1239/ 533 | 1239/ 166 | 13/ 10 | 336/ 216 | 15/ 9 |
| 28 | Mike MacFarlane | 400 5/ 2 | 7/ 4 | 4/ 2 | 7/ 0 | 7/ 4 | 7/ 1 | 0/ 0 | 3/ 2 | 0/ 0 |
| 99 | Oniz Concepcion | 215 343/ 74 | 365/ 99 | 312/ 17 | 365/ 20 | 365/ 114 | 365/ 24 | 9/ 6 | 128/ 52 | 20/ 15 |
| 02 | Angel Salazar | 180 304/ 55 | 315/ 67 | 248/ 15 | 315/ 27 | 315/ 77 | 315/ 53 | 3/ 2 | 82/ 35 | 12/ 11 |
| 30 | Dave Gumpert | 250 4/ 1 | 4/ 1 | 1/ 1 | 4/ 1 | 4/ 4 | 4/ 3 | 0/ 0 | 1/ 1 | 0/ 0 |
| 36 | Rondin Johnson | 320 25/ 8 | 26/ 9 | 22/ 3 | 26/ 1 | 26/ 11 | 26/ 3 | 0/ 0 | 6/ 3 | 1/ 0 |
| 45 | Steve Balboni | 223 855/ 198 | 940/ 253 | 605/ 136 | 940/ 53 | 940/ 438 | 940/ 228 | 0/ 0 | 217/ 139 | 0/ 0 |
| 35 | Lynn Jones | 256 82/ 21 | 91/ 31 | 74/ 4 | 91/ 12 | 91/ 34 | 91/ 8 | 0/ 0 | 27/ 10 | 2/ 2 |
| 32 | Bill Pecota | 360 25/ 9 | 26/ 10 | 21/ 1 | 26/ 1 | 26/ 13 | 26/ 3 | 0/ 0 | 7/ 2 | 0/ 0 |
| 07 | Ed Hearn | 212 33/ 7 | 35/ 9 | 29/ 3 | 35/ 1 | 35/ 13 | 35/ 4 | 0/ 0 | 5/ 3 | 1/ 1 |
| 22 | Jim Eisenreich | 186 59/ 11 | 61/ 13 | 47/ 9 | 61/ 5 | 61/ 24 | 61/ 8 | 0/ 0 | 19/ 12 | 1/ 1 |
| 09 | Jamie Quirk | 204 244/ 50 | 269/ 76 | 192/ 21 | 269/ 18 | 269/ 103 | 269/ 42 | 0/ 0 | 61/ 34 | 2/ 1 |
| 24 | Larry Owen | 136 73/ 10 | 81/ 19 | 46/ 7 | 81/ 5 | 81/ 22 | 81/ 21 | 0/ 0 | 15/ 10 | 5/ 4 |

## Batting-Order Report
### Kansas City Royals Against All Left-Handed Pitchers

| No. | Name | Batting Average | At Bats/ Hits | Ability to get on Base | RBI | Runs Scored | Total Bases Gained | Strike Outs | Stolen Bases | Advancing a Runner by Hitting | Advancing a Runner by Bunting |
|---|---|---|---|---|---|---|---|---|---|---|---|
| 04 | Danny Tartabull | 294 | 95/ 28 | 113/ 48 | 71/ 16 | 113/ 9 | 113/ 64 | 113/ 23 | 1/ 1 | 24/ 21 | 0/ 0 |
| 05 | George Brett | 276 | 431/ 119 | 480/ 168 | 374/ 66 | 480/ 48 | 480/ 240 | 480/ 48 | 2/ 2 | 118/ 82 | 1/ 0 |
| 06 | Willie Wilson | 299 | 468/ 140 | 485/ 159 | 391/ 34 | 485/ 57 | 485/ 215 | 485/ 69 | 18/ 13 | 89/ 56 | 9/ 5 |
| 99 | Oniz Concepcion | 172 | 151/ 26 | 161/ 38 | 134/ 8 | 161/ 11 | 161/ 47 | 161/ 10 | 4/ 4 | 47/ 19 | 2/ 1 |
| 21 | Lonnie Smith | 225 | 271/ 61 | 295/ 86 | 226/ 15 | 295/ 27 | 295/ 108 | 295/ 40 | 12/ 10 | 62/ 36 | 3/ 0 |
| 20 | Frank White | 292 | 448/ 131 | 479/ 163 | 383/ 47 | 479/ 26 | 479/ 215 | 479/ 55 | 2/ 1 | 135/ 75 | 5/ 2 |
| 27 | Thad Bosley | 350 | 20/ 7 | 25/ 12 | 12/ 2 | 25/ 0 | 25/ 14 | 25/ 8 | 0/ 0 | 4/ 5 | 1/ 1 |
| 37 | Charlie Liebrandt | 500 | 2/ 1 | 2/ 1 | 1/ 0 | 2/ 1 | 2/ 2 | 2/ 1 | 0/ 0 | 0/ 0 | 0/ 0 |
| 33 | Kevin Seitzer | 315 | 76/ 24 | 88/ 37 | 68/ 6 | 88/ 8 | 88/ 45 | 88/ 8 | 0/ 0 | 16/ 13 | 0/ 0 |
| 11 | Hal McRae | 299 | 397/ 119 | 448/ 173 | 324/ 71 | 448/ 30 | 448/ 247 | 448/ 63 | 0/ 0 | 104/ 69 | 0/ 0 |
| 16 | Bo Jackson | 301 | 63/ 19 | 71/ 27 | 39/ 6 | 71/ 4 | 71/ 38 | 71/ 24 | 0/ 0 | 13/ 10 | 0/ 0 |
| 45 | Steve Balboni | 264 | 352/ 93 | 403/ 145 | 245/ 54 | 403/ 26 | 403/ 244 | 403/ 98 | 0/ 0 | 88/ 50 | 0/ 0 |
| 35 | Lynn Jones | 234 | 111/ 26 | 117/ 32 | 100/ 14 | 117/ 5 | 117/ 41 | 117/ 11 | 0/ 0 | 34/ 18 | 3/ 3 |
| 24 | Larry Owen | 191 | 68/ 13 | 71/ 16 | 45/ 7 | 71/ 8 | 71/ 27 | 71/ 17 | 0/ 0 | 14/ 7 | 2/ 2 |
| 32 | Bill Pecota | 230 | 13/ 3 | 14/ 4 | 10/ 1 | 14/ 2 | 14/ 7 | 14/ 1 | 0/ 0 | 4/ 1 | 0/ 0 |
| 09 | Jamie Quirk | 238 | 21/ 5 | 23/ 7 | 15/ 0 | 23/ 1 | 23/ 8 | 23/ 6 | 0/ 0 | 4/ 2 | 0/ 0 |
| 07 | Ed Hearn | 148 | 27/ 4 | 34/ 11 | 21/ 4 | 34/ 0 | 34/ 13 | 34/ 6 | 0/ 0 | 4/ 1 | 1/ 1 |
| 02 | Angel Salazar | 246 | 150/ 37 | 150/ 38 | 131/ 12 | 150/ 6 | 150/ 53 | 150/ 16 | 0/ 0 | 43/ 23 | 0/ 0 |
| 36 | Rondin Johnson | 250 | 16/ 4 | 17/ 5 | 15/ 0 | 17/ 0 | 17/ 5 | 17/ 1 | 0/ 0 | 4/ 1 | 0/ 0 |
| 17 | Rick Anderson | 250 | 4/ 1 | 4/ 1 | 2/ 0 | 4/ 0 | 4/ 1 | 4/ 2 | 0/ 0 | 0/ 0 | 0/ 0 |

## Batting-Order Report
### Baltimore Orioles Against All Right-Handed Pitchers

| No. | Name | Batting Average | Ability to get on Base | RBI | Runs Scored | Total Bases Gained | Strike Outs | Stolen Bases | Advancing a Runner by Hitting | Advancing a Runner by Bunting |
|---|---|---|---|---|---|---|---|---|---|---|
| 08 | Cal Ripken, Jr. | 275 | 875/241 | 964/337 | 740/127 | 964/114 | 964/494 | 964/110 | 1/1 | 259/151 | 2/0 |
| 37 | Ron Washington | 317 | 104/33 | 109/38 | 87/14 | 109/3 | 109/51 | 109/15 | 1/1 | 21/17 | 0/0 |
| 19 | Fred Lynn | 270 | 517/140 | 589/213 | 421/81 | 589/56 | 589/327 | 589/82 | 3/3 | 130/80 | 0/0 |
| 09 | Jim Dwyer | 246 | 369/91 | 426/149 | 289/53 | 426/33 | 426/218 | 426/60 | 2/2 | 89/51 | 14/3 |
| 25 | Ray Knight | 257 | 424/109 | 460/147 | 358/48 | 460/14 | 460/188 | 460/53 | 1/1 | 131/80 | 2/1 |
| 03 | Bill Ripken | 241 | 29/7 | 32/10 | 24/2 | 32/4 | 32/11 | 32/4 | 1/1 | 10/4 | 0/0 |
| 02 | Alan Wiggins | 268 | 487/131 | 543/189 | 442/30 | 543/38 | 543/218 | 543/40 | 42/36 | 110/69 | 41/14 |
| 27 | Lee Lacy | 261 | 524/137 | 562/178 | 405/46 | 562/59 | 562/229 | 562/113 | 6/5 | 123/77 | 8/6 |
| 16 | Scott McGregor | 250 | 4/1 | 4/1 | 3/1 | 4/0 | 4/1 | 4/1 | 2/1 | 2/3 | 0/0 |
| 10 | Todd Cruz | 219 | 73/16 | 76/19 | 54/13 | 76/5 | 76/30 | 76/17 | 2/2 | 19/10 | 4/3 |
| 06 | Floyd Rayford | 251 | 231/58 | 240/70 | 177/31 | 240/25 | 240/109 | 240/49 | 2/2 | 63/37 | 2/2 |
| 43 | Mike Young | 227 | 418/95 | 463/140 | 306/63 | 463/40 | 463/223 | 463/108 | 3/2 | 107/71 | 5/3 |
| 33 | Eddie Murray | 290 | 765/222 | 874/332 | 658/129 | 874/93 | 874/499 | 874/96 | 4/2 | 225/144 | 0/0 |
| 15 | Terry Kennedy | 269 | 523/141 | 570/190 | 429/68 | 570/24 | 570/262 | 570/82 | 2/1 | 138/94 | 1/1 |
| 11 | Jackie Gutierrez | 206 | 247/51 | 256/61 | 206/20 | 256/1 | 256/69 | 256/37 | 11/10 | 71/30 | 13/9 |
| 38 | Ken Gerhart | 202 | 79/16 | 88/25 | 61/12 | 88/13 | 88/38 | 88/15 | 3/2 | 19/9 | 4/4 |
| 28 | Jim Traber | 314 | 70/22 | 83/35 | 60/13 | 83/21 | 83/54 | 83/8 | 0/0 | 28/18 | 0/0 |
| 01 | Rex Hudler | 133 | 15/2 | 15/2 | 15/0 | 15/0 | 15/2 | 15/0 | 2/2 | 5/1 | 2/2 |
| 30 | Ricky Jones | 100 | 10/1 | 11/2 | 7/1 | 11/0 | 11/3 | 11/3 | 0/0 | 1/2 | 0/0 |
| 18 | Larry Sheets | 290 | 434/126 | 465/158 | 361/85 | 465/58 | 465/265 | 465/65 | 0/0 | 135/88 | 0/0 |
| 99 | Leo Hernandez | 222 | 27/6 | 29/8 | 26/5 | 29/1 | 29/12 | 29/1 | 0/0 | 9/4 | 0/0 |
| 17 | Rick Burleson | 236 | 127/30 | 139/42 | 107/6 | 139/9 | 139/50 | 139/15 | 0/0 | 39/15 | 3/3 |
| 14 | Dave Van Gorder | 189 | 37/7 | 40/10 | 26/2 | 40/2 | 40/11 | 40/10 | 0/0 | 11/2 | 1/1 |
| 88 | Rene Gonzales | 142 | 28/4 | 28/4 | 20/2 | 28/5 | 28/7 | 28/7 | 0/0 | 8/2 | 1/1 |
| 47 | Luis Deleon | 200 | 5/1 | 5/1 | 5/0 | 5/0 | 5/1 | 5/0 | 0/0 | 3/0 | 1/1 |
| 49 | Tom Niedenfuer | 100 | 10/1 | 10/1 | 4/1 | 10/0 | 10/1 | 10/5 | 0/0 | 1/1 | 1/0 |

Batting-Order Report
Baltimore Orioles Against All Left-Handed Pitchers

| No. | Name | Batting Average | Ability to get on Base | RBI | Runs Scored | Total Bases Gained | Strike Outs | Stolen Bases | Advancing a Runner by Hitting | Advancing a Runner by Bunting |
|---|---|---|---|---|---|---|---|---|---|---|
| 08 | Cal Ripken, Jr. | 327 | 357/117 | 405/165 | 310/52 | 405/48 | 405/257 | 405/34 | 1/1 | 103/62 | 0/0 |
| 27 | Lee Lacy | 306 | 248/76 | 276/106 | 218/30 | 276/27 | 276/143 | 276/26 | 3/2 | 59/46 | 4/4 |
| 28 | Jim Traber | 280 | 25/7 | 31/13 | 19/7 | 31/4 | 31/16 | 31/4 | 0/0 | 5/7 | 0/0 |
| 02 | Alan Wiggins | 236 | 190/45 | 208/63 | 175/9 | 208/17 | 208/49 | 208/12 | 18/14 | 49/24 | 10/4 |
| 37 | Ron Washington | 225 | 93/21 | 97/26 | 80/6 | 97/3 | 97/47 | 97/11 | 2/2 | 26/4 | 3/3 |
| 11 | Jackie Gutierrez | 266 | 124/33 | 129/39 | 106/14 | 129/1 | 129/55 | 129/16 | 3/2 | 37/20 | 6/5 |
| 03 | Bill Ripken | 354 | 31/11 | 31/11 | 29/3 | 31/4 | 31/15 | 31/2 | 0/0 | 10/8 | 0/0 |
| 33 | Eddie Murray | 304 | 342/104 | 390/152 | 289/57 | 390/38 | 390/229 | 390/47 | 0/0 | 105/6 | 0/0 |
| 49 | Tom Niedenfuer | 500 | 2/1 | 2/1 | 2/0 | 2/0 | 2/1 | 2/0 | 0/0 | 0/0 | 1/1 |
| 25 | Ray Knight | 273 | 249/68 | 268/90 | 213/40 | 268/10 | 268/125 | 268/33 | 0/0 | 60/45 | 0/0 |
| 38 | Ken Gerhart | 192 | 83/16 | 86/19 | 66/3 | 86/4 | 86/25 | 86/12 | 2/1 | 19/4 | 4/2 |
| 43 | Mike Young | 273 | 238/65 | 267/94 | 188/29 | 267/20 | 267/135 | 267/44 | 1/0 | 65/34 | 3/1 |
| 09 | Jim Dwyer | 312 | 16/5 | 17/6 | 12/1 | 17/3 | 17/11 | 17/3 | 0/0 | 4/1 | 0/0 |
| 15 | Terry Kennedy | 263 | 182/48 | 192/60 | 138/23 | 192/7 | 192/89 | 192/40 | 0/0 | 45/33 | 0/0 |
| 18 | Larry Sheets | 234 | 64/15 | 66/17 | 49/11 | 66/7 | 66/25 | 66/13 | 0/0 | 17/9 | 0/0 |
| 99 | Leo Hernandez | 333 | 15/5 | 15/5 | 14/1 | 15/2 | 15/5 | 15/1 | 0/0 | 4/1 | 0/0 |
| 19 | Fred Lynn | 241 | 232/56 | 251/75 | 175/28 | 251/18 | 251/114 | 251/53 | 0/0 | 72/41 | 1/0 |
| 06 | Floyd Rayford | 258 | 139/36 | 144/41 | 100/20 | 144/11 | 144/72 | 144/35 | 0/0 | 35/19 | 1/1 |
| 17 | Rick Burleson | 226 | 106/24 | 114/32 | 92/8 | 114/5 | 114/42 | 114/11 | 0/0 | 21/10 | 2/1 |
| 10 | Todd Cruz | 235 | 34/8 | 37/11 | 30/1 | 37/0 | 37/11 | 37/4 | 0/0 | 12/6 | 3/1 |
| 14 | Dave Van Gorder | 157 | 19/3 | 20/4 | 12/2 | 20/1 | 20/7 | 20/6 | 0/0 | 6/3 | 0/0 |
| 88 | Rene Gonzales | 125 | 16/2 | 17/3 | 12/0 | 17/1 | 17/3 | 17/2 | 0/0 | 7/1 | 0/0 |
| 01 | Rex Hudler | 83 | 12/1 | 12/1 | 8/0 | 12/0 | 12/1 | 12/3 | 0/0 | 3/0 | 2/2 |

**Batting-Order Report**
**Atlanta Braves Against All Right-Handed Pitchers**

| No. | Name | Batting Average | Ability to get on Base | RBI | Runs Scored | Total Bases Gained | Strike Outs | Stolen Bases | Advancing a Runner by Hitting | Advancing a Runner by Bunting |
|---|---|---|---|---|---|---|---|---|---|---|
| 12 | Paul Runge | 363  66/24 | 75/33 | | 55/5 | 75/5 | 75/38 | 3/3 | 16/14 | 2/2 |
| 03 | Dale Murphy | 278  1213/338 | 1370/502 | 925/195 | 1370/155 | 1370/798 | 1370/259 | 35/34 | 300/203 | 0/0 |
| 10 | Dion James | 310  245/76 | 277/110 | 225/31 | 277/26 | 277/155 | 277/18 | 4/3 | 68/47 | 4/2 |
| 19 | Craig Nettles | 234  397/93 | 466/163 | 339/63 | 466/20 | 466/223 | 466/50 | 1/1 | 117/79 | 0/0 |
| 20 | Bruce Benedict | 258  502/130 | 572/200 | 439/55 | 572/26 | 572/230 | 572/42 | 3/3 | 142/81 | 12/7 |
| 01 | Albert Hall | 267  131/35 | 150/54 | 115/10 | 150/14 | 150/65 | 150/13 | 17/15 | 32/24 | 4/3 |
| 15 | Gary Roenicke | 250  160/40 | 184/64 | 133/18 | 184/7 | 184/90 | 184/23 | 3/3 | 51/22 | 2/1 |
| 28 | Gerald Perry | 235  544/128 | 621/206 | 472/54 | 621/48 | 621/250 | 621/58 | 28/25 | 164/92 | 4/1 |
| 22 | Ken Griffey | 288  662/191 | 714/245 | 579/95 | 714/47 | 714/341 | 714/69 | 13/10 | 216/133 | 3/1 |
| 16 | Rafael Ramirez | 260  1070/279 | 1117/330 | 949/96 | 1117/77 | 1117/408 | 1117/99 | 25/23 | 318/178 | 24/16 |
| 32 | Jeff Blauser | 307  13/4 | 13/4 | 10/3 | 13/2 | 13/5 | 13/2 | 1/1 | 0/3 | 1/1 |
| 14 | Andres Thomas | 216  208/45 | 214/52 | 166/26 | 214/20 | 214/68 | 214/34 | 5/5 | 64/37 | 1/1 |
| 17 | Glenn Hubbard | 253  944/239 | 1082/384 | 795/92 | 1082/81 | 1082/501 | 1082/122 | 12/8 | 260/136 | 20/13 |
| 24 | Ken Oberkfell | 265  771/205 | 866/302 | 707/55 | 866/67 | 866/380 | 866/47 | 5/3 | 245/118 | 5/5 |
| 06 | Darryl Motley | 216  443/96 | 465/121 | 358/49 | 465/14 | 465/187 | 465/74 | 5/4 | 113/60 | 1/1 |
| 34 | Zane Smith | 92  76/7 | 80/11 | 61/6 | 80/6 | 80/13 | 80/12 | 1/1 | 11/6 | 16/12 |
| 23 | Ted Simmons | 252  325/82 | 358/118 | 291/47 | 358/14 | 358/148 | 358/26 | 2/1 | 103/66 | 1/0 |
| 09 | Ozzie Virgil | 226  513/116 | 576/181 | 402/76 | 576/45 | 576/265 | 576/91 | 0/0 | 123/75 | 6/6 |
| 46 | David Palmer | 237  59/14 | 59/14 | 39/5 | 59/3 | 59/20 | 59/18 | 0/0 | 8/5 | 7/6 |
| 26 | Gene Garber | 176  17/3 | 19/5 | 14/1 | 19/0 | 19/5 | 19/3 | 0/0 | 4/3 | 2/2 |
| 42 | Rick Mahler | 175  137/24 | 141/28 | 108/10 | 141/8 | 141/34 | 141/25 | 0/0 | 31/13 | 13/12 |
| 45 | Charlie Puleo | 130  23/3 | 23/3 | 15/4 | 23/2 | 23/6 | 23/8 | 0/0 | 8/3 | 2/2 |
| 49 | Jeff Dedmon | 150  20/3 | 22/3 | 14/1 | 22/4 | 22/5 | 22/6 | 0/0 | 2/0 | 2/2 |
| 33 | Doyle Alexander | 68  29/2 | 30/3 | 21/2 | 30/0 | 30/4 | 30/8 | 0/0 | 5/3 | 4/3 |

## Batting-Order Report
## Atlanta Braves Against All Left-Handed Pitchers

| No. | Name | Batting Average | Ability to get on Base | RBI | Runs Scored | Total Bases Gained | Strike Outs | Stolen Bases | Advancing a Runner by Hitting | Advancing a Runner by Bunting |
|---|---|---|---|---|---|---|---|---|---|---|
| 24 | Ken Oberkfell | 294 197/ 58 | 226/ 89 | 161/ 27 | 226/ 16 | 226/ 108 | 226/ 26 | 2/ 2 | 55/ 34 | 2/ 1 |
| 22 | Ken Griffey | 260 215/ 56 | 226/ 68 | 185/ 36 | 226/ 17 | 226/ 97 | 226/ 24 | 1/ 1 | 71/ 41 | 3/ 2 |
| 28 | Gerald Perry | 252 91/ 23 | 101/ 33 | 77/ 12 | 101/ 4 | 101/ 42 | 101/ 14 | 2/ 2 | 28/ 18 | 2/ 1 |
| 10 | Dion James | 285 56/ 16 | 70/ 30 | 44/ 3 | 70/ 7 | 70/ 36 | 70/ 11 | 2/ 2 | 17/ 8 | 2/ 2 |
| 06 | Darryl Motley | 250 272/ 68 | 289/ 86 | 233/ 35 | 289/ 8 | 289/ 127 | 289/ 26 | 1/ 1 | 97/ 56 | 1/ 0 |
| 01 | Albert Hall | 235 85/ 20 | 93/ 28 | 72/ 8 | 93/ 12 | 93/ 31 | 93/ 12 | 5/ 5 | 22/ 11 | 4/ 1 |
| 03 | Dale Murphy | 267 464/ 124 | 554/ 215 | 350/ 62 | 554/ 62 | 554/ 316 | 554/ 106 | 11/ 9 | 100/ 66 | 0/ 0 |
| 14 | Andres Thomas | 232 112/ 26 | 117/ 32 | 88/ 7 | 117/ 6 | 117/ 42 | 117/ 14 | 1/ 1 | 36/ 20 | 2/ 1 |
| 16 | Rafael Ramirez | 263 455/ 120 | 478/ 147 | 400/ 48 | 478/ 40 | 478/ 179 | 478/ 40 | 5/ 4 | 132/ 76 | 4/ 2 |
| 12 | Paul Runge | 177 62/ 11 | 70/ 19 | 49/ 4 | 70/ 6 | 70/ 23 | 70/ 13 | 1/ 1 | 18/ 7 | 6/ 6 |
| 15 | Gary Roenicke | 286 237/ 68 | 289/ 120 | 195/ 66 | 289/ 25 | 289/ 193 | 289/ 27 | 0/ 0 | 56/ 52 | 0/ 0 |
| 32 | Jeff Blauser | 166 6/ 1 | 8/ 3 | 5/ 1 | 8/ 0 | 8/ 4 | 8/ 1 | 0/ 0 | 2/ 2 | 0/ 0 |
| 17 | Glenn Hubbard | 244 356/ 87 | 421/ 155 | 300/ 32 | 421/ 31 | 421/ 202 | 421/ 45 | 1/ 0 | 91/ 52 | 13/ 8 |
| 09 | Ozzie Virgil | 229 144/ 33 | 171/ 60 | 122/ 14 | 171/ 6 | 171/ 75 | 171/ 17 | 0/ 0 | 44/ 36 | 0/ 0 |
| 20 | Bruce Benedict | 251 195/ 49 | 216/ 71 | 182/ 16 | 216/ 15 | 216/ 85 | 216/ 9 | 0/ 0 | 51/ 21 | 3/ 3 |
| 23 | Ted Simmons | 209 167/ 35 | 179/ 49 | 149/ 23 | 179/ 9 | 179/ 64 | 179/ 16 | 0/ 0 | 61/ 36 | 3/ 1 |
| 31 | Ed Olwine | 500 2/ 1 | 2/ 1 | 1/ 0 | 2/ 0 | 2/ 1 | 2/ 1 | 0/ 0 | 0/ 0 | 0/ 0 |
| 19 | Craig Nettles | 223 103/ 23 | 112/ 32 | 82/ 9 | 112/ 3 | 112/ 50 | 112/ 19 | 0/ 0 | 37/ 17 | 0/ 0 |
| 46 | David Palmer | 125 32/ 4 | 33/ 5 | 24/ 4 | 33/ 2 | 33/ 8 | 33/ 7 | 0/ 0 | 8/ 4 | 6/ 5 |
| 34 | Zane Smith | 148 27/ 4 | 28/ 5 | 23/ 2 | 28/ 2 | 28/ 5 | 28/ 4 | 0/ 0 | 6/ 3 | 7/ 5 |
| 42 | Rick Mahler | 80 50/ 4 | 51/ 6 | 42/ 2 | 51/ 3 | 51/ 6 | 51/ 8 | 0/ 0 | 9/ 3 | 5/ 5 |
| 38 | Jim Acker | 100 10/ 1 | 10/ 1 | 4/ 0 | 10/ 1 | 10/ 1 | 10/ 6 | 0/ 0 | 2/ 1 | 1/ 1 |
| 49 | Jeff Dedmon | 83 12/ 1 | 12/ 1 | 10/ 0 | 12/ 0 | 12/ 1 | 12/ 2 | 0/ 0 | 3/ 1 | 1/ 1 |
| 33 | Doyle Alexander | 90 11/ 1 | 11/ 1 | 8/ 0 | 11/ 0 | 11/ 1 | 11/ 3 | 0/ 0 | 1/ 0 | 2/ 0 |

## Batting-Order Report
### Chicago Cubs Against All Right-Handed Pitchers

| No. | Name | Batting Average | Ability to get on Base | RBI | Runs Scored | Total Bases Gained | Strike Outs | Stolen Bases | Advancing a Runner by Hitting | Advancing a Runner by Bunting |
|---|---|---|---|---|---|---|---|---|---|---|
| 36 | Gary Matthews | 252  796/201 | 957/363 | 611/105 | 957/90 | 957/480 | 957/174 | 9/9 | 197/141 | 2/2 |
| 22 | Jerry Mumphrey | 325  679/221 | 738/282 | 584/93 | 738/51 | 738/388 | 738/94 | 9/8 | 195/133 | 1/0 |
| 23 | Ryne Sandberg | 298  1607/479 | 1747/630 | 1356/217 | 1747/218 | 1747/923 | 1747/227 | 101/88 | 436/288 | 9/4 |
| 10 | Leon Durham | 274  1251/344 | 1454/548 | 1019/204 | 1454/160 | 1454/829 | 1454/202 | 25/21 | 316/226 | 1/1 |
| 19 | Manny Trillo | 251  330/83 | 363/116 | 283/35 | 363/21 | 363/156 | 363/35 | 1/1 | 92/55 | 8/7 |
| 01 | Dave Martinez | 207  251/52 | 291/95 | 204/16 | 291/29 | 291/110 | 291/38 | 8/8 | 66/35 | 5/1 |
| 24 | Brian Dayett | 216  111/24 | 123/36 | 88/13 | 123/12 | 123/56 | 123/20 | 1/1 | 29/17 | 0/0 |
| 16 | Paul Noce | 333  36/12 | 38/14 | 31/1 | 38/4 | 38/18 | 38/4 | 1/1 | 8/2 | 4/3 |
| 12 | Shawon Dunston | 266  713/190 | 752/230 | 547/65 | 752/79 | 752/337 | 752/140 | 29/28 | 184/109 | 18/5 |
| 06 | Keith Moreland | 265  1484/394 | 1590/509 | 1294/241 | 1590/107 | 1590/700 | 1590/157 | 8/7 | 466/301 | 15/15 |
| 17 | Mike Brumley | 200  15/3 | 17/5 | 11/1 | 17/1 | 17/5 | 17/4 | 1/1 | 5/3 | 0/0 |
| 28 | Luis Quinones | 184  38/7 | 40/9 | 31/1 | 40/1 | 40/9 | 40/3 | 1/1 | 17/7 | 0/0 |
| 29 | Chico Walker | 220  168/37 | 181/52 | 127/11 | 181/25 | 181/66 | 181/38 | 16/13 | 36/20 | 8/3 |
| 08 | Andre Dawson | 266  665/177 | 708/222 | 543/121 | 708/42 | 708/358 | 708/98 | 11/7 | 188/123 | 2/1 |
| 40 | Rick Sutcliffe | 198  131/26 | 140/36 | 104/11 | 140/7 | 140/48 | 140/24 | 1/1 | 35/11 | 9/6 |
| 20 | Bob Dernier | 225  864/195 | 942/278 | 744/39 | 942/104 | 942/329 | 942/101 | 66/57 | 180/74 | 32/18 |
| 25 | Rafael Palmeiro | 263  91/24 | 102/35 | 80/20 | 102/13 | 102/55 | 102/11 | 0/0 | 35/21 | 0/0 |
| 07 | Jody Davis | 255  1318/337 | 1434/455 | 1027/204 | 1434/106 | 1434/711 | 1434/255 | 2/0 | 378/218 | 12/9 |
| 11 | Jim Sundberg | 236  558/132 | 610/185 | 438/48 | 610/12 | 610/246 | 610/106 | 0/0 | 136/64 | 7/5 |
| 31 | Greg Maddux | 178  28/5 | 28/5 | 26/1 | 28/1 | 28/5 | 28/2 | 0/0 | 11/6 | 7/4 |
| 49 | Jamie Moyer | 108  46/5 | 53/13 | 37/1 | 53/4 | 53/13 | 53/9 | 0/0 | 9/6 | 5/5 |
| 44 | Drew Hall | 200  5/1 | 5/1 | 2/0 | 5/1 | 5/1 | 5/1 | 0/0 | 1/1 | 5/5 |
| 21 | Scott Sanderson | 108  92/10 | 99/17 | 56/6 | 99/11 | 99/21 | 99/34 | 0/0 | 13/7 | 16/14 |
| 47 | Dickie Noles | 130  23/3 | 24/4 | 9/2 | 24/0 | 24/12 | 24/12 | 0/0 | 1/1 | 1/1 |
| 52 | Reggie Patterson | 100  10/1 | 11/2 | 7/0 | 11/0 | 11/2 | 11/3 | 0/0 | 2/1 | 1/1 |
| 50 | Les Lancaster | 200  10/2 | 10/2 | 5/1 | 10/0 | 10/3 | 10/4 | 0/0 | 0/0 | 0/0 |
| 34 | Steve Trout | 112  133/15 | 137/20 | 101/8 | 137/8 | 137/22 | 137/31 | 1/0 | 28/6 | 26/20 |
| 41 | Mike Mason | 142  7/1 | 7/1 | 6/0 | 7/1 | 7/1 | 7/1 | 0/0 | 3/3 | 3/3 |
| 37 | Ed Lynch | 89  7/1 | 7/1 | 0/0 | 7/1 | 7/1 | 7/1 | 0/0 | 0/0 | 9/8 |
| 33 | Frank DiPino | 90  56/5 | 58/7 | 33/0 | 58/0 | 58/8 | 58/23 | 0/0 | 6/3 | 9/8 |
| 60 | Ray Fontenot | 58  34/2 | 34/2 | 17/0 | 34/3 | 34/16 | 34/16 | 0/0 | 4/0 | 5/4 |
| 46 | Lee Smith | 47  21/1 | 22/2 | 8/0 | 22/0 | 22/2 | 22/13 | 0/0 | 5/1 | 3/3 |

## Batting-Order Report
## Chicago Cubs Against All Left-Handed Pitchers

| No. | Name | Batting Average | Ability to get on Base | RBI | Runs Scored | Total Bases Gained | Strike Outs | Stolen Bases | Advancing a Runner by Hitting | Advancing a Runner by Bunting |
|---|---|---|---|---|---|---|---|---|---|---|
| 36 | Gary Matthews | 307 299/ 92 | 344/ 138 | 248/ 53 | 344/ 36 | 344/ 199 | 344/ 42 | 6/ 6 | 85/ 71 | 0/ 0 |
| 07 | Jody Davis | 259 416/108 | 456/ 148 | 353/ 61 | 456/ 46 | 456/ 235 | 456/ 55 | 2/ 2 | 123/ 73 | 3/ 3 |
| 06 | Keith Moreland | 301 464/ 140 | 530/ 208 | 411/ 58 | 530/ 46 | 530/ 280 | 530/ 41 | 5/ 4 | 159/ 93 | 2/ 2 |
| 20 | Bob Dernier | 280 367/103 | 408/ 148 | 331/ 30 | 408/ 47 | 408/ 194 | 408/ 27 | 28/ 25 | 70/ 34 | 19/ 9 |
| 23 | Ryne Sandberg | 272 492/134 | 549/ 195 | 424/ 49 | 549/ 54 | 549/ 261 | 549/ 59 | 17/ 14 | 153/ 76 | 4/ 2 |
| 11 | Jim Sundberg | 226 230/ 52 | 258/ 82 | 183/ 31 | 258/ 10 | 258/ 122 | 258/ 43 | 1/ 1 | 56/ 28 | 3/ 2 |
| 10 | Leon Durham | 242 355/ 86 | 391/ 125 | 256/ 53 | 391/ 25 | 391/ 175 | 391/ 93 | 3/ 2 | 96/ 74 | 0/ 0 |
| 22 | Jerry Mumphrey | 280 164/ 46 | 183/ 66 | 141/ 16 | 183/ 1 | 183/ 75 | 183/ 21 | 4/ 3 | 55/ 28 | 2/ 2 |
| 08 | Andre Dawson | 280 214/ 60 | 230/ 77 | 178/ 41 | 230/ 25 | 230/ 137 | 230/ 31 | 6/ 3 | 63/ 36 | 0/ 0 |
| 12 | Shawon Dunston | 196 214/ 42 | 220/ 49 | 169/ 25 | 220/ 23 | 220/ 83 | 220/ 36 | 4/ 3 | 45/ 23 | 5/ 0 |
| 16 | Paul Noce | 125 8/ 1 | 9/ 2 | 6/ 0 | 9/ 0 | 9/ 2 | 9/ 2 | 2/ 1 | 2/ 1 | 0/ 0 |
| 29 | Chico Walker | 200 25/ 5 | 27/ 7 | 20/ 1 | 27/ 4 | 27/ 8 | 27/ 5 | 2/ 1 | 8/ 4 | 1/ 1 |
| 24 | Brian Dayett | 314 124/ 39 | 135/ 50 | 104/ 26 | 135/ 9 | 135/ 82 | 135/ 20 | 0/ 0 | 41/ 24 | 1/ 1 |
| 34 | Steve Trout | 135 37/ 5 | 39/ 8 | 25/ 5 | 39/ 6 | 39/ 8 | 39/ 12 | 0/ 0 | 2/ 2 | 5/ 4 |
| 01 | Dave Martinez | 266 15/ 4 | 15/ 4 | 11/ 2 | 15/ 2 | 15/ 7 | 15/ 3 | 1/ 1 | 4/ 3 | 0/ 0 |
| 21 | Scott Sanderson | 26 38/ 1 | 41/ 4 | 22/ 0 | 41/ 0 | 41/ 1 | 41/ 16 | 0/ 0 | 8/ 0 | 3/ 3 |
| 17 | Mike Brumley | 250 4/ 1 | 4/ 1 | 3/ 0 | 4/ 0 | 4/ 1 | 4/ 1 | 1/ 1 | 1/ 1 | 0/ 0 |
| 19 | Manny Trillo | 288 135/ 39 | 142/ 46 | 112/ 15 | 142/ 11 | 142/ 62 | 142/ 18 | 0/ 0 | 39/ 18 | 2/ 2 |
| 31 | Greg Maddux | 111 9/ 1 | 9/ 1 | 8/ 0 | 9/ 1 | 9/ 1 | 9/ 1 | 0/ 0 | 1/ 1 | 3/ 2 |
| 40 | Rick Sutcliffe | 173 52/ 9 | 53/ 10 | 33/ 3 | 53/ 6 | 53/ 12 | 53/ 18 | 0/ 0 | 9/ 7 | 6/ 6 |
| 49 | Jamie Moyer | 62 16/ 1 | 18/ 3 | 12/ 0 | 18/ 1 | 18/ 3 | 18/ 4 | 0/ 0 | 4/ 0 | 4/ 3 |
| 60 | Ray Fontenot | 125 8/ 1 | 8/ 1 | 3/ 0 | 8/ 2 | 8/ 1 | 8/ 5 | 0/ 0 | 2/ 0 | 0/ 0 |
| 37 | Ed Lynch | 90 11/ 1 | 13/ 3 | 4/ 0 | 13/ 0 | 13/ 3 | 13/ 7 | 0/ 0 | 1/ 0 | 0/ 0 |

# Index Of Players